Young Lambs are usually born between late February and early May.

CHARACTERISTICS Rams (male bighorn sheep) have big, curved horns; ewes' (females) horns are smaller and straighter.

Bighorn sheep can balance on mountain ledges that are only a few inches wide.

A ram's horns can be 30 inches long and weigh 30 pounds; as much as all the bones in its body.

California
Science

SCHOOL PUBLISHERS

Visit *The Learning Site!*
www.harcourtschool.com

California
Science

Bighorn sheep

Series Consulting Authors

Michael J. Bell, Ph.D.
Assistant Professor of Early Childhood Education
College of Education
West Chester University of Pennsylvania
West Chester, Pennsylvania

Michael A. DiSpezio
Curriculum Architect
JASON Academy
Cape Cod, Massachusetts

Marjorie Frank
Former Adjunct, Science Education
Hunter College
New York, New York

Gerald H. Krockover, Ph.D.
Professor of Earth and Atmospheric Science Education
Purdue University
West Lafayette, Indiana

Joyce C. McLeod
Adjunct Professor
Rollins College
Winter Park, Florida

Barbara ten Brink, Ph.D.
Science Specialist
Austin Independent School District
Austin, Texas

Carol J. Valenta
Senior Vice President
St. Louis Science Center
St. Louis, Missouri
Former teacher, principal, and Coordinator of Science Center Instructional Programs
Los Angeles Unified School District
Los Angeles, California

Barry A. Van Deman
President and CEO
Museum of Life and Science
Durham, North Carolina

Series Consultants

Catherine Banker
Curriculum Consultant
Alta Loma, California

Robin C. Scarcella, Ph.D.
Professor and Director, Program
    of Academic English and ESL
University of California, Irvine
Irvine, California

Series Content Reviewers

Paul Asimow, Ph.D.
Associate Professor, Geology and
    Geochemistry
California Institute of Technology
Pasadena, California

Larry Baresi, Ph.D.
Associate Professor
California State University,
    Northridge
Northridge, California

John Brockhaus, Ph.D.
Department of Geography and
    Environmental Engineering
United States Military Academy
West Point, New York

Mapi Cuevas, Ph.D.
Professor of Chemistry
Santa Fe Community College
Gainesville, Florida

William Guggino, Ph.D.
Professor of Physiology and
    Pediatrics
Johns Hopkins University, School
    of Medicine
Baltimore, Maryland

V. Arthur Hammon
Pre-College Education Specialist
Jet Propulsion Laboratory
Pasadena, California

Steven A. Jennings, Ph.D.
Associate Professor in Geography
University of Colorado at
    Colorado Springs
Colorado Springs, Colorado

James E. Marshall, Ph.D.
Professor and Chair, Department
    of Curriculum and Instruction
California State University,
    Fresno
Fresno, California

Joseph McClure, Ph.D.
Associate Professor Emeritus
Department of Physics
Georgetown University
Washington, D.C.

Dork Sahagian, Ph.D.
Professor of Earth and
    Environmental Science
Lehigh University
Bethlehem, Pennsylvania

Curriculum and Classroom Reviewers

Jay Bell
Science Specialist
Lodi Unified School District
Lodi, California

Ja-Na Castillo
Teacher
Florin Elementary School
Sacramento, California

Michael Lebda
Science Specialist
Fresno Unified School District
Fresno, California

Cherie Liu-Barba
Teacher
Strauch Elementary School
Sacramento, California

Ana G. Lopez
Science Specialist
Fresno Unified School District
Fresno, California

Thomas Monet Richardson
Teacher
Parkview Elementary School
San Jose, California

Printed in the United States of America

ISBN 13: 978-0-15-347121-6
ISBN 10: 0-15-347121-2

2 3 4 5 6 7 8 9 10 048 13 12 11 10 09 08 07 06

Big Idea Scientific progress is made by asking meaningful questions and conducting careful investigations.

Essential Questions

PHYSICAL SCIENCE

Elements and Compounds

56

Big Idea Elements and their combinations account for all the varied types of matter in the world.

Essential Questions

LIFE SCIENCE

UNIT 2 Structures of Living Things

Big Idea Plants and animals have structures for respiration, digestion, waste disposal, and transport of materials.

Essential Questions

Dairy farm, Arvin, California

EARTH SCIENCE

UNIT 3 — The Water Cycle 220

Big Idea Water on Earth moves between the oceans and land through the processes of evaporation and condensation.

Essential Questions

UNIT 4 — Weather 266

Big Idea Energy from the Sun heats Earth unevenly, causing air movements that result in changing weather patterns.

Essential Questions

EARTH SCIENCE

Big Idea The solar system consists of planets and other bodies that orbit the Sun in predictable paths.

Essential Questions

Surfing in Southern California

References

Getting Ready for Science

California Standards in This Unit

6 Scientific progress is made by asking meaningful questions and conducting careful investigations. As a basis for understanding this concept and addressing the content in the other three strands, students should develop their own questions and perform investigations. Students will:

6.a Classify objects in accordance with appropriate criteria.

6.b Develop a testable question.

6.c Plan and conduct a simple investigation based on a student-developed question and write instructions others can follow to carry out the procedure.

6.d Identify the dependent and controlled variables in an investigation.

6.e Identify a single independent variable in a scientific investigation and explain how this variable can be used to collect information to answer a question about the results of an experiment.

6.f Select appropriate tools (e.g., thermometers, metersticks, balances, and graduated cylinders) and make quantitative observations.

6.g Record data by using appropriate graphic representations (including charts, graphs, and labeled diagrams) and make inferences based on those data.

6.h Draw conclusions from scientific evidence and indicate whether further information is needed to support a specific conclusion.

6.i Write a report of an investigation that includes conducting tests, collecting data or examining evidence, and drawing conclusions.

What's the Big Idea?

Your observations can give you ideas for experiments. To plan and carry out an experiment, scientists ask certain questions. They also choose the right tools for finding the answers.

Essential Questions

Alameda

Hi, Jorge!

Today, we went to the Alameda Naval Air Museum. Check out this awesome picture of a Marine jet!

The USS Hornet, an aircraft carrier, is on display here, too. Thousands of planes took off and landed on it.

Now I'm wondering—how exactly do planes fly?

Your friend,

Lea

USA

How might a scientist find the answer to Lea's question? How is that related to the

Big Idea?

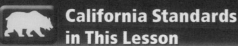

Investigation and Experimentation

6.c Plan and conduct a simple investigation based on a student-developed question and write instructions others can follow to carry out the procedure.

6.f Select appropriate tools (e.g., thermometers, metersticks, balances, and graduated cylinders) and make quantitative observations.

California Fast Fact

Lighter Than Air!

This blimp, hovering above Dodger stadium in Los Angeles, stays in the air because it is filled with helium. The blimp's shiny, flexible body, also known as an envelope, is almost 70 m (206 ft) long. It was painted by children around the region. In this lesson, you will learn about the tools scientists use to measure things like length.

LESSON

1

Essential Question

What Tools Do Scientists Use?

Dodger Stadium,
Los Angeles, California

qualitative observation
[KWAHL•uh•tayt•iv
ahb•zer•VAY•shuhn] An
observation that does not
involve measurements or
numbers (p. 6)

quantitative observation
[KWAHNT•uh•tayt•iv
ahb•zer•VAY•shuhn] An
observation that involves
numbers or measurements
(p. 6)

microscope [MY•kruh•skohp]
A tool that makes small
objects appear larger (p. 8)

balance [BAL•uhns] A tool that
measures an object's mass
(p. 11)

graduated cylinder
[GRA•joo•ayt•id SIL•uhn•der] A
tool used to make quantitative
observations of the volume of
liquids (p. 12)

3

Measuring Up!

Start with Questions

You use measurements every day. You wear clothes and shoes that have been measured to fit you. You eat foods and drinks that are packaged in measured amounts.

- What is measurement?

- What are some ways you can measure how high a kite flies?

Investigate to find out. Then read to find out more.

Prepare to Investigate

Investigation Skill Tip
When you measure, you select appropriate tools and use them to make quantitative observations. Which of the tools will best help you make observations about the balloon?

Materials

- balloon
- hand lens
- tape measure
- ruler
- spring scale

Make a Data Table

	Empty Balloon	Full Balloon
Hand lens		
Ruler		
Tape measure		
Spring scale		

Follow This Procedure

① **Observe** the empty balloon with the hand lens. Copy the chart, and **record** your observations.

② **Measure** the length and circumference of the balloon. **Record** your measurements.

③ Use the spring scale to **measure** the weight of the balloon. **Record** its weight.

④ Blow up the balloon.

⑤ Repeat the observations and **measurements** from Steps 1–3. **Record** your observations and measurements.

Draw Conclusions

1. How did the measurements change when you blew up the balloon? Why?

2. **Standards Link** Do you think that your measurement of the empty balloon or the blown-up balloon was more accurate? Why? `6.f`

3. **Investigation Skill** Work with another group to **measure** its balloon. Do you get different measurements? Why? `6.f`

Step 1

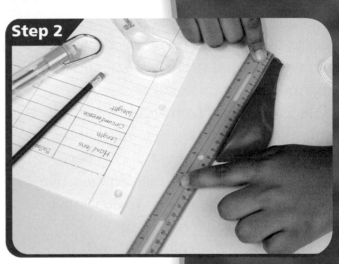
Step 2

Independent Inquiry   **Plan and Conduct an Investigation**

How can you find the volume of a blown-up balloon? Plan and conduct a simple investigation to find out. Be sure to write out instructions that others can follow to carry out the procedure. `6.c`

VOCABULARY
qualitative observation p. 6
quantitative
    observation p. 6
microscope p. 8
balance p. 11
graduated cylinder p. 12

SCIENCE CONCEPTS
▶ how tools are used to make better observations
▶ why a balance and a scale measure different things

Focus Skill MAIN IDEA AND DETAILS
Look for details about how and when each tool is used.

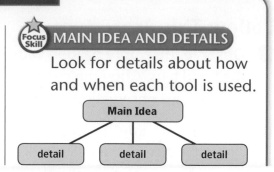

Using Science Inquiry Tools

People in many jobs must use tools. Cooks use pots and pans. Mechanics use screwdrivers and wrenches. Scientists use tools to measure and observe objects in nature. Some tools allow scientists to make observations that do not involve measurement or numbers. These observations are called **qualitative observations**. You can make qualitative observations with a hand lens.

Many useful tools allow scientists to measure, or make observations that use numbers. These observations are called **quantitative observations**. Thermometers and spring scales allow you to make quantitative observations.

Your Science Tool Kit includes a dropper to move liquids, as well as forceps to pick up solids. A hand lens and a magnifying box help you see details. You can measure temperature with the thermometer, length with the ruler or tape measure, and volume with the measuring cup. The spring scale measures weight.

Focus Skill MAIN IDEA AND DETAILS What are four tools you can use to make quantitative observations?

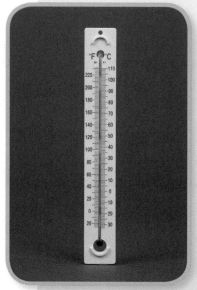

◀ A thermometer measures the temperature of liquids and the air. It measures in degrees Celsius (°C).

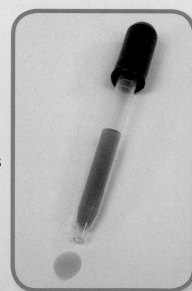

Use a dropper to move small amounts of liquid or to measure volume by counting drops. ▶

◀ A tape measure helps you measure the length of curved or irregular surfaces.

A ruler measures the length and width of objects in centimeters (cm) and millimeters (mm). ▼

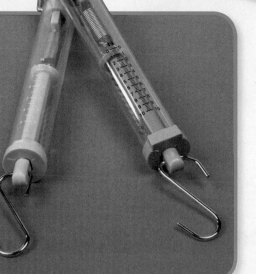

◀ A spring scale measures forces, such as weight or friction. It measures in units called newtons (N).

A measuring cup is used to measure the volume of liquids. It measures in liters (L) and milliliters (mL). ▼

▲ You can place an insect, pebble, or other small object in the magnifying box. Looking through the lid helps you see the object clearly.

A hand lens makes objects look larger and helps you see more detail. ▼

◀ Forceps help you pick up or hold small objects. They are handy for holding small objects under a hand lens.

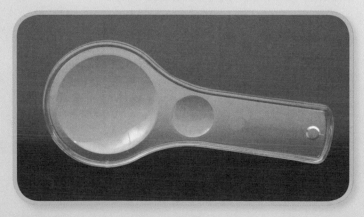

Microscopes

Without a telescope, you can't identify tiny-looking, distant objects in the sky. In the same way, you can't see tiny parts of an insect, all of the particles in a rock, or cells in a leaf without a microscope. A **microscope** is a tool that makes small objects appear larger. It lets you see details you couldn't see with your eyes alone.

People have known for a long time that curved glass can *magnify,* or make things look larger. An early Roman scholar read through a glass ball filled with water. People started making eyeglasses a thousand years ago. They called the curved glass a *lens* because it had the shape of a lentil—a kind of bean!

An early scientist named Anton van Leeuwenhoek used a lens to see creatures in a drop of pond water. He called them animalcules.

In the late 1500s, a Dutch eyeglass maker put a lens on each end of a hollow tube. Changing the length of the tube made tiny objects look three to nine times their actual size. This was probably the first "modern" microscope.

In the 1600s, Robert Hooke used a microscope to study thin slices of cork. He used the word *cell* to describe the tiny, boxlike structures he saw. Now we call the smallest unit of any living thing a cell.

Today's microscopes can magnify objects thousands of times. So a tiny "animalcule" might look as large as a whale!

Most classroom microscopes have several main parts. The

▲ Leeuwenhoek was the first person to see microscopic organisms. He placed tiny samples on the tip of a needle and looked at them through a single lens.

A simple microscope can make things look up to 400 times their actual size. ▼

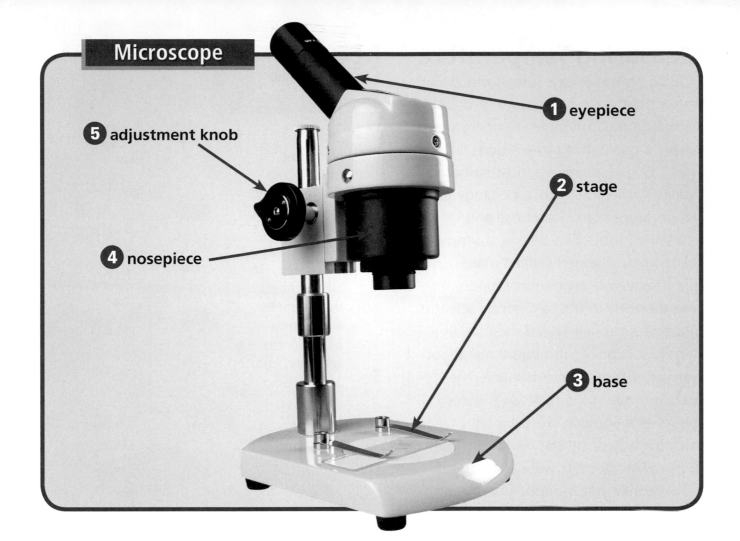

Microscope

5 adjustment knob

4 nosepiece

1 eyepiece

2 stage

3 base

numbers in the following list refer to the numbers in the diagram labels.

1 The eyepiece contains one lens and is mounted at the end of a tube.

2 The stage holds the slide or the object you are looking at.

3 The base supports the microscope. It usually holds a lamp or mirror that shines light through the object.

4 A nosepiece holds one or more lenses that can magnify an object up to 400 times.

5 Adjustment knobs help you focus the lens.

Focus Skill MAIN IDEA AND DETAILS What are the main parts of a microscope?

Research microscopes magnify objects up to 5000 times! These microscopes are used for everything from studying diseases to solving crimes. ▼

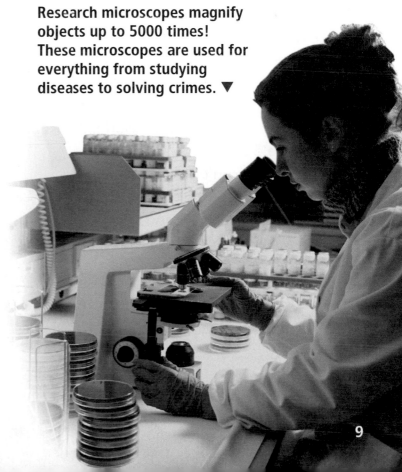

Measuring Temperature

"Boy, it's hot today! It feels much hotter than it was yesterday!" Is it really? Without a measurement, temperature is simply a qualitative observation.

In 1592, an Italian scientist named Galileo Galilei found that a change in temperature made water rise and fall in a sealed tube. This device, a simple *thermometer*, helped Galileo make quantitative observations of nature.

In the early 1700s, a German scientist named Fahrenheit sealed mercury in a thin glass tube. As this liquid metal got warmer, it took up more space. The mercury rose in the tube. As it cooled, the level of liquid in the tube fell. But how was this thermometer to be marked? What units were to be used?

Fahrenheit put the tube into freezing water and into boiling water and marked the mercury levels. Then he divided the difference between the two levels into 180 equal units—called degrees.

In 1742, a Swedish scientist named Celsius made a thermometer with 100 degrees between the freezing and boiling points of water. The Celsius scale is used in most countries of the world. It is also the scale used by all scientists.

Thermometers can't measure extreme temperatures. For example, many metals get to several thousand degrees before they melt. Scientists have other temperature-sensing tools to measure very hot and very cold objects.

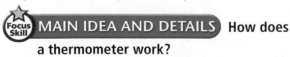 **MAIN IDEA AND DETAILS** How does a thermometer work?

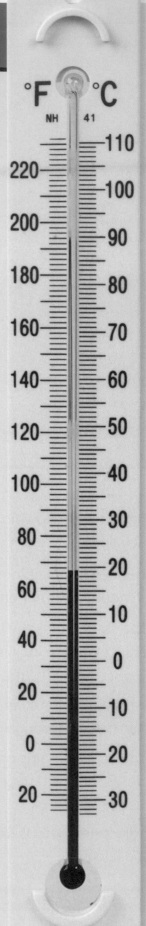

Temperature Scales

Measured on a Celsius thermometer, water boils at 100 degrees and freezes at 0 degrees. On a Fahrenheit thermometer, water boils at 212 degrees and freezes at 32 degrees.

Balance or Spring Scale

Suppose you're a merchant in California in the mid-1800s. A man wants food in exchange for some gold he panned from the bottom of the Yuba River. How much is the gold worth?

To find out, you use a tool that looks like a small seesaw. You place the gold at one end of a beam. Then you add objects with a known mass at the other end until the beam is level. The objects balance! A **balance** is a tool that measures the amount of matter in an object—the object's *mass.* Mass is measured in grams (g) or kilograms (kg).

The balance in your classroom measures mass by balancing an unknown object with one or more objects of known mass. To measure an object's weight, you use a spring scale. You hang the object from a hook on the scale and let gravity pull it down. Gravity is a force that pulls on all objects on or near Earth. Weight is a measure of the force of gravity's pull. The unit for this measurement is the newton (N).

People often confuse mass and weight. To see that they are different, think what happens to the mass of an astronaut as he or she travels from Earth to the International Space Station. Nothing happens! The astronaut's mass stays the same, even though his or her weight is less. The pull of gravity from Earth works against the space station's great speed in orbit.

Focus Skill **MAIN IDEA AND DETAILS** What does a balance measure? What does a spring scale measure?

▲ When you hang an object on the hook of the spring scale, you measure the force of gravity pulling on the object. This is the object's weight.

▲ Find an object's mass, or amount of matter, by first placing the object on one pan. Then add known masses to the other pan until the pointer stays in the middle.

Insta-Lab

Do They Balance?
Place a blown-up balloon on one pan of a balance and an empty balloon on the other pan. Do they have the same mass? Why or why not?

Reading a Graduated Cylinder

A **graduated cylinder** is a tool used to make quantitative observations of the volume of liquids. *Volume* is how much space something takes up. So, a graduated cylinder measures the amount of space a liquid takes up.

Graduated cylinders come in many sizes, measuring liquids in milliliters (mL) or liters (L). The cylinder usually has a wide bottom to keep it from tipping over. The cylinder's top usually has a lip to make pouring easier.

Markings on the cylinder show the units of volume.

When a liquid is poured into a cylinder, it forms a column. At the top, the column of liquid is curved. The curved top of a column of liquid is called the *meniscus* (muh•NIS•kuhs). To measure the volume of a liquid in a graduated cylinder, read the markings on the cylinder in the center of the meniscus, where the liquid is the most level.

 **MAIN IDEA AND DETAILS** What does a graduated cylinder measure?

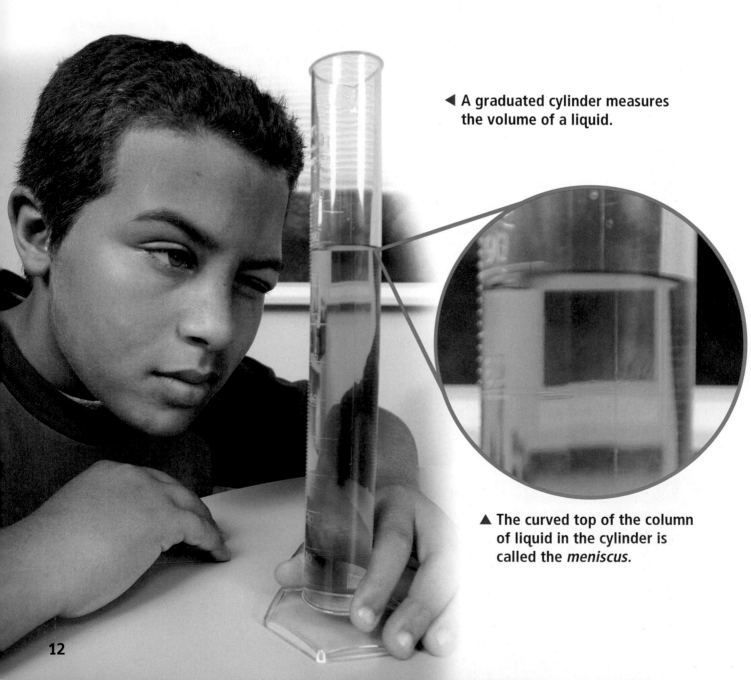

◀ A graduated cylinder measures the volume of a liquid.

▲ The curved top of the column of liquid in the cylinder is called the *meniscus.*

12

Safety in the Lab

Working in the lab is fun, but you need to be careful to stay safe. Here are some general rules to follow:

- Study all the steps of an investigation so that you know what to expect. If you have any questions, ask your teacher.
- Watch for safety icons, and obey all caution statements.

Scientists in the lab wear safety goggles to protect their eyes. Smart students do the same thing! When you work with chemicals or water, a lab apron protects your clothes.

Be careful with sharp objects!

- Scissors, forceps, and even a sharp pencil should be handled with care.
- If you break something made of glass, tell your teacher.
- If you cut yourself, tell your teacher right away.

Be careful with electricity!

- Be especially careful with electric appliances.
- Keep cords out of the way.
- Never pull a plug out of an outlet by the cord.

General Safety

- Pull long hair back and roll up long sleeves to keep them out of the way.
- Never eat or drink during a science activity.
- Don't drink from lab equipment.
- Never work in the lab by yourself.
- Wash your hands with soap and water after cleaning up your work area.

 **MAIN IDEA AND DETAILS** What are four ways to keep safe in the lab?

Standards Wrap-Up and Lesson Review

What tools do scientists use?

In this lesson, you learned about several tools scientists use to make qualitative and quantitative observations.

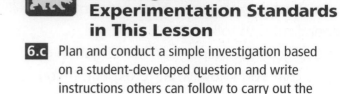

Investigation and Experimentation Standards in This Lesson

6.c Plan and conduct a simple investigation based on a student-developed question and write instructions others can follow to carry out the procedure.

6.f Select appropriate tools (e.g., thermometers, metersticks, balances, and graduated cylinders) and make quantitative observations.

1. **MAIN IDEA AND DETAILS** Draw and complete a graphic organizer to show the supporting details of this main idea: Tools are used to make observations in science. **6.f**

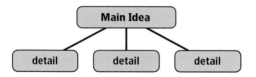

Main Idea — detail, detail, detail

2. **SUMMARIZE** Use your graphic organizer to write a lesson summary. **6.f**

3. **DRAW CONCLUSIONS** Why are different tools used to measure mass and weight? **6.f**

4. **VOCABULARY** Write one sentence describing each vocabulary term. **6.f**

5. **Critical Thinking** You are doing an investigation and spill water on the floor by accident. How could this be a safety problem? Explain. **6.f**

6. **Investigate and Experiment** Write a set of instructions about how to measure the volume of a liquid. Have another student follow your instructions to find the volume of a sample of liquid. **6.c**

7. Why is using a thermometer or graduated cylinder more scientific than estimating temperature or volume?

   A It is easier.

   B It is more accurate.

   C It looks more scientific.

   D It uses up more class time. **6.f**

8. In what ways do tools help scientists make observations? **6.f**

The Big Idea

 Writing ELA–W 2.1

Write a Report

Use reference materials to learn about the life of Anton van Leeuwenhoek. Write a report that includes what he is famous for and what kinds of things he observed by using a microscope.

 Math MG 1.0

Describing Data

A bottle is half full of water. Describe three things you could measure about the water, and name the tools used for the measurements.

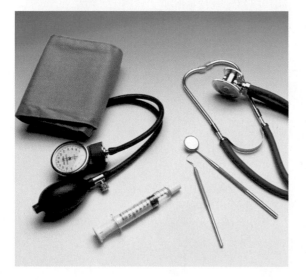

 Health

Measuring for Health

Science tools such as thermometers, balances, and spring scales are used outside of the science laboratory, too. Research how they are used in health care by doctors, nurses, and lab workers in hospitals.

 For more links and activities, go to **www.hspscience.com**

Investigation and Experimentation

6.b Develop a testable question.

6.c Plan and conduct a simple investigation based on a student-developed question and write instructions others can follow to carry out the procedure.

6.d Identify the dependent and controlled variables in an investigation.

6.e Identify a single independent variable in a scientific investigation and explain how this variable can be used to collect information to answer a question about the results of an experiment.

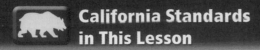

LESSON 2

Essential Question

What Inquiry Skills Do Scientists Use?

California Fast Fact

King of the Bay

Kite-flying is no longer just for kids. In the annual King of the Bay competition, people use kites for kiteboarding in San Francisco Bay. They do dramatic stunts such as midair spins and flips. The wind blowing on the kites gives the boarders the pull and lift they need. The event draws competitors and spectators from around the world.

"Flying" over San Francisco Bay, California

Vocabulary Preview

investigation [in•ves•tuh•GAY•shuhn] A procedure carried out to gather data about an object or event (p. 20)

inquiry [IN•kwer•ee] An organized way to gather information and answer questions (p. 21)

dependent variable [dee•PEN•duhnt VAIR•ee•uh•buhl] The part of an investigation that is being measured or controlled (p. 22)

control variable [kuhn•TROHLD VAIR•ee•uh•buhl] The part of an investigation that remains the same so that the dependent variable can be measured (p. 22)

experiment [ek•SPEHR•uh•muhnt] A procedure you carry out under controlled conditions to test a hypothesis (p. 23)

17

Make a Parachute!

Start with Questions

When scientists carry out investigations, they often ask questions about what they think will happen and why.

- What makes a parachute float slowly to the ground?

- How can you test a hypothesis about parachutes?

Investigate to find out. Then read to find out more.

Prepare to Investigate

Investigation Skill Tip
When you develop a testable question, you ask a question that can be answered by conducting a simple investigation.

Materials

- coffee filter
- hole punch
- string
- scissors
- empty film canister
- 3 marbles
- timer or stopwatch

Make a Data Table

Weight	Time
0 marbles	
1 marble	
2 marbles	
3 marbles	

Follow This Procedure

1 Carefully punch holes, equally spaced, around the edge of the filter.

2 Thread one piece of string through a hole, and tie a knot. Repeat until there is a piece of string tied to each hole.

3 Place the loose ends of the string in the film canister, and snap on the lid.

4 Launch your parachute. Have one group member **record** the time it takes for the parachute to reach the ground.

5 **Measure** and **record** your results.

6 Open the canister, and add a marble. Repeat Steps 3–5. Then repeat the procedure with two marbles and with three marbles in the canister.

Step 1

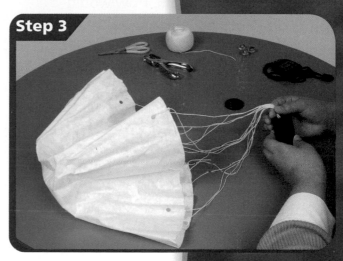
Step 3

Draw Conclusions

1. How did the amount of weight in the canister affect the travel time?

2. **Standards Link** What factor did you change in this investigation? 6.e

3. **Investigation Skill** How would changing the size of the parachute affect the time it stays in the air? **Develop a testable question** about changing the size of the parachute. 6.b

Independent Inquiry

Plan and Conduct an Investigation

Develop a testable question, and then plan and conduct a simple investigation to find out how the length of the strings affects the travel time of a parachute. 6.c

Write out instructions others can follow to carry out the procedure.

Understand Science

VOCABULARY
investigation p. 20
inquiry p. 21
dependent variable p. 22
controlled variable p. 22
experiment p. 23

SCIENCE CONCEPTS
▶ how inquiry skills help you gather information
▶ how an investigation differs from an experiment

Focus Skill **MAIN IDEA AND DETAILS**
Look for information about when to use different inquiry skills.

```
        Main Idea
       /    |    \
  detail  detail  detail
```

What Is Inquiry?

Suppose you wanted to learn about the way parachutes work. How would you begin? You might read a book about parachutes. You might also investigate the subject on your own. An **investigation** is a procedure that is carried out to gather data about an object or event. An investigation can be as simple as measuring an object or observing a change in the environment. At the beginning of this lesson, you investigated how weight affects the flight of a parachute.

How might you learn more about parachutes? Scientists begin an investigation with questions. They use inquiry skills to answer

Inquiry Skills

Observe—Use your senses to gather information about objects and events.

Measure—Compare the length, mass, volume, or another property of an object to a standard unit, such as a meter, gram, or liter.

Gather, Record, and Display Data—Gather data by making observations and measurements. Record your observations and measurements in an organized way. Display your data so others can understand and interpret it.

Use Numbers—Collect, display, and interpret data as numbers.

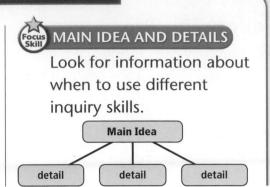

How does a parachute enable a person to jump from an airplane without getting hurt? ▶

their questions. **Inquiry** is an organized way to gather information so you can answer questions.

First, you might **observe** how parachutes are made. You could study diagrams in books or examine parachutes at a local airport. Then, you might **gather, record, and display data** you collected. You could **measure** and **use numbers** to express the data.

You might wonder how a round parachute **compares** to a parachute like the one shown on the previous page. What do they have in common? How are they different? What other shapes can a parachute have? Are parachutes with different shapes best for different jobs? You can **classify** the parachutes by using this information.

Now you've gathered a lot of data. The next step is to **interpret data**. For example, how does the size or shape of the parachute relate to its use? Is there any pattern in the data?

Data and observations can be used in many ways. It depends on what questions you want to answer! You can use the

data to draw conclusions about things you haven't directly observed. For example, you might notice that narrow parachutes are used for tricks. You might **infer** that narrow shapes are easier to control.

 **MAIN IDEA AND DETAILS** What are inquiry skills used for?

Inquiry Skills

Compare—Identify ways in which things or events are alike or different.

Classify—Group or organize objects or events into categories based on certain characteristics.

Interpret Data—Use data to look for patterns, to predict what will happen, or to suggest an answer to a question.

Infer—Use logical reasoning to come to a conclusion based on data and observations.

Predict—Use observations and data to form an idea of what will happen under certain conditions.

How does the size or shape of a parachute affect the way it works? ▶

Investigate

Suppose you were in a contest to find a way to drop a raw egg from a balcony without breaking the egg. First, you must **develop a testable question**, such as "What kind of parachute would you use?"

To answer this question, you might **plan and conduct a simple investigation**. In an investigation, one thing is being controlled or measured. This variable is called a **dependent variable**. In the egg-dropping investigation, the egg's characteristics are dependent variables. They include its size, its shape, and, most importantly, its breakability.

The part of an investigation that remains the same so that the dependent variable can be measured is called a **control variable**. In your investigation, you might make parachutes of different shapes and sizes. You might tie weights on them, drop them, and see how they behave. You could make observations and take measurements.

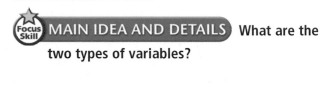 **MAIN IDEA AND DETAILS** What are the two types of variables?

You might wonder what type of parachute would let an egg fall to the ground without breaking. You could plan and conduct a simple investigation to help answer this question. ▼

Experiment

With the information from your investigation, you can **hypothesize**. What design has the best chance to protect the egg? You may think that a large, round parachute is the best design. You could conduct an **experiment** to test your hypothesis. An **experiment** is a procedure you carry out under controlled conditions to test a hypothesis.

An experiment involves more steps than a simple investigation. You have to write down what you do and how you do it. You have to test each control variable separately so that you know how it affects the results. You have to **record** all of your measurements and observations. You have to use your data to **draw conclusions**. What did the experiment show? Did it support your hypothesis?

Finally, you have to present your experiment to **communicate** your results to others. You might write a report and include tables of your data or diagrams of your parachute designs.

Focus Skill MAIN IDEA AND DETAILS How does an experiment differ from an investigation?

This experiment is testing hypotheses about the type of parachute that would keep an egg from breaking. What are the dependent variables? What are the controlled variables? ▶

Inquiry Skills

Develop a Testable Question—Ask a question that can be answered by conducting a simple investigation.

Plan and Conduct a Simple Investigation—Use inquiry skills to gather data and answer a question.

Hypothesize—Suggest an outcome or explanation that can be tested in an experiment.

Experiment—Design a procedure to test a hypothesis under controlled conditions.

Control Variables—Identify and control the factors that can affect the outcome of an experiment.

Draw Conclusions—Use data and experimental results to decide if your hypothesis is supported.

Communicate—Share results and information visually, orally, or electronically.

What testable question might you ask about this group of skydivers? ▲

More to Think About

Two other inquiry skills can help you with your investigation or experiment. For example, have you ever watched a leaf falling from a tree? You might think of a falling leaf as a model for a parachute. It could give you ideas about parachute design. You might **make a model** and test it before making an actual parachute. That can be very practical. Companies that build rockets, for example, save a lot of time and money by making and testing models before building the real ones.

How will your parachute interact with what is attached to it? Thinking about **time and space relationships** is an important inquiry skill. For example, how do you make sure the parachute in a model rocket pops out at the right time? There's a lot to think about! Inquiry skills are ways to make sure your thinking and tests really work.

 **MAIN IDEA AND DETAILS** How do models help an investigation?

 **Insta-Lab**

What Causes Lift?

Cut a strip of newspaper or notebook paper about 2–3 cm long. Hold one end of the strip in your hand, and blow gently over the top of it. What happens? How might the result relate to airplane wings?

Inquiry Skills

Make a Model—Make a mental or physical representation of a process or object. Use a model that someone else has built or something from nature that is similar to what you are investigating.

Use Time/Space Relationships—Think about ways in which moving and nonmoving objects relate to one another. Figure out the order in which things happen.

Using inexpensive models is a good way to test an idea before building the real thing. ▼

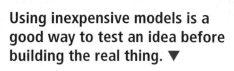

Standards Wrap-Up and Lesson Review

What inquiry skills do scientists use?

In this lesson, you learned about inquiry, investigations, and experiments. You learned about several inquiry skills scientists use to guide the way they answer questions.

Investigation and Experimentation Standards in This Lesson

6.b Develop a testable question.

6.c Plan and conduct a simple investigation.

6.d Identify the dependent and controlled variables in an investigation.

6.e Identify a single independent variable in an investigation and explain how this variable can be used to collect information.

1. **(Focus Skill) MAIN IDEA AND DETAILS** Draw and complete a graphic organizer to show the supporting details of this main idea: Scientists use inquiry skills to help them answer questions. **6.c**

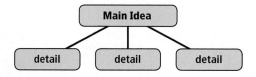

Main Idea

detail   detail   detail

2. **SUMMARIZE** Use your graphic organizer to write a lesson summary. **6.c**

3. **DRAW CONCLUSIONS** If you wanted to learn more about birds, would you be more likely to just make observations first or to experiment first? **6.b**

4. **VOCABULARY** Use the vocabulary terms in a paragraph describing how scientists study the natural world. **6.c**

5. **Critical Thinking** Andrea is testing balloon rockets by using balloons with different amounts of air. Identify three variables Andrea will need to control. **6.d**

6. **Investigate and Experiment** Alberto shines a red light on one group of plants and a blue light on another. He measures the plants each day. What question did he develop to investigate? **6.b**

7. What is the term for a factor that can affect the outcome of an experiment?
   A hypothesis
   B prediction
   C variable
   D model **6.d**

8. List and describe five inquiry skills scientists use. **6.c**

The Big Idea

 ## Writing **ELA–W 2.1**

Write a Report

You use inquiry skills all the time in your everyday life. Write a report about making a special breakfast for your family. Describe how you use inquiry skills to decide what to cook.

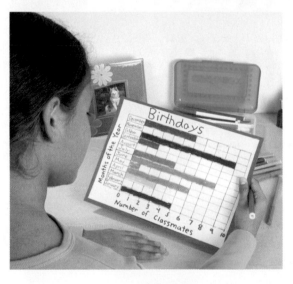

 ## Math **SDAP 1.2**

Display Data

How many of your classmates were born in each month of the year? Make three different charts, tables, or graphs that show this information. Which display gives you the clearest picture of differences between the months?

 ## Social Studies **HSS 5.1**

Make Inferences

Use reference materials to find out how archaeologists make inferences. What information do they use to infer what life was like for peoples in the past? Interview or email a local archaeologist to find out about current projects in your area.

 For more links and activities, go to **www.hspscience.com**

27

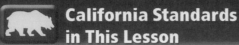

Investigation and Experimentation

6.a Classify objects in accordance with appropriate criteria.

6.b Develop a testable question.

6.d Identify the dependent and controlled variables in an investigation.

6.g Record data by using appropriate graphic representations (including charts, graphs, and labeled diagrams) and make inferences based on those data.

LESSON

3

Essential Question

How Do Scientists Record and Interpret Data?

California Fast Fact

Getting It Wright

This plane in the San Diego Aerospace Museum is a copy of the Wright *Flyer*, the first plane flown in controlled flight. Making the *Flyer* work took years of trial and error by Orville and Wilbur Wright. Long before their 1903 flight, the Wright brothers observed, experimented, and recorded. In this lesson, you'll learn about ways to record results of experiments.

San Diego Aerospace Museum

criteria [kry•TIR•ee•uh] The specific qualities that allow you to group items together (p. 32)

classify [KLAS•uh•fy] To group or organize objects or events into categories, based on criteria that are similar (p. 32)

conclusion
[kuhn•KLOO•zhuhn]
A decision you make, based on information (p. 33)

Design an Airplane

Start with Questions

When scientists carry out investigations, they need to record and interpret their findings. You need to do the same in your own investigations.

- How will you record your data?

- How will you use your results to evaluate your investigation?

Investigate to find out. Then read to find out more.

Prepare to Investigate

Investigation Skill Tip
When you **record data**, you do several things. You make observations and display the data in charts, graphs, or tables. You also **make inferences** based on the data.

Materials

- thick paper
- tape
- meterstick or tape measure
- stopwatch

Make a Data Table

Data Table		Airplane 1	Airplane 2
Trial			
1	time		
	distance		
2	time		
	distance		
3	time		
	distance		

Follow This Procedure

1. Design a paper airplane. Then fold a sheet of paper to make the plane.

2. **Measure** a distance of 10 m in an open area. Mark one end of the distance as a starting line. Place a marker every half meter from the starting line.

3. Test-fly your plane. Have a partner time the flight. **Record** the time in a table like the one shown.

4. **Measure** and **record** the distance the plane flew.

5. Repeat Steps 3 and 4 twice.

6. Make a second airplane with wings half as wide as those on your first plane.

7. Test-fly your second plane three times. **Record** all of your **measurements**.

Step 1

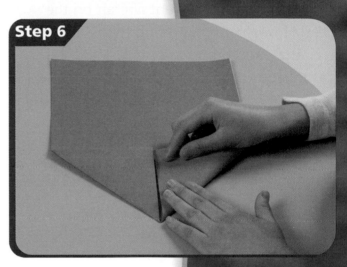

Step 6

Draw Conclusions

1. How did changing the width of the wings affect the way your plane flew?

2. **Standards Link** Identify the **dependent** and **control** variables.   **6.d**

3. **Investigation Skill** Some planes flew faster or farther than others. From the **data recorded**, what can you **infer** about the design of a paper airplane?   **6.g**

Independent Inquiry

Develop a Testable Question

What question might you ask about how the weight of a plane affects the way that the plane flies?   **6.b**

Plan and conduct a simple investigation to answer your question.

Understand Science

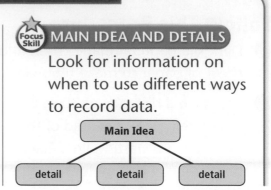

6.a, 6.b, 6.d, 6.g

VOCABULARY
criteria p.32
classify p. 32
conclusion p. 33

SCIENCE CONCEPTS
▶ how objects can be classified
▶ how data can be organized
▶ how organization helps with interpretation

MAIN IDEA AND DETAILS
Look for information on when to use different ways to record data.

Main Idea

detail detail detail

Classifying

Suppose you visit an airport. While there, you notice many different aircraft on the field. How might you group them? Some are large, and others are small. Some carry cargo, and others carry passengers. Some have one engine, and others have two, three, or even four engines. Some are military planes, and some are seaplanes.

The **criteria** you use to group objects together are the specific qualities you use to put the objects into groups. The criteria are also ways to compare the objects. When you **classify**, you actually put the objects into groups based on your criteria.

For example, at the airport, you might classify single-engine planes in one group and twin-engine planes in another. The groups are divided by the number of engines each plane has. Other criteria might be the planes' purposes, such as carrying cargo or passengers, and the size of the planes; two-seaters and jumbo jets.

MAIN IDEA AND DETAILS What information does classification give about the items grouped together?

What criteria would you use to classify these airplanes? ▶

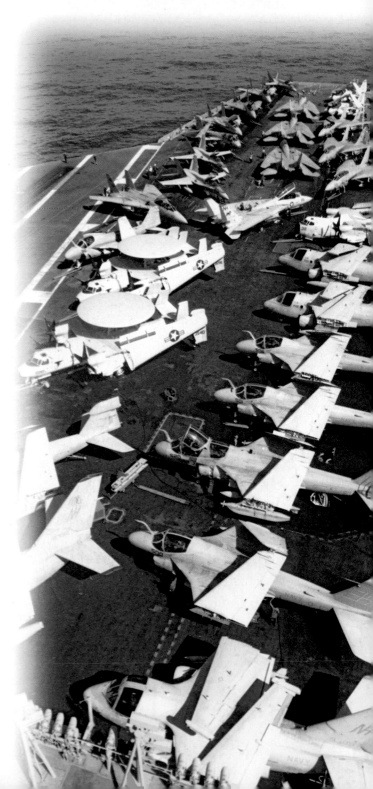

32

Tables and Charts

When you do an investigation in science, you need to use appropriate graphic representations to record the data that you collect. Tables and charts are good ways to organize data so that you and others can understand and interpret the data.

Suppose you're studying the wingspans of airplanes. Your assignment is to find the planes with the shortest and longest wingspans. As you collect information, you can record it in a table.

The table on this page shows the data you might collect. The title describes the information in the table. The headings below the title describe each kind of information. Each wingspan is shown to the right of the plane's name. Look for patterns. Which plane has the longest wingspan? Which has the shortest? You can easily interpret the data to draw a conclusion. A **conclusion** is a decision you make based on information.

 **MAIN IDEA AND DETAILS** How can tables help you draw conclusions?

◀ Tables and charts make it easy for you and other people to understand and interpret data.

Wingspans of Airplanes	
Type of Plane	Wingspan
Bumble Bee	1.9 m (6.3 ft)
Ryan M-2 (Spirit of St. Louis)	14 m (46 ft)
Boeing 727	32.9 m (108 ft)
Airbus A 380	79.8 m (262 ft)

Bar, Line, and Circle Graphs

Like a table, a bar graph can be used to compare information about different objects, events, or groups. To read a bar graph, use the labels as guides. Study the bars and compare the measurements. Look for patterns to help you draw conclusions.

Suppose you want to know how the speed of the U.S. Navy's Blue Angels demonstration planes has changed over time. A line graph can show these changes. In a line graph, the data is recorded as points along a line. Look for patterns by studying changes from point to point. Then draw conclusions.

Suppose you want to see how many of each kind of airplane are at an airport. You could use a circle graph. A circle graph shows the parts of data that form a whole. In this kind of graph, fractions or percentages are used, and the sum of the parts must equal 1, or 100 percent. To read a circle graph, look at the label for each section. It tells what the section shows. You can interpret the data by comparing the sizes of the sections. Then you can draw conclusions.

 MAIN IDEA AND DETAILS What do bar graphs, line graphs, and circle graphs have in common?

Wingspans of Airplanes	
Type of Plane	Wingspan
Bumble Bee	1.9 m (6.3 ft)
Ryan M-2 (Spirit of St. Louis)	14 m (46 ft)
Boeing 727	32.9 m (108 ft)
Airbus A 380	79.8 m (262 ft)

A bar graph can organize the data from a table in a different way. ▼

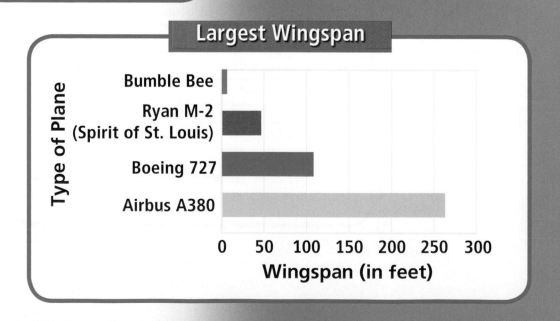

This line graph shows how the speed of airplanes has changed over time. ▼

Airplane Speed		
Year	Plane	Speed
1965	C-130 Hercules	602 km/hr (347 mi/hr)
1970	F-14 Tomcat	3344 km/hr (1520 mi/hr)
1978	F/A-18 Hornet	2640 km/hr (1200 mi/hr)
2010 (est.)	F/A-18G Growler	2640 km/hr (1200 mi/hr)

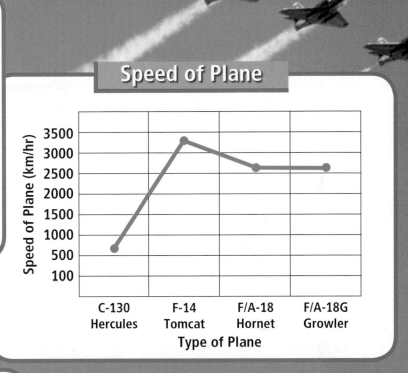

Speed of Plane

Airline Fleet	
Type of Plane	Percentage
Commercial Jetliners	62%
Single-engine corporate jets	28%
Twin-engine commuter planes	6%
Twin-engine cargo planes	4%

Both the table and the bar graph show the percentage of airplanes of each type that make up an airline's fleet. The sum of the percentages is 100 percent. ▶

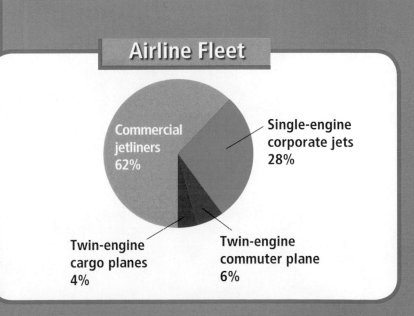

Airline Fleet

35

Diagrams

Suppose you decide to write a report about how helicopters work. To begin, you decide to investigate the structure of a helicopter. You use library and Internet sources to learn more.

As you read, you find a great deal of complex information about the parts of helicopters and how they work together. How can you share this information with your classmates in a way that they can understand?

A *diagram* is a drawing, sketch, or other visual representation that shows an idea or object. Diagrams are usually simple, so they help make complex things easier to understand. Diagrams can also show the parts of an object. A photograph shows the whole object, but a diagram can identify the parts of an object.

Using a diagram of a helicopter, you can show your classmates the moving parts of the machine. The diagram can help you explain how they work together to make the helicopter fly.

 **MAIN IDEA AND DETAILS** How do diagrams make it easier to communicate?

▲ In this photograph, you can see a U.S. Coast Guard helicopter.

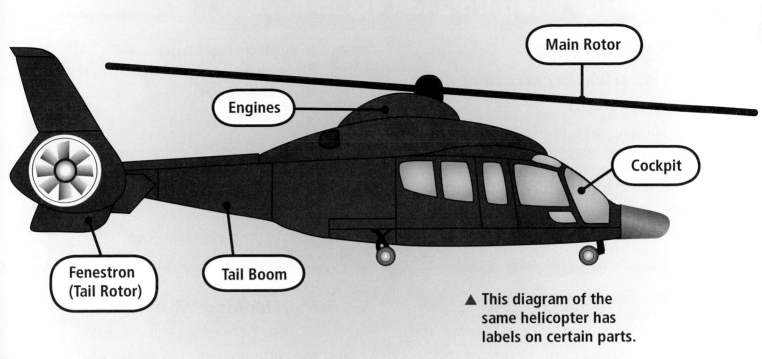

Main Rotor

Engines

Cockpit

Fenestron
(Tail Rotor)

Tail Boom

▲ This diagram of the
same helicopter has
labels on certain parts.

Make a Helicopter

Cut a piece of paper 3 cm wide and
13 cm long. Draw lines on the paper
like those on the diagram above. Cut
along all the solid lines. Fold one flap
forward and one flap to the back.
Fold the base up to add weight at
the bottom. Drop your helicopter, and
watch it fly. How does adding a paper
clip to the bottom change the way the
helicopter flies?

How do scientists record and interpret data?

In this lesson, you learned ways that objects and events can be grouped, as well as how observations and measurements can be recorded and interpreted.

Investigation and Experimentation Standards in This Lesson

6.a Classify objects.

6.b Develop a testable question.

6.d Identify the dependent and controlled variables in an investigation.

6.g Record data by using appropriate graphic representations and make inferences.

1. **(Focus Skill) MAIN IDEA AND DETAILS** Draw and complete a graphic organizer to show the supporting details of this main idea: Scientists use different ways to share data. **6.g**

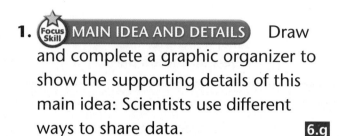

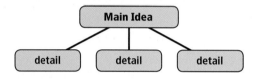

2. **SUMMARIZE** Use your graphic organizer to write a lesson summary. **6.a, 6.g**

3. **DRAW CONCLUSIONS** Suppose you gathered information about how the number of B–727 airplanes has decreased over time. How would you display your data? Why? **6.g**

4. **VOCABULARY** Write one sentence that uses all the vocabulary terms. **6.a**

5. **Critical Thinking** What is the relationship between a hypothesis and the data recorded in tables and graphs? **6.b, 6.g**

6. **Investigation and Experimentation Skill** A fifth-grade class is studying the growth of plants. Light is the students' controlled variable, and the students are measuring the growth of two plants. How might they record their measurements so that they can best compare the results? **6.g**

7. Which of the following allows you to organize information according to specific criteria?
   A graphing   **C** measuring
   B diagraming   **D** classifying **6.a**

8. How is classifying like showing data in tables, charts, and graphs? **6.a, 6.g**

The Big Idea

 Writing ELA–W 1.2

Write a Composition
Scientists record and interpret data in their investigations and experiments. You also interpret data—in fact, every day! Think of your closet. How could you organize it so you can see patterns? Write a short composition describing to a friend how you could organize your closet in different ways.

 Math MR 2.3

Display Data
Circle graphs are often called pie charts because the wedges for the data look like slices of a pie. Use the data at the left to make a circle graph (pie chart). Then write a sentence describing the information.

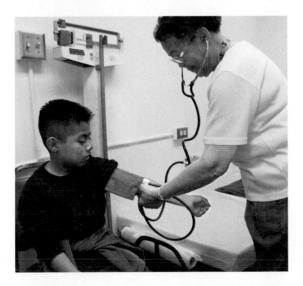

 Health

Graphing for Good Health
Investigate how health-care workers in hospitals record temperature, blood pressure, and pulse rates. Ask a nurse or doctor how this information is gathered, recorded, and interpreted in hospitals.

 For more links and activities, go to **www.hspscience.com**

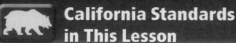

Investigation and Experimentation

6.b Develop a testable question.

6.c Plan and conduct a simple investigation based on a student-developed question and write intructions others can follow to carry out the procedure.

6.d Identify the dependent and controlled variables in an investigation.

6.h Draw conclusions from scientific evidence and indicate whether further information is needed to support a specific conclusion.

6.i Write a report of an investigation that includes conducting tests, collecting data or examining evidence, and drawing conclusions.

California Fast Fact

Reaching for the Stars

In October of 2004, *SpaceShipOne* traveled nearly 112 km (70 mi) above the surface of Earth. The ship reached a speed of Mach 3— three times the speed of sound. It was launched from and landed in the Mojave Desert. *SpaceShipOne* wasn't built or launched by a government or a major aerospace company. It was the first successful private spaceship!

LESSON 4

Essential Question

What Is the Scientific Method?

Mojave Desert, California

scientific method
[sy•uhn•TIF•ik METH•uhd] A series of steps used to plan and carry out an experiment (p. 44)

hypothesis [hy•PAHTH•uh•sis] A testable possible answer to a scientific question (p. 45)

evidence [EV•uh•duhns] Information, collected during an investigation, to support a hypothesis (p. 48)

Build a Rocket

Directed Inquiry ## Start with Questions

When scientists carry out investigations, they often make predictions about what will happen. In this investigation, you'll build a balloon rocket.

- How do you think your balloon rocket will travel?

- What do you think you can do to affect the way the balloon rocket travels?

Investigate to find out. Then read to find out more.

Prepare to Investigate

Investigation Skill Tip
When you draw conclusions from scientific evidence, you should also indicate whether further information is needed to support your conclusion.

Materials

- safety goggles
- string, 5 m
- drinking straw
- 2 chairs
- tape measure
- balloon
- tape
- stopwatch or timer

Make a Data Table

Trial	Amount of Air	Travel Time	Distance Traveled
1			
2			
3			

Follow This Procedure

CAUTION: In Steps 3–7, wear safety goggles.

1 Thread the string through the straw.

2 Place the chairs about 4 m apart, and tie one end of the string to each chair.

3 Blow up the balloon and pinch it shut.

4 Have a partner tape the balloon to the straw, with the balloon's opening near one chair.

5 Release the balloon. Use the stopwatch to time how long the balloon rocket keeps going.

6 **Measure** and **record** the distance and time the balloon rocket travels.

7 Repeat Steps 3–6 with more air in the balloon and then with less air.

Step 2

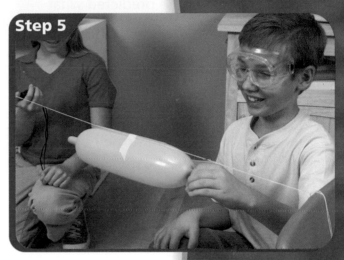

Step 5

Draw Conclusions

1. Why did the balloon rocket move?

2. **Standards Link** How did the amount of air in the balloon affect the time and distance the balloon rocket traveled? `6.g`

3. **Investigation Skill** Would changing the shape of the balloon affect the distance the balloon rocket travels? **Draw a conclusion** from the evidence you collected, and then decide whether more information is needed to support your conclusion. `6.h`

Independent Inquiry — Write a Report

Plan and conduct a simple investigation to find out how the angle of the string affects the travel time and distance of the balloon rocket. Then write a report of the investigation. Include the tests you conducted, the data or evidence you collected, and your conclusions. `6.i`

VOCABULARY
scientific method p. 44
hypothesis p. 45
evidence p. 48

SCIENCE CONCEPTS
▶ what steps are in the scientific method
▶ how scientists use the scientific method

Focus Skill **MAIN IDEA AND DETAILS**
Look for information on the steps of the scientific method.

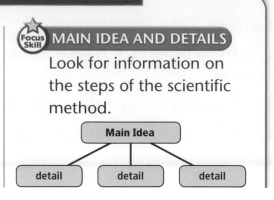

Observe / Ask Questions

In the Investigate, you predicted what would happen if you changed the shape of the balloon in your rocket. How can you tell if your prediction is right? As a scientist, you would follow a series of steps called the **scientific method**.

Scientists use the scientific method to plan and carry out investigations. Some of the steps are the same as inquiry skills. Some other inquiry skills are also used in planning experiments.

There are five steps in the scientific method:

1. Observe, and ask questions.
2. Form a hypothesis.
3. Plan an investigation.
4. Conduct the investigation.
5. Draw conclusions, and write a report.

All investigations start with a testable question. In the Investigate, you were asked how changing the shape of a balloon would affect the way a rocket flies. This is a logical question that came from the Investigate. It can be tested in another investigation.

Focus Skill **MAIN IDEA AND DETAILS** What can help you form a testable question?

1. Use your senses to make observations. Then write *one* question you would like to answer.

A possible answer to your question is a *hypothesis*. A hypothesis is a statement that can be tested.

Form a Hypothesis

After you've formed your question, the next step in the scientific method is to form a hypothesis. A **hypothesis** is a possible answer to your question. It is a statement and must be testable. In the Investigate, you might have hypothesized that a rocket with a round balloon would not travel as far as one with a long balloon. When you make a hypothesis, you don't have to worry about whether it is right or wrong. The results of an investigation will either support the hypothesis or fail to support it.

 **MAIN IDEA AND DETAILS** What is a hypothesis?

Flying Objects

Write a hypothesis about which will travel farther: a rocket with a long balloon or one with a round balloon. Use the scientific method to test your hypothesis.

Plan an Investigation

Suppose you've decided to test your hypothesis that a rocket with a round balloon will travel a shorter distance than a rocket with a long balloon. How can you test this hypothesis?

You can plan an investigation by first deciding what variables you will control. Remember that many variables can affect the outcome of your investigation. In your investigation, the balloon shape will change. All of the other variables must stay the same, so that you know that your results are due to the shape.

After deciding what variables you will control, plan your procedure. Write down the steps you will follow to do your test. Note the materials you will need, and decide how you will gather and record your data.

 **MAIN IDEA AND DETAILS** What steps go into planning an investigation?

46

Conduct an Investigation

By the time you reach the step where you're ready to conduct an investigation, you've already asked a question and given a likely answer. You've decided how to test your hypothesis, written instructions for the procedure, chosen materials, and planned how you will measure and record your data.

Now the fun begins! As you follow your planned procedure, observe and measure carefully. Record everything that happens. Write down what you observe and what you measure. Finally, record your data in a way that is easy to understand and interpret.

 **MAIN IDEA AND DETAILS** What is done during an investigation?

4 Carry out your investigation by following the procedure you wrote down. Record all of your observations and measurements.

Draw Conclusions

After you collect your data, organize it by using appropriate graphic representations. Use charts, tables, or graphs to display your findings.

For your balloon investigation, you might make a table and then a bar graph. They would help you analyze your observations and the data you collected. Try to identify patterns in the data. These can help you determine whether the **evidence**—the information you gathered during the investigation—supports your hypothesis.

If your data does not support your hypothesis, that's OK! Remember, your investigation was designed to answer a question. Your hypothesis was just one possible answer to that question. Even if the data does not support the hypothesis, you have still gathered important information.

Focus Skill **MAIN IDEA AND DETAILS** How do tables, graphs, and charts help you draw conclusions?

5 Organize and analyze your observations and data. Does the evidence support your hypothesis?

5 Your report should be detailed enough to enable others to repeat your investigation.

Write a Report

The final part of the scientific method is writing a report of your findings. In your report, describe your test—what you did and how you did it. Use your charts, tables, and graphs to display your data. Describe the evidence you used to draw conclusions about whether the investigation supported your hypothesis. Communicate clearly, and finish with a statement about whether your hypothesis was supported.

A good report will allow others to carry out the same investigation so that they can see if they get the same results. This is how scientists check each other's investigations to make sure that conclusions are correct.

 **MAIN IDEA AND DETAILS** Why is it important to write a report?

49

Standards Wrap-Up and Lesson Review

Essential Question

What is the scientific method?

In this lesson, you learned that the scientific method is a series of steps used to plan and conduct an investigation.

Investigation and Experimentation Standards in This Lesson

6.b Develop a testable question.

6.c Plan and conduct a simple investigation.

6.d Identify the dependent and controlled variables.

6.h Draw conclusions from scientific evidence and indicate whether further information is needed.

6.i Write a report of an investigation.

---

1. **(Focus Skill) MAIN IDEA AND DETAILS** Draw and complete a graphic organizer to show the supporting details of this main idea: The scientific method has five steps. `6.b, 6.c, 6.d, 6.h, 6.i`

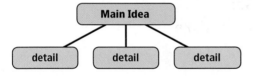

2. **SUMMARIZE** Use your graphic organizer to write a lesson summary. `6.b, 6.c, 6.d, 6.h, 6.i`

3. **DRAW CONCLUSIONS** During which step of the scientific method would you identify variables and figure out how to control them? `6.d`

4. **VOCABULARY** For each letter in *scientific method*, write a science-related word starting with the same letter. Skip repetitions of a letter. `6.b, 6.c, 6.d, 6.h, 6.i`

5. **Critical Thinking** You have done an investigation, and the data does not support your hypothesis. How might you use the information you gathered? `6.b, 6.c, 6.d, 6.h, 6.i`

6. **Investigate and Experiment** Karla concluded from an experiment that for making ice cubes, room-temperature water is better than hot water because it freezes faster. What other evidence might she need to support this conclusion? `6.h`

7. What does an investigation test?
   A a fact
   B a hypothesis
   C a conclusion
   D an experiment `6.c`

8. How does asking questions help you plan an investigation? `6.b, 6.c, 6.d, 6.h, 6.i`

The **Big** Idea

50

 ## Writing ELA–W 2.4

Write a Persuasive Letter

Write a letter to a friend, explaining how he or she could use the scientific method to test a balloon rocket.

 ## Math MR 2.3

Display Data

In the Investigate, you made a table to display how long and how far each balloon rocket flew. Make a graph of the times and a graph of the distances.

 ## Social Studies HSS 5.4

Changes in Method

One of the founders of the United States was known for his scientific experiments. Learn more about how Benjamin Franklin conducted his investigations. Then compare them with the scientific method described in this lesson.

 For more links and activities, go to **www.hspscience.com**

51

▶ Visual Summary

Tell how each picture helps explain the **Big Idea**.

The Big Idea

Scientific progress is made by asking meaningful questions and conducting careful investigations using the scientific method.

6.a, 6.f

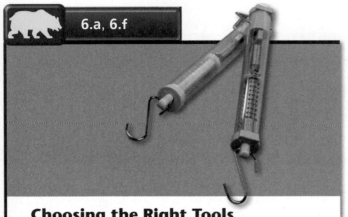

Choosing the Right Tools

This spring scale is just one of the many tools that scientists use to gather information and classify objects.

6.b, c, d, e, h, i

Inquire and Investigate

To answer your questions, you can plan and conduct a simple investigation.

6.g

Recording Data

Using tables, charts, and graphs helps organize data to make it easier to spot patterns.

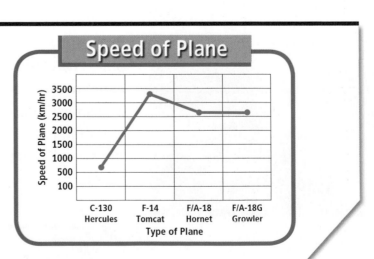

Speed of Plane

Speed of Plane (km/hr)

3500
3000
2500
2000
1500
1000
500
100

C-130 Hercules | F-14 Tomcat | F/A-18 Hornet | F/A-18G Growler

Type of Plane

Show What You Know

Unit Writing Activity

Write an Essay

Greek philosopher and scientist Aristotle was among the first to state that observations using the senses should be used to diagnose, or identify, illnesses. Yet, his ideas were limited by what he and other people believed 2,000 years ago. Use library resources to learn more about how Aristotle answered scientific questions. Then write an essay that compares his "scientific method" with the scientific method used today.

Unit Project

Plan and Conduct an Investigation

How do boomerangs come back when they are thrown? What other kinds of objects fly or float besides airplanes? Research different types of flying objects and design some of your own. See what types of objects fly the farthest, or stay in the air the longest.

Vocabulary Review

Use the terms below to complete the sentences. The page numbers tell you where to look in the unit if you need help.

qualitative observation p. 6

quantitative observation p. 6

balance p. 11

experiment p. 23

classify p. 32

conclusion p. 33

hypothesis p. 45

evidence p. 48

1. A tool used to measure the mass of an object is a _____. `6.f`

2. An observation that does not involve measurements is a _____. `6.f`

3. A procedure you carry out under controlled conditions to test a hypothesis is an _____. `6.c`

4. When you group objects or ideas according to criteria, you _____. `6.a`

5. An observation that involves measurement is a _____. `6.f`

6. A decision you make based on information is a _____. `6.h`

7. A possible answer to a question is a _____. `6.b`

8. Information collected during an investigation is _____. `6.h`

Check Understanding

Choose the best answer.

9. **MAIN IDEA AND DETAILS** Which of the following investigation steps is done first? `6.b`
   A test a hypothesis   **C** interpret data
   B form a hypothesis   **D** ask questions

10. **MAIN IDEA AND DETAILS** Classifying, measuring, and recording data are all examples of what process? `6.a, f, g`
    A communicating
    B inquiry
    C hypothesizing
    D conclusion

11. Why are tables, charts, diagrams, and graphs useful? `6.g`

Use the image below to answer questions 12 and 13.

12. Identify Tool R and its function. How is it read? `6.f`

13. Identify Tool S and its function. How is it used? `6.f`

14. Why do scientists classify objects using specific criteria? `6.a`

15. Why are safety goggles important when doing an investigation with liquids or glass? `6.f`

16. Describe why you should write a report after conducting an investigation. `6.i`

Investigation Skill

17. Andrea is testing balloon rockets with different amounts of air. What is the dependent variable in her investigation? What will she need to control? `6.c, d, e`

18. Which boat do you think will finish second in the race? Write a hypothesis. `6.b`

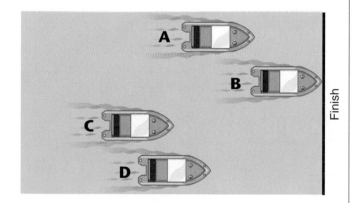

Critical Thinking

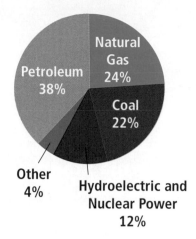

19. Suppose wind, geothermal, and solar energy make up some of the "other" energy sources in the United States. Will they be a greater or lesser part of U.S. energy sources in the future? Why? `6.h`

20. The diagram shows an experiment. Different amounts of water were placed in four beakers. The beakers were heated at the same rate. The data shows how long it took each beaker to boil.

The Big Idea

2.0 min.   4.0 min.   6.0 min.   7.9 min.

What variables were controlled in the experiment? What conclusion is supported by the experiment? Explain.

Elements and Compounds

California Standards in This Unit

1 Elements and their combinations account for all the varied types of matter in the world. As a basis for understanding this concept:

1.a *Students know* that during chemical reactions the atoms in the reactants rearrange to form products with different properties.

1.b *Students know* all matter is made of atoms, which may combine to form molecules.

1.c *Students know* metals have properties in common, such as high electrical and thermal conductivity. Some metals, such as aluminum (Al), iron (Fe), nickel (Ni), copper (Cu), silver (Ag), are pure elements; others, such as steel and brass, are composed of a combination of elemental needs.

1.d *Students know* that each element is made of one kind of atom and that the elements are organized in the periodic table by chemical properties.

1.e *Students know* scientists have developed intruments that can create discrete images of atoms and molecules that show that atoms and molecules often occur in well-ordered arrays.

1.f *Students know* differences in chemical and physical properties of substances are used to separate mixtures and identify compounds.

1.g *Students know* properties of solid, liquid, and gaseous substances, such as sugar ($C_6H_{12}O_6$), water (H_2O), helium (He), oxygen (O_2), nitrogen (N_2), and carbon dioxide (CO_2).

1.h *Students know* living organisms and most materials are composed of just a few elements.

1.i *Students know* the common properties of salts, such as sodium chloride (NaCl).

This unit also includes these Investigation and Experimentation Standards: **6.a 6.b 6.c 6.g 6.h**

What's the Big Idea?

There are about 100 different kinds of matter called elements. When these elements combine in different ways, they form all the other types of matter, including living things.

Essential Questions

Shasta Valley, California

Dear Julio,

You won't believe what we did today! For my birthday, we went for a balloon ride. They filled the balloon with hot air. We rode in a basket underneath.

Now I know how a bird feels. I could see for miles, and it was really quiet. It was noisy only when the pilot lit a fire so we could go higher! Wow!

Your friend,

Taber

What did the pilot burn to make the balloon go higher? How does that relate to the **Big Idea?**

Unit Inquiry

Freezing Point of Water

When roads are covered with ice, people pour salt on the ice to melt it. The salt combines with the ice, forming salt water. The ice melts because salt water freezes at a lower temperature than fresh water does. What happens to the freezing point of water when other substances are added? Plan and conduct an experiment to find out.

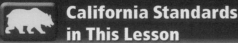
Science Content

1.b *Students know* all matter is made of atoms, which may combine to form molecules.

1.d *Students know* that each element is made of one kind of atom and that the elements are organized in the periodic table by their chemical properties.

1.f *Students know* differences in chemical and physical properties of substances are used to separate mixtures and identify compounds.

Investigation and Experimentation

6.a Classify objects (e.g., rocks, plants, leaves) in accordance with appropriate criteria.

6.b Develop a testable question.

California Fast Fact

Colorful Elements

Some theme parks in California have fireworks displays. Fireworks are very colorful because they contain different elements. Each element burns with a different color. The element strontium burns with a red color. Calcium burns orange, and sodium produces a yellow color.

LESSON 1

Essential Question

What Are Atoms and Elements?

Fireworks at Disneyland in Anaheim, California

Vocabulary Preview

atom [AT•um] The smallest unit of an element that has the properties of that element (p. 62)

element [EL•uh•muhnt] A substance made of only one kind of atom (p. 62)

periodic table [pir•ee•AHD•ik TAY•buhl] A table that shows the elements arranged by their atomic numbers (p. 64)

compound [KAHM•pownd] A substance made of two or more different elements (p. 66)

molecule [MAHL•uh•kyool] A group of two or more atoms that are joined (p. 66)

physical property [FIZ•ih•kuhl PRAHP•er•tee] A trait—such as color, shape, or hardness—that describes a substance by itself (p. 68)

mixture [MIKS•cher] A combination of two or more different substances (p. 69)

59

Classifying and Organizing Matter

Start with Questions

When you use different kinds of objects to build a sculpture, the pieces don't always fit together.

- What determines the ways in which objects fit together?

- Do these ways in which objects fit together affect the things that can be made from them?

Investigate to find out. Then read to find out more.

Prepare to Investigate

Investigation Skill Tip
When scientists classify, they group objects into categories based on specific properties.

Materials

Small plastic bag containing:

- small, medium, and large metal nails
- small, medium, and large bolts
- small, medium, and large washers
- small, medium, and large metal nuts

Make an Observation Chart

Follow This Procedure

1. Copy the chart on page 60. Make each box in the chart large enough to hold the largest nail or bolt.

2. Empty the bag onto the top of a chart. Group the objects by their physical properties.

3. **Classify** the objects by placing them together, in your chart, to form columns and rows. Items in the same row should have similar properties.

4. **Observe** the groups that you made in your chart. Improve the chart by putting all the items that have the same properties into the same column. You may move objects, but leave them in the same rows.

Draw Conclusions

1. Write a sentence describing your groups. How did you decide on ways to group the objects?

2. **Standards Link** What properties affect the ways that objects can fit together to make larger objects? `1.f`

3. **Investigation Skill** What properties did you use to **classify** and organize your objects? How did you improve your classification? `6.a`

Step 2

Step 3

Independent Inquiry > **Develop a Testable Question**

What question might you ask about how the simple objects listed in your chart could be combined to make objects that are more complex? `6.b`

Plan and conduct a simple investigation to answer your own question.

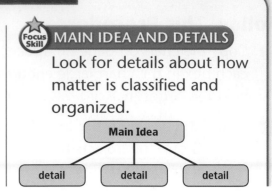
VOCABULARY
atom p. 62
element p. 62
periodic table p. 64
compound p. 66
molecule p. 66
physical property p. 68
mixture p. 69

SCIENCE CONCEPTS
▶ what atoms and molecules are
▶ how compounds are formed

Focus Skill **MAIN IDEA AND DETAILS)**
Look for details about how matter is classified and organized.

| Main Idea |
| detail | detail | detail |

Atoms and Elements

Have you ever used charcoal to draw a picture? If so, you probably had a fine black powder on your fingers when you were done. The powder was probably so fine, you couldn't see each grain of it. Suppose, however, that you could get to see each grain. How small would a piece of the powder be?

Charcoal is made of a single type of matter called carbon. Centuries ago, Greek thinkers wondered about the smallest unit of matter. They didn't know how small that unit was, but they called it an *atom*.

An **atom** is the smallest unit of an element that still has the properties of that element. An **element** is the simplest form of matter because it contains only one type of atom. Carbon, oxygen, iron, and hydrogen are all elements.

The Greeks thought that atoms couldn't be broken down any smaller. Today, we know that atoms are made of smaller particles—*protons, neutrons, and electrons*.

All protons are alike. All neutrons are alike. All electrons are alike. They don't have the properties of any element. An element's properties are created when these particles combine.

You may know that you can combine flour, milk, sugar, and eggs in different

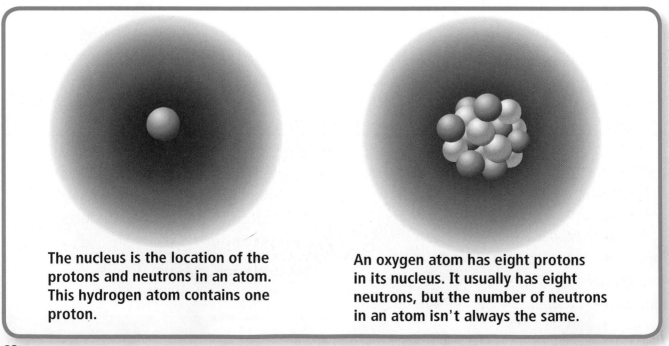

The nucleus is the location of the protons and neutrons in an atom. This hydrogen atom contains one proton.

An oxygen atom has eight protons in its nucleus. It usually has eight neutrons, but the number of neutrons in an atom isn't always the same.

Science Up Close

For more links and animations, go to **www.hspscience.com**

Carbon

All carbon atoms are alike. They combine in different ways with one another and with other elements to form many kinds of matter. A carbon atom has 6 protons.

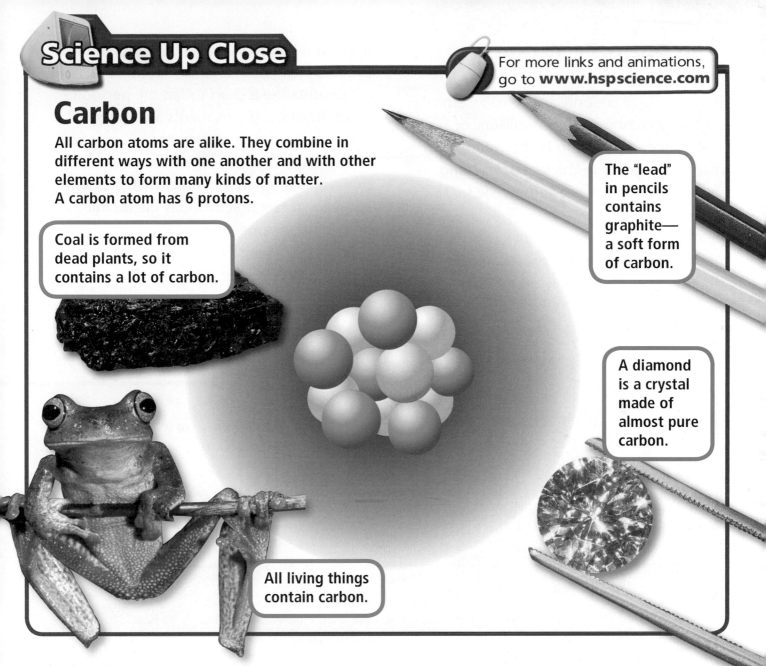

Coal is formed from dead plants, so it contains a lot of carbon.

The "lead" in pencils contains graphite— a soft form of carbon.

A diamond is a crystal made of almost pure carbon.

All living things contain carbon.

amounts to make either a cake or cookies. In the same way, protons, neutrons, and electrons combine in different ways. The number of protons an atom has determines what element it is.

Each type of atom has the properties of a certain element. Carbon atoms have the properties of carbon. Gold atoms have the properties of gold.

The early Greeks thought there were four elements—earth, air, fire, and water. Today, we know that there are more than 100 elements. In nature, only a few of them are found in pure states.

Each element name can be written in a short form—with one, two, or three letters that stand for that element. For many elements, such as carbon (C) and aluminum (Al), the symbol is the first few letters of the name. For others, such as iron (Fe), the symbol comes from the original Latin or Greek name for the element. The name for iron in Latin is *ferrum*.

Focus Skill **MAIN IDEA AND DETAILS** How are atoms and elements related?

63

The Periodic Table

Elements are the building blocks of matter. There are only about 100 elements, but they combine to form millions of substances. Everything in the world, from the tiniest insect to the largest building, is made from combinations of the same elements.

Atoms of each element have a certain number of protons. For example, each hydrogen atom has only one proton. Each iron atom has 26 protons. The number of protons in an atom is its *atomic number*.

Scientists use a chart called the **periodic table**, in which the elements are arranged in order of atomic number. Atomic numbers increase as you move across a row and down a column. In the table, each element has its own box that includes the atomic number, the name, and the symbol. Which element has atoms with 79 protons? What is the atomic number for copper?

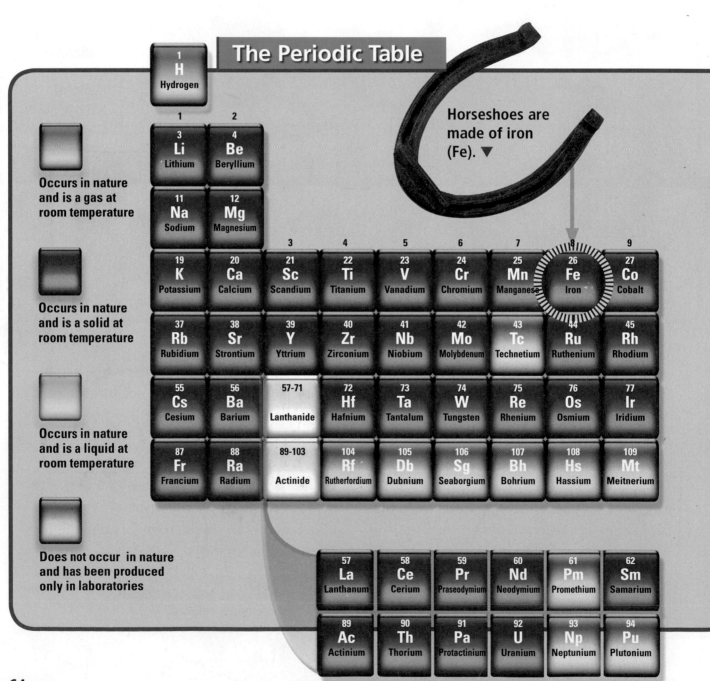

Horseshoes are made of iron (Fe). ▼

The periodic table tells us a lot about each element. All the elements on the left side, except for hydrogen, are metals. The elements on the far right side of the table are nonmetals. Many of these are gases. The blue color shows which are gases.

Only two elements are liquids at room temperature. Which ones are they? Where in the table are the elements that have been made only in labs?

The elements in each column of the table have similar properties. For example, look at column 1 in the table. Lithium, sodium, and potassium are all soft metals that can be cut with a knife. Look in column 17. Find fluorine. All of the elements in that column combine very easily with the elements in the first column.

The word *periodic* means "repeating in a pattern." Scientists use the patterns in the periodic table to predict what the elements will be like.

Focus Skill **MAIN IDEA AND DETAILS** How are elements arranged in the periodic table?

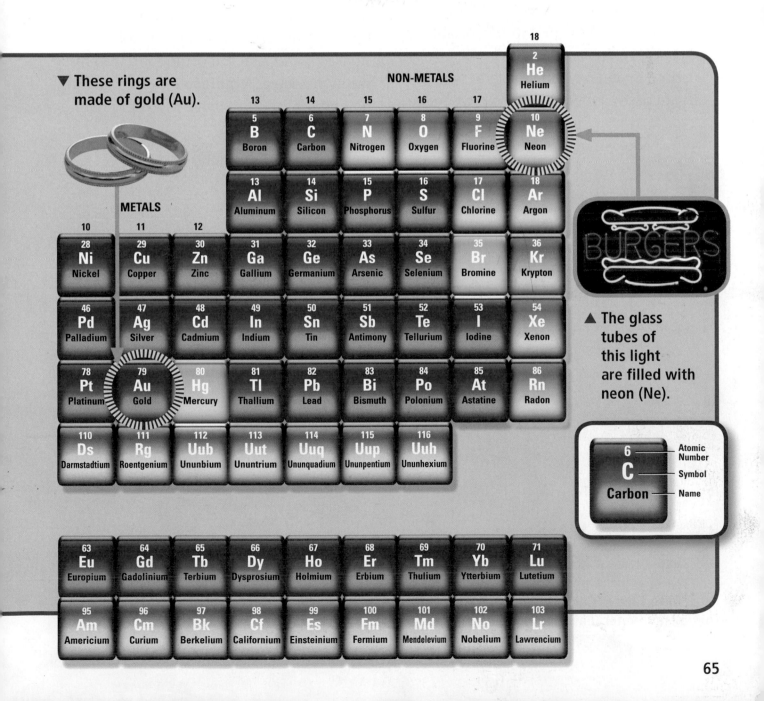

▼ These rings are made of gold (Au).

METALS

NON-METALS

▲ The glass tubes of this light are filled with neon (Ne).

The glass tubes of this light are filled with neon (Ne).

6 — Atomic Number
C — Symbol
Carbon — Name

65

Molecules and Compounds

Elements are rarely found in their pure forms in nature. Most are found in compounds. A **compound** is a substance made of atoms from two or more elements that have been combined chemically. A compound has a *formula*—symbols that show how many atoms of each element are present. For example, H_2O and $NaCl$ are the formulas for water and table salt.

At one time, people thought that water was an element. Later, scientists found that water can be broken apart into hydrogen and oxygen atoms.

Hydrogen and oxygen are elements. Both are gases. If hydrogen and oxygen are mixed together, nothing happens. But if a little energy in the form of a flame is added, atoms of hydrogen and oxygen make water.

The same atoms can sometimes combine to form different compounds. For example, carbon and hydrogen can combine in many different ways. The combination CH_4, called *methane*, is found in natural gas. Natural gas is mostly methane. C_3H_8 is propane, the gas used for heating in some homes and for cooking.

Pure substances include elements and compounds. In a pure substance, all particles are alike. The smallest particle of the element carbon is a carbon atom. The smallest particle of the compound water is a water molecule. A **molecule** is the smallest unit of a compound that can exist in nature.

A water molecule is made up of two hydrogen atoms and one oxygen atom.

Yosemite Falls in California has billions of water molecules in it.

Elements in a Compound

The mineral halite is a compound of sodium and chlorine. It's also known as rock salt. It's mined where ancient seas and salt lakes evaporated millions of years ago. ▼

◄ Table salt is a compound of of sodium (Na) and of chlorine (Cl). Its chemical formula is NaCl.

◄ The element sodium is a metal.

The element chlorine is a gas. ▶

SODIUM

Chlorine

The numbers after the element's symbol tell how many atoms are in a single molecule.

Some atoms of gases, such as hydrogen, oxygen, and nitrogen, are found in nature in pairs. Two atoms of the same element bond to form a molecule. That's why those gases have a formula such as N_2. They are still elements, because they are made of only one type of atom.

Focus Skill MAIN IDEA AND DETAILS How can there be so many different types of matter when there are so few elements?

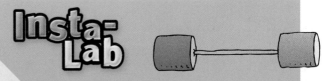

Insta-Lab

Marshmallow Models
Use different-colored mini-marshmallows to represent atoms of hydrogen (H) and oxygen (O). With short lengths of toothpicks, make models of two water molecules. How does the compound differ from the original elements?

Physical Properties

How would you describe your favorite food? You might describe its shape, color, texture, taste, or smell. You use your senses to observe these things. They are all physical properties of the food.

Physical properties are the traits that describe a substance by itself, not by the way it combines with other substances. For example, fur is soft. Wood is solid. Water is wet. These are all physical properties.

Some physical properties can't be observed directly. You can't see the temperature of a teapot. You can't feel how much mass an elephant has. Temperature and mass are physical properties, but you have to use a thermometer or a balance to observe those properties.

The way many substances look can change. For example, water can be a solid, a liquid, or a gas. Water is still H_2O in any of these forms, or states, even as solid ice, although it looks different in each state. The state in which matter exists is a physical property, and a change in state is a physical change. A *physical change* is a change in which a substance remains the same substance. Its form changes, but not its chemical makeup.

Solubility, or the ability to dissolve, is also a physical property. Sugar can dissolve in water. Sand can't. When sugar dissolves, the sugar molecules are still there. The sugar just breaks into pieces too small to see.

Math in Science
Interpret Data

Melting and Boiling Points

- Which substance in the table has the greatest difference between its melting and boiling points?
- Which substance boils at the lowest temperature?

Element or Compound	Melting Point (°C)	Boiling Point (°C)
Water	0	100
Table salt	801	1465
Aluminum	660	2467
Nitrogen	−210	−196

At very high temperatures, aluminum melts.

Nitrogen boils at very low temperatures.

Alcohol and water mix. Oil and water don't. The words *dissolve* and *mix* are clues that a physical change has happened. The substances don't change.

A **mixture** is a combination of two or more substances in which the substances themselves aren't changed. The substances undergo a physical change when they mix, but they can be separated from the mixture. They will be the same as they were before they were mixed.

Most materials found in nature are mixtures. For example, sand at the beach is a mixture of rocks, broken shells, and other materials. You can separate the materials in the sand by sifting or by other methods. The original pieces keep their own properties.

Some mixtures are blended so well that it's hard to see the parts. A sugar-and-water mixture looks as if it contains only water. The sugar seems to disappear. A mixture in which all the parts are mixed evenly is called a *solution*.

Focus Skill **MAIN IDEA AND DETAILS** What are some ways you can tell that a change is a physical one?

Solid carbon dioxide doesn't melt. It "sublimes," or changes directly from a solid to a gas. That's why it's called dry ice. ▼

▲ A mixture can be formed from a combination of solids, liquids, or gases. For example, a coin is a mixture of different metals.

Standards Wrap-Up and Lesson Review

What are atoms and elements?

In this lesson, you learned that atoms are the smallest particles of an element that have the properties of that element. All matter in the world is made up of combinations of elements.

 Science Content Standards in This Lesson

1.b *Students know* all matter is made of atoms . . .

1.d *Students know* . . . elements are organized . . . by their chemical properties.

1.f *Students know* . . . properties . . . are used to separate mixtures and identify compounds.

1. (**Focus Skill**) **MAIN IDEA AND DETAILS** Draw and complete a graphic organizer to show the supporting details of this main idea: There are more than 100 elements. `1.b, 1.d, 1.f`

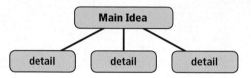

2. **SUMMARIZE** Use the completed graphic organizer to write a lesson summary. `1.b, 1.d, 1.f`

3. **DRAW CONCLUSIONS** How could physical properties be used to separate the parts of a salad? `1.f`

4. **VOCABULARY** Write a paragraph that contains four of the vocabulary terms from the lesson. `1.b, 1.d, 1.f`

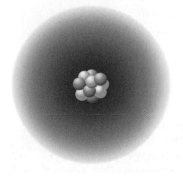

5. **Critical Thinking** The formula for one kind of sugar is $C_6H_{12}O_6$. The formula for potato starch is $C_6H_{10}O_5$. Which statement is true about these two compounds?

   A Both are listed in the periodic table

   B Both have the same physical properties.

   C Both are made of hydrogen, carbon, and oxygen atoms.

   D One molecule of each has the same number of hydrogen atoms. `1.b`

6. **Investigate and Experiment** How is the classification in the Investigate like the periodic table? `6.a`

7. Which of the following does **not** appear in the periodic table?

   A atomic name

   B atomic number

   C element's symbol

   D date discovered `1.d`

8. Explain how elements and compounds can form so many different types of matter. `1.b`

The Big Idea

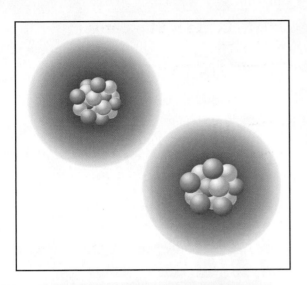

Writing

ELA–W 1.2

Dramatic Writing

Write a conversation between an oxygen atom and a carbon atom. Have them discuss their most important properties or facts. Then write your conversation as dialogue in the form of a script.

Melting and Boiling Points

Element or Compound	Melting Point (°C)	Boiling Point (°C)
Water	0	100
Table salt	801	1465
Aluminum	660	2467
Nitrogen	−210	−196

Math

MR 1.2

Display Data

Communicate the data in this table in the form of a bar graph. Be sure to label the axes of your graph, and include a title and a key.

Health

Essential Elements

Study the nutrition labels on cereal boxes. Look for these elements that are needed for good health: iron, phosphorus, and calcium. How much of each of these elements does a serving of one kind of cereal provide?

For more links and activities, go to **www.hspscience.com**

Dream Machines

Welcome to the car showroom of the future! Step right up and take a look at some of our new models. If going fast is your thing, climb into this superfast car that can zip along at 405 km (252 miles) per hour! Say goodbye to smog with these cars. The AUTOnomy runs on clean-burning hydrogen instead of gasoline. The Hypercar runs on gasoline and hydrogen.

Drive, He Said
The cars of the future are already here as "prototypes." The real thing might even be ready once you get your driver's license.

Zoom, Zoom, Zoom

A European carmaker recently unveiled its 1001-horsepower ultrafast supercar, which can reach a top speed of 405 km (252 miles) per hour. The car is made of lightweight materials. It also has specially made tires that won't melt when the car hits high rates of speed.

Engineers designed the bottom of the car to create the "venturi effect." The venturi effect is a downward pull that helps keep the car on the road.

H Is for "Hydrogen Power"

Can engineers design a car that doesn't cause pollution? An American carmaker thinks it can. The carmaker is working to build cars that operate on hydrogen-powered fuel cells.

Fuel cells, like batteries, store energy. Unlike batteries, however, fuel cells never lose power and never need to be recharged as long as there is enough hydrogen fuel. Fuel cells create energy through the combination of hydrogen and oxygen. That energy can power an electric car motor.

The new AUTOnomy car runs on a series of hydrogen fuel cells. Instead of producing pollution, the AUTOnomy produces water vapor. Scientists expect AUTOnomy's hydrogen-powered system to get the equivalent of 161 km (100 miles) per gallon of hydrogen.

Another type of hydrogen-powered car is the Hypercar, which will run on a fuel system based on gasoline and hydrogen. Scientists say the vehicle will be able to travel 482 km (300 mi) on a gallon of gas.

The design of the Hypercar is friendly to the environment, too. The vehicle is made from lightweight materials called composites—two or more substances that strengthen the individual properties of each material. The Hypercar is not as heavy as a typical vehicle, so it needs less energy to accelerate.

 ## Think and Write

❶ How might cars powered by fuel cells help prevent pollution? `1.a`

❷ How might using lighter materials to build a car help with fuel efficiency? `1.c`

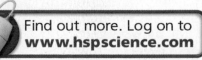
Find out more. Log on to
www.hspscience.com

Science Content

1.c *Students know* metals have properties in common, such as high electrical and thermal conductivity. Some metals, such as aluminum (Al), iron (Fe), nickel (Ni), copper (Cu), silver (Ag), and gold (Au), are pure elements; others, such as steel and brass, are composed of a combination of elemental metals.

1.e *Students know* scientists have developed instruments that can create discrete images of atoms and molecules that show that the atoms and molecules often occur in well-ordered arrays.

Investigation and Experimentation

6.g Record data by using appropriate graphic representations and make inferences based on those data.

6.h Draw conclusions from scientific evidence and indicate whether further information is needed to support a specific conclusion.

California Fast Fact

Bright and Shiny

The dome on San Francisco's City Hall is taller than the dome on the U.S. Capitol building in Washington, D.C.! The dome was originally covered with gold leaf over copper. Today, the dome is covered with gold leaf over paint.

LESSON 2

Essential Question

What Are Metals?

San Francisco City Hall

metal [MET•uhl] A substance that transfers heat and electricity well and is malleable (p. 78)

nonmetal [nahn•MET•uhl] A substance that does not transfer heat and electricity well and is not malleable (p. 78)

malleable [MAL•ee•uh•buhl] Easy to shape or to form (p. 79)

alloy [AL•oy] A solid solution in which a metal or a nonmetal dissolves in a metal (p. 84)

metalloid [MET uh•loyd] A substance that has some of the properties of a metal and some of the properties of a nonmetal (p. 85)

Testing Metals and Nonmetals

Start with Questions

Before you connect a wire to a light, you must "strip" the wire.

- Why must you strip the wire before using it?

- What would happen if you didn't strip the wire?

Investigate to find out. Then read to find out more.

Prepare to Investigate

> **Investigation Skill Tip**
> Scientists record data by using appropriate graphic representations in order to make inferences based on the data.

Materials

- light bulb holder
- battery
- battery holder
- light bulb
- 3 lengths of insulated wire with bare ends
- 3-cm length of bare copper wire
- straightened paper clip
- piece of graphite (pencil lead)
- short strips of aluminum foil, cardboard, foam, rubber tubing, and plastic

Make an Observation Chart

Test Object	Appearance	Lights the Bulb	Bends Without Breaking
wire			
paper clip			
graphite			

Follow This Procedure

1. Copy the table. **Observe** each of the materials, and try to bend each one. **Record** your observations in the table.

2. Use the three insulated wires to connect the battery holder and the light bulb holder as shown in the picture. Leave the two free wire ends separated.

3. Screw in the light bulb, and place the battery in the holder. Touch the ends of the free wires together. **Observe**, and **record** your observations.

4. Separate the wires. Place one of the other test objects between the two wires so that both wires are touching it. **Record** what happens.

5. Repeat Step 4 with each of the other test objects.

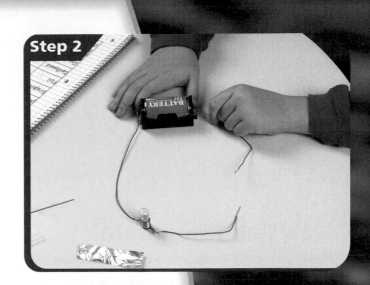

Step 2

Step 4

Draw Conclusions

1. Why is copper a good choice for connecting parts of an electrical device?

2. **Standards Link** Which type of material was able to conduct electricity? `1.c`

3. **Investigation Skill** What other graphic organizer could you have used to **record** your **data** in this Investigate? `6.g`

Independent Inquiry

Draw Conclusions from Scientific Evidence

For which tested item or items do you need more information before listing the item(s) in a certain group? `6.h`

Plan and conduct a simple investigation to test the item(s) in order to have enough information to support a specific conclusion.

VOCABULARY
metal p. 78
nonmetal p. 78
malleable p. 79
alloy p. 84
metalloid p. 85

SCIENCE CONCEPTS
▶ what metals, nonmetals, and metalloids are
▶ what some properties of metals are

Focus Skill **MAIN IDEA AND DETAILS**
Look for details about the properties of metals.

Main Idea

detail | detail | detail

Metals and Nonmetals

Have you ever touched a metal slide on a hot summer day? The slide was probably hot, too. A **metal** is a substance that is a good conductor of heat and electricity. Metals heat up quickly, and electricity passes through them easily.

About 75 percent of all elements are metals. Metals are grouped together in the periodic table on the left side and in the middle. Hydrogen is an exception. Hydrogen and the elements found on the far right side of the periodic table are nonmetals. **Nonmetals** are substances

Common Metals

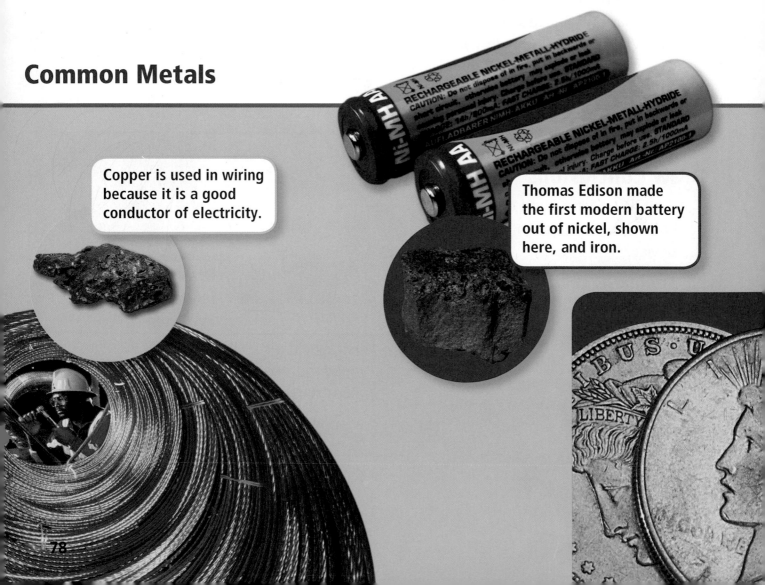

Copper is used in wiring because it is a good conductor of electricity.

Thomas Edison made the first modern battery out of nickel, shown here, and iron.

that don't have the properties of metals. On a warm day, a metal slide feels much hotter than a plastic slide does. Plastic—a substance made of nonmetals—doesn't conduct heat or electricity very well.

Substances that look like metals are called *metallic*. Metals reflect light and are often shiny. Gold and silver are good examples. New pennies are shiny because they are coated, or covered, with the metal copper.

Most metals are silver or gray in color. Gold and copper are the most common nongray metals. Metals are also **malleable**. They are easy to shape, or form. They can be hammered or rolled into very thin sheets. The gold on the San Francisco City Hall dome is less than one millimeter thick.

In the Investigate, you used metal wires. Metals are *ductile* (DUHK•tuhl). This means that they can be pulled into thin strands—such as wires—without breaking.

Gold was probably the first metal used by humans, more than 8,000 years ago. This is because gold doesn't rust and is often found in nature as a pure element. It also doesn't tarnish, or change colors. As humans learned to work with metals, other forms of technology improved, too. Today, people are able to build tall buildings, safe cars, and strong homes by using metals.

 **Focus Skill** **MAIN IDEA AND DETAILS** How can you tell whether a substance is a metal?

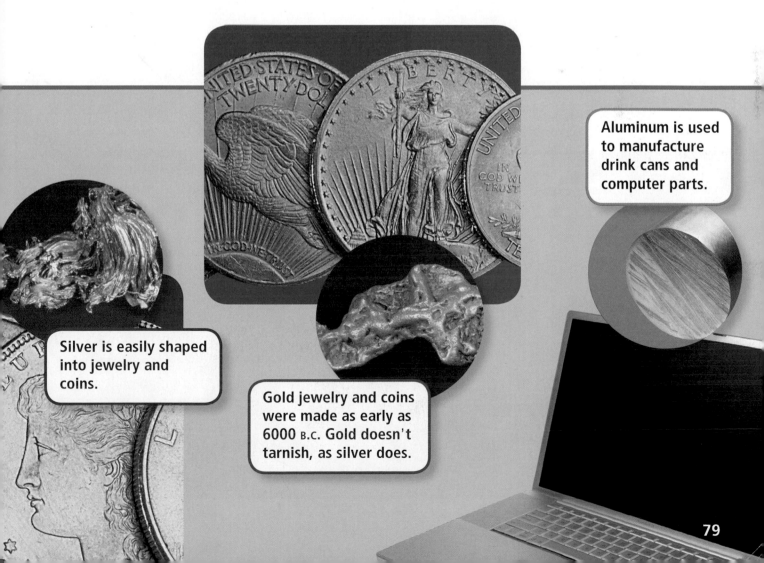

Silver is easily shaped into jewelry and coins.

Gold jewelry and coins were made as early as 6000 B.C. Gold doesn't tarnish, as silver does.

Aluminum is used to manufacture drink cans and computer parts.

Properties of Metals

All the elements in the same column of the periodic table are called a "family." Like members of a real family, these elements are related. Most metals in a family have the same physical properties. For example, lithium and other metals in the first column are the most active metals. When they are exposed to air, some of them start burning!

Other physical properties of metals include their melting and boiling points. One metal, mercury, is a liquid at room temperature. When mercury is heated or cooled, it expands or shrinks evenly. Because of this, mercury was once used in thermometers.

Many cooking pans are made of metal. Metals are good conductors of heat. They have a high *thermal conductivity*.

The handles of pans are often covered with plastic or wood. This is because nonmetals don't conduct heat well. Heat doesn't transfer from the pan to your hand as fast if the pan has a nonmetal handle.

Another important use of metals is in electrical wiring. When you look at the cord on an appliance, you see rubber or plastic. Inside, the wire is made of metal, usually copper. Copper allows electricity to pass easily through it. Metals are good conductors of electricity. That is, they have a high *electrical conductivity*. Silver has better

Melting Points of Metals

Mercury	Gallium	Tungsten
−39°C (−38°F)	30°C (86°F)	3410°C (6170°F)

Mercury remains a liquid at the outdoor temperatures of most places. Because of this, it is used in outdoor thermometers and barometers.	Some computer parts such as transistors and semiconductors, are made of gallium.	Tungsten's high melting point makes it perfect for light bulb filaments.

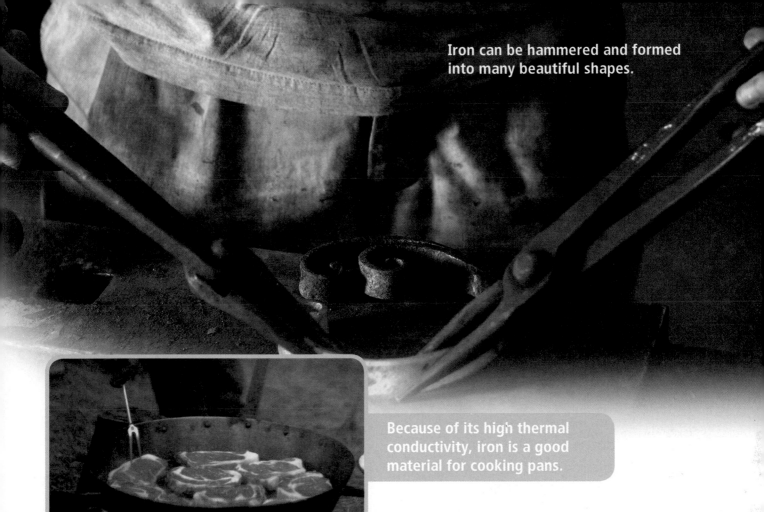

Iron can be hammered and formed into many beautiful shapes.

Because of its high thermal conductivity, iron is a good material for cooking pans.

aluminum airplane into the air than it would to lift one made of iron or copper.

electrical conductivity than copper. But, making wires out of silver costs too much.

In the Investigate, you found that plastic and rubber kept the light bulb from lighting. Those materials don't conduct electricity. Materials that don't conduct electricity or heat well are called *insulators*. The plastic or rubber covering on electrical cords and plugs is an insulator, which keeps you from getting a shock!

Some metals, such as aluminum and titanium, are much less dense than others. This means that the same volume of metal has much less mass. Metals such as these are very light. They are often used in airplanes and other objects in which weight is important. It takes a lot less fuel to lift an

Focus Skill MAIN IDEA AND DETAILS How do the properties of metals affect the ways they are used?

Insta-Lab

Conductors of Heat

Put hot water into two cups. Place a piece of graphite (from a mechanical pencil) in one cup. Put a copper wire in the other. After a few minutes, carefully touch the graphite and the copper. Can you feel a difference? What does this experiment tell you about metals and nonmetals?

Seeing Metal Atoms

Atoms are really small! Twenty million large atoms placed side by side would measure only one centimeter. How can scientists study something that small?

Most microscopes magnify only about 1000 times. In the 1930s, scientists built an electron microscope that could magnify more than 50,000 times. An *electron microscope* uses a stream of electrons to produce images of objects. Scientists could then see objects—such as the parts of cells—in great detail.

In the 1980s, a new type of microscope gave scientists their first look at atoms. A *scanning tunneling microscope*, or STM, uses a probe to examine the surface of a material. It produces an image based on how many electrons move from each part of the surface to the probe. At first, the images of atoms looked like fuzzy balls projected onto a television screen. Scientists could infer that atoms were separate objects that had rounded shapes. They could also see that atoms in solids were arranged in specific patterns.

As STMs have improved, images of atoms have gotten much clearer. Scientists can even use an STM to move individual atoms on the surface of a metal. They hope to make new materials in this way.

The properties of an object depend on how its atoms join with one another. With an STM, scientists can watch atoms form natural crystals and arrays. An *array* is a

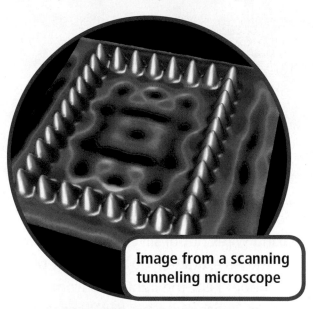

Image from a scanning tunneling microscope

Can you find the place where atoms are missing? The empty space could cause this metal to be weak.

An electron microscope doesn't have an eyepiece. Images are projected onto a screen.

pattern of atoms. Sometimes, a well-ordered array has a missing piece, or flaw. Scientists can use STMs to learn how and where flaws form. They can see and remove atoms that don't belong in a metal.

This technology may become very helpful to people. For example, scientists hypothesize that sulfur atoms may have been mixed with the iron that was used to build the *Titanic* in the early 1900s. The sulfur made the iron weak, so when the *Titanic* struck the iceberg, the iron pieces broke apart and the ship sank. Today, with STMs, scientists can check materials for flaws before the materials are used.

Scientists can also use STMs to observe molecules. They can see the shapes of the molecules and learn why certain elements will or won't join together. Understanding how atoms work together can help scientists improve all kinds of electronic devices.

Focus Skill **MAIN IDEA AND DETAILS** Why do scientists want to be able to see atoms?

This mask is made of billions of iron and copper atoms.

This piece of iron is not pure. There are copper atoms mixed in.

The smallest part of an array of iron is shaped like a cube.

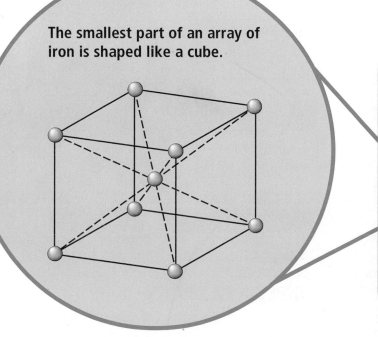

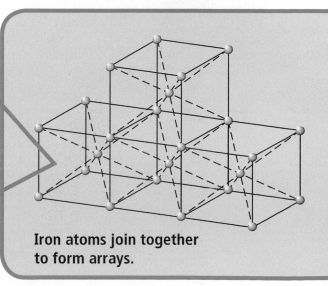

Iron atoms join together to form arrays.

83

Alloys and Metalloids

Do you use "silverware" to eat your meals? Your forks and spoons may actually be made of stainless steel. Some good flatware still contains silver—but steel costs a lot less!

Steel is an alloy. An **alloy** is a solid solution made by combining metals or a metal and a nonmetal. An alloy has properties that are different from the elements that the alloy contains. Iron is the main metal in many steel alloys, but iron is not very hard. When it is made into steel by adding carbon, it is much stronger.

The first alloys were different kinds of bronze. Mixing tin with copper makes bronze, which is harder, stronger, and less likely to corrode than copper. To

corrode means "to combine with things—like oxygen—and to break materials down." Many large statues are made of bronze. They can be outside in extreme weather for years without corroding. Ship propellers are made of bronze that contains the metal manganese. This alloy resists corrosion by sea water. Another form of bronze contains aluminum. This alloy doesn't cause sparks when it's hit. This is useful around materials that burn easily.

There are many different forms of steel. High-carbon steel is strong and flexible. It is used for wire springs. Low-carbon steel can be formed into shapes, such as gas tanks.

High-quality stainless steel has chromium in it. Stainless steel doesn't rust, and it won't combine with the chemicals in food. The alloy is easy to keep clean.

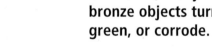

brass

bronze

Over time, many bronze objects turn green, or corrode. ▶

Some Common Alloys

Name	Main Substances	Properties
Brass	copper zinc	bright yellow, soft
Bronze	copper tin	resists corrosion, hard
Pewter	tin antimony copper	silver-colored, shiny
Steel	iron manganese carbon	much stronger than iron
Stainless Steel	steel chromium nickel	strong as steel, but will not corrode

The metalloid silicon is a semiconductor. It is used to make computer chips.

▲ The elements that are used in steel alloys depend on how the steel will be used.

There are even stainless steels that don't contain iron! You can use a magnet to see if your spoons and forks contain iron. If they do, the magnet will attract them.

Metalloids are elements that have some properties of metals and some of nonmetals. They are also called *semimetals*. Silicon is one example. It looks shiny, but it isn't as strong as a metal. It breaks when you hit it with a hammer. It conducts electricity, but not as well as copper or silver, so the flow of electricity can easily be controlled. Metalloids with this property, including silicon and germanium, are called semiconductors. Semiconductors are used in computers and in portable devices such as digital music players.

MAIN IDEA AND DETAILS How do we determine which metals and other elements to use to make an alloy?

Standards Wrap-Up and Lesson Review

1. **(Focus Skill) MAIN IDEA AND DETAILS** Draw and complete a graphic organizer to show the supporting details of this main idea: Metals have different physical properties. **1.c**

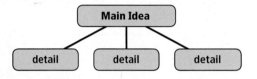

Main Idea — detail, detail, detail

2. **SUMMARIZE** Summarize the lesson by using the five vocabulary terms in a paragraph. **1.c**

3. **DRAW CONCLUSIONS** What properties do arrays of metals have that makes metals in things like sewing needles, pans, and even skyscrapers? **1.e**

4. **VOCABULARY** Use the words *metal* and *alloy* in a sentence. **1.c**

5. **Critical Thinking** Colonists used a metallic substance called pewter to make plates and cups. Pewter is not shown on the periodic table. What can you infer about pewter?

A It's really a nonmetal.

B It's an alloy.

C It's a plastic.

D It has another name. **1.c**

6. **Investigate and Experiment** Think about what you learned in the Investigate. How would you change your conclusions about whether the test objects would conduct electricity? **6.h**

7. Which of the following substances is an alloy?

A iron   **C** chromium

B bronze   **D** manganese **1.c**

8. Explain how you use metals in your daily life. **1.c**

The Big Idea

 Writing ELA–WA 2.3

Write a Report

Some metals, such as lead, have been known since ancient times, but some were discovered more recently. Find out how one of these metals was discovered or produced and how it got its name. Write a report about what you find.

9÷3 **Math** MG 2.1

Mass Math

A block of lead and a block of aluminum are the same size. The block of lead has a mass of 11.4 g. The block of aluminum has a mass of 2.7 g. How many times the mass of the aluminum block does the block of lead have?

 Art VPA–VA 2.4

Make a Piece of Art

Create a piece of art out of common metal objects. The art should be abstract, but it should have some theme that expresses an idea or an emotion. Are some metals easier to work with than others?

 For more links and activities, go to **www.hspscience.com**

Yuan Tseh Lee

▶ **YUAN TSEH LEE**

▶ **Former researcher at Lawrence Berkeley Lab**

▶ **Won Nobel Prize for work on chemical reactions**

▶ Wants university researchers to study ways to make the world better

As a student in Taiwan, Yuan T. Lee was a member of his school's baseball team and a championship table-tennis player. He played trombone in the marching band. Lee was also a serious reader. He was very inspired by a biography of Marie Curie. Her dedication to science and belief that science could make the world better convinced Lee to be a scientist.

After earning his Ph.D. in chemistry at the University of California at Berkeley, Lee continued to do research at that university and at the Lawrence Berkeley National Laboratory. In 1986, Lee and two other scientists won the Nobel Prize for their study of chemical reactions.

After winning the prize, Lee returned to Taiwan to help that country develop. He thinks scientists and researchers at universities should be concerned about the future of humankind. "We need to become good citizens in the global village instead of competing," he said. "What are we competing for—to drive more cars, eat more steaks? That will destroy the world." He thinks we should be researching things that will make people's lives better and help the world become a safer place.

✍ Think and Write

1 How do you think Marie Curie's ideas affected Yuan Lee and his career in science?

2 What kinds of things do chemical researchers spend the most time on?

1.a

In a chemical reaction, reactants combine to form products faster than the eye can blink. Yuan T. Lee won the Nobel Prize for figuring out what happens during that brief time.

Dmitri Mendeleev

When you're the youngest of 17 children, you have to do something to be noticed. Dmitri Mendeleev became a good student and was especially good at chemistry. In 1864, he became a professor of chemistry, but he couldn't find a textbook he liked. So he decided to write one!

▶ **DMITRI MENDELEEV**

▶ **Developed the periodic table**

▶ Predicted properties of elements that had not yet been discovered

While writing his book, Mendeleev tried to classify elements by their properties. He noticed that if elements are arranged in order, their properties repeat themselves. By writing the elements in rows and columns, he found that elements in the same column, or family, have similar properties. His chart enabled chemists to study not only each element itself, but also the relationships between elements. Today, we call his chart the periodic table.

Mendeleev's table had gaps because some elements hadn't been discovered yet. Instead of becoming discouraged, though, he predicted what those elements would be like when they were discovered. Within 20 years, three "missing" elements were discovered. They all had the properties he had predicted!

In Mendeleev's time, people didn't know about protons and atomic numbers. The order of the elements on today's periodic table is slightly different from Mendeleev's, but the table is just as useful.

✍️ Think and Write

1. How did Mendeleev's chart help him predict the properties of undiscovered elements? **1.d**

2. What do you think was Mendeleev's greatest contribution to the knowledge of matter?

> Mendeleev discovered the law of periodicity—the idea that properties of elements repeat themselves in a regular pattern.

89

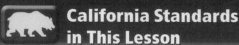
Science Content

1.g *Students know* properties of solid, liquid, and gaseous substances, such as sugar ($C_6H_{12}O_6$), water (H_2O), helium (He), oxygen (O_2), nitrogen (N_2), and carbon dioxide (CO_2).

1.h *Students know* living organisms and most materials are composed of just a few elements.

Investigation and Experimentation

6.c Plan and conduct a simple investigation based on a student-developed question and write instructions others can follow to carry out the procedure.

6.g Record data by using appropriate graphic representations (including charts, graphs, and labeled diagrams) and make inferences based on those data.

California Fast Fact

Get Your Fresh Fruit Here!

There are more than 350 farmers' markets around California. You can buy many things, including flowers, freshly baked pies, and spices. Many of the markets sell foods that were grown organically. This means that no chemical fertilizers or pesticides were used to grow them. Chemical fertilizers and pesticides have properties that may affect foods that are grown using them.

Essential Question

What Are the Properties of Some Common Substances?

gas [GAS] The state of matter that does not have a definite shape or volume (p. 94)

liquid [LIH•kwid] The state of matter that has a definite volume but no definite shape (p. 96)

solid [SAHL•id] The state of matter that has a definite shape and a definite volume (p. 98)

Farmers' market, San Francisco, California

Speedy Bubbles

Start with Questions

When you open a bottle of soda or carbonated water, bubbles appear. Sometimes there are a lot and sometimes just a few.

- What determines how many and how fast bubbles appear?

Investigate to find out. Then read to find out more.

Prepare to Investigate

Investigation Skill Tip
When you record data, you use appropriate graphic representation to help you make inferences based on the data.

Materials

- 3 250-mL beakers
- 300-mL cold carbonated drink
- hot tap water
- small bucket or deep bowl
- measuring cup
- sugar

Make a Data Table

	room temperature water	hot water	sugar water
before			
after			

Follow This Procedure

1. Label the first beaker *room temperature*, the second beaker *hot water*, and the third beaker *sugar*.

2. Place 100 mL of the carbonated drink in each of the three beakers. Wait until the bubbling has stopped.

3. Set the first beaker aside on the table. Let it stand undisturbed, and **observe** it from time to time, until you complete the other steps.

4. Set the second beaker in the container without shaking it. Place enough hot tap water in the bucket or bowl so the water is even with the carbonated drink. **Observe and record** what happens in the beaker.

5. Add a teaspoon of sugar to the third beaker. Don't stir. **Record** your **observations**.

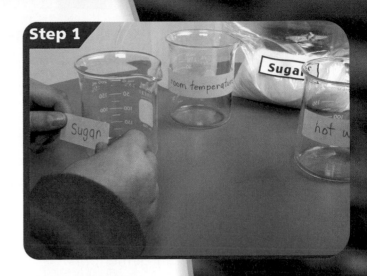

Step 1

Step 4

Draw Conclusions

1. How did your observations of the three beakers compare?

2. **Standard Link** What affects how fast the bubbles come out of a carbonated drink? **1.g**

3. **Investigation Skill** What kind of graph or table could you use to **record data** in this Investigate? What other data would you need to make a graph? **6.g**

Independent Inquiry

Develop a Testable Question

Think about what you have observed. What other question could you test? Plan and conduct a simple investigation to answer the question. **6.c**

Write a procedure for the investigation that another student could follow. Be sure to include materials, steps to follow, and things to look for.

VOCABULARY
gas p. 94
liquid p. 96
solid p. 98

SCIENCE CONCEPTS
▶ what properties common liquids and gases have
▶ what elements are found in living things

Focus Skill **MAIN IDEA AND DETAILS**
Look for properties of familiar substances.

Main Idea		
detail	detail	detail

Common Gases

Air is invisible. Without it, there would be no life on Earth. Air isn't an element or a compound. It is a mixture of gases. A **gas** is a state of matter that has no definite shape or volume. There's no formula for air. The air in a big city may contain gases that you won't find in country air. But the overall makeup of air is roughly the same all over the Earth.

About 78 percent of air is nitrogen (N_2). Nitrogen is a gas that reacts with other elements to form many compounds. These compounds are needed by many living things.

About 21 percent of air is oxygen (O_2).

Oxygen is the element other substances combine with when they burn. All animals need oxygen—even fish! Fish take in oxygen that is dissolved in water. Plants release oxygen when they make food.

A less common form of oxygen is ozone (O_3). *Ozone* is a pale blue gas with a sharp odor. It is poisonous even in small amounts. Fortunately, most of Earth's ozone is in the upper atmosphere. It absorbs some of the more harmful energy from the sun. It also helps keep Earth at a constant temperature.

There is no hydrogen (H_2) in the air. That's a good thing, because when a flame gets too close to a mixture of hydrogen and oxygen, it explodes! However,

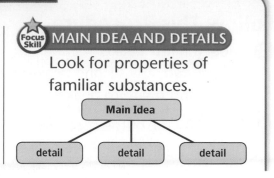

The balloon filled with helium weighs less than the same balloon filled with air, so it floats!

Gases in the Atmosphere

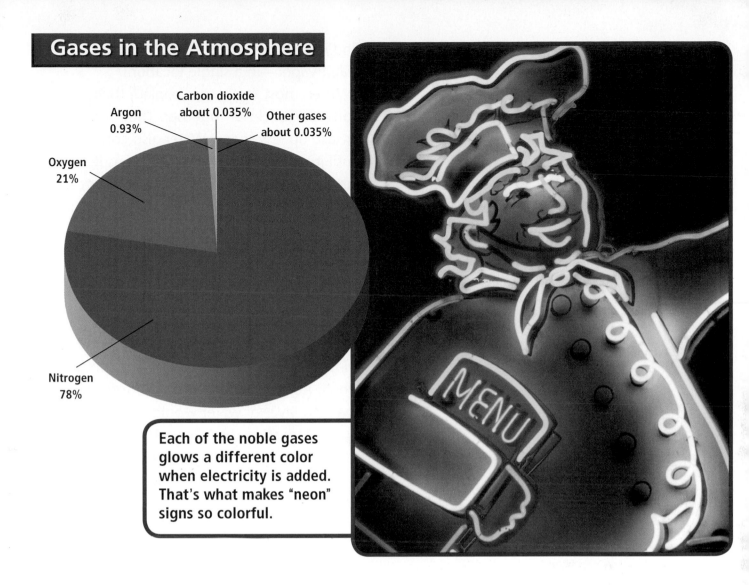

Carbon dioxide about 0.035%

Argon 0.93%

Other gases about 0.035%

Oxygen 21%

Nitrogen 78%

Each of the noble gases glows a different color when electricity is added. That's what makes "neon" signs so colorful.

there's a lot of hydrogen in space. In fact, hydrogen is the most common element in the universe. It combines with other elements to form hundreds of thousands of compounds.

Look back at the periodic table on pages 64–65. The last column contains the elements helium (He), neon (Ne), argon (Ar), krypton (Kr), and xenon (Xe). They are called the noble gases. They don't combine with other elements, but they are still useful.

You've probably seen giant balloons in parades. They are filled with helium gas. Helium is also used in lighter-than-air craft, such as blimps and weather balloons.

The noble gases are used in the kind of signs people call "neon signs." They're really not all neon signs, because each of the colors is produced by a different noble gas.

Two common gases are compounds containing carbon. They are carbon dioxide (CO_2) and methane (CH_4). Carbon dioxide makes up much of the gas you exhale. It's also the gas used in some fire extinguishers. Many homes use natural gas furnaces or stoves.

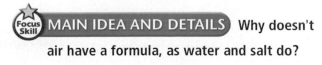 **MAIN IDEA AND DETAILS** Why doesn't air have a formula, as water and salt do?

Common Liquids

Oceans cover more than 70 percent of Earth, making water the most common liquid on the planet. A **liquid** is a state of matter that has a definite volume, but no definite shape.

Have you heard the expression "Water, water everywhere, and not a drop to drink"? The oceans, which account for 97% of all the water on Earth, are salt water. We don't drink salt water. The salt has to be removed first.

Another 2 percent of Earth's water is frozen in glaciers and ice caps. Only 1 percent of Earth's water is in a form that humans and animals can use. This water is found in lakes, rivers and groundwater.

Water has other interesting properties. It is the only compound on Earth that you can find in all three states—liquid water, ice, and water vapor—in a single location!

When most liquids are cooled, their particles get closer together. They contract, or take up less space. Water also contracts—until it reaches about 4°C (39°F). As it cools further, it expands! As the water changes to ice, the molecules form rings with holes in the middle. The rings take up more space than the loose molecules.

That's why ice cubes take up more room in an ice cube tray than the water from which they were made. It's also why ice floats. What would happen to a lake in winter if ice didn't float? The water on top would freeze and sink to the bottom. Then the next layer of water would freeze and sink. Pretty soon the lake would freeze from top to bottom. Nothing could live in it.

These monkeys are enjoying this hot spring even with ice on their heads. There's water vapor in the air. Water is present in all three states.

What would happen if you used water as the liquid in a thermometer? If the temperature dropped below freezing, the water would become a solid! It wouldn't make a very useful thermometer.

Mercury is the only metallic element that is a liquid at the temperatures that are common on Earth. Mercury stays a liquid at a colder temperature than water does. Mercury expands and contracts the same amount with every degree its temperature changes. Because of this, early thermometers contained mercury. However, mercury is also poisonous. So instead, colored alcohol is now used in most thermometers.

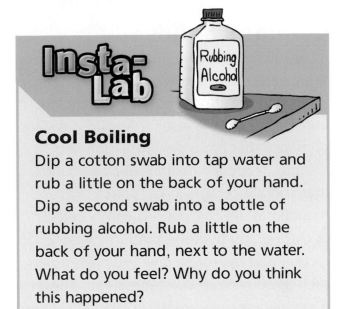

Insta-Lab

Cool Boiling

Dip a cotton swab into tap water and rub a little on the back of your hand. Dip a second swab into a bottle of rubbing alcohol. Rub a little on the back of your hand, next to the water. What do you feel? Why do you think this happened?

(Focus Skill) MAIN IDEA AND DETAILS What are some unusual properties of water?

Mercury was used in thermometers for many years. ▶

▲ Older thermostats used mercury switches to turn a furnace off and on.

Common Solids

The element carbon makes up a very small percent of Earth's crust. However, it is the sixth most common element in the universe. Carbon is a solid. A **solid** is a state of matter that has a definite shape and volume. There are millions of compounds that contain carbon. Coal, petroleum, and natural gas are compounds composed of carbon and hydrogen. Add oxygen to carbon and hydrogen and you have sugars, such as corn syrup and table sugar. These three elements also make up starches, found in plants.

Why is carbon present in so many compounds? One reason is that each carbon atom can combine with four other atoms at once. That increases the different compounds that can be formed with carbon as their base.

Even the element carbon itself is found in several useful forms. It may be hard to believe, but charcoal, the "lead" in your pencil, and the diamond in a ring are all carbon. The only difference is the way the carbon atoms join together.

What do you think the most common solid on Earth is? You're standing on it! It's

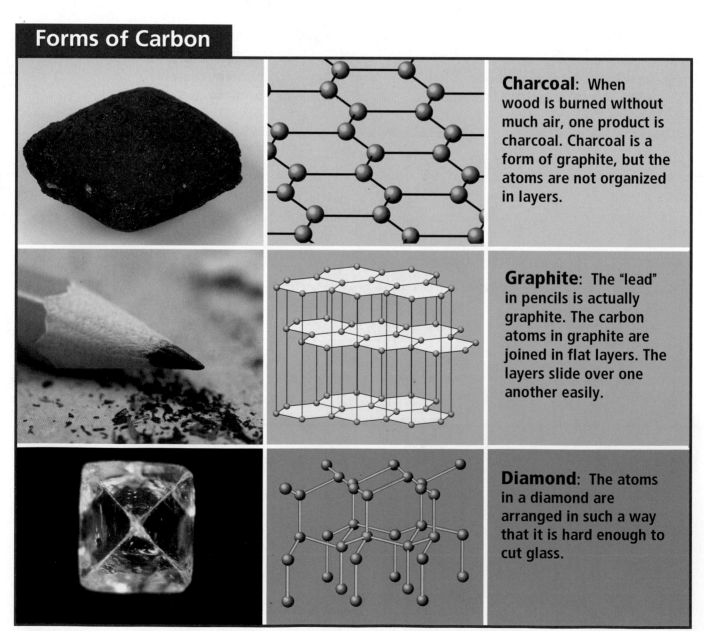

Forms of Carbon

Charcoal: When wood is burned without much air, one product is charcoal. Charcoal is a form of graphite, but the atoms are not organized in layers.

Graphite: The "lead" in pencils is actually graphite. The carbon atoms in graphite are joined in flat layers. The layers slide over one another easily.

Diamond: The atoms in a diamond are arranged in such a way that it is hard enough to cut glass.

Oxygen is a nonmetal. Silicon is a metalloid. About what percent of Earth's crust is made up of metals?

Element	Approximate % by weight
Oxygen	46.6
Silicon	27.7
Aluminum	8.1
Iron	5.0
Calcium	3.6
Sodium	2.8
Potassium	2.6
Magnesium	2.1
All others	1.5

Many useful minerals are mined from open pits or quarries, such as this one.

Earth itself—though not all of Earth is solid. Many elements, except the artificial ones, are found in Earth's crust. Some of them are found only in small amounts.

Oxygen and seven other elements make up 98.5 percent of Earth's crust. Yet more than 3500 minerals are known to be in Earth's crust. Many of the elements and compounds needed to make familiar objects are dug from the Earth. For example, the copper and nickel in coins and the stone in fireplaces are mined. The aluminum in soda cans and the silicon in the glasses you drink from originally came from Earth's crust. Gemstones, such as rubies and emeralds, are also mined from the ground.

Look around your kitchen. The metal and plastic in every appliance originally came from materials found in Earth's crust. Think of the spices, meats, fruits, and vegetables you eat. Many of them are made up of just a handful of elements, but those elements combine together in thousands of different ways.

Focus Skill **MAIN IDEA AND DETAILS** Where do most of the objects you use in your life originally come from?

Molecules of Life

Without carbon, Earth would be lifeless. There would be no plants or animals. Even the tiniest one-celled bacteria are 50 percent carbon. Carbon is the building block around which the molecules of life are built.

About 98.8 percent by weight of the human body is composed of only 6 elements. Oxygen, with 65 percent, is at the top. Carbon is second, at 18.5 percent. Hydrogen, nitrogen, calcium, and phosphorus are the other four. The remaining 1.2 percent of the body is composed of tiny amounts of 30 other elements. Each one of them is necessary for good health.

For example, there is very little iron in the body. Because atoms are so tiny, though, that "very little" is still billions of iron atoms. Iron atoms are found in your red blood cells and enable them to carry oxygen throughout your body. Red blood cells wear out over time. Your bones keep making new ones, so they need a constant supply of iron. Iron is found in the foods you eat.

Your hair, fingernails, and muscles are all made of proteins. Proteins contain carbon, hydrogen, nitrogen, and oxygen, combined

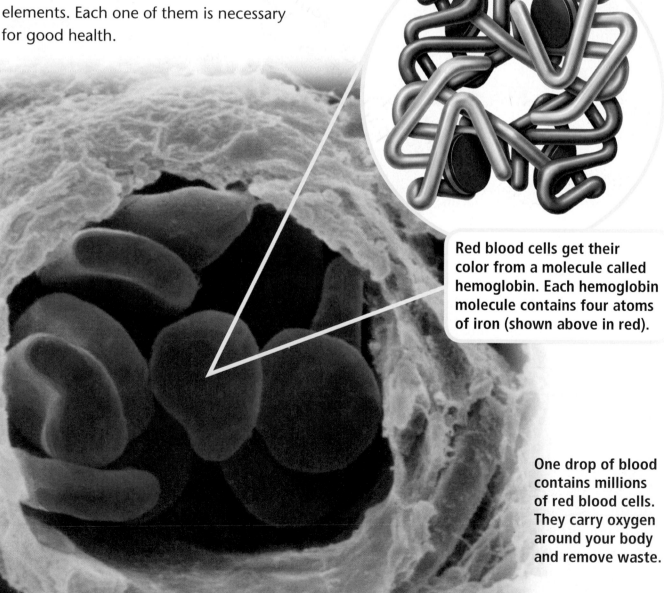

Red blood cells get their color from a molecule called hemoglobin. Each hemoglobin molecule contains four atoms of iron (shown above in red).

One drop of blood contains millions of red blood cells. They carry oxygen around your body and remove waste.

in dozens of different ways. Each protein has a different job to do in the body. Some carry messages throughout the body. Others respond when a virus or bacteria attacks.

DNA is one of the most complex molecules in your body. However, it is made from just a few elements, too. DNA is found in the nucleus of each cell. It makes sure that new cells your body makes are like the original ones.

DNA is a huge molecule that looks like a twisted ladder. Each colored ball in the diagram of DNA shown represents a different element. Notice that there are just five colors. DNA contains only five elements—carbon, hydrogen, oxygen, nitrogen, and phosphorus.

Focus Skill **MAIN IDEA AND DETAILS** What is the most common element in both Earth's crust and the human body?

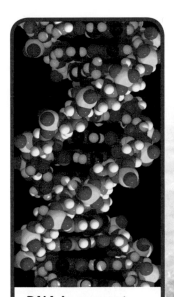

DNA is present in the nucleus of every cell. It carries genetic information.

Elements in the Human Body

Element	Symbol	Weight by Percentage
Oxygen	O	65.0
Carbon	C	18.5
Hydrogen	H	9.5
Nitogen	N	3.3
Calcium	Ca	1.5
Phosphorus	P	1.0

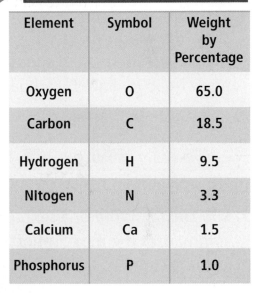

A healthful diet and exercise are needed for good health.

Standards Wrap-Up and Lesson Review

Essential Question

What are the properties of some common substances?

In this lesson you learned that Earth has many common gases, liquids, and solids. Many of the objects you use in your daily life come from just a few elements found in Earth's crust.

Science Content Standards in This Lesson

1.g *Students know* properties of solid, liquid, and gaseous substances, such as sugar ($C_6H_{12}O_6$), water (H_2O), helium (He), oxygen (O_2), nitrogen (N_2), and carbon dioxide (CO_2).

1.h *Students know* living organisms and most materials are composed of just a few elements.

---

1. **(Focus Skill) MAIN IDEA AND DETAILS** Draw and complete a graphic organizer to show the supporting details of this main idea: There are three states of matter—solid, liquid, and gas. **1.g**

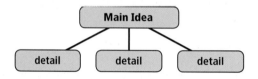

2. **SUMMARIZE** Write one sentence that summarizes the most important point in this lesson. **1.g, 1.h**

3. **DRAW CONCLUSIONS** Why is it a good idea to recycle metals such as aluminum cans? **1.g**

4. **VOCABULARY** Which state of matter has no definite shape or volume?
   A liquid **B** element
   C gas **D** solid **1.g**

5. **Critical Thinking** When you digest food, your body breaks the food down into its elements and compounds. Why do you think it is important to have protein in your diet? **1.h**

6. **Investigate and Experiment** Plan a simple investigation for a testable question about the effect sugar has on how fast bubbles form. **6.c**

7. Which of the following elements is present in DNA?
   A iron
   B mercury
   C nitrogen
   D aluminum **1.h**

8. **Explain** why Earth's crust and the human body are good examples of the fact that many forms of matter can be made up of just a few elements. **1.h**

The Big Idea

Writing · ELA–WA 2.4

Write a Friendly Letter

Telling someone else what you have learned often helps you understand it better. Write a friendly letter explaining what you learned in this lesson.

Math · MR 3.3

Reason It Out

One mL of water has a mass of 1 gram. Is the mass of 1 mL of ice greater than, equal to, or less than 1 gram? How do you know?

Health

The Risks of Lead

The paint used for walls and furniture once contained lead, but lead is no longer used in paint. Find out more about why lead shouldn't be used in paint, particularly in rooms or on furniture used by infants. Prepare a brief speech on the subject for your classmates or family.

For more links and activities, go to **www.hspscience.com**

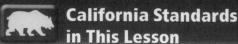

Science Content

1.f *Students know* differences in chemical and physical properties of substances are used to separate mixtures and identify compounds.

Investigation and Experimentation

6.h Draw conclusions from scientific evidence and indicate whether further information is needed to support a specific conclusion.

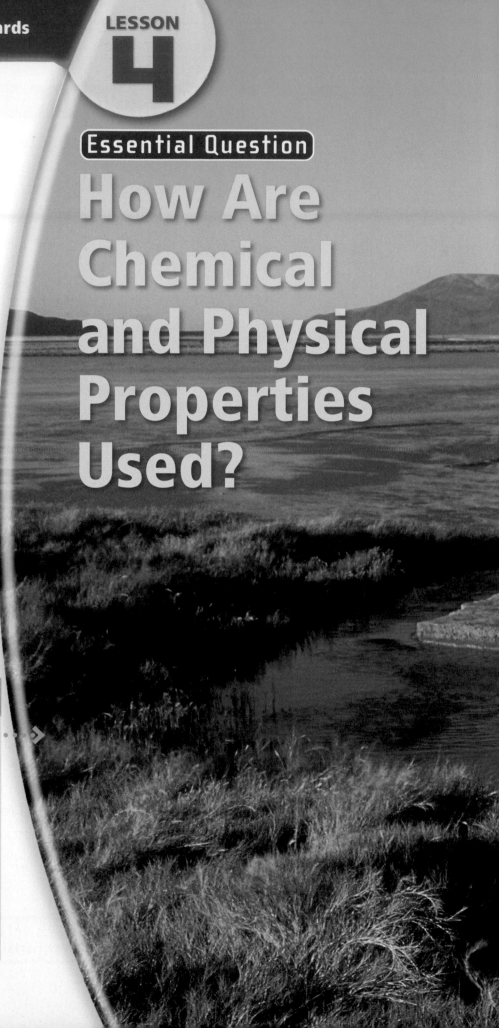

LESSON 4

Essential Question

How Are Chemical and Physical Properties Used?

California Fast Fact

Super Salty

A glass company in California uses this pond to produce salt. Energy from the sun evaporates the water, leaving the salt behind. The salt—which is sodium carbonate, not sodium chloride (table salt)—is used to make detergents, cleaning products, and glass.

A salt evaporation pond near Owens Lake, California

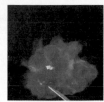

chemical property
[KEM•ih•kuhl PRAHP•er•tee]
A trait that involves the way a substance combines with other substances to form new substances (p. 108)

acid [AS•id] A chemical compound that turns blue litmus paper red and has a pH of less than 7 (p. 110)

base [BAYS] A chemical compound that turns red litmus paper blue and has a pH of more than 7 (p. 110)

105

Chemical Properties

Start with Questions

Cornstarch and baking soda look nearly the same. Suppose they were in unmarked boxes and you needed baking soda for a recipe.

• How would you know which box to use?

• Are there any tests you could do?

Investigate to find out. Then read to find out more.

Prepare to Investigate

Investigation Skill Tip
When you draw conclusions from scientific evidence, you should decide whether more information is needed to support a specific conclusion.

Materials

• apron
• safety goggles
• 9 test tubes
• 3 plastic spoons
• baking soda
• 3 droppers
• water
• vinegar
• iodine solution
• cornstarch
• baby powder

Make a Data Table

	Baking Soda	Cornstarch	Baby Powder
Water			
Vinegar			
Iodine Solution			

Follow This Procedure

CAUTION: Wear an apron and safety goggles.

1 Label three test tubes *water*, three *vinegar*, and three *iodine*. Use a spoon to put a *tiny* bit of baking soda in one test tube of each kind.

2 Add three drops of water to the test tube labeled *water*. **Record** your **observations**.

3 Add three drops of vinegar to the test tube labeled *vinegar*. **Record** your **observations**.

4 Add three drops of iodine solution to the test tube labeled *iodine*. **Record** your **observations**.

5 Using a clean spoon, put a tiny bit of cornstarch in one clean test tube of each kind. Repeat Steps 3–5.

6 Using a clean spoon, put a tiny bit of baby powder in one clean test tube of each kind. Repeat Steps 3–5.

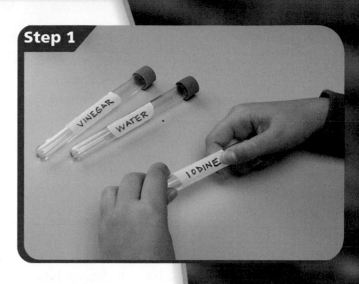

Step 1

Step 2

Draw Conclusions

1. What effect did vinegar have on the baking soda? Did any other combination show the same effect?

2. Standards Link How could you identify which of the two unmarked boxes had baking soda? **1.f**

3. Investigation Skill In which combinations can you **conclude** that a chemical change took place? What tests would you need to do to be sure? **6.h**

Independent Inquiry **Draw Conclusions from Scientific Evidence**

What does iodine solution help you identify? How? What information is needed to support your conclusion? **6.h**

Get a "mystery powder" from your teacher. Test it with iodine solution. Use your observations to draw conclusions about what the powder is.

VOCABULARY
chemical property p. 108
acid p. 110
base p. 110

SCIENCE CONCEPTS
▶ how physical properties are used
▶ how chemical properties are used

Focus Skill **MAIN IDEA AND DETAILS**
Look for details about how mixtures are separated.

Main Idea
detail detail detail

Separating Mixtures

Suppose you don't like raisins, but the only breakfast cereal you have at home has raisins in it. What can you do?

Cereal with raisins is a mixture. All the substances in a mixture keep their physical properties. It's easy to see the dark raisins against the lighter flakes. All you have to do is pick them out.

That isn't so easy with a mixture of flour and sugar. However, you can still use their physical properties to separate them. Sugar dissolves in water. Flour doesn't. You can add water to the mixture and stir it until the sugar dissolves. Let it sit until the flour falls to the bottom. Pour off the solution into a second container, and let the water evaporate. The sugar is left.

Most materials found in nature are mixtures. Sand at the beach is a mixture. You can separate the parts of sand by sifting. The diagram at the right shows how a mixture of salt, iron, rocks, and dirt can be separated.

Chemical properties can also be used to separate mixtures. A **chemical property** involves the way a substance reacts, or combines, with other substances to form new substances. Most metals in nature are found in ores, which contain minerals. These ores are chemical compounds. For example,

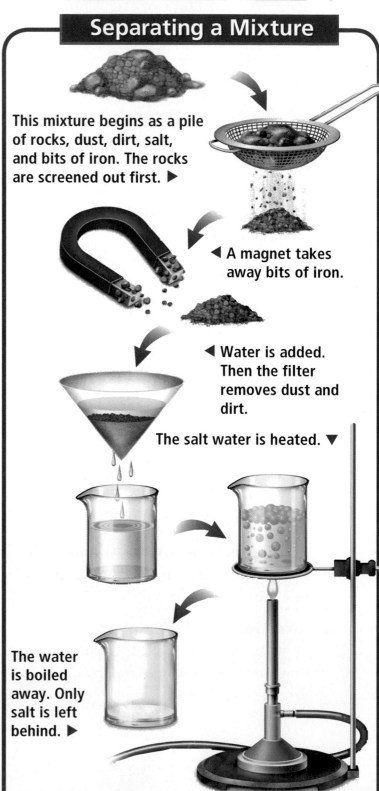

Separating a Mixture

This mixture begins as a pile of rocks, dust, dirt, salt, and bits of iron. The rocks are screened out first. ▶

◀ A magnet takes away bits of iron.

◀ Water is added. Then the filter removes dust and dirt.

The salt water is heated. ▼

The water is boiled away. Only salt is left behind. ▶

in nature, copper is usually combined with oxygen or sulfur. The metals in ores must be removed before they can be used. How this is done depends on the chemical properties of the elements in the ore.

One way to get pure copper begins by crushing its ore into a fine powder. Water and other chemicals are added to the powder. The other chemicals make the copper compounds in the powder stick to air bubbles, which rise. The bubbles are taken away and dried, leaving a block of copper ore.

Next, the ore is combined with a weak acid to remove the copper. The copper dissolves. Then it can be removed from the acid by using electricity.

MAIN IDEA AND DETAILS What are some ways physical properties are used to separate mixtures?

Splitting Water

Attach a paper clip to one bare end of a piece of insulated wire. Repeat with another wire. Use tape to attach the other ends of the wires to the two poles of a 9-volt battery. Use the paper clips to attach two pieces of "lead" (graphite) from a mechanical pencil to the inside of a plastic cup filled with salt water. Make sure the pieces extend into the water and don't touch each other. What do you observe in the cup? What do you think is happening?

Much of the copper found in nature is combined with other elements. ▶

Crushed copper ore is heated to get rid of other elements. This is called smelting.

After the impurities are removed, the melted copper is poured into molds, where it cools into bars. Copper bars are about 25 cm (10 in.) long. They weigh up to 10 kg (22 lb).

Identifying Elements and Compounds

You can use chemical properties to identify elements and compounds. For example, you can tell an acid from a base by using *litmus paper*. Litmus paper contains chemicals that change color. An **acid** is a substance that turns blue litmus paper red. A **base** is a substance that turns red litmus paper blue.

Some acids and bases are stronger than others. Scientists rank acids and bases on a scale called the *pH scale*, giving each a number from 0 to 14. An acid has a pH of less than 7, while a base has a pH of more than 7. Some substances, such as water, have a pH of 7. They are *neutral*, which means that they are neither acids nor bases.

How can you identify common acids and bases? If you touch the substance with an indicator known as pH paper, the paper changes color. You compare the paper to a color chart to tell if the substance is an acid or a base. You can also tell from the chart if the substance is either strong or weak.

Sometimes, scientists use physical properties to identify substances. Color is

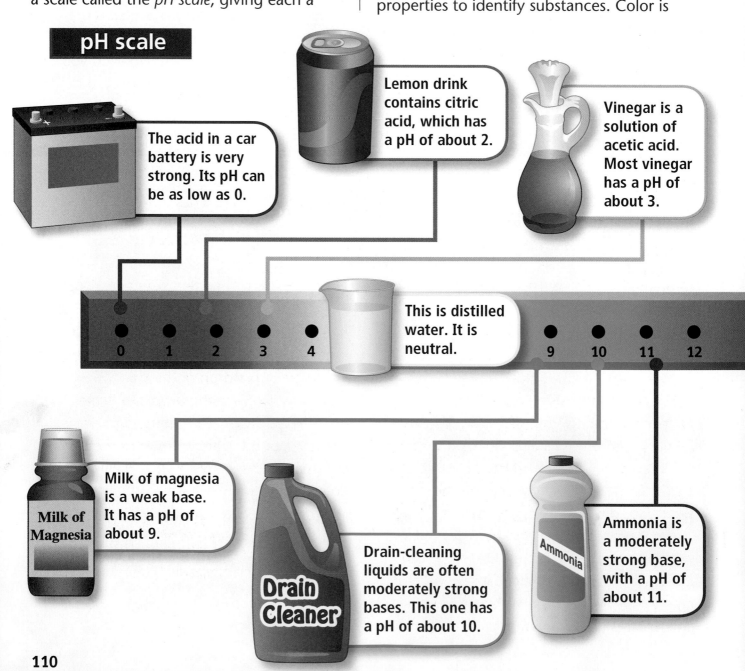

pH scale

The acid in a car battery is very strong. Its pH can be as low as 0.

Lemon drink contains citric acid, which has a pH of about 2.

Vinegar is a solution of acetic acid. Most vinegar has a pH of about 3.

This is distilled water. It is neutral.

0 1 2 3 4   9 10 11 12

Milk of magnesia is a weak base. It has a pH of about 9.

Milk of Magnesia

Drain-cleaning liquids are often moderately strong bases. This one has a pH of about 10.

Drain Cleaner

Ammonia is a moderately strong base, with a pH of about 11.

Ammonia

▲ Solutions that contain metals burn with flames of different colors. Sodium burns bright yellow, potassium burns blue-purple, and copper burns blue-green.

◀ Compounds can be identified by their solubility. More than five times as much sugar as salt will dissolve in the same amount of water at the same temperature.

useful with some elements, including gold, copper, and chlorine. Melting points can help you identify metals. Texture is also a physical property. Some substances are *brittle*—they break or crush easily.

Solubility can also help you identify elements and compounds. Sugar dissolves in water very easily. Salt dissolves less easily.

To use a chemical property to identify a substance, you have to change the substance. For example, you can tell magnesium from iron because they react with acid at different rates. Once you test a metal in this way, though, it's used up! It reacts with the acid to produce hydrogen and another compound.

One chemical test that uses very little material is called a flame test. Suppose you have a white solid, but you don't know what it is. First, dissolve a little of it in water. Then, pick up a drop of the solution in a loop of wire. Place the drop in a flame. The color of the flame tells you what metal is in the compound. Different metals burn with different colors. Fireworks get their brilliant colors from different metals.

Focus Skill MAIN IDEA AND DETAILS What are some properties you can use to identify an element or a compound?

Standards Wrap-Up and Lesson Review

Essential Question

How are chemical and physical properties used?

In this lesson, you learned that scientists use chemical and physical properties to separate mixtures and to identify unknown elements and compounds.

 Science Content Standards in This Lesson

1.f *Students know* differences in chemical and physical properties of substances are used to separate mixtures and identify compounds.

1. **MAIN IDEA AND DETAILS** Draw and complete a graphic organizer to show the supporting details of this main idea: Chemical properties help scientists identify substances. **1.f**

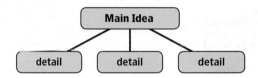

2. **SUMMARIZE** Write three sentences summarizing the lesson. **1.f**

3. **DRAW CONCLUSIONS** Which would be easier to separate from the rock in which it's found—gold or copper? Why? **1.f**

4. **VOCABULARY** Which of the following describes an acid?
   A It has a pH of more than 7.
   B It has a pH of less than 7.
   C It is the same as a base.
   D It is a neutral substance. **1.f**

5. **Critical Thinking** You have a solution of a compound. You know the compound contains a metal. How can you find out what metal it is? **1.f**

6. **Investigate and Experiment** Suppose you add a fourth white powder to the powders in the Investigate. What new information will you need to identify all four powders? **6.h**

7. Which of the following would be best for separating a mixture of aluminum and steel cans?
   A a magnet
   B a strainer
   C a microscope
   D a beaker of water **1.f**

8. Explain how there can be so many kinds of matter made of only a handful of elements. **1.f**

 The **Big** Idea

112

 Writing ELA–WA 2.3

Write a Description

Find out more about one element. Write a description of the element, but don't name it. Use enough details for a reader to identify the element without its being named. Share your description with your classmates.

 Math SDAP 2.3

Make a Bar Graph

Make a bar graph to show the solubility of each of four substances in 100 mL of water at room temperature. Use this data: sugar, 204 g; salt, 36 g; baking soda, 7 g; and sand, 0 g.

Drama HSS 5.1

Iron Age

People have been shaping iron for hundreds of years. Research the history of iron. What were some of the first things people made out of iron? Draw pictures of some of these objects and present them to the class on a poster.

 For more links and activities, go to **www.hspscience.com**

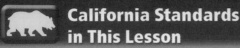

LESSON 5

Essential Question

What Are Chemical Reactions?

California Fast Fact

A Big Painting Job

The Golden Gate Bridge was first painted when it was completed, in 1937. Until 1965, the paint was just touched up now and then. Over the next 30 years, the original paint was replaced with paint that would better protect the bridge from corrosion. The bridge is now touched up all year long by a crew of 38 painters.

Golden Gate Bridge, San Francisco, California

chemical reaction
[KEM•ih•kuhl ree•AK•shuhn] A change in which one or more new substances are formed (p. 118)

reactant [ree•AK•tuhnt] A substance that changes during a chemical reaction (p. 120)

product [PRAHD•uhkt] A substance that is formed by a chemical reaction (p. 120)

salt [SAWLT] A substance that is made by combining an acid and a base (p. 124)

Chemical Changes

Start with Questions

Burning is one of the most obvious examples of a chemical change taking place.

- Why will a match light only once?

- As a candle burns, what happens to the wax?

Investigate to find out. Then read to find out more.

Prepare to Investigate

> **Investigation Skill Tip**
> Scientists develop testable questions they can answer by doing investigations.

Materials

- safety goggles
- plastic gloves
- plastic knife
- water
- 3 droppers
- plastic wrap
- hydrogen peroxide
- baby food jar
- plastic stirring spoon
- ammonia

- apron
- avocado
- small plastic bag
- green food coloring
- bleach
- raw hamburger
- Epsom salts
- measuring spoons

Make an Observation Chart

Material	Observations
Avocado	
Colored water	
Hamburger	
Epsom salts	

Follow This Procedure

CAUTION: Put on goggles, gloves, and an apron. Avoid breathing the bleach and the ammonia.

1 Use the plastic knife to cut a slice from the avocado. **Observe** the color. Observe again after 2 min. **Record** your observations.

2 Fill the plastic bag with tap water. Use a dropper to add 1 drop of food coloring. Use a clean dropper to add 2 drops of bleach. **Record** your **observations**.

3 Place a small piece of raw hamburger on a sheet of plastic wrap. Use a clean dropper to place 1 or 2 drops of hydrogen peroxide on the hamburger. **Observe** and **record**.

4 Half-fill the baby food jar with water. Add $\frac{1}{2}$ teaspoon of Epsom salts. Stir until it dissolves. Stir in 2 teaspoons of household ammonia. **Observe** for 4 or 5 min. **Record** your observations.

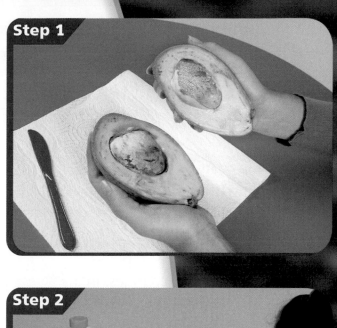

Step 1

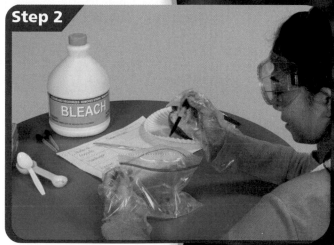

Step 2

Draw Conclusions

1. What do all four observations have in common? How do you know?

2. **Standards Link** How is lighting a match similar to what you observed in the Investigate? **1.a**

3. **Investigation Skill** What is one **testable question** you could develop for this investigation? **6.b**

Independent Inquiry

Plan and Conduct a Simple Investigation

Think about what you observed in this investigation. What is another question you could develop? Plan and conduct a simple investigation to answer the question. **6.c**

Write a procedure for the investigation. Be sure to include the materials needed, the steps to take, and what to look for.

117

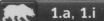
VOCABULARY
chemical reaction p. 118
reactant p. 120
product p. 120
salt p. 124

SCIENCE CONCEPTS
▶ how chemical and physical changes are different
▶ how acids and bases are different

Focus Skill **COMPARE AND CONTRAST**
Look for the difference between reactants and products.

alike ——— different

Changing Properties

Paper tears. Glass breaks. Sugar dissolves in water. Water boils at 100°C (212°F). These are all descriptions of physical changes, not chemical changes. In a *chemical change*, the substance changes. It's not just the appearance that changes. The substance itself is no longer the same.

A **chemical reaction** is a chemical change that results in one or more new substances. If you touch a lit match to wood, the wood burns. When something burns, it combines with oxygen. The compounds in the wood combine with oxygen in the air to produce other gases. The gases escape into the air. You may not see the gases, but you know that something is gone, because all that is left are ashes. You know that a chemical change took place because the properties of the materials are different. New substances with different properties have formed.

Hydrogen and oxygen are colorless, odorless gases. If you mix them in a balloon, nothing happens—but if you touch a match to the balloon, boom! The hydrogen burns so fast that it explodes. A new substance,

Chemical Properties

Water
- made up of hydrogen and oxygen
- reacts with some metals to produce bases

Silver
- reacts with few substances
- does not react with air
- reacts with ozone or sulfur to form tarnish

Iron
- reacts easily with many substances
- reacts with oxygen to form the minerals hematite and magnetite
- reacts with oxygen in presence of water to form rust

Sulfur
- reacts with any liquid element
- reacts with any solid element except gold and platinum
- reacts with oxygen to form sulfur dioxide, a form of air pollution

▲ Mixing the dry ingredients for bread is a physical change. It might be hard to separate them again, but you can do it. Baking the bread is a chemical change. A new substance forms.

Physical Properties

• colorless • odorless • liquid at room temperature	• boils at 100°C • melts at 0°C
• shiny • soft • silver in color	• boils at 2163°C • melts at 962°C
• shiny • hard • grayish silver in color	• boils at 2861°C • melts at 1538°C
• dull • brittle • yellow	• boils at 445°C • melts at 115°C

water, forms. As elements, hydrogen and oxygen can burn, but combined as water, they can be used to put out fires. That's quite a difference in properties!

Baking bread and frying an egg are also chemical changes. You may think that the substances change only their state. But if you want to change a substance from its liquid state to its solid state, you *take away* energy. In the case of the egg and the bread, you *add* energy. You can tell these are chemical changes, because you can't get back the bread dough or the raw egg.

All the changes you observed in the Investigate were chemical changes. You saw gas bubbles form. When you left the avocado in the air, a new brown substance formed. Neither hamburger nor hydrogen peroxide is a gas, but together they produced a gas. When you added two clear liquids, a solid formed.

Bubbles, color changes, and the appearance of a solid when two liquids are mixed are clues that a chemical change has taken place. In each case, the properties of the substances changed.

 COMPARE AND CONTRAST

How are a chemical change and a physical change different?

Chlorine

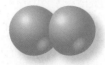

+

Sodium

—

Reactants and Products

Every chemical reaction begins with one or more reactants. A **reactant** is one of the starting materials in a chemical reaction. For example, suppose you pass an electric charge through water. Bubbles of hydrogen gas and oxygen gas form. In this case, there is only one reactant—water. Hydrogen and oxygen are the products. A **product** is one of the ending materials of a chemical reaction.

Suppose the reactants are the elements sodium and chlorine. Sodium is a soft, shiny metal. Chlorine is a greenish-yellow gas. What is the product?

The photographs below show the reaction between sodium and chlorine. If you just place the sodium in a container with chlorine, nothing happens. Water is added to the flask through the glass tube. The water makes the sodium react with the chlorine. You can tell there is a chemical change, because a lot of energy is released.

The last picture shows the product. The product of this reaction is sodium

Salt Formation

The bottle is filed with chlorine. Chlorine is a greenish yellow gas.

A small chunk of sodium is lowered into the chlorine gas. Sodium is a soft, shiny, silvery metal.

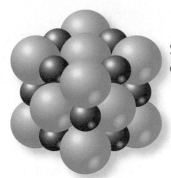

Sodium chloride crystal

 +

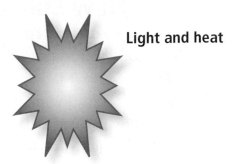

Light and heat

chloride—table salt. It doesn't look much like table salt, but it is! It's just that the crystals are so tiny, they look like smoke.

What are the reactants in a nail that's rusting? You can see the iron—the nail. The other reactant is invisible. It's the oxygen in the air. The iron and oxygen combine to form a new product—iron oxide, or rust.

The properties of iron oxide are very different from those of iron and oxygen.

When silver tarnishes, the product is silver sulfide. The reactants are the element silver and the compound hydrogen sulfide.

COMPARE AND CONTRAST What is the difference between the reactants and the products in a chemical reaction?

The sodium begins to react with the chlorine. The reaction gives off energy in the form of light and heat.

When the reaction is complete, white crystals are formed. The reactants, sodium and chlorine, have combined to form a new product. It is sodium chloride, or table salt.

Making New Substances

The way elements and compounds react with one another produces all the kinds of matter in the world. Many of the reactions fall into four groups. In one group, a compound breaks apart into its elements. Suppose you begin with water (H_2O), a compound that contains two elements. During a chemical change, the compound breaks apart into the elements hydrogen and oxygen. If you begin with sodium chloride (NaCl), or table salt, the elements will be sodium and chlorine.

In another kind of reaction, two elements combine to make a compound. Hydrogen combines with oxygen to make water. As you can see, this is the reverse of the first type of reaction.

What if you start with an element and a compound? The single element switches

Science Up Close

Chemical Reactions

Two Compounds React
One compound dissolves in water and forms a clear solution. Another compound dissolves in water and forms a yellow solution. When the two solutions are mixed, two solids form. One dissolves in the water, so you never see it. The other is a bright, reddish solid.

An Element Reacts with a Compound
Silver reacts with hydrogen sulfide in the air to form silver sulfide, or tarnish.

places with one of the elements in the compound. After the reaction, the products are still an element and a compound, but both are now different. For example, if you place a strip of magnesium (Mg) in hydrochloric acid (HCl), the products are magnesium chloride ($MgCl_2$) and hydrogen gas (H_2).

If two compounds react, two of the elements switch partners. The same elements are present in both the original compounds and the products. They're just combined in different ways. Suppose the reactants are hydrochloric acid (HCl) and sodium hydroxide (NaOH). The products will be salt (NaCl) and water (H_2O).

Elements and compounds combine in other ways to form new compounds. For example, many carbon compounds contain long chains of molecules, like paper clips linked together. These chains are found in plastics, proteins, and DNA.

 COMPARE AND CONTRAST Describe two ways in which elements, compounds, or both can react with one another.

A Compound Comes Apart
Nitrogen dioxide is a brown gas. When it's heated above 140°C (284°F), it comes apart into two colorless gases.

Two Elements Combine
You've seen the result of the reaction between sodium, a soft metal, and chlorine, a yellowish gas. When these two elements react, the product is sodium chloride— table salt.

 For more links and animations, go to **www.hspscience.com**

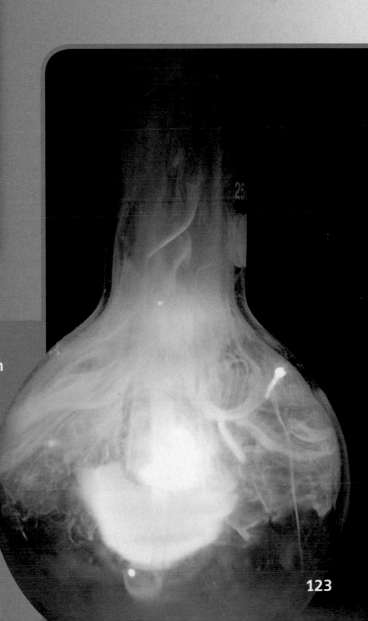

Salts

In the Lesson 4, you learned that litmus paper can help you tell an acid from a base. Which everyday substances are acids, and which are bases? Some acids are safe to eat or drink. However, you should NEVER taste a substance to find out what it is. Orange juice, for example, is an acid. So is the vinegar in salad dressing. Household ammonia, detergent, soap, shampoo, and drain cleaner are all bases. Strong bases are as dangerous as strong acids. They can burn skin.

What happens when you add vinegar to baking soda? You get bubbles. A chemical property of acids and bases is that they react with one another.

Think back to Lesson 4. What new substances are made when the base sodium hydroxide reacts with hydrochloric acid? The products are water and sodium chloride—table salt. A **salt** is the product that occurs when an acid and a base react.

There are many salts other than table salt. For example, the stomach contains an acid that digests food. Sometimes, the acid in the stomach gets too strong. This gives people "heartburn." Antacid tablets contain a base. When a person who has heartburn takes an antacid, the antacid reacts with the acid and gets rid of the extra acid. What's left is water and a salt. The heartburn is gone!

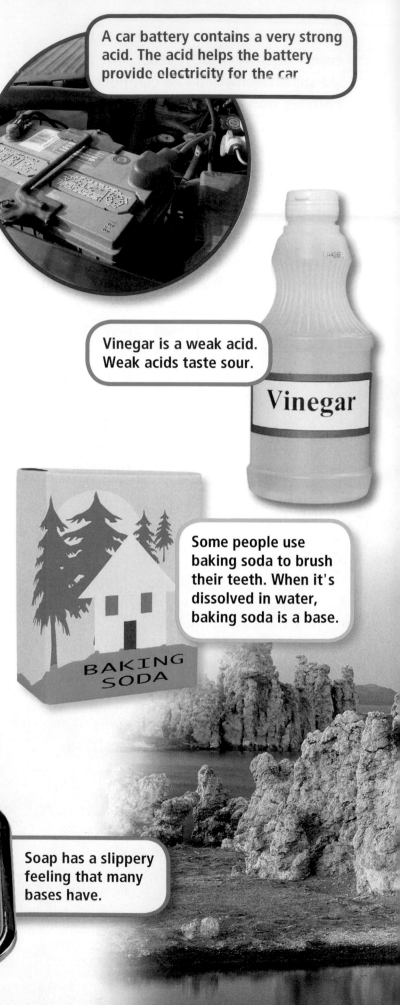

A car battery contains a very strong acid. The acid helps the battery provide electricity for the car

Vinegar is a weak acid. Weak acids taste sour.

Vinegar

BAKING SODA

Some people use baking soda to brush their teeth. When it's dissolved in water, baking soda is a base.

Soap has a slippery feeling that many bases have.

Most salts are made when strong acids react with strong bases. Salts also form when some metals react with strong acids. The elements that react in these ways are usually ones from column 1 or 2 of the periodic table, combining with elements from column 17. The elements in column 1, except hydrogen, and column 2 are metals. The elements in column 17 are nonmetals.

Most salts have similar physical and chemical properties. Salts are hard but brittle—they break easily. Salts also dissolve easily in water. Salt solutions have high electrical conductivity. Pure water is a poor conductor of electricity.

Salts also change the freezing point of water. Fresh water freezes at 0°C (32°F). When a salt is added, water remains a liquid at 0°C. This is why salt is used on icy roads in winter. Salt melts the ice and snow, preventing the roads from becoming dangerous.

Have you ever made ice cream? Salt is mixed into the ice in the machine to lower the temperature of the ice. Milk and cream freeze at a lower temperature than water. Without salt, the cream wouldn't change from a liquid to a solid.

Salts are also used to preserve foods and to improve the taste of some foods. Salts preserve foods by preventing the growth of bacteria. Salt water can kill plants by drying them out, but animals need salt to survive. However, not all salts are safe to eat. Some are actually poisonous.

Focus Skill **COMPARE AND CONTRAST** How are salts alike? How are they different?

The rocks in Earth's crust contain different salts. The salts dissolve in ocean or lake water. When salt water washes onto the shore, the water evaporates. The salts are left behind.

Milk and cream freeze at a lower temperature than water does. Salt is used to lower the temperature of the ice to make ice cream.

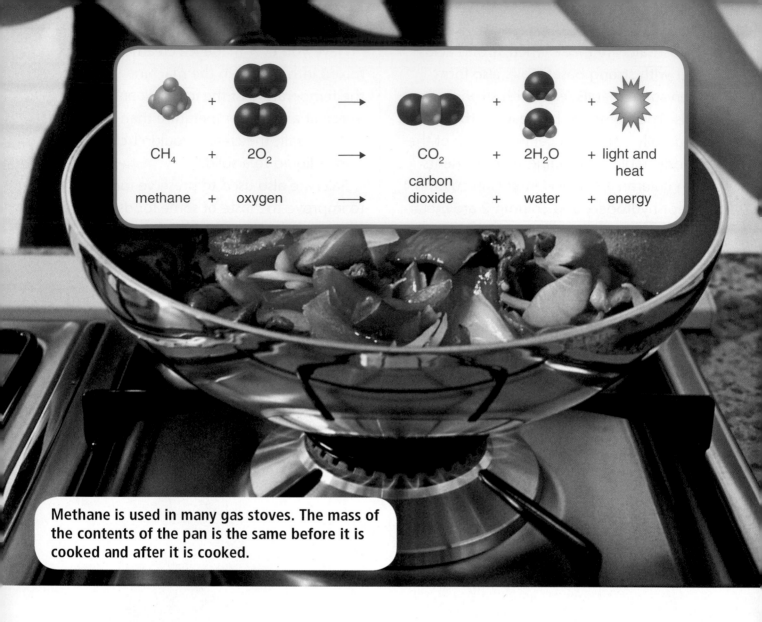

$$CH_4 + 2O_2 \longrightarrow CO_2 + 2H_2O + \text{light and heat}$$

methane + oxygen $\longrightarrow$ carbon dioxide + water + energy

Methane is used in many gas stoves. The mass of the contents of the pan is the same before it is cooked and after it is cooked.

Conservation of Mass

During a chemical change, new substances form. These substances are not new matter. The same atoms that were present in the reactants are still present in the products. They're just combined in different ways.

Suppose that you measure the total mass of the sodium metal and chlorine gas on page 120. After the reaction is over, you measure the mass of the sodium chloride. The masses are exactly the same. No new matter is made, and no matter is destroyed. This is called the *Law of Conservation of Mass.*

When iron rusts, it gains mass. It might appear that new matter is made. Actually, though, the iron has combined with oxygen from the air. Suppose that you could find out the mass of the oxygen and add it to the mass of the iron. If you compared the total to the mass of the rusted iron, they would be the same.

A marshmallow has less mass after it burns than it did before. Was any matter destroyed? No. The sugar in the marshmallow combined with oxygen in the air. The products of this reaction were gases—water vapor and carbon dioxide. They escaped into the air.

What if you burned the marshmallow in a sealed box that was filled with air? If you measured the mass of the box and its contents before and after burning, you would find that they are the same. The total mass of the water vapor, carbon dioxide, and burned marshmallow is the same as the total mass of the air and the marshmallow before burning.

In any chemical reaction, no new matter is made and no matter is destroyed. Matter is *conserved.* The amount of matter remains the same.

 **COMPARE AND CONTRAST** Compare the products in a chemical reaction and the masses of the reactants.

Bubble, Bubble

Push an antacid tablet through the neck of a balloon. Stretch the neck of the balloon over a plastic soda bottle that contains some water. Tape the neck of the balloon in place. Let the balloon hang to one side of the bottle. Find the mass of the bottle and balloon. Then tip the balloon so that the tablet drops into the water. Observe what happens. When the reaction is finished, find the mass of the bottle and balloon again. How do the masses compare?

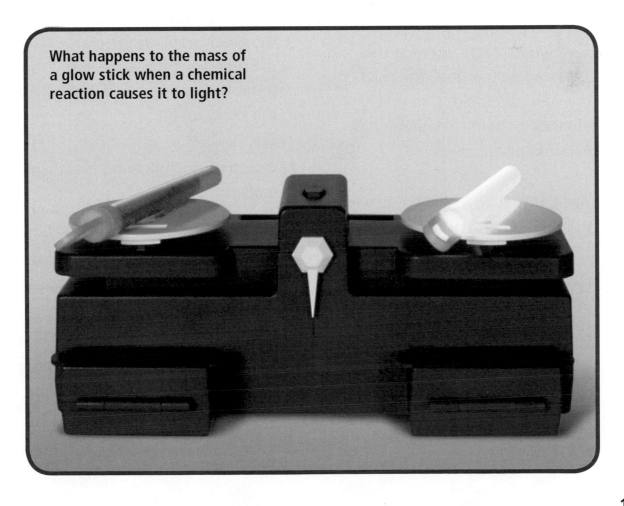

What happens to the mass of a glow stick when a chemical reaction causes it to light?

Standards Wrap-Up and Lesson Review

In this lesson, you learned that chemical reactions take place when two substances react. The reactants make products. When acids and bases react, they produce a salt.

Science Content Standards in This Lesson

1.a *Students know* that during chemical reactions the atoms in the reactants rearrange to form products with different properties.

1.i *Students know* the common properties of salts, such as sodium chloride (NaCl).

1. **(Focus Skill) COMPARE AND CONTRAST** Draw and complete a graphic organizer to compare and contrast reactants and products. **1.a**

```
  alike  ——————  different
```

2. **SUMMARIZE** Write a sentence that tells the most important information in this lesson. **1.a**

3. **DRAW CONCLUSIONS** A pan contains a cloudy white solid. You heat the pan. After a few minutes, the solid becomes a clear liquid. Can you tell whether a chemical change has occurred? Explain. **1.a**

4. **VOCABULARY** Which of the following occurs when an acid and a base are combined?

   A a reactant   **B** a strong acid
   C a salt   **D** a weak base **1.i**

5. **Critical Thinking** Liquid A turns litmus paper blue. Liquid B turns litmus paper red. Liquids A and B are mixed together in a glass. After the glass stands for several days, the liquid is gone. A white solid remains in the glass. What would you infer happened? **1.i**

6. **Investigate and Experiment** In the Investigate, you added bleach to the green water in the plastic bag, and the green color disappeared. What testable question could you ask about this observation? **6.b**

7. Which of the following is a chemical reaction?

   A wood burning
   B clouds forming
   C salt dissolving
   D meat freezing **1.a**

8. How do chemical reactions affect the number of different types of matter in the world? **1.a**

The **Big** Idea

  Writing ELA–W 1.2

Expository Writing

Write an expository paragraph about why burning a candle is an example of a chemical change and not a physical change. Include an explanation about how burning a candle demonstrates the law of conservation of mass.

  Math NS 2.0

Solve a Problem

If 55.9 g of iron react with oxygen to produce 71.9 g of rust, what is the mass of the oxygen that has reacted?

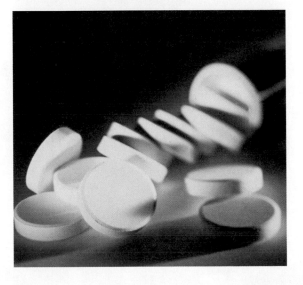

  Health

How Antacids Work

Find out more about antacids. Write a report, explaining when antacids should and shouldn't be used, and how they work.

 For more links and activities, go to **www.hspscience.com**

NATIONAL FUEL CELL RESEARCH CENTER

Suppose you could make electricity without burning a fuel or creating pollution. Suppose you could do it quietly and without wasting a lot of the energy produced. Scientists at the National Fuel Cell Research Center (NFCRC) are working to make this possible. Someday your home may have no power lines running to it. You may refill your car's fuel tank with hydrogen rather than gasoline. Instead of a battery, you'll plug a new fuel cell into your CD player. How does a fuel cell work? How is it used?

A fuel cell produces energy without burning fuel.

The National Fuel Cell Research Center (NFCRC) is at the University of California in Irvine.

ENGINEERING LABORATORY

323

How Fuel Cells Work

Fuel cells are similar to batteries. However, instead of storing chemical energy and changing it to electricity when the battery is activated, a fuel cell produces electricity constantly. Fuel cells work by combining a fuel, such as hydrogen, with oxygen from the air without burning the hydrogen. The products are water vapor, heat, and electricity. Because fuel cells have no moving parts, no energy is wasted through friction.

Benefits, Uses, and Challenges

Fuel-cell energy can be generated on site, so energy is not lost in moving it from power plants to places where it is to be used. Costs are reduced because power plants and transmission lines aren't needed. Fuel cells are more efficient than the burning of fuels, and they produce little pollution.

Scientists at NFCRC are developing large stationary fuel cells. These cells can be used in buildings to provide light and to run electrical devices. Heat produced by the cells could be used to heat water. When used in this way, the fuel cells are more than 80 percent efficient because little fuel is wasted. Automobile companies work with NFCRC to develop fuel cells to power cars. Small fuel cells can replace batteries in things such as cell phones.

Before fuel cells can become common, their cost must be reduced. They must work with more common fuels, and scientists must find new methods to hold the fuels safely. NFCRC is working to solve these problems.

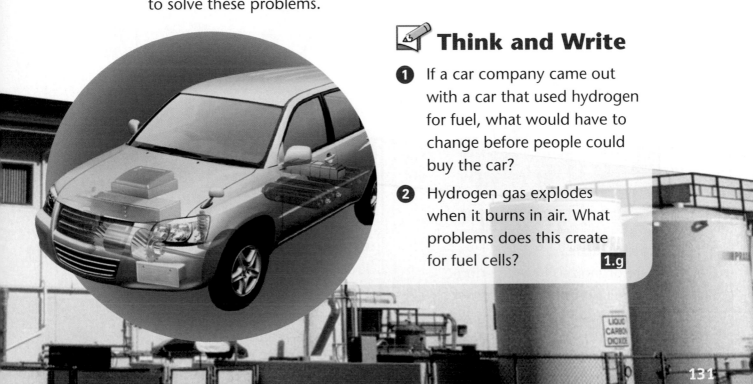

✍️ Think and Write

1. If a car company came out with a car that used hydrogen for fuel, what would have to change before people could buy the car?

2. Hydrogen gas explodes when it burns in air. What problems does this create for fuel cells? **1.g**

Visual Summary

Tell how each picture helps explain the **Big Idea**.

The Big Idea Elements and their combinations account for all the varied types of matter in the world.

1.a, 1.b, 1.d, 1.e

Atoms, Elements, and Compounds

The smallest particle of a substance is an atom. Each element has only one kind of atom. Atoms combine to form molecules. Compounds contain two or more elements.

1.c, 1.d, 1.h

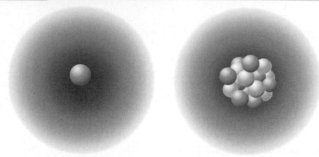

The Periodic Table

Elements are organized in the periodic table by atomic number. Elements with similar properties are grouped together.

1.f, 1.g, 1.i

Chemical and Physical Properties

Properties of substances can be used to separate mixtures and to identify elements and compounds, such as sugar, water, and salts.

Show What You Know

 Unit Writing Activity

Identify a Substance

Suppose you find a substance that you've never seen before. You're not sure whether it's an element or a compound. If it's an element, where would it be placed in the periodic table? Write a research report that presents questions you would ask about the substance and describes the steps you might take to answer them. Include details, examples, and explanations in your report.

Unit Project

Making Sugar Crystals

Have you ever tried sugar crystal candy? It is made by boiling sugar water until the water evaporates. Design an experiment to grow different-sized sugar crystals. Write your plan in a form similar to the Investigate. List the materials and the procedure. Describe the variables you will control and those you will measure. Predict what your experiment will show. Design a table to record your data and a graph to display your data. If your teacher approves of your plan, carry out your experiment.

Vocabulary Review

Use the terms below to complete the sentences. The page numbers tell you where to look in the unit if you need help.

periodic table p. 64

metal p. 78

alloy p. 84

liquid p. 96

chemical property p. 108

chemical reaction p. 118

reactant p. 120

salt p. 124

1. When you say that iron rusts, you are describing a _____ of iron. **1.f**

2. Stainless steel is an _____. **1.c**

3. A substance with a definite volume but no definite shape is a _____. **1.e**

4. One or more new substances form during a _____. **1.a**

5. An element that is a good conductor of heat and electricity is a _____. **1.c**

6. The chart that scientists use to organize the elements is the _____. **1.d**

7. A substance made when an acid and a base combine is called a _____. **1.i**

8. A starting material in a chemical reaction is a _____. **1.a**

Check Understanding

Choose the best answer.

9. **COMPARE AND CONTRAST** Which of the substances shown in this table would both be liquids at 1000°C? **1.g**

Element or Compound	Melting Point (°C)	Boiling Point (°C)
Water	0	100
Table salt	801	1465
Aluminum	660	2467
Nitrogen	−210	−196

A water and nitrogen

B table salt and water

C aluminum and nitrogen

D table salt and aluminum

10. **MAIN IDEA AND DETAILS** Which of the following contains only one kind of atom? **1.b**

A an alloy

B an element

C a solution

D a compound

11. A sealed box containing air and a piece of wood has a mass of 750 g. The box remains sealed as the wood is burned. What would be the mass of the box after the wood is burned? **1.a**

A a little less than 750 g

B much less than 750 g

C more than 750 g

D exactly 750 g

This diagram shows part of the periodic table. Use the diagram to answer questions 12 and 13

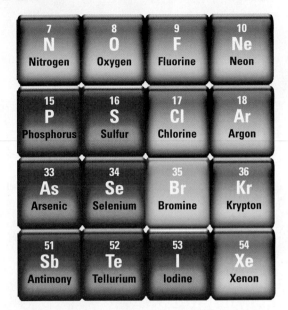

7 **N** Nitrogen	8 **O** Oxygen	9 **F** Fluorine	10 **Ne** Neon
15 **P** Phosphorus	16 **S** Sulfur	17 **Cl** Chlorine	18 **Ar** Argon
33 **As** Arsenic	34 **Se** Selenium	35 **Br** Bromine	36 **Kr** Krypton
51 **Sb** Antimony	52 **Te** Tellurium	53 **I** Iodine	54 **Xe** Xenon

12. Most of the elements shown in the diagram are what type of element? **1.d**

A alloys

B metals

C nonmetals

D human-made elements

13. Which of the elements shown is most likely to have properties of both metals and nonmetals? **1.c**

A helium

B oxygen

C krypton

D arsenic

14. Which of these is a mixture? **1.f**

A soil   **C** water

B oxygen   **D** copper

15. Which elements are important parts of an insect, a tree, and a human? **1.h**

A argon and helium

B carbon and oxygen

C aluminum and bromine

D hydrogen and californium

16. Which of the following is a chemical property of water? **1.g**

A Water freezes at 0°C.

B Water expands as it freezes.

C Electricity can be used to separate water into hydrogen and oxygen.

D Sugar and many types of salts can dissolve in water.

Investigation Skills

17. What are several properties you can use to classify metals and nonmetals? **6.a**

18. A clear, green liquid has been added to a clear, white liquid. A white solid forms, and the green color disappears. What conclusion can you draw from these observations? Explain. **6.h**

Critical Thinking

Use the images below to answer question 19.

A

B

C

19. The pictures show models of three different molecules. Which model shows a molecule of an element? Explain your answer. **1.b**

20. Explain several ways in which all the different types of matter in the world can be made up of so few elements.

The **Big** Idea

135

UNIT 2 · LIFE SCIENCE
Structures of Living Things

What's the Big Idea?

Plants and animals have structures for respiration, digestion, waste disposal, and transport of material.

Essential Questions

Giant Redwoods

Dear Emma,

The race this morning was amazing. Running through these redwoods was awesome.

As I drank my water, I thought: How does water get from the ground to the top of a redwood? How do the trees get food?

Well, I'm off to have dinner. After all that running, I'm starving!

Lily

USA

How do the trees Lily wrote about get food and water? How does this relate to the

Big Idea?

Unit Inquiry

Plant Growth

Living organisms respond to factors in their environments. A plant's roots grow down because they respond to gravity. Another environmental factor plants respond to is light. How do plants respond to light? For example, will plants grow toward a light source? Plan and conduct an experiment to find out.

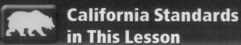
Science Content

2.a *Students know* many multicellular organisms have specialized structures to support the transport of materials.

Investigation and Experimentation

6.a Classify objects (e.g., rocks, plants, leaves, cells) in accordance with appropriate criteria.

California Fast Fact

Cells That Bloom

This photo of very tiny organisms called diatoms was taken through a microscope. Diatoms, which look somewhat like jewels, are hard-shelled, single-cell organisms. Their populations can increase quickly, or bloom. When this happens, diatoms can change the color of California's coastal waters.

LESSON

1

Essential Question

How Do Organisms Transport Materials?

Pacific Ocean diatoms

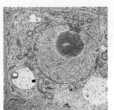

cell [SEL] The basic unit of structure and function of all living things (p. 142)

tissue [TISH•oo] A group of cells that work together to perform a certain function (p. 146)

organ [AWR•guhn] A group of tissues that work together to perform a certain function (p. 146)

organ system [AWR•guhn SIS•tuhm] A group of organs that work together to do a job for the body (p. 147)

Observing Cells

Start with Questions

Each part of an organism works with all the other parts to help the organism carry out its life functions.

- How do organisms get the energy they need for activities, such as rock climbing?

- How are the building blocks of all organisms alike and different?

Investigate to find out. Then read to find out more.

Prepare to Investigate

Investigation Skill Tip
Objects can be classified, or grouped, by characteristics that you observe. Before you classify, think about what characteristics you should use to group the objects.

Materials

- dropper
- red food coloring
- microscope slide
- onion skin
- prepared slide of animal skin
- coverslip
- paper towels
- microscope
- colored pencils

Make an Observation Chart

Plant Cell	Animal Cell

Follow This Procedure

CAUTION: Avoid getting food coloring on your clothing, since it can cause stains.

Step 1

① Use the dropper to place one drop of food coloring on the slide. Place a piece of onion skin in the drop of food coloring. Gently lower the coverslip at an angle over the onion skin. Use a paper towel to remove any excess food coloring.

② **Observe** the onion skin under the microscope. Use colored pencils to **record** your observations on the chart you made.

③ Then **observe** the animal skin slide under the microscope. Use colored pencils to **record** your observations on the chart.

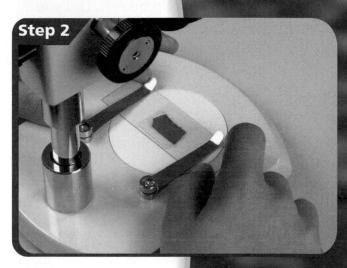
Step 2

Draw Conclusions

1. **Compare** the onion skin and the animal skin. What is each made up of?

2. **Standards Link** Describe some of the structures inside the cells you observed. Are any of them the same in both kinds of cells? `2.a`

3. **Investigation Skill** Animal and plant cells have similarities and differences that you can use to **classify** them. For example, in the center of most cells, there are structures that control the functions of the cell. Based on what you observed, how many kinds of these structures do plant cells have? How many do animal cells have? `6.a`

Independent Inquiry — Classify Objects

Think about your observations during this investigation. What structures helped you classify plant and animal cells?

Develop a method to classify the structures seen within cells. Decide what characteristics you will use for your classification. Try to classify the structures within plant and animal cells. `6.a`

VOCABULARY
cell p. 142
tissue p. 146
organ p. 146
organ system p. 147

SCIENCE CONCEPTS
▶ how living things are made of cells
▶ what structures for transport are in multicellular organisms

Focus Skill **MAIN IDEA AND DETAILS**

Look for details about the structure of living organisms.

Main Idea

detail   detail   detail

Cells as Building Blocks

You've probably seen cork stoppers in bottles or cork on bulletin boards. Did you know that cork comes from the bark of an oak tree? In 1665, Robert Hooke, an English scientist, observed a thin layer of cork through a microscope. He saw the same kind of structures you observed in the onion skin. Because Hooke thought the structures looked like tiny rooms, he named them cells. A **cell** is the basic unit of structure and function in living things.

Most cells are microscopic—they can be seen only with a microscope. The microscope you used in the Investigate helped you observe and compare cells from an animal and cells from a plant.

Hooke's description of cells made scientists want to know more about them. Using microscopes, they learned that all living things are made of cells. They found that all cells share some characteristics. They also discovered that different kinds of cells do different jobs.

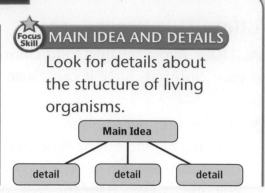

Robert Hooke's microscope, made in the 1600s, looks very different from the microscopes we use today. Both help us see cells—the building blocks of living things.

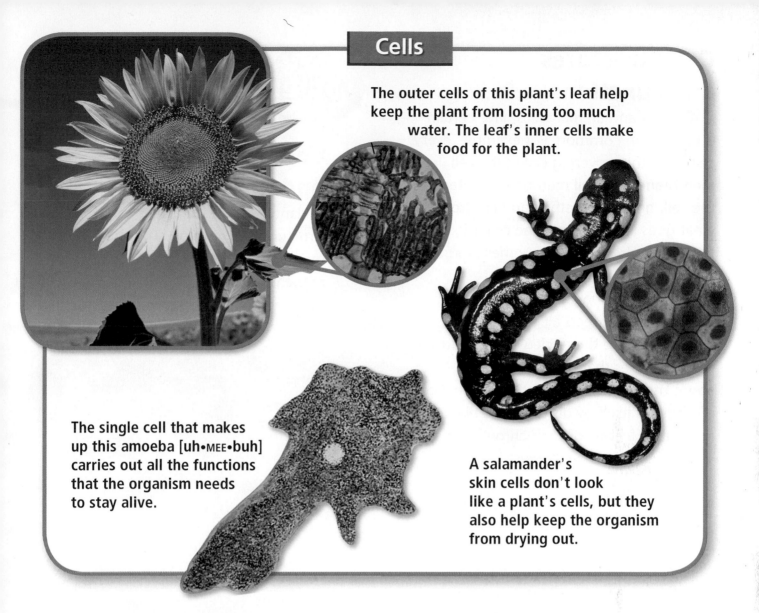

The outer cells of this plant's leaf help keep the plant from losing too much water. The leaf's inner cells make food for the plant.

The single cell that makes up this amoeba [uh•MEE•buh] carries out all the functions that the organism needs to stay alive.

A salamander's skin cells don't look like a plant's cells, but they also help keep the organism from drying out.

Every living thing, or *organism,* is made up of cells. Some simple organisms are just a single cell. Most plants and animals contain many cells.

Plants and animals have different types of cells, each with its own job. The different cells work together to carry out life functions that keep an organism alive and healthy. For example, your body has cells that help you break down food. It has cells that carry oxygen to other cells. It also has cells that carry away waste materials.

To perform its own functions, each cell contains structures called *organelles.* Each type of organelle has a certain function that helps keep the cell alive.

MAIN IDEA AND DETAILS How do cells keep organisms alive and healthy?

A Cell Model

Carefully use a plastic knife to cut a peeled hard-boiled egg in half. Compare it to the animal cells that you observed in the Investigate. Why is a hard-boiled egg a good model for an animal cell?

Cell Structures and Functions

All plant and animals cells have certain organelles in common. For example, every cell has a thin covering called the cell membrane. The cell membrane protects the cell, holds it together, and controls what goes into or out of the cell. Most organelles also have membranes around them.

Plant and animal cells have a *nucleus*. This organelle directs all of a cell's activities. Inside the nucleus are threadlike chromosomes that have information about the cell's characteristics. When a cell reproduces itself by dividing, the nucleus first makes a copy of each chromosome. The new cell gets the copies.

Between the cell membrane and the nucleus is the cytoplasm, a material like jelly. Cytoplasm contains chemicals that help keep a cell healthy.

Several kinds of organelles float in the cytoplasm. Mitochondria are the "powerhouses" of plant and animal cells. They release energy from nutrients. Vacuoles store nutrients, water, or waste materials in plant cells. Vesicles have a similar function in animal cells.

Plant cells have some structures that are not found in animal cells. A thick cell wall helps support a plant cell. The cell wall lies outside the cell membrane. In the cytoplasm of many plant cells, there are chloroplasts. Chloroplasts make food for plant cells.

 **MAIN IDEA AND DETAILS** What organelle directs all the functions of a cell?

Comparing Plant and Animal Cells

Plant cells and animal cells have certain structures in common. They all have a cell membrane, cytoplasm, a nucleus, and mitochondria. Study and compare the plant cells and animal cells in the pictures.

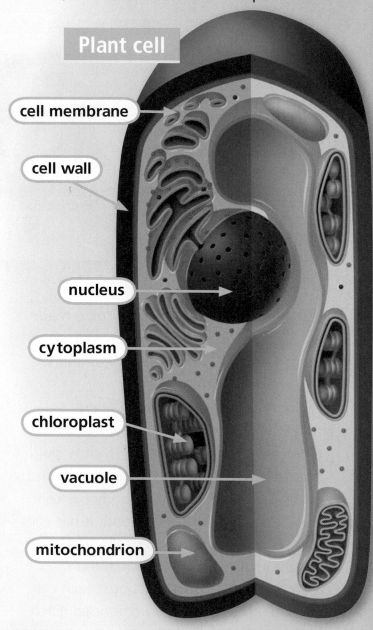

Plant cell

cell membrane

cell wall

nucleus

cytoplasm

chloroplast

vacuole

mitochondrion

Plant cells have different sizes, shapes, and functions, but most have the same organelles.

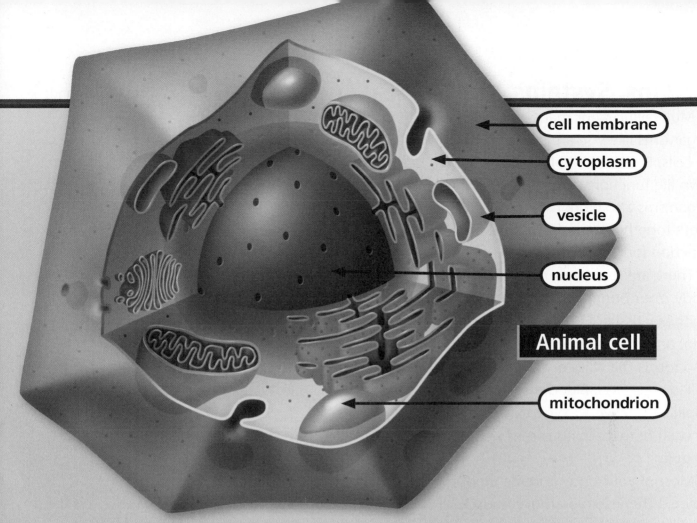

cell membrane

cytoplasm

vesicle

nucleus

Animal cell

mitochondrion

Cell Structures

Organelle	Function	Kind of Cell
Nucleus	directs a cell's activities	plant and animal
Chromosome	inside nucleus; contains information about cell	plant and animal
Cell membrane	holds a cell together and separates it from its surroundings	plant and animal
Cell wall	supports and protects a plant cell	plant
Cytoplasm	a jellylike substance containing chemicals that help the cell stay healthy	plant and animal
Chloroplast	makes food for the cell	plant
Vacuole	stores food, water, or wastes	plant
Vesicle	stores food, water, or wastes	animal
Mitochondria	release energy from nutrients	plant and animal

Like plant cells, animal cells have different sizes, shapes, and functions. They also have many of the same organelles. How is an animal cell different from a plant cell?

For more links and animations, go to **www.hspscience.com**

Cells, Tissues, Organs, Systems

Multicellular—or many-celled—organisms like you are made up of trillions of cells. Each cell is able to carry out its own life functions. The cells in multicellular organisms also work together. Cells that work together to perform a specific function form a **tissue**.

There are four kinds of tissues in your body. Your body is covered and lined with epithelial tissue. Epithelial tissue is in your skin, and it lines your internal organs. It also forms the walls of tiny blood vessels called *capillaries.* Blood that flows through capillaries delivers oxygen and nutrients to each body cell and carries wastes away from it.

Most of your body is made up of muscle tissue. Whenever you move, muscle tissue contracts and relaxes to move your skeleton.

The bones and cartilage of your skeleton are made of connective tissue. Blood is also a type of connective tissue.

Signals from nervous tissue make muscles contract. Nervous tissue also helps you think, talk, and see. It is found in the brain, spinal cord, and nerves.

Together, the four kinds of tissues make up structures. The structures carry out digestion of food, breathing, waste disposal, and transport of materials throughout the body.

Just as cells work together in tissues, tissues work together in organs. An **organ** is several kinds of tissues that work

The lungs are made of epithelial and connective tissues. These tissues work together to take in oxygen from the air and move it into the blood. ▼

The heart is an organ made of muscle tissue, epithelial tissue, nervous tissue, and connective tissue. These work together to pump blood to all parts of the body. ▼

together to carry out a certain function. Your stomach is an organ. It is a muscular sac that is lined and covered with epithelial tissue. Muscle and epithelial tissues work together to add chemicals and squeeze and churn the food you eat. That helps break it down into a form that your body can use.

Your heart is an organ that pumps blood to all parts of your body. It contains each of the different kinds of tissue. The heart is mostly muscle tissue, but it also has connective tissue. It is lined and covered with epithelial tissue, too. Nervous tissue in the heart receives signals from the brain to make the heart beat faster or slower.

The lungs are organs that take in oxygen from the air. They are made of epithelial and connective tissues.

The lungs, the heart, and all other organs rely on another kind of connective tissue—blood. The red cells in blood deliver oxygen to all other cells of the body. The liquid part of blood, called plasma, delivers nutrients to body cells and helps remove wastes from the body.

Organs that work together to do a job for the body form an **organ system**. Your body has many organ systems. You will learn more about some of them in the next few lessons.

 **MAIN IDEA AND DETAILS** What life functions do tissues and organs carry out?

◀ Tissues in the digestive system work together to break down food. The result is what the body can use for energy.

Transport in Multicellular Organisms

All of the cells in plants and animals have the same basic needs. They need oxygen, water, nutrients, and food. Most plants and animals have structures to transport these materials to each cell.

In many animals, including humans, the structures that make up the circulatory system transport needed materials to each of the body's cells. They also take away wastes.

The *circulatory system* is made up of the heart, the blood vessels, and the blood. Together, these organs and tissues transport oxygen and nutrients to each body cell. They also remove wastes made by each cell. The circulatory system works with the excretory system, the respiratory system, and the digestive system to do this.

The nutrients from food and the waste products from cells dissolve in the plasma. Plasma carries the nutrients to the body's cells. Waste products are carried away from the cells so that they can be removed from the body. The solid part of blood includes red blood cells. Red blood cells carry oxygen to all of the body's cells.

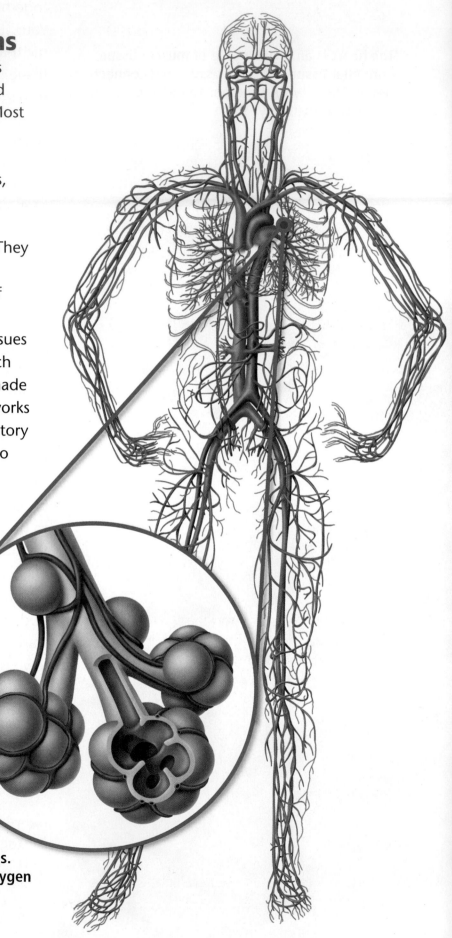

Blood vessels of the circulatory system reach all parts of the body, such as the lungs. In the lungs, the blood receives oxygen and gives up carbon dioxide. ▶

148

Plant cells also need water, nutrients, and food. The water that a plant's roots absorb is carried throughout the plant. Food is carried from the leaves to each cell, too. In most plants, specialized tissues transport these materials.

The transport structures of many plants, like those of the tree shown here, form a system of tubes. The tubes go to all parts of the plant. These tubes are made up of two kinds of tissue. One tissue carries water and minerals from the roots to the leaves. Another tissue carries sugar made in the leaves to each of the plant's cells.

What causes water to move through this transport tissue? In a leafy plant, losing water from the leaves into the air causes negative pressure, or suction. This pulls water up through the plant. You can model this process by sipping water through a straw.

Water pressure also causes sugar to move through a plant. When a solution is more concentrated, or dense, in one area, water flows into that area by a process called osmosis (ahz•MOH•suhs). The water dilutes the solution, or makes it less dense. The sugar in a plant's leaves is very concentrated. It pulls in water. The added water increases the pressure, causing the sugar solution to move to areas where it is needed.

Focus Skill **MAIN IDEA AND DETAILS** What are the functions of transport tissues in plants and animals?

From a plant's roots, water and nutrients move upward through tubes. These tubes extend into the leaves, where they make up the veins.▼

Standards Wrap-Up and Lesson Review

Essential Question

How do organisms transport materials?

In this lesson, you learned that all living things are made up of cells. You also learned that multicellular organisms have specialized tissues, organs, and systems that transport materials to, and remove wastes from, all cells in the organism.

 Science Content Standards in this Lesson

2.a *Students know* many multicellular organisms have specialized structures to support the transport of materials.

1. 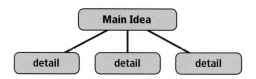 **MAIN IDEA AND DETAILS** Draw and complete a graphic organizer to show the supporting details of this main idea: Transport structures in plants and animals **2.a**

```
            Main Idea
         /     |      \
    detail   detail   detail
```

2. **SUMMARIZE** Write a sentence that explains what different kinds of cells do. **2.a**

3. **DRAW CONCLUSIONS** You are studying a slide under a microscope, and you observe cells that don't have cell walls or chloroplasts. What kind of cells are you probably looking at? **2.a**

4. **VOCABULARY** Use lesson vocabulary and related terms to make a crossword puzzle. **2.a**

5. **Critical Thinking** What is the relationship between the circulatory system in humans and the transport tubes in an oak tree? **2.a**

6. **Investigate and Experiment** Write a plan for an investigation to classify plant and animal cells according to their structures. **6.a**

7. Which of the following is **not** a function of the circulatory system?
   A carrying oxygen to body cells
   B delivering nutrients to body cells
   C breaking down food
   D removing wastes from body cells **2.a**

8. Of the following choices, which is a function of both plant and animal structures?
   A making food
   B transporting materials
   C removing blood cells
   D simulating sleep **2.a**

The Big Idea

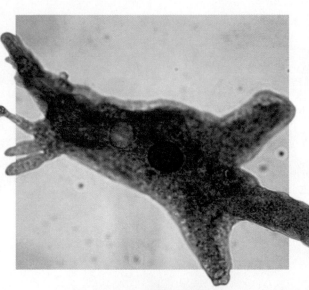

 Writing ELA–W.1.2

Write a Report

The word *cytoplasm* contains the word parts *cyto-* and *-plasm.* Use a dictionary to find the meanings of the parts. How do these meanings relate to the meaning of the whole word *cytoplasm*? Write a report that explains what you found out.

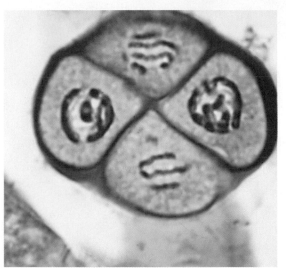

 Math NS 1.0

Extend a Pattern

Imagine that a single cell divides into two cells every 15 minutes. If each of these cells also divides into two, and so on, how long will it take for a single cell to produce 500 cells?

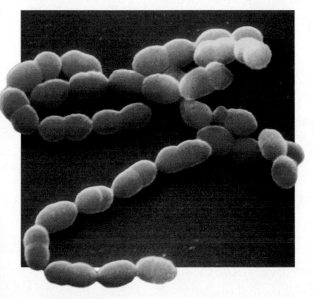

 Health

Bacteria

Bacteria are single-celled organisms that are neither plants nor animals. Most bacteria promote health, but some cause disease. Use the library or trusted Internet resources to investigate the organisms that cause strep throat. What do those cells have in common with plant cells? How are they like animal cells?

 For more links and activities, go to **www.hspscience.com**

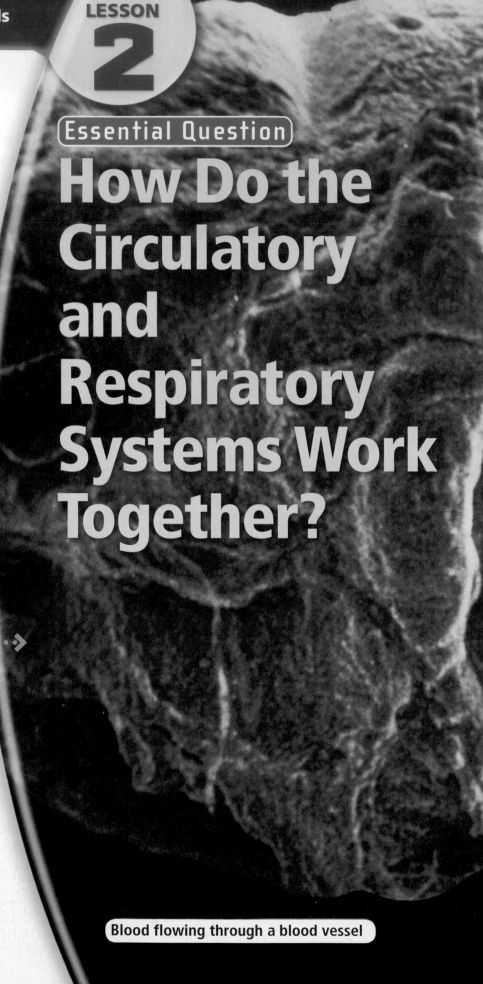

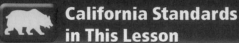
Science Content

2.b *Students know* how blood circulates through the heart chambers, lungs, and body and how carbon dioxide (CO_2) and oxygen (O_2) are exchanged in the lungs and tissues.

Investigation and Experimentation

6.c Plan and conduct a simple investigation based on a student developed question and write instructions others can follow to carry out the procedure.

6.d Identify the dependent and controlled variables in an investigation.

California Fast Fact

Miles of Open Highway

A human body contains about 113,000 km (70,000 mi) of blood vessels. That's enough to stretch the length of California about 90 times! Blood flows best in clean, open vessels like the one shown. Scientists at the University of California have found a surprising substance that may help keep blood vessels open and healthy—and it's found in chocolate!

LESSON

2

Essential Question

How Do the Circulatory and Respiratory Systems Work Together?

Blood flowing through a blood vessel

152

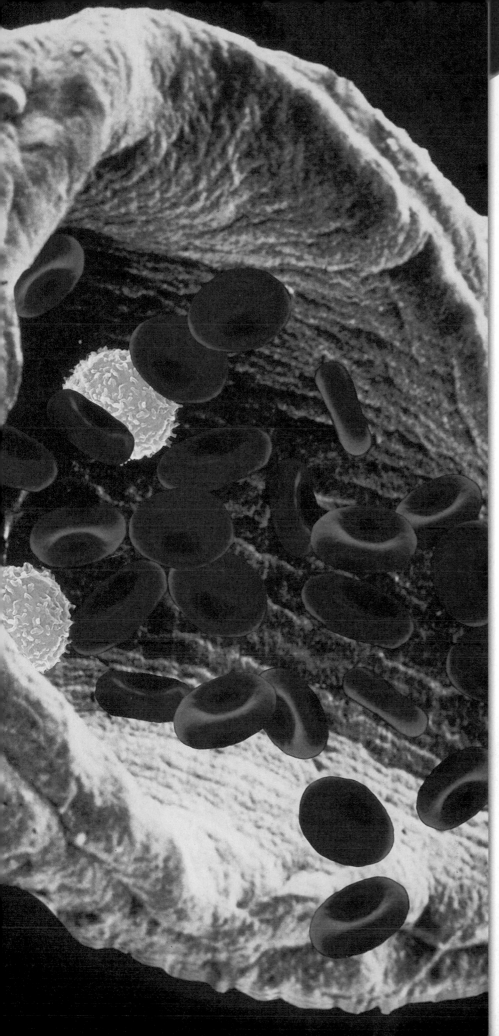

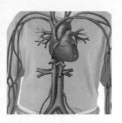

circulatory system
[SER•kyoo•luh•tawr•ee sis•tuhm] A group of organs that transports needed materials throughout the body (p. 158)

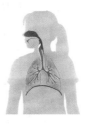

respiratory system
[RES•per•uh•tawr•ee sis•tuhm] A group of organs and tissues that exchanges oxygen and carbon dioxide between your body and the environment (p. 160)

Pulse Rates

Start with Questions

At the doctor's office, someone may take your blood pressure and pulse.

- What do you think blood pressure and pulse measure?

- What information can they give you about the health of your circulatory system?

Investigate to find out. Then read to find out more.

Prepare to Investigate

Investigation Skill Tip
To conduct a valid investigation, you need to Identify the dependent and controlled variables.

Materials

- stopwatch, timer, or clock with second hand

Make a Data Table

Activity	Pulse Rate After 1 Minute
Sitting	
Marching	
Running	

Follow This Procedure

1. Make a table like the one shown.

2. After sitting for at least 1 minute, find the pulse on your wrist. Count the number of times your heart beats in 15 seconds. **Using that number**, multiply by 4 to find how many times your heart beats in 1 minute while you are resting. **Record** the result in your table.

3. Stand up and march in place for 1 minute. As soon as you stop, find your pulse. Count your heartbeats for 15 seconds. **Use the number** to calculate the beats per minute. **Record** the result.

4. Rest. Then run in place for 1 minute. As soon as you stop, find your pulse. Count your heartbeats for 15 seconds. **Use the number** to calculate the beats per minute. **Record** the result.

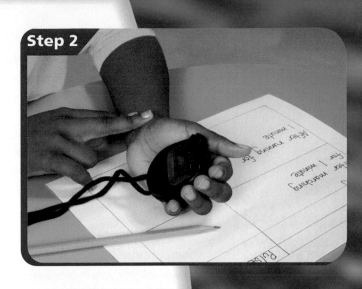

Step 2

Step 3

Draw Conclusions

1. **Compare** the effects of the activities on your pulse rate. After which activity was your pulse rate the highest? After which was it the lowest?

2. **Standards Link** How does exercise affect your heart?　　2.b

3. **Investigation Skill** Scientists **identify the dependent and controlled variables** when they conduct an investigation. What was the dependent variable in this Investigate?　　6.d

Independent Inquiry

Plan and Conduct a Simple Investigation

How do you think exercise affects breathing rates? Plan an investigation to answer this question. Then carry out your plan.　　6.c

155

VOCABULARY
circulatory system p. 158
respiratory system p. 160

SCIENCE CONCEPTS
► how the circulatory and respiratory systems work together
► how they deliver oxygen to the body's cells and remove carbon dioxide from them

 **SEQUENCE**
Note the order of events in circulation and respiration.

▭ → ▭ → ▭

The Heart

As you did the Investigate, you felt—on the outside of your body—evidence that your heart was beating inside your body. You observed that the heart beats with a rhythm and that it keeps going. Why is it so important for the heart to keep working all the time?

All animal cells need oxygen and nutrients to survive. Animals that have bodies made up of many cells have structures that carry the oxygen and nutrients to each cell. One of these structures—the heart—is the pumping organ.

Some animals' hearts are very simple. A earthworm's heart, for example, is just a thick, muscular part of a large blood vessel. When the thick area contracts, or squeezes, it forces blood through the vessel. As you can see in the pictures below, other hearts are more complex.

The human heart is a double pump made up of four parts, or chambers. It normally beats at a steady rate, sending blood to all parts of the body. As you observed in the Investigate, you can feel your heartbeat by taking your pulse.

Before your heart beats, two of the

A crayfish's heart has only two chambers. Even though it is a simple structure, it is very good at pumping blood to all cells in the crustacean's body.

A pig's heart is more complex, with four chambers.

Blood Flow Through the Heart

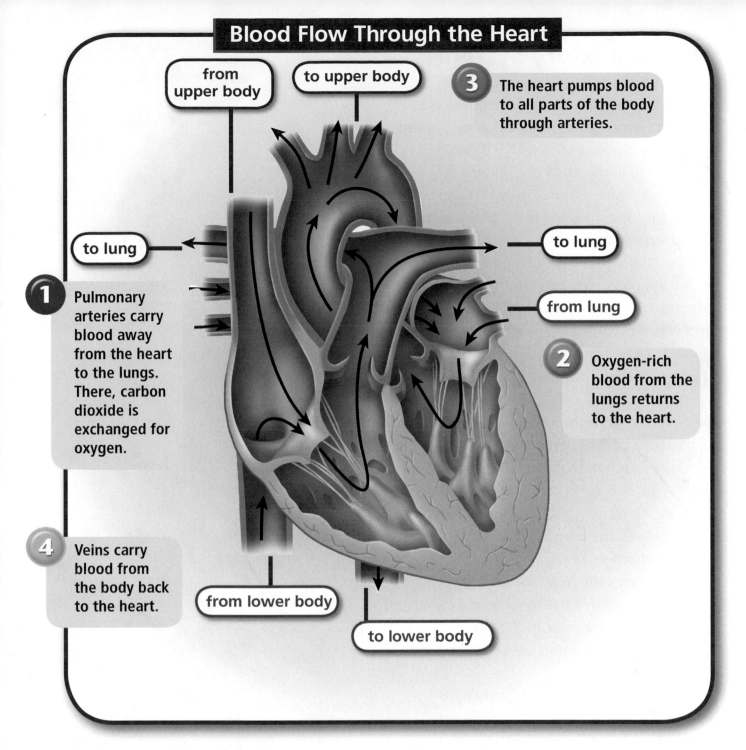

from upper body

to upper body

3 The heart pumps blood to all parts of the body through arteries.

to lung

to lung

from lung

1 Pulmonary arteries carry blood away from the heart to the lungs. There, carbon dioxide is exchanged for oxygen.

2 Oxygen-rich blood from the lungs returns to the heart.

4 Veins carry blood from the body back to the heart.

from lower body

to lower body

chambers fill with blood. Then the heart contracts and squeezes blood into large tubes, or blood vessels. The pulse you felt at your wrist was caused when your heart contracted and pushed blood through a vessel in your arm.

Blood travels in a certain path. Blood from the body returns to the right side of the heart. The heart then pumps it to the lungs. There, carbon dioxide is exchanged for oxygen. The oxygen-rich blood goes to the left side of the heart. Then it is pumped to all body cells.

Focus Skill **SEQUENCE** What path does blood follow between the time it returns to the heart from the body and the time it is pumped from the heart to the body?

The Circulatory System

Though all of the body's systems are important, the circulatory system is one of the most important. The **circulatory system** transports blood loaded with oxygen and nutrients to each cell of the body. It also takes away wastes from the cells. The circulatory system is made up of the heart, blood vessels, and blood.

Blood is a connective tissue made up of several parts. The liquid part, called plasma, is mostly water. Nutrients from food and waste products from cells dissolve in plasma. The plasma carries the nutrients to the body's cells. It carries away the waste products from the cells. Then the wastes can be removed from the body.

The solid part of blood includes red blood cells, white blood cells, and platelets. Red blood cells carry oxygen to all body cells. White blood cells help fight infection. Platelets help the blood clot and stop bleeding from wounds.

Blood leaves the heart through blood vessels called *arteries*. Arteries lead to small vessels called *capillaries*. In the capillaries, materials are exchanged between the blood and body cells.

Capillaries have thin walls and come into direct contact with every body cell. Materials move through the thin walls

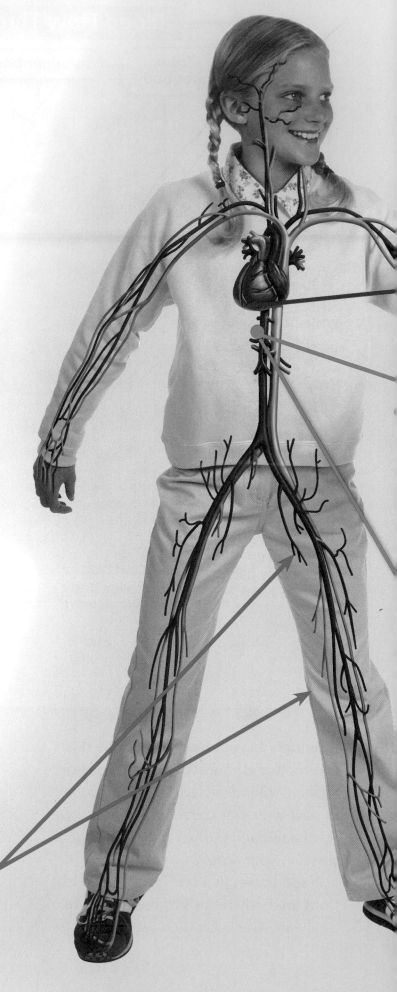

The circulatory system is made up of the heart, blood, capillaries, veins, and arteries. Together, these organs and tissues provide your body's cells with the oxygen and nutrients they need. They also help body cells get rid of wastes. ▶

and cross the membranes of the cells. Nutrients, oxygen, and wastes move from areas of high concentration to areas of low concentration. So, nutrients and oxygen move from the capillaries into the cells where they are needed. Waste materials move from the cells into the capillaries.

◄ Your heart beats at a steady rate, pushing blood into your arteries. You can feel this push as a pulse in the arteries in your wrist and neck.

Capillaries lead to large blood vessels called *veins* (VAYNZ). Veins return blood to the heart.

 **SEQUENCE** What path does blood take after being pumped from the heart to the body cells?

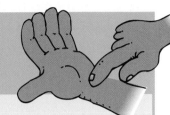

Pulse Check

Measure the pulse at your wrist, and record it. Then measure and record the pulse through an artery on your neck, the top of your foot, and behind your knee. Compare the rates. What can you infer about the heart from your results?

◄ Blood is a kind of connective tissue that is part of the circulatory system. It travels through blood vessels, carrying oxygen and nutrients to body cells and taking wastes away from body cells. Blood vessels are some of the structures that animals have for the transport of materials.

For a more detailed look at the circulatory system, see the Health Handbook.

The Respiratory System

Think of all the things you do each day. You go to school, you might play on a sports team, you take part in clubs, you play outdoors, and you do homework. You need a lot of energy! To produce that energy, your cells need a lot of oxygen. The **respiratory system** is a group of organs and tissues that exchanges oxygen and carbon dioxide between your body and the environment.

Put your hand over your heart and take a deep breath. Do you feel your chest rise and fall? Breathing causes this movement.

A muscle called the *diaphragm* (DY•uh•fram), located near the bottom of your rib cage, helps pull air into your body. The air that enters your body contains the oxygen your cells need.

Air travels from your nose or mouth into the trachea (TRAY•kee•uh). The trachea branches into smaller and smaller tubes that lead into your lungs. The lungs are the main organs of your respiratory system. In the lungs, the tubes end in tiny air sacs.

 **SEQUENCE** What path does air take when you inhale?

The cells of this athlete's body must get a lot of oxygen to meet their energy needs. The body gets this oxygen by breathing rapidly.

Math in Science
Interpret Data

Air is a mixture of gases, one of which is very important to life. Study the graph. How much additional oxygen is needed for athletic training compared to moderate exercise?

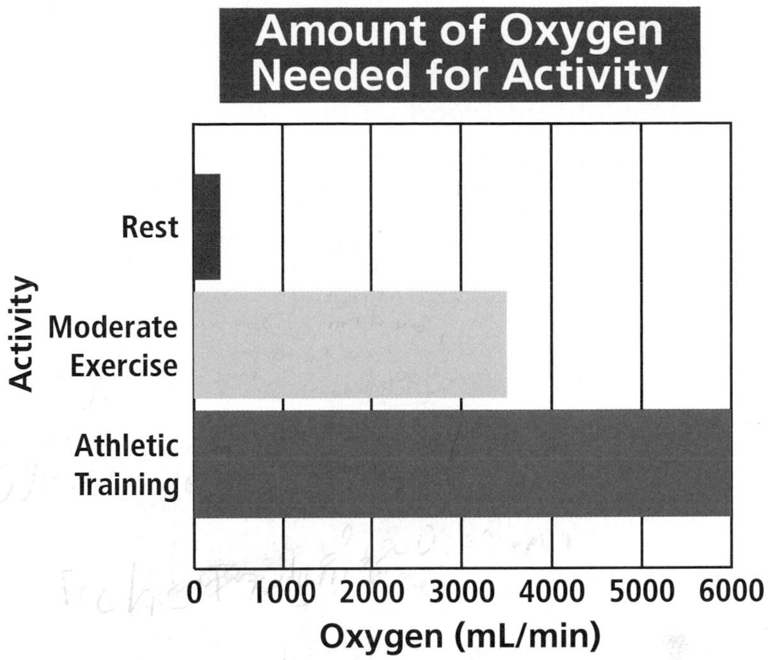

Amount of Oxygen Needed for Activity
Activity
Rest
Moderate Exercise
Athletic Training
0
1000
2000
3000
4000
5000
6000
Oxygen (mL/min)

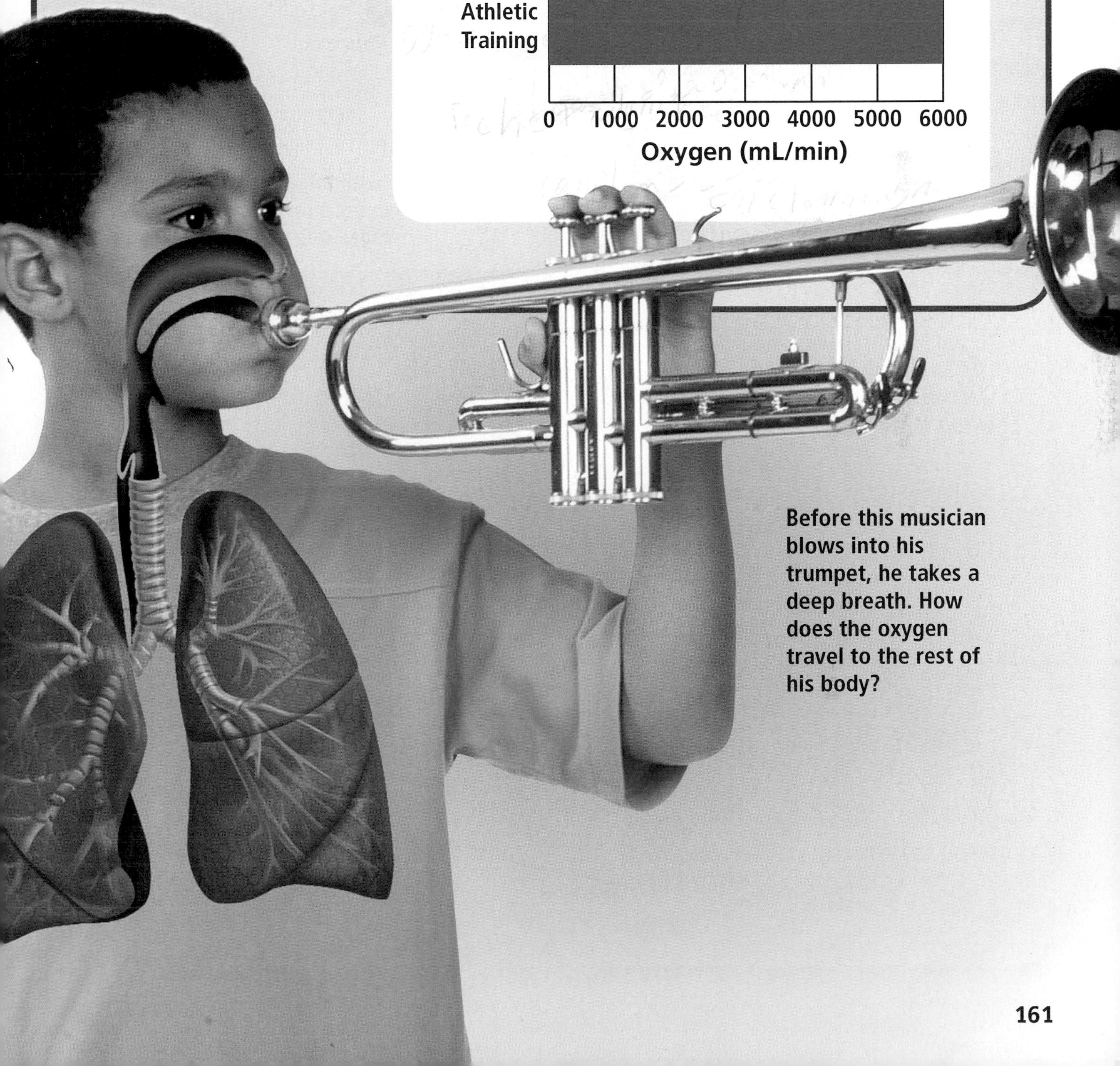

Before this musician blows into his trumpet, he takes a deep breath. How does the oxygen travel to the rest of his body?

Working Together

How does the circulatory system work with the respiratory system? The oxygen in the air that you inhale moves from the respiratory system into the blood. At the same time, carbon dioxide moves from the blood into the respiratory system. Your body produces carbon dioxide as a waste product. Carbon dioxide leaves the body when you exhale.

This exchange of gases takes place in air sacs in the lungs. Capillaries wrap around each air sac. The air sacs and the capillaries have thin walls that let gases move through them.

The capillaries at the air sacs receive oxygen-poor blood from the heart. This blood contains a lot of carbon dioxide. Carbon dioxide passes from the blood plasma into the air sacs. When you exhale, your body gets rid of the carbon dioxide. When you inhale, oxygen from the air passes into the blood, and red blood cells pick it up. Oxygen-rich blood travels back to the heart. From the heart, it is pumped throughout the body, to every body cell.

Focus Skill **SEQUENCE** How does oxygen get from the air into your blood?

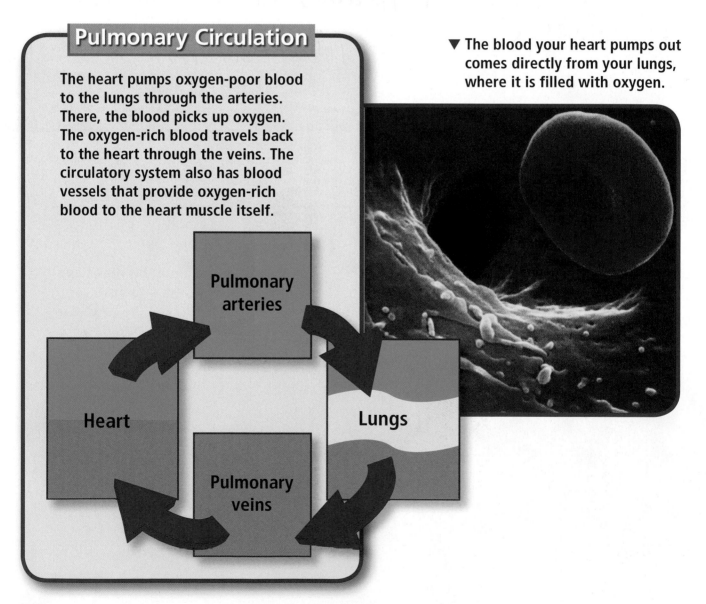

Pulmonary Circulation

The heart pumps oxygen-poor blood to the lungs through the arteries. There, the blood picks up oxygen. The oxygen-rich blood travels back to the heart through the veins. The circulatory system also has blood vessels that provide oxygen-rich blood to the heart muscle itself.

Heart

Pulmonary arteries

Pulmonary veins

Lungs

▼ The blood your heart pumps out comes directly from your lungs, where it is filled with oxygen.

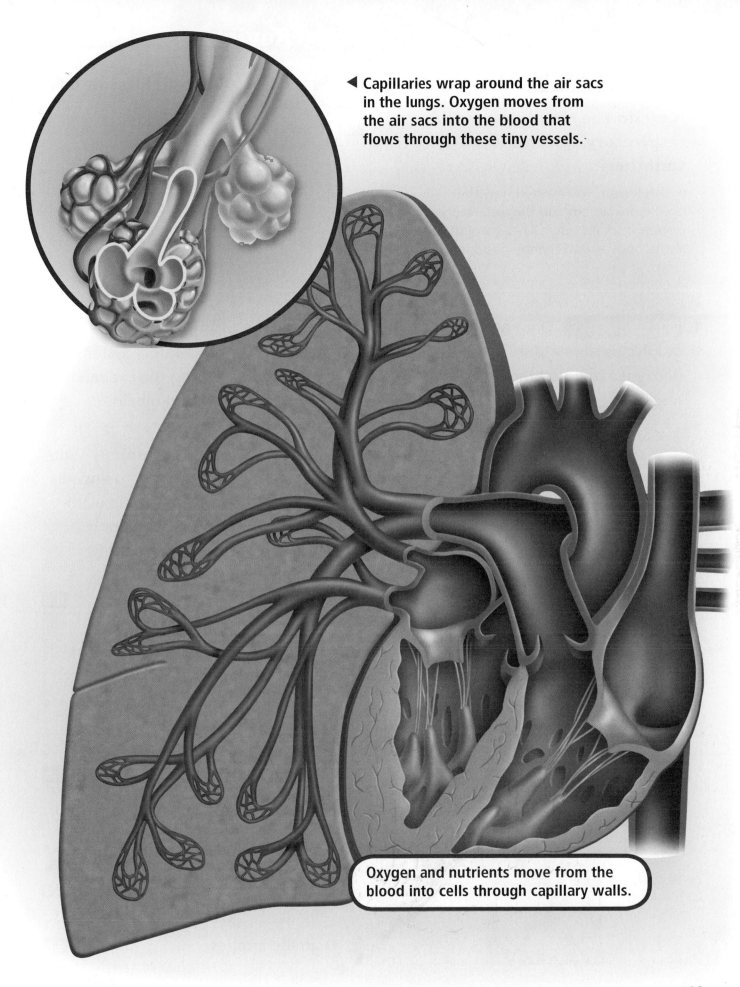

◀ Capillaries wrap around the air sacs in the lungs. Oxygen moves from the air sacs into the blood that flows through these tiny vessels.

Oxygen and nutrients move from the blood into cells through capillary walls.

Standards Wrap-Up and Lesson Review

How do the circulatory and respiratory systems work together?

In this lesson, you learned how the circulatory system and the respiratory system work together. They carry materials in the body and exchange gases in the lungs.

Science Content Standards in This Lesson

2.b *Students know* how blood circulates through the heart chambers, lungs, and body and how carbon dioxide (CO_2) and oxygen (O_2) are exchanged in the lungs and tissues.

1. **(Focus Skill) SEQUENCE** Draw and complete a graphic organizer to show the sequence of oxygen transport through the respiratory and circulatory systems. **2.b**

   ⬭ → ⬭ → ⬭

2. **SUMMARIZE** Write two sentences that tell what this lesson is mainly about. **2.b**

3. **DRAW CONCLUSIONS** The trachea branches into smaller and smaller tubes that lead to air sacs in your lungs. Why do you think there are many air sacs and not just one big air sac? **2.b**

4. **VOCABULARY** Write a definition for each vocabulary term. **2.b**

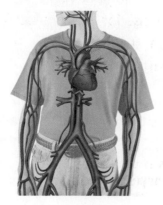

5. **Critical Thinking** How do the circulatory and respiratory systems work together during the exchange of oxygen and carbon dioxide? **2.b**

6. **Investigate and Experiment** Write a plan for an investigation to answer this question: How do the circulatory and respiratory systems respond to exercise? Be sure you identify the dependent and controlled variables. **6.d**

7. Which of the following is the main organ of the circulatory system?
   - **A** the heart
   - **B** arteries
   - **C** veins
   - **D** blood **2.b**

8. Where does gas exchange take place in the body?
   - **A** in the trachea
   - **B** in the liver
   - **C** in the air sacs
   - **D** in the arteries **2.b**

The **Big** Idea

  Writing **ELA–W 2.1**

Write a Narrative

Write a narrative about the travels of an oxygen molecule. Describe how it moves from the air, into your mouth or nose, and through your body to a body cell.

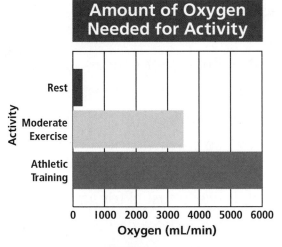

Amount of Oxygen Needed for Activity

Activity

Rest

Moderate Exercise

Athletic Training

0   1000 2000 3000 4000 5000 6000

Oxygen (mL/min)

9÷3 **Math** **SDAP 1.4**

Interpret Data

The table shows the amount of oxygen your body needs during various activities. How does physical activity affect the amount of oxygen needed?

 Health

Pogo A-Go-Go!

You can improve the health of your circulatory system by lowering your resting heart rate. Measure your heart rate at rest. Then exercise for 30 minutes every day for a month. By how much does your resting heart rate drop?

For more links and activities, go to **www.hspscience.com**

▶ **DR. JEWEL PLUMMER COBB**

▶ **Trustee Professor, California State University at Los Angeles**

▶ **President and Professor of Biological Sciences, Emerita, California State University at Fullerton**

▶ Studied skin pigments to find new drugs for cancer

▶ Is a mentor for minority students

Jewel Plummer Cobb

What does skin color have to do with scientific achievement? For Jewel Plummer Cobb, it was the subject of her achievement. As a cell physiologist—a scientist who studies how the parts of a cell work together—Dr. Cobb focused on melanin. This dark skin pigment helps protect skin from the cancer-causing effects of the sun. Dr. Cobb's research led to the development of important cancer-fighting medicines.

Dr. Cobb's influence extends beyond the laboratory. She offers science students the same encouragement her family offered her. When her career began, it was unusual for an African American woman to choose a career in science. She wants minority students to learn that they, too, have opportunities for careers in science. While she was president of California State University at Fullerton, she encouraged diversity, raising funds to allow many more minority students to study science.

Think and Write

1 How has Dr. Cobb improved the lives of others?

2 How are the timing and focus of Dr. Cobb's career historically important?

Dr. Jewel Plummer Cobb has made her mark not only with her research but also with her care for others. She encourages all students interested in science careers to pursue their dreams.

Wei Shi

All cells carry out the same basic life functions. But in organisms made of many cells, each cell also has a special function. What "tells" a cell to do its job? What makes the cells in the respiratory system carry out their respiratory functions?

Dr. Wei Shi, a molecular scientist who started his education in China, may have asked himself these questions. Dr. Shi wondered why breathing problems are so common in babies under a year of age. He wanted to learn whether certain substances affect the ability of respiratory cells to carry out their jobs. He became interested in learning which of the molecules called growth factors affect normal respiratory structure to form and function in a baby.

Dr. Shi's research showed how two substances help the lungs form. His discoveries gave doctors a better understanding of respiratory illnesses in newborns.

▶ **DR. WEI SHI**

▶ **Assistant Professor of Research, Developmental Biology Program, Saban Research Institute of Children's Hospital Los Angeles and University of Southern California**

▶ Researches how the lungs develop and mature before and after birth

▶ Has Increased understanding of lung disease in babies

 Think and Write

1 How does molecular biology help solve medical mysteries?

2 Why is it important to understand the breathing problems that affect babies? **2.b**

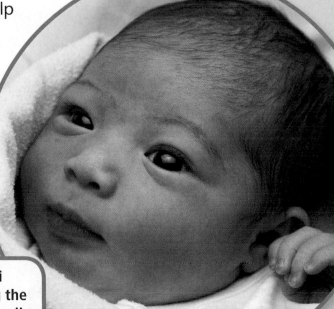

A tireless researcher, Dr. Wei Shi has spent several years studying the molecules that "tell" respiratory cells to do their special jobs.

Science Content

2.c *Students know* the sequential steps of digestion and the roles of teeth and the mouth, esophagus, stomach, small intestine, large intestine, and colon in the function of the digestive system.

Investigation and Experimentation

6.b Develop a testable question.

6.g Record data by using appropriate graphic representations (including charts, graphs, and labeled diagrams) and make inferences based on those data.

California Fast Fact

A Large Intestine!

There's an amazing woman in California. Tess, a 15-m (50-ft) model, gives a glimpse into the inner workings of the body. Through holes in her "skin," visitors can see her digestive system, including her large intestine. And what a large intestine it is! Tess is 9.3 times as tall as the average adult American woman, so her digestive system is about 22 m (74 ft) long.

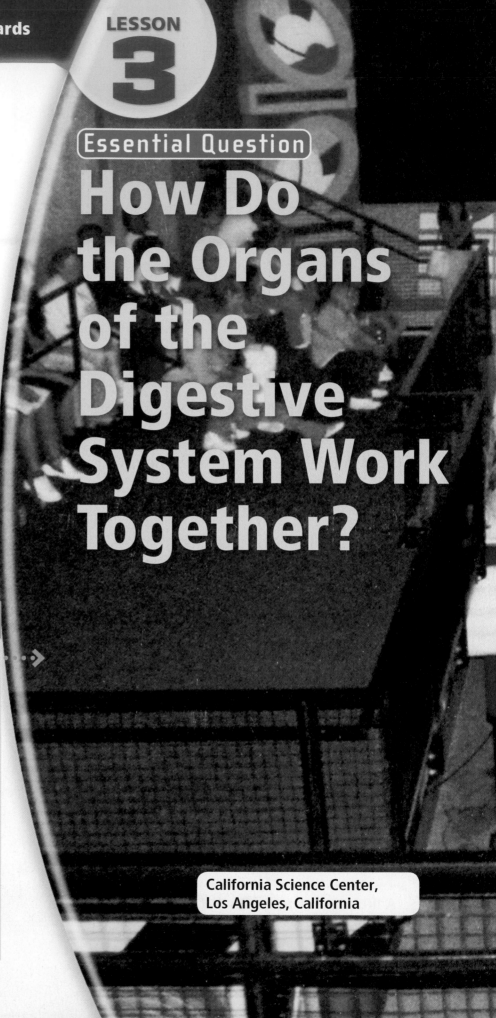

LESSON 3

Essential Question

How Do the Organs of the Digestive System Work Together?

California Science Center, Los Angeles, California

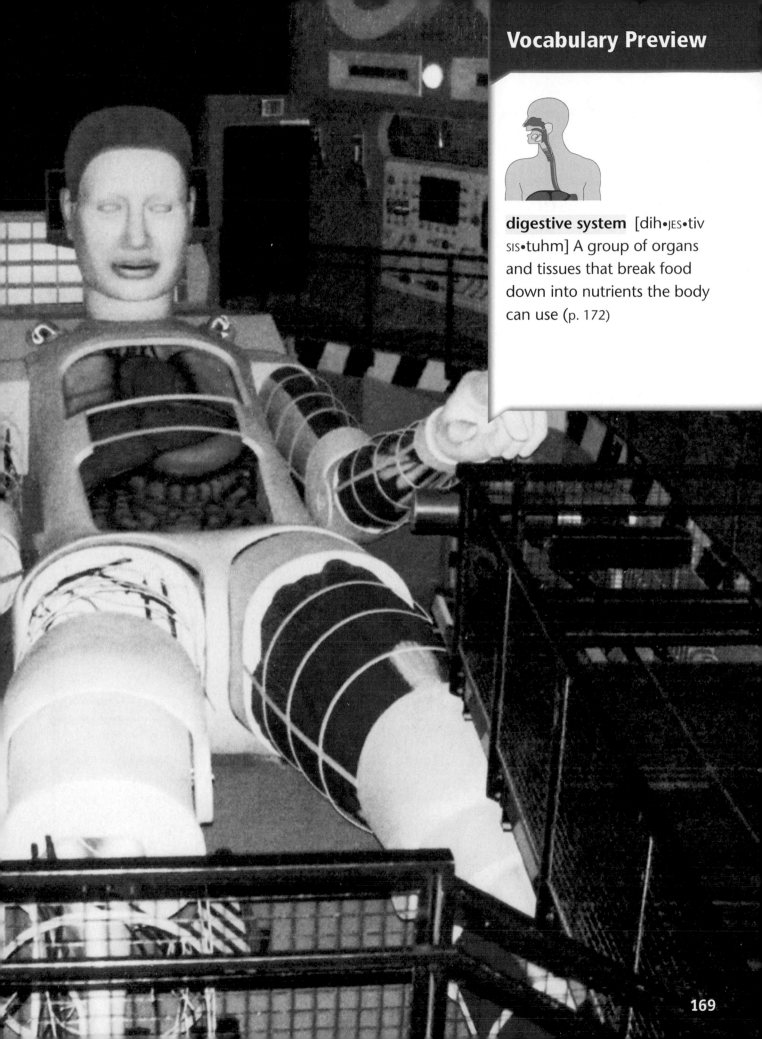

digestive system [dih•JES•tiv SIS•tuhm] A group of organs and tissues that break food down into nutrients the body can use (p. 172)

Breakdown

Start with Questions

Carrying a heavy backpack requires a lot of energy. You get this energy from the food you eat.

- How does your body change food into a form it can use?

- What organs break down food?

Investigate to find out. Then read to find out more.

Prepare to Investigate

> **Investigation Skill Tip**
> If you carefully observe and record data from an investigation, you can make inferences based on the data.

Materials

- 2 soda crackers
- paper towel
- 2 droppers
- amylase solution
- colored pencils
- iodine solution

Make an Observation Chart

Cracker Without Amylase	Cracker Treated with Amylase
After 5 minutes:	After 5 minutes:
After treatment with iodine:	After treatment with iodine:

Follow This Procedure

CAUTION: Iodine stains fabrics. Don't get any on your clothing.

1. Place the crackers on the paper towel. Use a dropper to place 5 drops of amylase solution on one cracker. Wait 5 minutes. **Observe** the cracker. Use the colored pencils to **record** your observations.

2. Use the other dropper to place 2 drops of iodine solution on each cracker. **Observe** the changes that occur. Use the colored pencils to **record** your observations.

Step 1

Step 2

Draw Conclusions

1. **Compare** the crackers. Which one changed to a dark color when iodine was added?

2. **Standards Link** Which cracker appeared to break down—the one treated with amylase or the one without amylase? **2.c**

3. **Investigation Skill** Crackers are starchy. Iodine detects the presence of starch in foods. Based on your observations and the data you recorded, what **inference** can you make about amylase? **6.g**

Independent Inquiry

Develop a Testable Question

Think about what you observed in this investigation. What other question about the breakdown of food could you test? **6.b**

Write a plan to test your question. Your plan should include the following:

- **the materials you will need**
- **the steps of your investigation**

VOCABULARY
digestive system p. 172

SCIENCE CONCEPTS

▶ how the digestive system helps break down food into nutrients

Focus Skill SEQUENCE

Note the order of events in digestion.

☐ → ☐ → ☐

Food Breaks Down

Remember that an organ system is a group of organs working together to do a job for the body. One of the 10 major organ systems in your body systems is the **digestive system**. The organs of the digestive system include the mouth, esophagus, stomach, small intestine, and large intestine.

Digestion begins in the mouth. There, your teeth and tongue break food into smaller pieces. Saliva helps soften the food and also begins the digestion of starches.

In the small intestine, digestion is completed. The nutrients pass into capillaries in the villi (VIL•eye) and then go to your body's cells.

In the stomach, food mixes with digestive juices. When the food is nearly liquid, it passes into the small intestine.

The digestive system digests food, or breaks it down into chemical nutrients that body cells need. First, chemicals break food down into nutrients. Then, nutrients are moved into the blood. The blood transports the nutrients to each of the body's cells.

Most people think the stomach is the first body organ involved in digestion. Actually, digestion of certain foods starts as soon as you take a bite! As you chew, your teeth grind food into smaller pieces. Your mouth produces *saliva* (suh•LY•vuh). Saliva contains amylase—a chemical that begins the digestion of starchy foods, just as the amylase in the Investigate did.

From the mouth, food travels down the *esophagus* (ih•SAHF•uh•guhs), a long tube that leads to the stomach. The stomach is a baglike organ with walls of smooth muscle. In the stomach, strong muscles mix the food with digestive juices. The food becomes almost liquid.

From the stomach, food moves into another long tube of muscle. This is the *intestine* (in•TES•tuhn).

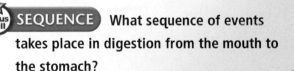 **SEQUENCE** What sequence of events takes place in digestion from the mouth to the stomach?

How Sweet It Is Chew an unsalted soda cracker as long as you can without swallowing it. Note its flavor when you first bite into it. Compare this flavor to the flavor that develops as you chew the cracker. What do you think causes the change?

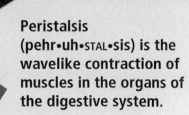

Peristalsis (pehr•uh•STAL•sis) is the wavelike contraction of muscles in the organs of the digestive system.

Water and Nutrients Are Absorbed

There are actually two intestines. Each is a long tube. The first tube, the small intestine, is connected to the stomach at one end. Partly digested food flows from the stomach into the small intestine, where chemicals from the liver and the pancreas (PAN•kree•uhs) are added.

Nutrients pass into the blood through the thin walls of the villi in the small intestine.

The strong contractions of the small intestine mix these chemicals with the food and break it down further. This process produces molecules that the body can easily use.

The small intestine is lined with fingerlike bumps called villi. Villi increase the surface area of the small intestine. This helps the transport of nutrients, because it means there are more places for nutrients to be absorbed into the blood.

Villi are full of capillaries. Nutrients move from the villi of the small intestine into these capillaries. Then, blood carries them throughout the body.

Study the graph on this page. How does body size relate to the length of the small intestine? Organisms with larger bodies have longer small intestines than organisms with smaller bodies. This is because larger organisms need more energy and nutrients.

Some materials cannot be broken down further by the actions of muscles or chemicals in the small intestine. These materials move into the large intestine. This movement occurs because of the strong, wavelike muscle contraction called peristalsis. (Food also moves through the esophagus from the mouth to the stomach because of peristalsis.)

In the large intestine, water from the remaining undigested food is absorbed into the body. Peristalsis moves the solid waste, called *feces*, to the lower part of the *colon*. There, it is stored until it is eliminated from the body.

Focus Skill **SEQUENCE** What events occur after food moves from the stomach into the small intestine?

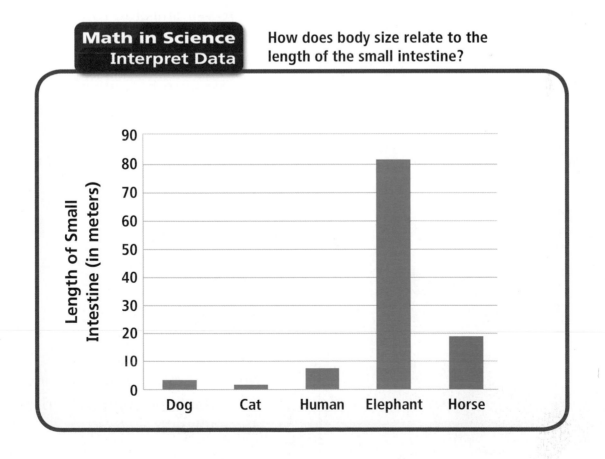

Math in Science
Interpret Data

How does body size relate to the length of the small intestine?

Standards Wrap-Up and Lesson Review

How do the organs of the digestive system work together?

In this lesson, you learned how organs of the digestive system work together in the digestion of food and the absorption of nutrients.

Science Content Standards in This Lesson

2.c *Students know* the sequential steps of digestion and the roles of teeth and the mouth, esophagus, stomach, small intestine, large intestine, and colon in the function of the digestive system.

1. (Focus Skill) **SEQUENCE** Draw and complete a graphic organizer that shows the sequence of food's movement through the digestive system. **2.c**

2. **SUMMARIZE** Write two sentences that tell what this lesson is mainly about. **2.c**

3. **DRAW CONCLUSIONS** What part of the digestive system is not working properly in people who can't absorb nutrients? Explain. **2.c**

4. **VOCABULARY** Use the lesson vocabulary and other lesson terms to write a paragraph about the digestive system. **2.c**

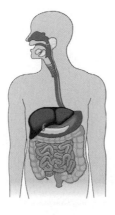

5. **Critical Thinking** What is the relationship between the digestive and circulatory systems? **2.c**

6. **Investigate and Experiment** What testable question could you develop to investigate why certain foods break down more rapidly in the mouth than other foods? **6.b**

7. How are villi similar to roots?
   A Both absorb nutrients.
   B Both distribute nutrients.
   C Neither absorbs nutrients.
   D Both are found only in animals. **2.c**

8. What might happen if the stomach lost its ability to contract? **The Big Idea**
   A Food would be thoroughly mixed with digestive juices.
   B It would take less time for digestion to be completed.
   C Food would not be well digested when it moved to the intestines.
   D Food would be completely broken down when it moved. **2.c**

Writing   ELA–W 1.3

Write a Report

Hippocrates (460–377 B.C.) is known as the father of medicine. Use library or Internet resources to learn about Hippocrates' beliefs about diet, nutrition, and health. Write a short report, and share your findings with the class.

9÷3 Math   MG 1.4

Find Area

Compare the area of a flat surface to the area of a surface with "villi." Place several sheets of paper end to end on the floor. Then fold other sheets of paper like a fan and place them on the flat sheets. How many folded "villi" sheets do you need to cover the flat "small intestine" sheets? How do you think villi affect the absorption of nutrients?

Health

The Right Stuff

Use library or Internet resources to identify the vitamins and minerals your body needs in small amounts. Make a chart. For each nutrient, show the amount your body needs every day and good sources of it. Also, show ways to help ensure it is absorbed, such as eating it with another nutrient.

For more links and activities, go to **www.hspscience.com**

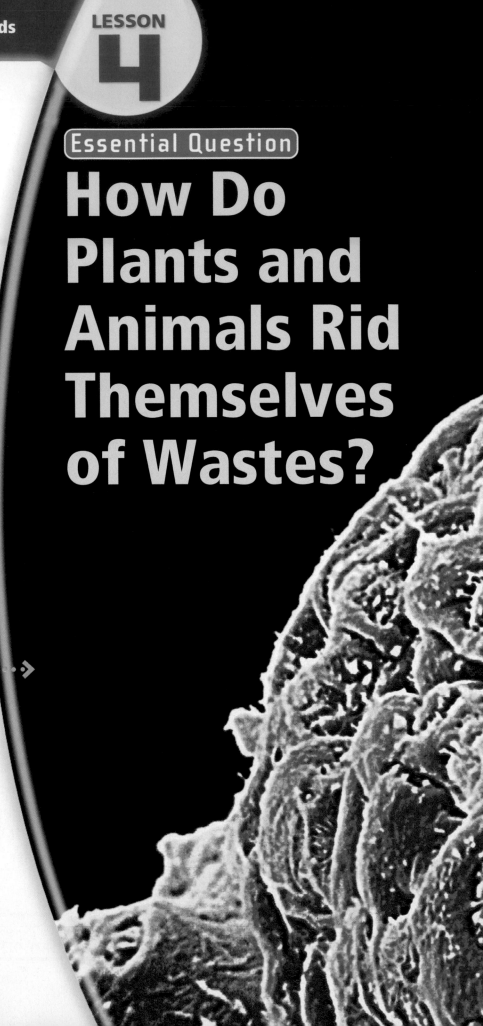

LESSON
4

Science Content

2.d *Students know* the role of the kidney in removing cellular waste from the blood and converting it to urine, which is stored in the bladder.

Investigation and Experimentation

6.c Plan and conduct a simple investigation based on a student-developed question and write instructions others can follow to carry out the procedure.

6.g Record data by using appropriate graphic representations and make inferences based on those data.

Essential Question

How Do Plants and Animals Rid Themselves of Wastes?

California Fast Fact

Laughter Is the Best Medicine

Dialysis (dy•AL•uh•sis) is the way wastes are removed from the blood when the kidneys no longer work properly. The uncomfortable procedure takes about 3 hours three times a week. Since 2002, the group called Rx Laughter, at UCLA, has entertained children having dialysis, decreasing their fear and pain.

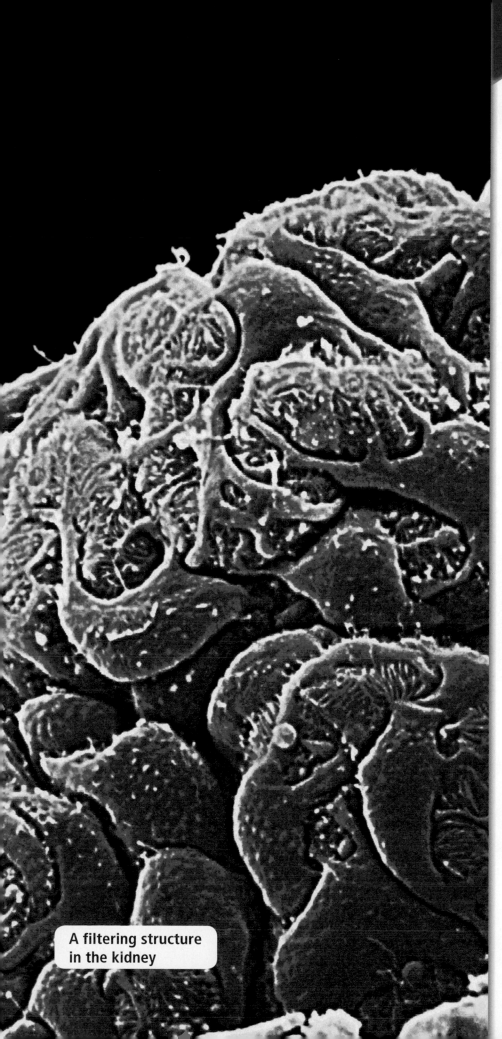

A filtering structure
in the kidney

excretory system
[EKS•kruh•tawr•ee SIS•tuhm]
The organ system that
removes wastes from the
body (p. 182)

kidney [KID•nee] The main
organ of the excretory system
(p. 183)

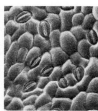

transpiration
[tran•spuh•RAY•shuhn] The
process by which water
moves out of plants through
tiny holes in the leaves
(p. 185)

Water Movement

Start with Questions

Your body is more than 70 percent water! There is a balance between all that water and other substances in your body. The right amount of water helps your body stay healthy and get rid of wastes.

- How does the body produce a water balance?

- How are wastes removed from animals and plants?

Investigate to find out. Then read to find out more.

Prepare to Investigate

Investigation Skill Tip
Record data in appropriate graphics, such as tables and charts. Then make inferences from the data.

Materials

- 2 cups
- water
- spoon
- salt
- 2 stalks of *Elodea*
- colored pencils

Make an Observation Chart

Elodea in fresh water	Elodea in salt water

Follow This Procedure

1. Label the cups *salt water* and *fresh water*. Fill each cup with water. To one cup, add a spoonful of salt.

2. Add a stalk of *Elodea* to each cup. **Predict** the changes that will occur.

3. After 5 minutes, **observe** the changes. Use the colored pencils to record your observations.

Draw Conclusions

1. **Compare** the changes in the stalks of *Elodea*.

2. **Standards Link** What would likely happen to the *Elodea* in the salt water if it were rinsed off and placed into a cup with fresh water? **2.d**

3. **Investigation Skill** Cytoplasm is a solution that has a lesser amount of dissolved salts in it—a lower concentration of salts and a higher concentration of water—than salt water has. Based on the data you recorded, **make inferences** about the movement of water into or out of cells. **6.g**

Step 1

Step 2

Independent Inquiry ▶ **Plan and Conduct a Simple Investigation**

The movement of water through a membrane, such as a cell membrane, is called osmosis. Plan and conduct a simple investigation based on a question you have about osmosis. **6.c**

In your plan, include written instructions that others can follow to carry out your procedure.

VOCABULARY
excretory system p. 182
kidney p. 183
transpiration p. 185

SCIENCE CONCEPTS
▶ how the excretory
  system removes wastes
  in animals
▶ how plants rid
  themselves of wastes

Focus Skill COMPARE AND CONTRAST
Note the ways animals and
plants rid themselves of
wastes and how those ways
are alike and different.

[alike]———[different]

The Excretory System

You know that body systems work
together to carry out life functions. The
respiratory system takes in the oxygen all
cells need. The digestive system breaks
down food to release nutrients. The
circulatory system carries nutrients from
the digestive system and oxygen from the
respiratory system to each of the body's
cells. It also carries away waste products
made by the cells.

How are the wastes removed from
the body? Carbon dioxide, a waste gas,
is removed when you exhale. However,
other cellular wastes cannot be
exhaled. These wastes include
ammonia, which results from
the breakdown of proteins.

Ammonia is removed
from the body by the
excretory system. It is
dissolved in plasma and
carried by the blood
to the liver. There, the
ammonia is converted to
urea. This waste product is
carried by the blood to the
excretory system and is then
removed from the body.

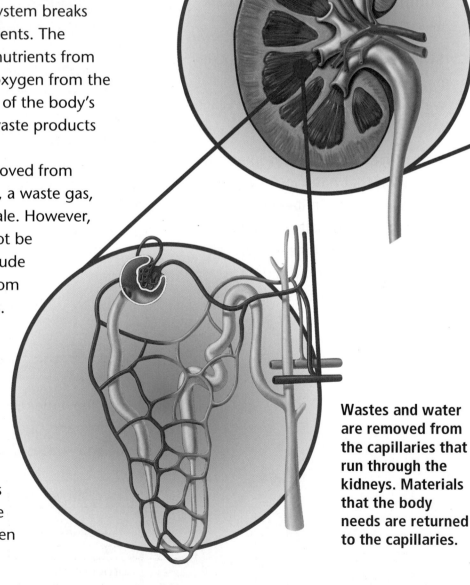

**Wastes and water
are removed from
the capillaries that
run through the
kidneys. Materials
that the body
needs are returned
to the capillaries.**

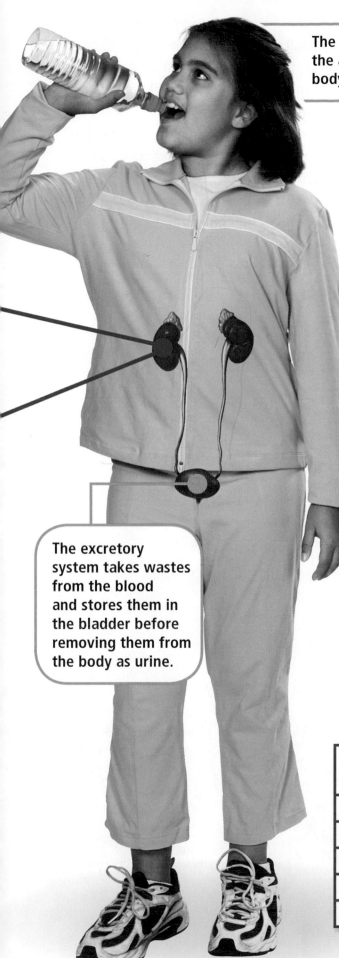

The excretory system keeps the amount of water in the body fairly constant.

The excretory system takes wastes from the blood and stores them in the bladder before removing them from the body as urine.

The excretory system is made up of the kidneys, ureters, bladder, and urethra. The **kidney** is the main organ of this system. There are two of these bean-shaped organs. They are under the rib cage, in the middle of the back, behind the liver and the stomach.

As blood flows through the capillaries in the kidneys, urea and water enter tubes called nephrons. Nephrons are filters that remove urea, water, and other wastes from the blood. These materials move from an area of higher concentration—the blood—to an area of lower concentration. Materials also move from an area of higher pressure—the capillaries— to an area of lower pressure—the nephrons. This movement is called *diffusion*.

The result of the filtering process is *urine*. Urine flows through tubes called ureters (yoo•REET•erz) to a saclike muscular organ called the bladder. There it is stored. When the bladder is full, urine flows out of the body through the urethra (yu•REE•thruh).

Focus Skill COMPARE AND CONTRAST How is the movement of fluid in the kidney like the movement you observed in *Elodea* in the Investigate?

Daily Water Gain and Water Loss in Adults			
Water Gain		Water Loss	
From cell activities	400 mL	In solid wastes	100 mL
From eating	900 mL	From skin and lungs	1000 mL
From drinking	1300 mL	As urine	1500 mL
Total	2600 mL	Total	2600 mL

How Plants Rid Themselves of Wastes

All cells need water and nutrients. Both plants and animals have structures to carry these materials to each cell. In multicellular animals, the circulatory system moves the needed materials to the cells. It also removes wastes from the cells. The excretory system then removes cell wastes from the body.

Like animal cells, plant cells produce wastes. Also like animals, vascular plants have structures that remove wastes. However, plants do not have an excretory system. Instead, they store cell wastes until the wastes can be removed.

Some plants store wastes in organs that will fall off, such as leaves that drop off in the autumn. For example, the mariposa lily stores wastes in the stems and leaves that die each year. Only an underground bulb remains. Most plants store wastes in a large central vacuole in each cell.

Like animal cells, plant cells need water, nutrients, and energy. Also like animal cells, plant cells produce wastes. Plants get rid of some of these wastes through their leaves.

Waste materials in plants include oxygen and water. These are produced by cell processes. Unlike animals, plants do not have lungs to exhale waste gas. They do not have kidneys to filter and remove water. These materials move out of plants through tiny holes, called *stomata,* on the undersides of leaves. Water moves out of plants in a process called **transpiration**. In transpiration, water moves up through a plant, passes through the tiny holes, and evaporates.

 **COMPARE AND CONTRAST** What are different ways that plants rid themselves of wastes?

Unlike animal cells, plant cells have a large central vacuole. Here, wastes are stored until they are removed from the plant.

Insta-Lab

Diffusion
Gently place 3 to 5 drops of red food coloring into a container of warm water. Then, for 10 minutes, watch the movement of the coloring. Do not stir or disturb the water as you watch. Describe and explain the movement of the coloring.

Standards Wrap-Up and Lesson Review

How do plants and animals rid themselves of wastes?

In this lesson, you learned about the excretory system in animals and the role of the kidney in removing wastes. You also learned how plants remove wastes.

Science Content Standards in This Lesson

2.d *Students know* the role of the kidney in removing cellular waste from the blood and converting it to urine, which is stored in the bladder.

1. **(Focus Skill) COMPARE AND CONTRAST** Draw and complete a graphic organizer that compares and contrasts the waste products of animals and plants and how the waste products are removed. **2.d**

   alike ——— different

2. **SUMMARIZE** Write a summary of this lesson. Begin with this sentence: Plants and animals have different waste removal processes. **2.d**

3. **DRAW CONCLUSIONS** In the Investigate, how was the movement of water in elodea like the movement of materials in the excretory system? **2.d**

4. **VOCABULARY** Use the lesson vocabulary and other lesson terms to write a paragraph about how animals rid their bodies of waste. **2.d**

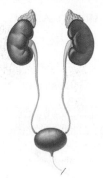

5. **Critical Thinking** How is the role of the circulatory system in digestion like its role in waste removal from the body? How does this role differ between the two processes? **2.d**

6. **Investigate and Experiment** Write a plan for an investigation to answer this question: If the stomata on a plant's leaves were blocked, what would happen to the plant? **6.c**

7. How is a plant cell's central vacuole like an animal's bladder?
   A Both filter wastes.
   B Both store wastes.
   C Both form urine.
   D Both occur in all living things. **2.d**

8. In animals, what is the main organ of the excretory system?
   A capillary
   B nephron
   C kidney
   D bladder **2.d**

The **Big** Idea

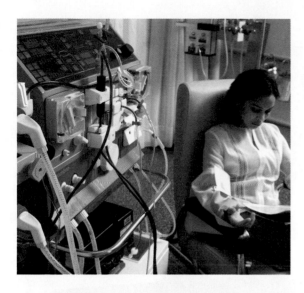

 Writing ELA–WA 2.3

Write a Report

Peritoneal dialysis (pehr•uh•tuh•NEE•uhl dy•AL•uh•sis) is one way to remove wastes in people whose kidneys do not work. Use the library or the Internet to learn how wastes diffuse across a membrane and are removed in peritoneal dialysis. Prepare a brief report of your findings.

 Math NS 1.2

Draw Conclusions

Study the table of daily water gain and water loss in adults on p. 183. What percentage of the water taken in each day comes from foods? What percentage comes from drinking? What percentage of water is lost in urine?

 Health

Exercise and Fluid Loss

You weigh more before recess than you do after recess. Why is this? What are different factors that affect fluid loss? Use library or other school resources to find out about why and how people lose fluid throughout the day. How do these fluids get replaced in the body? What is the best way to replace these fluids?

 For more links and activities, go to **www.hspscience.com**

Saving Stephanie

Most kids love to eat pizza, hamburgers, and French fries. But until she was 8 years old, Stephanie Singh couldn't eat any of those foods. In fact, she couldn't eat any solid foods. Stephanie could be fed only through a tube inserted in her arm. Then an amazing operation changed Stephanie's life.

Stephanie's Favorite Foods
- pizza
- macaroni and cheese
- homemade soups

Eating Through a Tube

Stephanie was born with visceral myopathy (VIS•er•uhl my•AHP•uh•thee), a rare condition in which the intestines don't develop properly. The intestines are made up of two main parts. The first part, the small intestine, is connected to the stomach at one end. Partly digested food flows from the stomach into the small intestine. The small intestine absorbs nutrients from the food. Food that can't be digested any further then flows into the large intestine. The large intestine then eliminates the undigested food wastes from the body.

Because of Stephanie's condition, her small intestine couldn't break down any food into nutrients. Stephanie would have starved, even if she had eaten plenty of food. To keep her alive, Stephanie's doctors connected a tube to her arm. The tube put nutrient-rich fluids directly into her bloodstream.

A Lifesaver

To help Stephanie, doctors performed an intestine transplant. Doctors perform many different types of transplant operations, including heart, liver, and kidney transplants. However, an intestine transplant is risky and dangerous.

The intestines have special cells that protect a person's body from bacteria in food. When a healthy but different intestine is put into a patient's body, the patient's immune system attacks the transplanted organ. In turn, those special bacteria-fighting cells in the intestine fight against the body's immune system. As the cells fight one another, the patient's body tries to reject the transplanted organ.

After Stephanie's operation, doctors gave her drugs to keep her immune system from attacking the transplanted intestine. Since the operation, Stephanie has been able to eat anything she wants.

Think and Write

1 What is the role of the small intestine in digestion? **2.c**

2 Why would the human body fight to reject a transplanted organ?

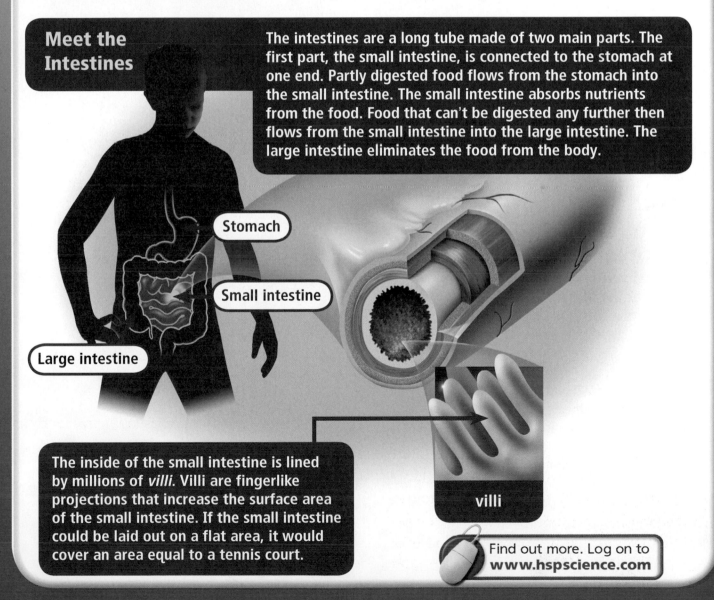

Meet the Intestines

The intestines are a long tube made of two main parts. The first part, the small intestine, is connected to the stomach at one end. Partly digested food flows from the stomach into the small intestine. The small intestine absorbs nutrients from the food. Food that can't be digested any further then flows from the small intestine into the large intestine. The large intestine eliminates the food from the body.

Stomach

Small intestine

Large intestine

The inside of the small intestine is lined by millions of *villi*. Villi are fingerlike projections that increase the surface area of the small intestine. If the small intestine could be laid out on a flat area, it would cover an area equal to a tennis court.

villi

Find out more. Log on to
www.hspscience.com

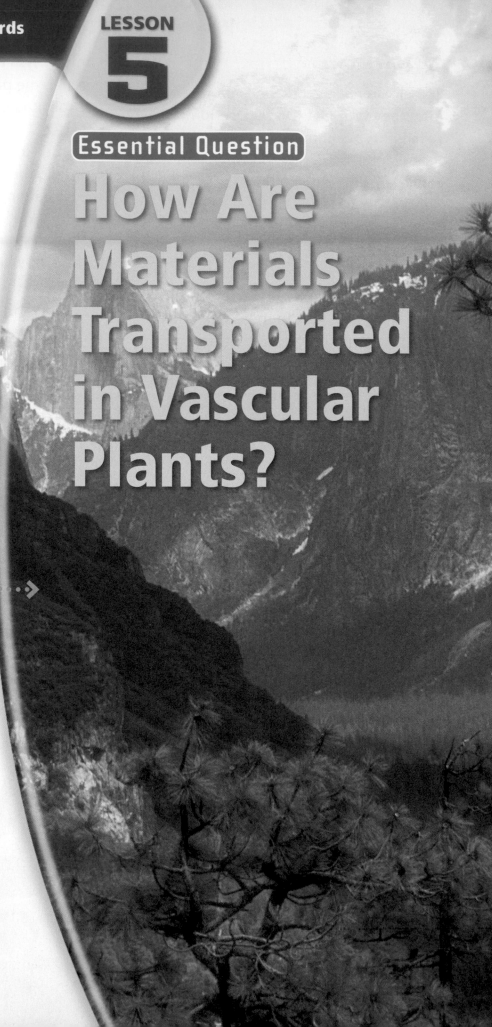

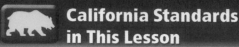
Science Content

2.e *Students know* how sugar, water, and minerals are transported in a vascular plant.

Investigation and Experimentation

6.b Develop a testable question.

6.g Record data by using appropriate graphic representations (including charts, graphs, and labeled diagrams) and make inferences based on those data.

California Fast Fact

Yosemite National Park

From the chaparral (shap-uh-RAL) of the foothills to the forests of the higher elevations, many different types of plants are found in Yosemite National Park. In the chaparral environment, the plant life is adapted to hot, dry summers and rainy, mild winters. The water transport systems in these plants are adapted to conserve water in dry conditions.

LESSON 5

Essential Question

How Are Materials Transported in Vascular Plants?

The Yosemite Valley in Yosemite National Park

vascular tissue [VAS•kyuh•ler TISH•oo] Tissue that supports a plant and carries water and food throughout the plant (p. 195)

xylem [ZY•luhm] Vascular tissue that carries water and nutrients from roots to the other parts of a plant (p. 195)

phloem [FLOH•em] Vascular tissue that carries food from leaves to the other parts of a plant (p. 195)

Water Transport

Directed Inquiry

Start with Questions

You have learned that all cells need certain materials.

- How do these materials reach all the cells of a plant?

- How do water and food move through a plant?

Investigate to find out. Then read to find out more.

Prepare to Investigate

Investigation Skill Tip
When you infer, you develop an explanation of events by using recorded data, observations, and what you know.

Materials

- stalk of celery
- plastic knife
- 2 containers
- water
- dropper
- red food coloring
- blue food coloring
- paper towels
- hand lens

Make an Observation Chart

Time	Observations

Follow This Procedure

CAUTION: Food coloring stains fabrics. Avoid getting it on your clothing.

1. Use the plastic knife to trim the end off the celery stalk. Split the celery from the middle of the stalk to the bottom.

2. Half-fill each container with water. Add 15 drops of red food coloring to one container. Add 15 drops of blue food coloring to the other container.

3. Place one part of the celery stalk in each container of colored water.

4. **Observe** the celery every 15 minutes for an hour. **Record** your observations in your chart.

5. After you have completed your chart, put a paper towel on your desk. Take the celery out of the water. Cut about 2 cm off the bottom of the stalk. Use the hand lens to **observe** each of the pieces of stalk and the freshly cut end of the stalk.

Step 1

Step 3

Draw Conclusions

1. How fast did the water travel? How do you know?

2. **Standards Link** In what part of the stalk did the water travel? How do you know? **2.e**

3. **Investigation Skill** Based on this investigation, what can you **infer** about the function of the tubes in the celery stalk? **6.g**

Independent Inquiry **Develop a Testable Question**

Think about what you did in this investigation. Then develop a testable question about changing a flower's color into several different colors. **6.b**

Write a plan to test your question. Your plan should include the following details:

- **the materials you will need**
- **the steps of your investigation**

VOCABULARY
vascular tissue p. 195
xylem p. 195
phloem p. 195

SCIENCE CONCEPTS
▶ how plants transport water
▶ how the parts of vascular plants function together

Focus Skill **MAIN IDEA AND DETAILS**
Look for details about plant structures and how they function.

Main Idea

detail   detail   detail

Nonvascular and Vascular Plants

Have you ever seen a rock or log covered with a moist, green, velvety plant? What you saw was really not one plant but many tiny moss plants.

Mosses are what we call *nonvascular plants*. Nonvascular plants don't have true roots, but they are anchored in the ground by small, rootlike structures. They have parts that look like stems but aren't true stems. In addition, they have small, leaflike structures that make food but aren't true leaves. These parts aren't true roots, stems, and leaves because they don't have tubes for transporting materials. In fact, nonvascular plants don't have any tissue for carrying materials throughout the plant.

Nonvascular plants absorb water and nutrients from their surroundings. Water carries food and nutrients directly from cell to cell. Because of this, nonvascular plants can't grow very tall. With their small size, they can absorb just enough water to carry materials throughout the plants. When there is not enough water, nonvascular plants quickly dry out and turn brown. When it rains, they absorb water and turn green again.

Mosses grow on rocks, trees, and other places where they can absorb nutrients and moisture. If you look at moss with a hand lens, you can see the individual plants.

Trees, such as the one shown here, are more complex than mosses. Trees are *vascular plants*—plants with vascular tissue, or tissue with transport tubes. **Vascular tissue** supports a plant and carries water and food. Roots, stems, and leaves all contain vascular tissue.

There are two kinds of vascular tissue. **Xylem** carries water and nutrients from roots to the other parts of a plant. **Phloem** carries food from leaves to the other parts of a plant. With these tissues, vascular plants do not have to depend on water moving from cell to cell, as nonvascular plants do.

There are more kinds of vascular plants than nonvascular plants. They include tiny duckweed—which is only a fraction of an inch long—and giant redwoods. They also include the cacti that live, with little water, in California's deserts, and the orchids that grow in the rain forests of Hawai`i.

Focus Skill MAIN IDEA AND DETAILS What transport tissues do vascular plants have?

Xylem cells in the trunk of a tree transport water and nutrients. Phloem cells, just under the bark, transport food. Each year, new layers of xylem and phloem grow. You can tell the age of a tree by counting the rings of xylem.

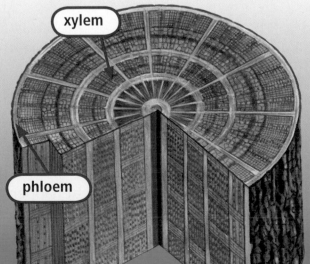

xylem

phloem

cross-section of a root

xylem

phloem

Fibrous roots spread out and absorb water from near the surface.

Taproots anchor plants firmly and can absorb water from deep in the ground.

Roots and Stems

Roots have vascular tissue that absorbs water and nutrients from the soil. In large roots, the vascular tissue is arranged in rings. If you've ever observed the roots of a potted plant, you may have noticed tiny hairs covering them. Root hairs absorb water and nutrients. Xylem cells take the water and nutrients from the root hairs and move them to the stem.

Roots are adapted to the environment and the needs of the plant. A taproot is one large, strong root that pushes deep into the soil. It anchors the plant firmly. Some taproots also store food. The plants use the stored food when they make flowers and fruits.

Other plants have fibrous roots. Fibrous roots are thin and branching. They form a thick mat just below the surface of the

ground. The mat spreads out and absorbs water from a large area. It holds the plant in place and keeps the soil from washing away. Grasses have a lot of fibrous roots, so people often plant grasses to hold soil in place.

Water Movement

Break several toothpicks in the middle, but make sure the halves remain connected. Arrange the toothpicks as shown. Wet the center of the pile with several drops of water, and observe what happens. Explain how the result relates to water moving through a stem.

Like roots, stems also have vascular tissues. The xylem and phloem in stems connect to the same tissues in roots. Together they act like a pipeline, transporting needed materials between the roots and the leaves. In the stems of some plants, such as trees, vascular tissue is gathered into rings. You can see these rings in the enlarged view below. In some smaller, softer vascular plants, bundles of xylem and phloem are scattered throughout the stem.

In addition to transport, stems also provide support for the plant. They usually grow from the ground and hold the leaves up to the sunlight. Trees and other tall plants have woody cells in their stems, making the stems strong. In plants without woody stems, water pressure holds the stems upright. A droopy stem is a clue that a plant needs water. Some plants, such as cacti, store water and food in fleshy stems.

 **MAIN IDEA AND DETAILS** What functions do roots perform?

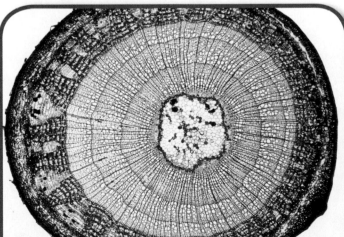

The inner part of a tree trunk, called heartwood, is filled with woody xylem cells. These cells provide support but no longer carry water, as xylem cells in the outer part do.

Tall trees have strong trunks and branches. Vascular tissues run through the trunks and branches and carry water and food to all parts of the plant.

197

Leaves

Remember that all cells have the same needs. They need water and nutrients. In organisms with many cells, these materials must reach every cell. You've learned that water and nutrients are carried by xylem from the roots. Along with these, plant cells, like animal cells, also need to have food delivered to them.

By just looking at a leaf, you'd never know that it makes all the food it needs and even has some left over. Leaves use sunlight, carbon dioxide, and water to make sugar.

Food making takes place inside the chloroplasts in leaf cells. Chloroplasts contain a green pigment that absorbs the light energy the leaves need. The carbon dioxide they need comes from the air, and the water comes from the ground.

The transport tissues in leaves are found in structures called veins. Xylem carries water and nutrients to the leaves. Phloem carries the sugar made in the leaves to each of the plant's cells.

MAIN IDEA AND DETAILS What is the relationship between transport tissues and a plant's food-making leaves?

These eucalyptus trees in San Diego's Balboa Park make food in their leaves. The food is then transported to all parts of the plant. ▼

Notice the veins on these leaves. Different kinds of leaves have different patterns of veins. The veins connect to the leaf stalk, which connects to the vascular tissue in the plant stem. ▶

xylem

phloem

stomata

▲ Xylem in leaf veins help bring water and nutrients from the soil to the leaf. Phloem carries food made in the leaf to the rest of the plant.

Standards Wrap-Up and Lesson Review

How are materials transported in vascular plants?

In this lesson, you learned how the parts of vascular plants transport water, nutrients, and food. You also learned how nonvascular plants get water and nutrients.

 Science Content Standards in this Lesson

2.e *Students know* how sugar, water, and minerals are transported in a vascular plant.

1. (Focus Skill) **MAIN IDEA AND DETAILS** Draw and complete a graphic organizer to show this main idea: Vascular tissues connect all parts of a plant. **2.e**

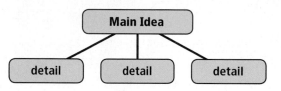

2. **SUMMARIZE** Use the vocabulary terms to write a summary of this lesson. **2.e**

3. **DRAW CONCLUSIONS** Suppose a plant with a taproot and a plant with fibrous roots are growing next to each other in the ground. After a while, you notice that the leaves of the plant with fibrous roots have turned brown, but the other plant's leaves have not. What conclusion can you draw about the fibrous roots? **2.e**

4. **VOCABULARY** Describe the two kinds of vascular tissue in plants. **2.e**

5. **Critical Thinking** How does a taproot help a plant meet its needs? **2.e**

6. **Investigate and Experiment** What testable question can be asked to investigate why placing the stem of a white carnation in blue water causes the petals to turn blue? **6.b**

7. What type of tissue are both xylem and phloem?
   A transport tissue
   B epithelial tissue
   C vascular tissue
   D root tissue **2.e**

8. Why do nonvascular plants remain small in size?

   A They must be small enough for water to move freely to all their cells.
   B They grow only in small spaces.
   C Their roots cannot grow deep into the soil.
   D They grow only on rocks and trees. **2.e**

Writing   ELA–W 2.1

Write a Narrative

Write about the journey of a water drop from the soil to a leaf. You might also research what happens to the water after it gets to the leaf and include that information in your narrative.

Math   MG 2.1

Collect, Organize, and Display Data

Observe and measure the movement of water through a plant stem. Fill a clear glass jar with water. Add a few drops of food coloring. Carefully cut the bottom from a carnation's stem, and place the flower in the water. Measure the movement of the colored water through the xylem every two hours for eight hours. Graph your results.

Art   VPA–VA 2.2

Leaf Rubbings

Gather a collection of fallen leaves. Place them, vein side up, in a pleasing pattern on a flat surface. Lay a piece of plain white paper on top. Hold the paper in place with one hand. With the other, use a flat part of a crayon to color the surface of the paper. Use enough pressure to pick up the leaves' impressions.

For more links and activities, go to **www.hspscience.com**

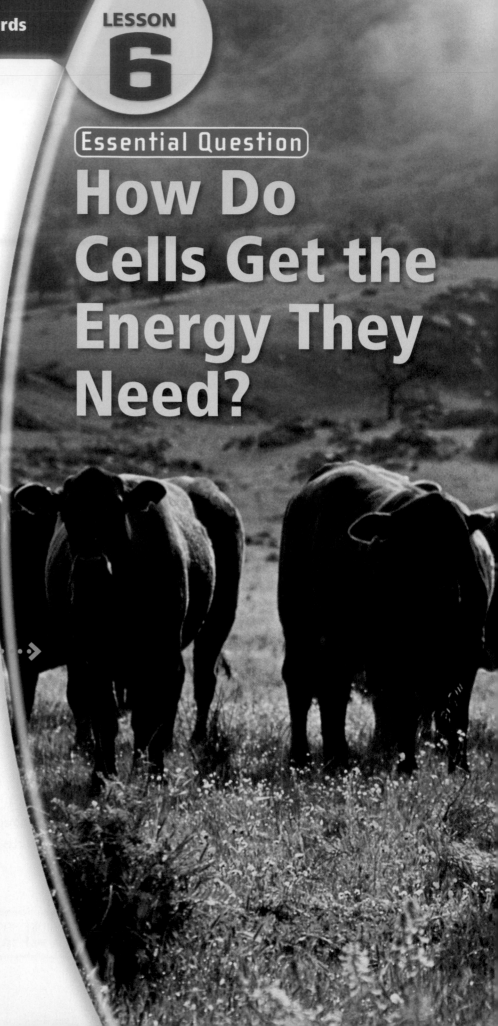

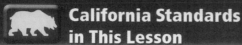
Science Content

2.f *Students know* how plants use carbon dioxide (CO_2) and energy from sunlight to build molecules of sugar and release oxygen.

2.g *Students know* plant and animal cells break down sugar to obtain energy, a process resulting in carbon dioxide (CO_2) and water (respiration).

Investigation and Experimentation

6.e Identify a single independent variable in a scientific investigation and explain how this variable can be used to collect information to answer a question about the results of the experiment.

California Fast Fact

Much to Moo About

Many people rely on milk for good nutrition. California's dairy cows each produce 23–30 L (6–8 gal) of milk every day. That's enough to meet the dairy needs of more than 40 people! How do cattle get the energy to meet their own needs, as well as those of people? The cattle do this by feeding on plants that have stored the sun's energy.

Essential Question

How Do Cells Get the Energy They Need?

Cows grazing in a field near Arvin, California

photosynthesis

[foht•oh•SIN•thuh•sis] The process by which plants make food from sunlight, carbon dioxide, and water and release oxygen into the air (p. 206)

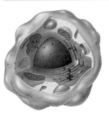

cellular respiration

[SEL•yoo•ler res•puh•RAY•shuhn] The process by which cells use oxygen for breaking down sugar to release energy (p. 208)

fermentation

[fer•muhn•TAY•shuhn] The process that releases energy from sugar in the absence of oxygen (p. 209)

Using Carbon Dioxide

Directed Inquiry

Start with Questions

As you know, all cells need water, nutrients, and energy. You know how water and nutrients get to cells.

- By what process do cells get the energy they need?

- What else is produced during this process?

Investigate to find out. Then read to find out more.

Prepare to Investigate

Investigation Skill Tip
Whenever you identify the independent variable, you identify and isolate the factor that affects the outcome of an investigation.

Materials

- safety goggles
- 2 plastic cups
- water
- dropper
- bromothymol blue (BTB)
- plastic straw
- 2 capped tubes
- *Elodea*
- funnel

Make an Observation Chart

BTB Solution with Elodea	BTB Solution without Elodea

Follow This Procedure

CAUTION: Wear safety goggles. Do not suck on the straw. If the solution gets into your mouth, spit it out and rinse your mouth with water.

1. Fill one cup about two-thirds full of water. Use the dropper to add BTB until the water is blue.

2. Put the straw into the cup, and blow into the straw.

3. **Observe**, and **record** your observations.

4. Put the *Elodea* in one test tube. Use the funnel to fill both tubes with the BTB solution. Cap both tubes.

5. Turn the test tubes upside down, and put them in the empty cup. Place the cup on a sunny windowsill. **Predict** what changes will occur in the tubes.

6. After 1 hour, **observe** both test tubes, and **record** your observations.

Step 2

Step 5

Draw Conclusions

1. What changes did you **observe** in the BTB solution?

2. **Standards Link** Why did the BTB solution with the *Elodea* show a change while the other test tube with the BTB solution did not? **2.f**

3. **Investigation Skill** What **variable** can you **identify** as the difference you set up between the two test tubes? **6.e**

Independent Inquiry — Identify a Variable

What variable caused the BTB solution to change color? Identify another variable that could provide information about this process.

Write a plan that tests the effect of that variable. **6.e**

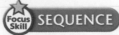
VOCABULARY
photosynthesis p. 206
cellular respiration p. 208
fermentation p. 209

SCIENCE CONCEPTS
► how plants make food
► how living things get energy

 **SEQUENCE**
Note the order of events in photosynthesis and cellular respiration.

[ ] → [ ] → [ ]

Photosynthesis

As you know, all cells need food. Plants make food in a process that uses water from the soil, carbon dioxide from the air, and energy from sunlight. This process, called **photosynthesis**, produces food for the plant—and for animals that eat plants. Photosynthesis also releases oxygen into the air.

Recall that many plant cells have organelles called chloroplasts. These contain a green pigment called *chlorophyll*. Chlorophyll allows a plant cell to use light to make food. It also gives plants their green color.

Photosynthesis begins when sunlight is absorbed by chloroplasts. The energy causes water molecules to split. Then carbon dioxide combines with hydrogen from the water to form food—a sugar called glucose. Cells need glucose to live and grow.

Photosynthesis also produces oxygen and water. They are released into the air through the leaves' stomata. About 90 percent of the oxygen in the air you breathe comes from photosynthesis.

SEQUENCE What sequence of events takes place during photosynthesis?

Science Up Close

Photosynthesis

Sunlight provides energy for plants to make food.

Plants take in carbon dioxide from the air.

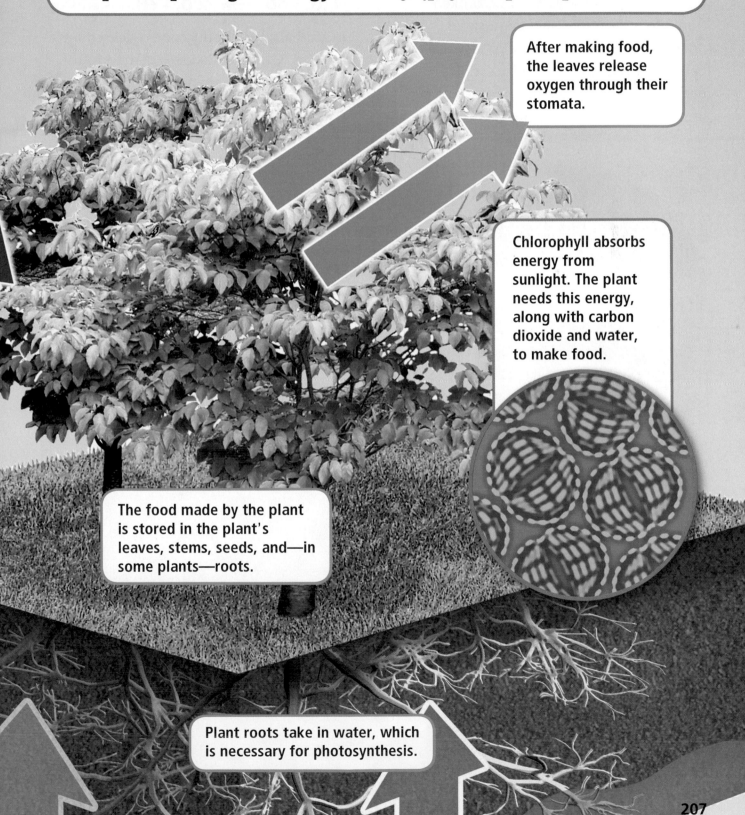

carbon dioxide + water + sunlight $\longrightarrow$ glucose + oxygen + water
$6CO_2 + 12H_2O +$ light energy $\longrightarrow C_6H_{12}O_6 + 6O_2 + 6H_2O$

After making food, the leaves release oxygen through their stomata.

Chlorophyll absorbs energy from sunlight. The plant needs this energy, along with carbon dioxide and water, to make food.

The food made by the plant is stored in the plant's leaves, stems, seeds, and—in some plants—roots.

Plant roots take in water, which is necessary for photosynthesis.

207

Cellular Respiration

All living things get the energy they need from the sun. Plants use light energy to make sugar. They "feed" themselves, and they feed animals.

However, the sugar made by plants during photosynthesis must be broken down to a form that cells can use for energy. This takes place in a process called **cellular respiration**. The process, like breathing, involves oxygen. It takes place in the mitochondria of both plant and animal cells. Cellular respiration is basically the reverse of photosynthesis. Oxygen helps break down sugar, releasing energy. In addition, carbon dioxide and water are produced. The process can be summarized by this equation:

$$C_6H_{12}O_6 + 6O_2 \longrightarrow 6CO_2 + 6H_2O + energy$$

In animals, the products are released into the blood. Carbon dioxide is carried to the lungs, where it is exchanged for oxygen in the alveoli. Water is carried to the kidneys, where it is removed in urine.

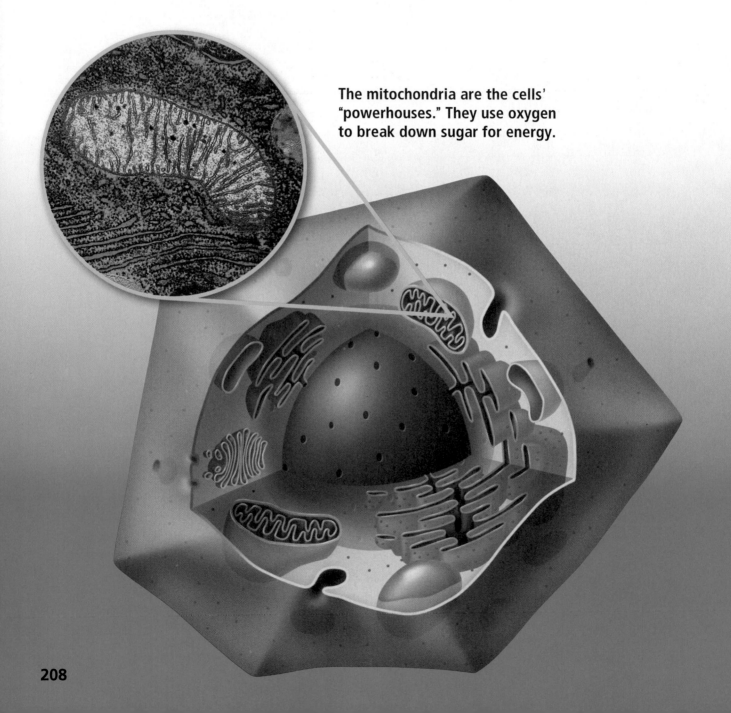

The mitochondria are the cells' "powerhouses." They use oxygen to break down sugar for energy.

Cellular respiration cannot always meet the body's energy needs. When there is not enough oxygen to release energy from sugar, the energy is released by a type of fermentation.

Think of a time when you exercised hard. Your breathing got deeper and more rapid. This brought more oxygen into your body. Sometimes, though, when the muscles are worked hard, there is not enough oxygen to meet the cells' energy needs. When this occurs, another process takes place.

Like cellular respiration, **fermentation** breaks down sugar and releases energy. However, it doesn't require oxygen. It produces less energy and more waste products than cellular respiration does.

Fermentation is helpful to humans in many ways. For example, it is used to make bread. When yeast cells ferment the carbohydrates in flour, they release carbon dioxide. This causes the bread to rise. Fermentation is also used to make yogurt, cheese, and many other foods and drinks.

Focus Skill SEQUENCE What is the sequence of events during and after cellular respiration?

▼ Yeast cells get energy by fermentation. This process breaks down sugar without the help of oxygen. One product of fermentation, carbon dioxide, causes bread to rise.

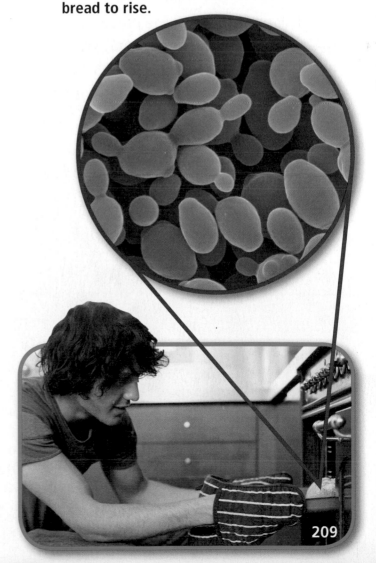

The Carbon-Oxygen Cycle

Plants make food, and both plants and animals use that food for energy. In nature, living organisms use and then reuse many materials. You can think of the use and reuse of carbon and oxygen as a kind of recycling. In the carbon-oxygen cycle, carbon and oxygen move among plants, animals, and the environment.

The recycling of carbon and oxygen through the environment depends on two processes. These are photosynthesis and respiration. During photosynthesis, plants take in carbon dioxide from the air. With the help of energy from the sun, the carbon is turned into food, and oxygen is released into the environment. Carbon, as food, is stored by plants or passed along to animals that eat plants.

Cellular respiration is the process that releases energy from food. During respiration, oxygen is taken from the air or water, and carbon dioxide is released into the environment.

Focus Skill **SEQUENCE** How are photosynthesis and respiration tied together in the carbon-oxygen cycle?

FUELS Over millions of years, the carbon in some decaying ocean organisms turned into petroleum.

PHOTOSYNTHESIS Microscopic plantlike organisms make their own food by photosynthesis. These organisms take in carbon dioxide and release oxygen. Oceans contain so many of these organisms that almost 90 percent of the oxygen in the atmosphere comes from photosynthesis in the oceans.

RESPIRATION All ocean organisms use oxygen and release carbon dioxide during respiration, the process that turns food into energy.

RESPIRATION All land organisms use oxygen and release carbon dioxide during respiration.

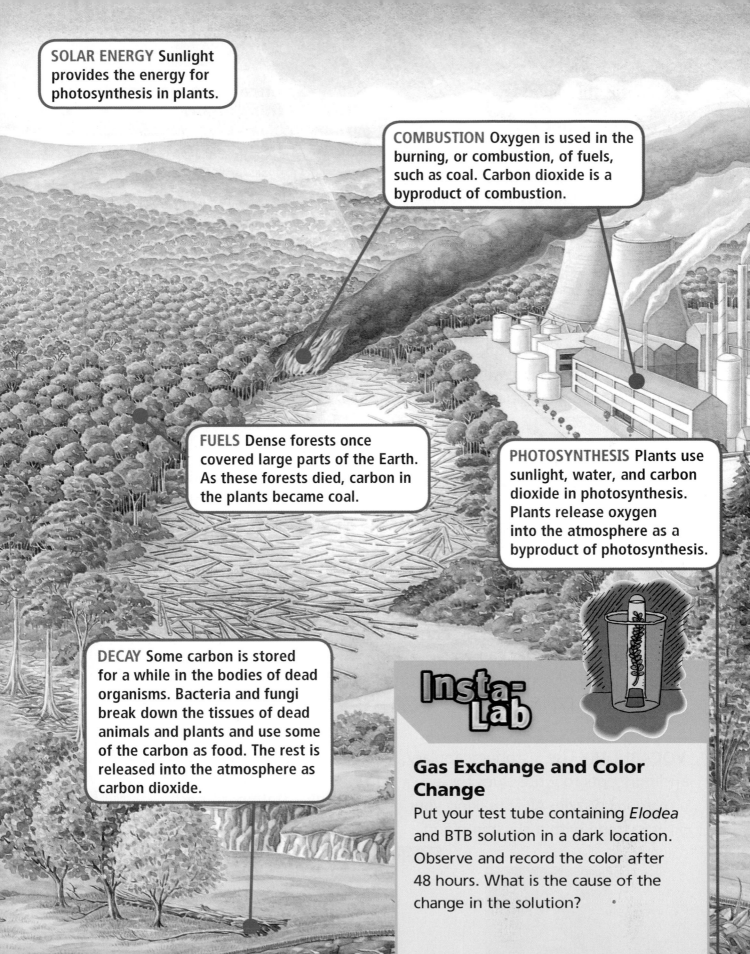

SOLAR ENERGY Sunlight provides the energy for photosynthesis in plants.

COMBUSTION Oxygen is used in the burning, or combustion, of fuels, such as coal. Carbon dioxide is a byproduct of combustion.

FUELS Dense forests once covered large parts of the Earth. As these forests died, carbon in the plants became coal.

PHOTOSYNTHESIS Plants use sunlight, water, and carbon dioxide in photosynthesis. Plants release oxygen into the atmosphere as a byproduct of photosynthesis.

DECAY Some carbon is stored for a while in the bodies of dead organisms. Bacteria and fungi break down the tissues of dead animals and plants and use some of the carbon as food. The rest is released into the atmosphere as carbon dioxide.

Insta-Lab

Gas Exchange and Color Change

Put your test tube containing *Elodea* and BTB solution in a dark location. Observe and record the color after 48 hours. What is the cause of the change in the solution?

Standards Wrap-Up and Lesson Review

Essential Question

How do cells get the energy they need?

In this lesson, you learned about photosynthesis, in which plants store the sun's energy in food. You also learned about cellular respiration, in which cells release energy stored in food. You learned how photosynthesis and cellular respiration are related in the carbon-oxygen cycle.

Science Content Standards in this Lesson

2.f *Students know* how plants use carbon dioxide (CO_2) and energy from sunlight to build molecules of sugar and release oxygen.

2.g *Students know* plant and animal cells break down sugar to obtain energy, a process resulting in carbon dioxide (CO_2) and water (respiration).

1. (Focus Skill) **SEQUENCE** Draw and complete a graphic organizer showing the sequence of steps in photosynthesis.

 **2.f**

2. **SUMMARIZE** Use the information in your graphic organizer to write a summary of photosynthesis. **2.f**

3. **DRAW CONCLUSIONS** Suppose you exercise hard on Monday. On Tuesday, you notice that your muscles are sore. What can you conclude about Monday's activity and fermentation? Explain. **2.g**

4. **VOCABULARY** Use lesson vocabulary and concepts to write clues for a crossword puzzle. After making your puzzle, trade with a classmate and solve. **2.f, 2.g**

5. **Critical Thinking** Suppose you were able to add chloroplasts to animal cells. Predict how this might change an animal's behavior. **2.f, 2.g**

6. **Investigate and Experiment** Suppose you're making bread. You put some yeast in each batch without measuring. After the loaves are baked, you notice that they are different in volume. What variable caused this to occur? **6.e**

7. Which of the following is **not** a product of photosynthesis?
   A carbon dioxide **C** sugar
   B oxygen **D** water **2.f**

8. Which statement best describes cellular respiration?
   A It produces sugar and oxygen.
   B It stores energy for later use.
   C It releases energy.
   D It causes fermentation. **2.g**

The Big Idea

 Writing **ELA–W 1.2**

Write a Composition
Suppose you are a rose bush. Write a "recipe" for photosynthesis. List the "ingredients" you need. Then write the procedure, explaining how you use the ingredients to make your own food.

 Math **NS 2.2**

Solve a Problem
Two mature oak trees can produce enough oxygen for a family of four. A mature tree produces about 118 kg (260 lb) of oxygen a year. About how much oxygen does one person use in a year?

 Health

California's Kelp
Kelp is an important California resource. It has many uses that affect people's health. Use library or Internet resources to learn what kelp is, where it is found, and how it is used. Share your findings with the class.

 For more links and activities, go to **www.hspscience.com**

THE SALK INSTITUTE FOR BIOLOGICAL STUDIES

Dr. Jonas Salk became a hero for making a vaccine to prevent the disabling disease called polio. Soon after, he set his sights on another major goal. He dreamed of having a place where scientists could work together to answer questions about life. His dream came true when the Salk Institute for Biological Studies opened its first laboratory in 1963. The institute's buildings, just west of the University of California, San Diego, were completed in 1967.

Studying the Mysteries of Life

At the Salk Institute, scientists work together to solve the mysteries of life. They study three broad areas of biology: molecular biology and genetics, neuroscience, and plant biology. Jonas Salk himself focused on the first area. His understanding of how the body fights diseases helped him study diseases in which the body's defense system attacks itself. It also helped him work on developing a vaccine for AIDS. Jonas Salk died in 1995, but other scientists continue his work.

The Salk Institute is different from many places where people study and learn. The scientists who study there do not graduate or receive degrees. However, they do enjoy the gift of working with and learning from some of the world's leading experts. The institute has educated more than 2000 scientists, 5 of whom have won Nobel Prizes. Many others have become leaders at research centers and universities.

Jonas Salk wanted his institute to be a place where scientists felt free to explore their questions about life.

Think and Write

1. Why would knowledge about the structures of living things be useful in finding cures for diseases?

   2.b **2.c** **2.d** **2.g**

2. How is the Salk Institute different from most schools?

Wrap-Up

▢ Visual Summary

Tell how each picture helps explain the **Big Idea**.

The Big Idea Plants and animals have structures that help them carry out life functions, keeping them alive and healthy.

2.a, 2.b

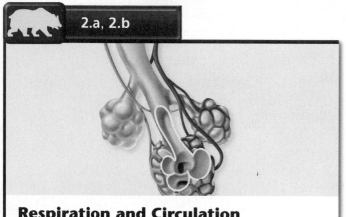

Respiration and Circulation

In the respiratory system, tiny blood vessels wrap around air sacs in the lungs. Oxygen moves from the air sacs to the blood and then to all body cells.

2.a, 2.c

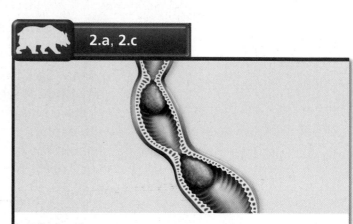

Digestion

During digestion, food is broken down into molecules that diffuse into capillaries and are carried to each body cell.

2.a, 2.d

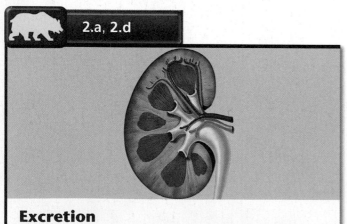

Excretion

Excretory organs take wastes from blood, store them in the bladder, and then remove them from the body as urine.

2.a, 2.e, 2.f

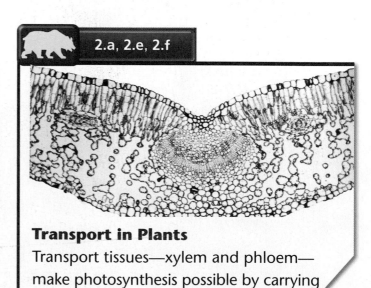

Transport in Plants

Transport tissues—xylem and phloem—make photosynthesis possible by carrying materials to where they are needed.

Show What You Know

Job Hunting

Suppose the human body is a corporation. You are in charge of hiring the "employees," or tissues, that make it run well. Write a job description for blood. Identify its roles, and emphasize the ways it interacts with other "employees."

Unit Project

Body Systems

Use colored pencils to draw the organs of the respiratory, circulatory, digestive, and excretory systems on an outline of a human body. Label each organ and system. Describe how the four systems work together to deliver oxygen to all body cells and to remove wastes from them.

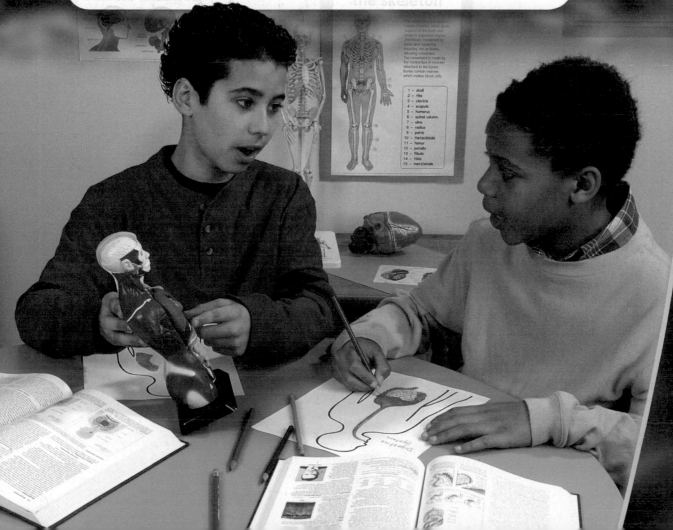

Vocabulary Review

Use the terms below to complete the sentences. The page numbers tell you where to look in the unit if you need help.

cell p. 142   **xylem** p. 195

tissue p. 146   **photosynthesis** p. 206

organ system p. 147 **cellular respiration** p. 208

respiratory system p. 160

transpiration p. 185

1. A group of organs and tissues that exchange oxygen and carbon dioxide between your body and the environment _____.   **2.b**

2. Organs that work together to do a job for the body form an _____.   **2.a**

3. Cells that work together to perform a certain function form a _____.   **2.a**

4. Water moves out of plants through their leaves during _____.   **2.e**

5. The process that makes food and releases oxygen is _____.   **2.f**

6. The basic unit of structure and function in living things is the _____.   **2.a**

7. A process that uses oxygen to break down food for energy is _____.   **2.g**

8. Vascular tissue that carries water and nutrients from the roots to other parts of the plant is called _____.   **2.e**

Check Understanding

Choose the best answer.

9. **COMPARE AND CONTRAST** In a comparison of photosynthesis and cellular respiration, which is **not** true?   **2.f, 2.g**
   A The processes are opposite.
   B One releases and one uses oxygen.
   C The processes are identical.
   D They both involve energy.

10. **DRAW CONCLUSIONS** Heart attacks damage the muscle of the heart. What is a likely result of this damage?   **2.b**
    A The heart will not pump as well.
    B Blood will not return to the heart.
    C Blood will not be oxygenated
    D The lungs will not receive blood.

11. Where does gas exchange occur?   **2.b**
    A in phloem
    B in the bronchi
    C in the heart
    D in air sacs

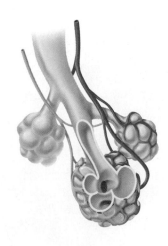

12. What process is shown in the equation below? **2.g**
A fermentation
B photosynthesis
C respiration
D excretion

$$C_6H_{12}O_6 + 6O_2 \longrightarrow 6CO_2 + 6H_2O + energy$$

13. What is released during the process shown in question 12? **2.g**
A oxygen   C sugar
B energy   D carbon monoxide

14. How does photosynthesis help feed humans? **2.f**
A Humans make food by photosynthesis.
B Humans eat plants that make food by photosynthesis.
C Humans eat animals that make food by photosynthesis.
D Photosynthesis does not help feed humans.

15. Why is an organ made of different tissues? **2.a**
A to make the organ more flexible
B so that the organ can work alone
C to hold the organ together
D because each does a different job

16. Which system helps the excretory system rid the body of wastes? **2.d**
A digestive   C respiratory
B circulatory   D skeletal

Investigation Skills

17. Develop a testable question concerning the function of the villi in the absorption of nutrients. **6.b**

18. What do students using a microscope need to **observe** to decide if a slide contains a plant cell or an animal cell? **6.a**

Critical Thinking

19. The drawings show a bean seed and a young bean plant. In which of these does photosynthesis occur? Explain. **2.g**

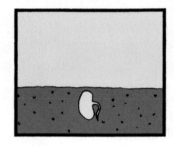

20. The transport of nutrients, oxygen, and waste products is very important to organisms. Why is the circulatory system so important in this process? Explain. **2.a**

The **Big** Idea

219

UNIT 3
EARTH SCIENCE

The Water Cycle

California Standards in This Unit

3 Water on Earth moves between the oceans and land through the processes of evaporation and condensation. As a basis for understanding this concept:

3.a *Students know* most of Earth's water is present as salt water in the oceans, which cover most of the Earth's surface.

3.b *Students know* when liquid water evaporates, it turns into water vapor in the air and can reappear as liquid when cooled or as a solid if cooled below the freezing point of water.

3.c *Students know* water vapor in the air moves from one place to another and can form fog or clouds, which are tiny droplets of water or ice, and can fall to Earth as rain, hail, sleet or snow.

3.d *Students know* that the amount of fresh water located in rivers, lakes, underground sources, and glaciers is limited and that its availability can be extended by recycling and decreasing the use of water.

3.e *Students know* the origin of the water used by their local communities.

This unit also includes these Investigation and Experimentation Standards: **6.c** **6.d** **6.e** **6.g** **6.h** **6.i**

What's the Big Idea?

Water on Earth moves between the oceans and land through the processes of evaporation and condensation.

Essential Questions

Joshua Tree National Park

Dear Ginny,

During spring break, my dad and I went on a camping trip to Joshua Tree National Park. We had a great time, but boy, was it dry!

We brought 30 gallons of water with us! We needed the water for drinking, cooking, bathing, and washing dishes. I never realized before just how important water is!

Your friend,
Maria

USA

Is the desert part of the water cycle? How might this relate to the **Big Idea?**

Unit Inquiry

Cleaning Up Pollution

Living organisms interact with each other and with the physical environment. Human activity can sometimes pollute the physical environment. How can visible pollution be removed from water? Can certain materials be used to filter polluted water? Plan and conduct an experiment to find out.

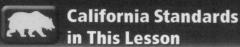
Science Content

3.a *Students know* most of Earth's water is present as salt water in the oceans, which cover most of Earth's surface.

3.b *Students know* when liquid water evaporates, it turns into water vapor in the air and can reappear as liquid when cooled or as a solid if cooled below the freezing point of water.

3.c *Students know* water vapor in the air moves from one place to another and can form fog or clouds, which are tiny droplets of water or ice, and can fall to Earth as rain, hail, sleet or snow.

Investigation and Experimentation

6.h Draw conclusions from scientific evidence and indicate whether further information is needed to support a specific conclusion.

6.i Write a report of an investigation that includes conducting tests, collecting data or examining evidence, and drawing conclusions.

California Fast Fact

Where Land Meets Sea

As the McWay Waterfall cascades down this cliff at Big Sur, water makes its way back into the Pacific Ocean. Where does the water in the waterfall come from? What happens to it after it reaches the ocean?

LESSON

1

Essential Question

How Does Water Move from Earth to the Air and Back Again?

McWay Falls, Big Sur, California

water cycle [WAW•ter SY•kuhl] The constant movement of water from Earth's surface to the atmosphere and back to Earth's surface (p. 228)

water vapor [WAW•ter VAY•per] The gas form of water (p. 228)

evaporation [ee•vap•uh•RAY•shuhn] The process by which a liquid changes into a gas (p. 230)

condensation [kahn•duhn•SAY•shuhn] The process by which a gas changes into a liquid (p. 231)

223

From Salt Water to Fresh Water

Start with Questions

Most of the Earth is covered with salt water. However, we don't drink salt water.

- How is drinkable water different from ocean water?

- Can ocean water be changed into drinkable water?

Investigate to find out. Then read to find out more.

Prepare to Investigate

Investigation Skill Tip
Draw conclusions from scientific evidence, and decide whether more information is necessary to support your conclusion.

Materials

- large bowl ● 500 mL of warm water
- spoon ● salt ● cotton swabs
- small glass jar ● plastic wrap
- large rubber band ● small ball
- masking tape

Make an Observation Chart

Day	Observations
1	
2	

Follow This Procedure

CAUTION: Do not share swabs. Throw swabs away after use.

1. In the bowl, stir two spoonfuls of salt into the warm water. Dip a cotton swab into the mixture. Touch the swab to your tongue. **Record** what you **observe**.

2. Place the jar in the center of the bowl.

3. Put plastic wrap over the bowl, but don't let the wrap touch the jar. Use the rubber band to keep the wrap on.

4. Put the ball on the wrap above the jar.

5. Place tape on the outside of the bowl to mark the level of the salty water. Set the bowl in the sun for a day.

6. Remove the plastic wrap and the ball. Use a clean swab to taste the water in the jar and in the bowl. **Record** what you **observe**.

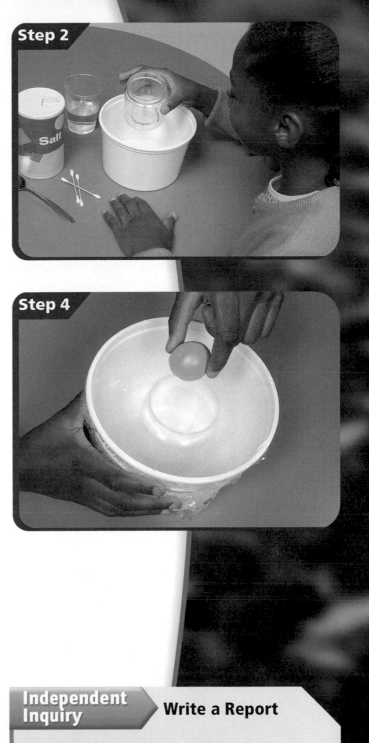

Step 2

Step 4

Draw Conclusions

1. What did you **observe** during the investigation?

2. **Standards Link** How did the water get into the jar? **3.b**

3. **Investigation Skill** Scientists **draw conclusions** from scientific evidence. What **conclusions** can you **draw** about using ocean water as drinkable water? **6.h**

Independent Inquiry   **Write a Report**

What would happen if you left the bowl and jar in the sun for several days? Develop a testable question. Then plan and conduct the investigation, collect data, and write a report about the investigation. Be sure to describe your evidence and conclusions. **6.i**

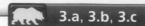
VOCABULARY	SCIENCE CONCEPTS	MAIN IDEA AND DETAILS

VOCABULARY
water cycle p. 228
water vapor p. 228
evaporation p. 230
condensation p. 231

SCIENCE CONCEPTS
▶ where water is located on Earth
▶ what processes make up the water cycle

Focus Skill MAIN IDEA AND DETAILS
Look for details about how water moves between the air and Earth's surface.

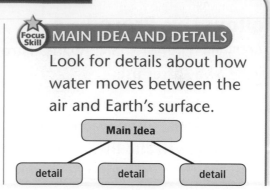

The Water Planet

Water covers almost three-fourths of Earth's surface. Because of this, Earth is sometimes called the water planet. A little more than 97 percent of Earth's water is found in the oceans. Ocean water is salty. Salt water is also found in some lakes. For example, California's Salton Sea is a saltwater lake.

The rest of Earth's water is fresh water. Fresh water is water that has very little salt dissolved in it. People need fresh water to live. For instance, we use fresh water for drinking, washing, and growing plants. However, less than 3 percent of all Earth's water is fresh water. Where on Earth can fresh water be found?

Most of the fresh water on Earth is frozen in ice caps and *glaciers*. Glaciers are huge sheets of ice. Most glaciers are near Earth's poles. They can also be found in other

Math in Science
Interpret Data

What percent of Earth's liquid water is fresh water?

Groundwater, 0.5%
Ice, 2.19%
Soil moisture, 0.005%
Atmosphere, 0.001%
Inland lakes, 0.018%
Rivers, 0.000096%

Oceans, 97.3%

◀ From space, Earth looks blue. That's because most of Earth's surface is covered with water.

▲ Glaciers and ice caps are both made of frozen fresh water. However, their water can't be used by many people because glaciers and ice caps are usually far away from cities and towns.

cold places, such as on mountaintops. The frozen water in glaciers is almost impossible for people to use.

Most of the remaining fresh water is underground. In fact, underground water is the only source of fresh water for many people around the world. To get to this water, people have to pump it up to Earth's surface.

We are most familiar with fresh water that is in the air, soil, rivers, and freshwater lakes. However, only 0.5 percent of all the fresh water on Earth is found in these familiar places.

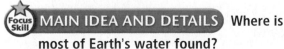 **MAIN IDEA AND DETAILS** Where is most of Earth's water found?

How Much Water?

Fill a 1-L container with water. This represents all of the water on Earth. Add 4 drops of food coloring. Put 28 mL of the water into a small, clear container. This represents all of the fresh water on Earth. From the small container, put 7 mL of the water into another small, clear container. This is all of the liquid fresh water on Earth. Observe how much water is in each container. How important do you think it is to protect our freshwater resources?

The Water Cycle

Water moves constantly through the environment. It moves from Earth's surface to the air and back to Earth's surface again in a never-ending process called the **water cycle**. The water cycle is also known as the *hydrologic cycle.*

Energy from the sun drives the water cycle. When the sun's energy warms water on Earth's surface, some of the water changes from a liquid to a gas.

The gaseous form of water, called **water vapor**, moves into the air. When water vapor cools, it becomes liquid water again. When the liquid water drops are heavy enough, they fall back to Earth.

Water may fall back into the ocean, into lakes or rivers, or onto the ground. When it falls on land, it can soak into the ground or run off the surface into rivers and lakes. Some water can also quickly recycle back to the atmosphere if the sun heats it and it turns into water vapor again. This is how the water cycle continues.

Science Up Close

For more links and animations, go to **www.hspscience.com**

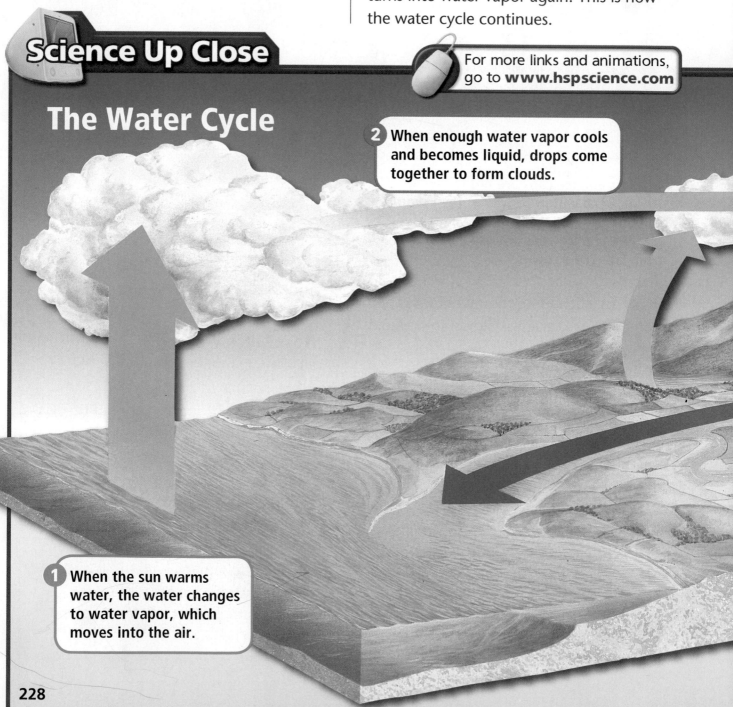

The Water Cycle

2 When enough water vapor cools and becomes liquid, drops come together to form clouds.

1 When the sun warms water, the water changes to water vapor, which moves into the air.

Most of the water moving through the water cycle comes from the oceans. The sun's energy heats water on the ocean's surface and turns it into water vapor. Winds carry the water vapor over land, where it becomes liquid water and falls as rain, snow, sleet, or hail.

Most rainwater comes from the oceans. So why isn't rain salty? When water in the ocean turns into water vapor, all of the salts dissolved in the water stay in the ocean. When the water vapor in the air cools, it becomes liquid again. Drops of fresh water form and fall to Earth.

Some water drops fall on land. These drops dissolve small amounts of salts and minerals on the land. The water with the dissolved salts and minerals runs off into rivers. Rivers carry the water to the oceans. Over time, all the salts build up in the ocean. That is why the oceans are salty.

Focus Skill **MAIN IDEA AND DETAILS** How does salt water become fresh water again?

3 In clouds, water droplets join to make larger drops. When the drops become heavy enough, they fall to Earth.

4 Some rain soaks into the ground. Rainwater can also run over the ground and flow into creeks, rivers, lakes, and, in time, back into the ocean.

Ice is water in its solid state.

As ice warms, it melts into liquid water.

Heat Makes a Difference

Evaporation

Suppose it's a hot day. To cool off, you take a swim. When you get out of the water, you dry off with a towel. You lay the towel in a sunny spot. The towel dries. Where did the water go?

The water evaporated. **Evaporation** is the process by which a liquid changes into a gas. Water evaporates because heat changes it from a liquid to a gas, or water vapor. It is hard to see evaporation happening because water vapor is invisible. However, you can infer that water has evaporated when it seems to disappear, like the water in the towel.

A large amount of water evaporates from Earth's oceans, lakes, and rivers every day. Water also evaporates from the soil, from puddles, from plants, and even from your skin as you sweat.

Water vapor mixes with other gases in the air. When the wind blows, the air moves. The water vapor moves with the air. It has become part of the air.

MAIN IDEA AND DETAILS Where does water go when it evaporates?

As the water is heated in the teapot, the liquid boils and becomes a gas—water vapor. As this water vapor cools, it condenses back into tiny droplets of water, called steam.

Condensation

When water vapor becomes part of the air, it moves with the air. Air can carry water vapor very long distances. It can also carry water vapor high into the atmosphere. Changes in air temperature affect the moving water vapor. As air and water vapor move up, they cool. When the water vapor gets cold enough, condensation occurs. **Condensation** is the process by which a gas changes into a liquid.

Air has dust particles in it. When water vapor cools, it condenses, or changes to liquid, on the dust particles. The condensed water and dust particles form clouds or fog. *Fog* is a cloud that forms near the ground.

Clouds that form very high up may be made of tiny ice crystals instead of water droplets. That is because the air is below the freezing point of water.

Clouds stay in the air because the ice crystals and water droplets are tiny. Additional condensation causes the droplets to grow. The droplets join to make larger, heavier drops. When the drops become too heavy to float, they fall to Earth as rain.

Water may also fall to Earth as snow, sleet, or hail if the air is cold enough for water to freeze. For example, if the air temperature is below freezing, water vapor becomes a solid without becoming a liquid first. This forms snow. Raindrops can form sleet or hail if they freeze as they fall to Earth.

 **MAIN IDEA AND DETAILS** How do clouds form?

Sweat is evaporating from this boy's face. At the same time, water vapor condenses on his cold drink glass. ▶

Standards Wrap-Up and Lesson Review

Essential Question

How does water move from Earth to the air and back again?

In this lesson, you learned that most water on Earth is salt water. You also learned about the water cycle and how water moves between the oceans and the land by the processes of evaporation and condensation. Water vapor can move from one place to another as fog or clouds and can fall to Earth as rain, hail, sleet, or snow.

 Science Content Standards in This Lesson

3.a *Students know* most of Earth's water is present as salt water in the oceans, which cover most of Earth's surface.

3.b *Students know* when liquid water evaporates, it turns into water vapor in the air and can reappear as liquid when cooled or as a solid if cooled below the freezing point of water.

3.c *Students know* water vapor in the air moves from one place to another and can form fog or clouds, which are tiny droplets of water or ice, and can fall to Earth as rain, hail, sleet or snow.

1. ⭐ **MAIN IDEA AND DETAILS** Draw and complete a graphic organizer to show the supporting details of this main idea: Water on Earth is found in many different places. **3.a, 3.c**

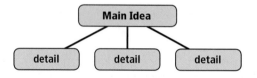

2. **SUMMARIZE** Draw a diagram that summarizes the water cycle. **3.c**

3. **DRAW CONCLUSIONS** Most rainwater comes from the ocean, but rainwater is not salty. Explain. **3.a**

4. **VOCABULARY** Write one sentence that uses all the vocabulary terms in this lesson. **3.b**

5. **Critical Thinking** On which type of day will the most pond water evaporate? **3.b**
   A hot and sunny **C** cool and rainy
   B hot and cloudy **D** cool and cloudy

6. **Investigate and Experiment** Your glass of ice water has left a ring of water on the table. Which conclusion can you draw by examining this evidence? **6.h**
   A Liquid water evaporated.
   B Water vapor from inside the glass condensed on the outside.
   C The air was warmer than the glass.
   D The air was cooler than the glass.

7. Where is most of Earth's water found?
   A the air   **B** the oceans
   C underground **D** polar ice caps **3.a**

8. How can water in an ocean end up in a freshwater lake? **3.c**

 The **Big** Idea

 Writing ELA–W 1.0

Write a Report

Describe how the water cycle occurs in your area during different parts of the year. Include a discussion of the seasons in your region. Explain how the seasons affect the water cycle.

 Math SDAP 1.1

Describe Patterns

City	Average Snowfall in December (in.)	Average Temperature in December (°F)
Blue Canyon	38.8	39
Fresno	0.0	45
Long Beach	0.0	57
Mount Shasta	21.9	35
Redding	2.2	45

Look at the table at the left, showing the average snowfall and temperature in five California cities during December. What conclusions can you draw about snowfall and temperature?

 Social Studies HSS 1.1

Water and Culture

Find a world map. Research one of the major bodies of water you see, and report one way it has influenced the culture of the people living near it.

For more links and activities, go to **www.hspscience.com**

233

Meltdown

Few plants or animals live on the icy mountaintops in southern Argentina and Chile. This South American region is cold, desolate, and snowy and is home to dozens of glaciers. These glaciers—many of them in the Andes Mountains—are in danger of melting away.

Slipping Away

The glaciers in South America are some of the largest, outside of the polar regions. Because of harsh weather and the area's rockiness, scientists have trouble reaching the area by foot. To study the melting of the South American glaciers, scientists have recently used satellite technology.

Scientists used satellites to take pictures of the glaciers. Those pictures were compared with earlier information. What scientists found was that the glaciers in this area are rapidly wasting, or melting. In fact, they are melting twice as fast as they were just a few years ago. Erik Rignot, a glacier expert, referred to the South American ice fields as the "fastest area of glacial retreat on Earth."

As the glaciers in South America—and in other areas—retreat, their water flows into lakes or oceans. As a result, the meltdown is causing the levels of Earth's oceans to rise.

If ocean levels rise by even one foot, coastal cities around the world could be flooded.

The Heat Is On

What is causing the glaciers to disappear? Scientists say that warmer temperatures and less snowfall are to blame for the meltdown. The warmer temperatures cause some glaciers to break off into the ocean as icebergs. That process, called calving, has increased in recent years. It's not just the South American glaciers that are "on thin ice." Scientists warn that about 90 percent of the world's glaciers are melting from global warming.

Think and Write

❶ How do you think a melting glacier might change Earth's surface? **3.d**

❷ What other surface features of Earth could scientists study with satellites?

Find out more. Log on to
www.hspscience.com

Frosty Facts

Glaciers are large sheets of snow and ice that move slowly over land. Glaciers are found in the polar regions and elsewhere around the world in mountain valleys.

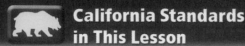
Science Content

3.e *Students know* the origin of the water used by their local communities.

Investigation and Experimentation

6.c Plan and conduct a simple investigation based on a student-developed question and write instructions others can follow to carry out the procedure.

6.g Record data by using appropriate graphic representations and make inferences based on those data.

California Fast Fact

Water Power

Shasta Dam, on the Sacramento River, is the largest dam in California. The dam was built to help store river water for use by local communities. The dam is a *hydroelectric* dam. This means that it uses the energy of moving water to produce electricity. Hydroelectric dams produce more than 15 percent of California's electricity.

Essential Question

How Do Californians Get the Water They Need?

236

Shasta Dam, California

Vocabulary Preview

watershed [WAW•ter•shed] The area of land in which water runs off into a particular system of creeks and rivers (p. 242)

dam [DAM] A barrier across a river that controls the river's flow (p. 242)

reservoir [REZ•uhr•vwahr] A body of water stored for future use (p. 242)

aqueduct [AK•wuh•duhkt] A pipe or channel that is used to transport water (p. 242)

groundwater [GROWND•waw•ter] Water that is in soil and rocks below Earth's surface (p. 244)

237

Exploring Groundwater

Start with Questions

People dig wells and use pumps to get to ground water.

- Have you ever used a pump?

- Have you ever used a hand pump to get water from a campground's well?

- How does water get into the ground in the first place?

Investigate to find out how water gets into the ground. Then read to find out more.

Prepare to Investigate

Investigation Skill Tip

Before you plan and conduct an investigation, think about the question you are testing. This will help you gather useful data during your investigation.

Materials

- clay soil
- gravel
- water
- food coloring
- book
- clear plastic box
- sand
- potting soil
- watering can
- spoon

Make an Observation Chart

Step	Observation
3	
5	

Follow This Procedure

1 Place a layer of clay soil in the plastic box. Pack the clay firmly. Place a layer of gravel on top of it. Cover the gravel with a layer of sand. Add a layer of potting soil.

2 Pour water into the watering can. Add food coloring to the water.

3 Sprinkle water into the box. Soak the soil. Look through the side of the box to **observe** the water moving through the soil layers.

4 **Model** a "pond" at one end of the box. With a spoon, remove soil from the top layer to make a low spot. Tilt the box by placing a book beneath the end opposite the dip.

5 Sprinkle water gently over the raised end of the box. Through the side of the box, **observe** the movement of the water. Stop the "rain" when a pond forms.

Step 1

Step 3

Draw Conclusions

1. Describe how the rain soaked into the soil layers and formed a pond.

2. **Standards Link** What would happen to the pond in your **model** if there were no more "rain?" `3.e`

3. **Investigation Skill** Scientists often use **models** in their investigations. Using your **model, plan and conduct an investigation** about how local soils and physical features might affect your area's water supply. `6.c`

Independent Inquiry ▸ Make Inferences

Water your model more than usual over several days. Use a lot of water. Record the data. Then allow your model to dry out for several days. Record and compare the data with the earlier results.

Look over the data you recorded. Use your data to infer how the amount of rain in your area might affect the water supply. `6.g`

VOCABULARY
watershed p. 242
dam p. 242
reservoir p. 242
aqueduct p. 242
groundwater p. 244

SCIENCE CONCEPTS
▶ how people use water resources
▶ where freshwater resources are located in local communities

Focus Skill **MAIN IDEA AND DETAILS**
Look for details about the sources of the water used in local communities.

Main Idea

detail | detail | detail

Water Resources

Did you know that the human body is made up of 60 to 75 percent water? That means that you may have about 40 L (10 gal) of water flowing around inside you! Fresh water is vital to human health. It is also necessary for growing many kinds of plants that people rely on for food.

Another important use for fresh water is bathing and showering. People also use fresh water to wash dishes, clothes, and even the family car. Several other ways that people use fresh water are shown in the table below.

Freshwater resources are important, but people use saltwater resources, too. For

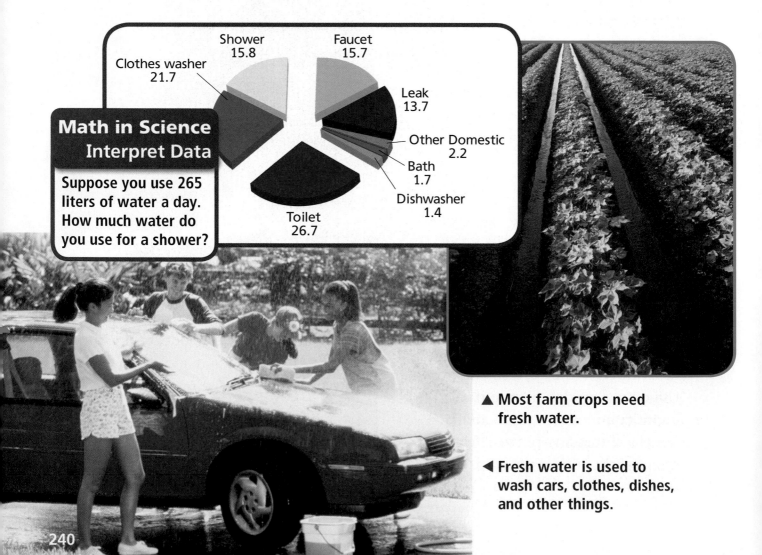

Math in Science
Interpret Data

Suppose you use 265 liters of water a day. How much water do you use for a shower?

Shower 15.8
Faucet 15.7
Clothes washer 21.7
Leak 13.7
Other Domestic 2.2
Bath 1.7
Dishwasher 1.4
Toilet 26.7

▲ Most farm crops need fresh water.

◀ Fresh water is used to wash cars, clothes, dishes, and other things.

▲ This fishing boat is gathering saltwater animals to be used as food. Saltwater animals are also gathered for nonfood products, such as pearls, which are taken from oysters.

example, people who live in places that have very little fresh water may use ocean water. They use it after the salt and other minerals in the water have been removed.

Saltwater animals, such as fish, shrimp, squid, and lobsters are very important to many people's diets. All of these organisms are gathered from the oceans.

Another important resource from ocean water is sea salt. It is used for cooking and can be used to preserve foods like fish or meat. Salt is also used to make chemicals.

Oceans are also used for recreation. Popular saltwater activities include surfing, sailing, and scuba diving.

Focus Skill **MAIN IDEA AND DETAILS** How do people use freshwater resources?

▲ Many people use the oceans for recreation.

Local Water Sources

Where do communities get the fresh water that people need? Most communities in California get it from lakes and rivers. That means the communities' water supplies depend on how much rain and snow falls during a year. In the Investigate, you saw how rain affects the water level in bodies of water on the surface.

When rain or snow falls, it collects in a watershed. A **watershed** is an area of land in which water runs off into a particular system of creeks and rivers. For example, as snow melts from the top of a mountain, it flows down in small creeks. The creeks join to form rivers. The rivers join to form larger rivers. This system of creeks and rivers "drains" the watershed.

A community may be able to take its water directly from the rivers of a watershed. However, the amount of water in a river changes from season to season. For instance, during the spring, rivers may have plenty of water from melted snow. However, during dry seasons, the water level may be low. There may not be enough water to meet a community's needs.

Many communities build dams to store water for dry seasons. A **dam** is a barrier across a river that controls its flow. In California, dams are often used to hold water. Water collects behind a dam to form a reservoir. A **reservoir** is a body of water stored for future use.

California's largest reservoir is Shasta Lake. It was formed when Shasta Dam was built in 1945. Now towns around the lake pump the water to homes, businesses, and farms.

If a community uses more water than is available from its watershed, the community may need to bring in water from another watershed through an aqueduct. An **aqueduct** is a pipe or channel used to transport water.

Los Angeles uses two large aqueducts. Its first major aqueduct was built in the early 1900s. It carried water 363 km (226 mi) from the Owens River Valley to Los Angeles.

As the city grew, so did its water needs. In 1970, a second aqueduct was completed. It also brought water from the Owens River Valley watershed.

MAIN IDEA AND DETAILS How has Los Angeles provided its citizens with water?

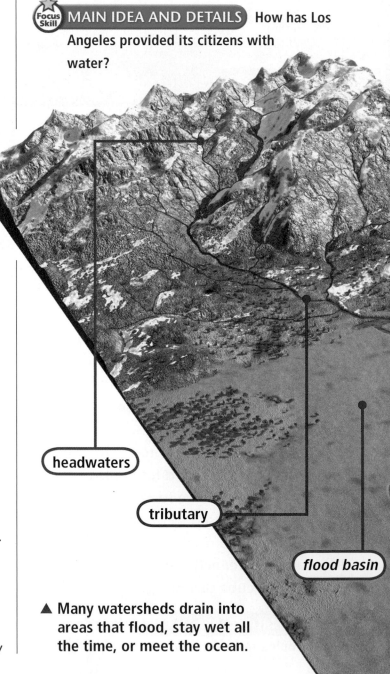

headwaters

tributary

flood basin

▲ Many watersheds drain into areas that flood, stay wet all the time, or meet the ocean.

242

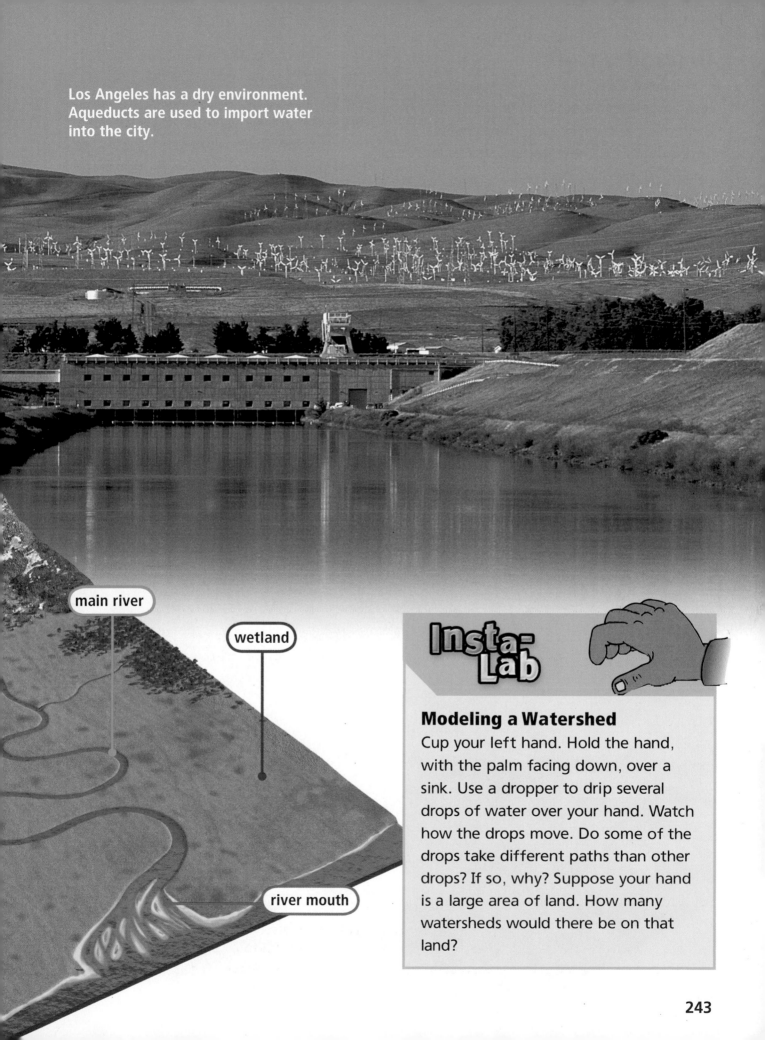

Los Angeles has a dry environment. Aqueducts are used to import water into the city.

main river

wetland

river mouth

Insta-Lab

Modeling a Watershed

Cup your left hand. Hold the hand, with the palm facing down, over a sink. Use a dropper to drip several drops of water over your hand. Watch how the drops move. Do some of the drops take different paths than other drops? If so, why? Suppose your hand is a large area of land. How many watersheds would there be on that land?

Groundwater

Not all of California's water supply is surface water. About 40 percent of California's population uses groundwater. **Groundwater** is water under Earth's surface located in the spaces between rocks and soil.

Remember that not all the rain that falls on land runs off into creeks and rivers. Some soaks into the ground, where it enters tiny air spaces in the soil and inside rocks.

As water moves through these spaces, some of it sticks to soil particles. Most of the water, however, continues moving downward. In time, it reaches an area where all the spaces are filled with water.

This is the top of the *water table.* You can think of the water table as a line underneath the ground. The ground above that line has air gaps in it. The ground below that line is completely filled with water. The water table rises during wet seasons. It drops during dry seasons.

Groundwater is found in rocks that have pores, or small openings, in them and spaces between them. The pores and spaces allow water to move through them. A rock layer that can store a lot of water and let it flow through is called an *aquifer.* California has many aquifers. Water can be obtained from them by drilling wells.

Rainwater moves down through the ground to form a body of groundwater. Many people rely on groundwater for their water needs. ▼

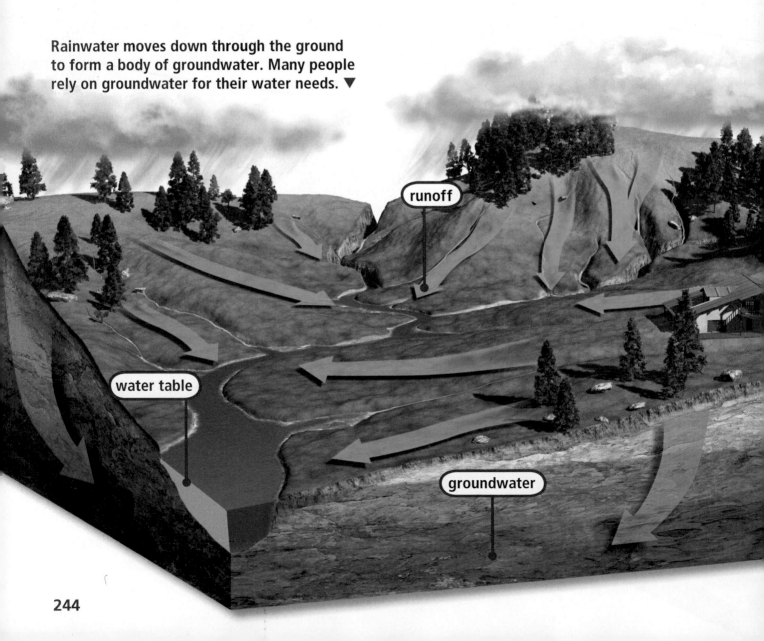

runoff

water table

groundwater

Sometimes, pressure in an aquifer is so great that the water comes out of a well without being pumped. This type of well is called an artesian well. Where water comes to the surface naturally, it forms an artesian spring.

well

A well is drilled from the surface to a spot below the water table. A pump is then used to bring the water up to the surface. A well can supply water for one home, one farm, one neighborhood, or a whole city.

If too much water is removed from a well, however, the water table will drop. Over time, the well may become dry. This happens when the water table drops below the depth of the well.

Because overpumped wells can become dry, people who use wells should try not to remove more water than is replaced naturally by rainfall. If an area's groundwater is used up, it will take a very long time for the water to be replaced by rain.

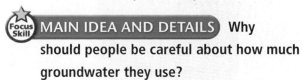 **MAIN IDEA AND DETAILS** Why should people be careful about how much groundwater they use?

245

Standards Wrap-Up and Lesson Review

How do Californians get the water they need?

In this lesson, you learned how local communities in California get the fresh water they need.

 Science Content Standards in This Lesson

3.e *Students know* the origin of the water used by their local communities.

1. **Focus Skill** **MAIN IDEA AND DETAILS** Draw and complete a graphic organizer to show the supporting details of this main idea: People use water for many different things. **3.e**

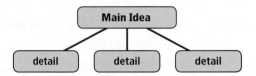

2. **SUMMARIZE** Write a paragraph explaining why fresh water is important to people and how people get fresh water. **3.e**

3. **DRAW CONCLUSIONS** What most likely happens to California's water table during a drought? **3.e**

4. **VOCABULARY** What is the name for a pipe or channel that people use to import water?

   A reservoir   **C** aquifer

   B watershed   **D** aqueduct   **3.e**

5. **Critical Thinking** Which is true of snow that falls on a mountain peak? **3.e**

   A Its height makes it salty.

   B It is a freshwater resource for towns below.

   C Its weight creates a reservoir.

   D It is frozen and can never be used.

6. **Investigate and Experiment** Write a plan for an investigation that would model how water moves through a large watershed. Include a list of needed materials in your plan. **6.c**

7. Which of the following is a man-made source of fresh water?

   A a river

   B an aquifer

   C a reservoir

   D a watershed   **3.e**

8. Can dams change the water cycle? Explain your answer. **3.e**

 **The Big Idea**

Writing   ELA–W 2.4

Write a Report

Keep a water usage journal for a week. Then write a report suggesting ways to decrease the amount of water you use.

9÷3 Math   NS 1.2

Solve Problems

About 550,000 L of water flow through Settler's Creek during the spring. If this amount of water is 40 percent of all the water that flows through the creek during a year, how much water does the creek carry during a year?

Music   VPA–M 2.3

Water Music

Trace the water you use during the day to its source or sources. Then write a song about the water's journey from its source to your tap.

For more links and activities, go to **www.hspscience.com**

Martha Conklin

▶ **DR. MARTHA CONKLIN**

▶ **Professor in the School of Engineering at the University of California, Merced**

▶ Water scientist

▶ Leading researcher in water quality

Dr. Martha Conklin, of the University of California, had a big goal. She wanted to monitor the water quality of every stream and river across the state of California. To do this, she needed a lot of help. So Conklin turned to the state's scientists-in-training: middle school science students.

Conklin says, "It's vital to educate the next generation about the environment and encourage them to go into science and engineering." She began working with Global Learning and Observations to Benefit the Environment (GLOBE), an organization that helps scientists work with students in elementary, middle, and high schools. For Conklin's studies, students measure local stream and air temperatures regularly. They send their data to Conklin, and she uses it in her water quality research.

What Conklin hopes to learn through her research is how metals, fertilizers, and other chemicals move through California's water cycle. All of these chemicals affect an area's water quality. Conklin's research on chemical flow may help environmental planners protect California's freshwater resources in the future.

 ## Think and Write

❶ How do middle school students benefit from helping researchers?

❷ How is Conklin's research connected to the water cycle?

`3.b, 3.d`

Students help in researching California rivers and streams.

Hugo Loaiciga

Homeowners who use wells know that if they pump too much groundwater, their wells will run dry. But just how much water can they pump without using up all the water in an aquifer? Until recently, homeowners had no way of knowing. That bothered Dr. Hugo Loaiciga of the University of California. If people didn't know how much water they could safely pump from their wells, they might not conserve enough groundwater to save the resource.

▶ **DR. HUGO LOAICIGA**

▶ **Professor in the Geography Dept. at UC, Santa Barbara**

▶ Water scientist

▶ Leading researcher in water conservation

To solve this problem, Loaiciga came up with an equation that models how quickly groundwater can be replaced. Loaiciga then made computer software based on his model. With a little information about an aquifer and the way it's used, homeowners and business owners can use the software to calculate the amount of water they can take from an aquifer without having it dry up.

Loaiciga hopes that people will start using his software to limit their groundwater consumption. If everybody uses only the amount of water that is naturally replaced, the aquifers will never dry out. This conservation would go a long way to solving California's freshwater resource problems.

✎ Think and Write

1 How might Loaiciga's software be used to help people conserve water? **3.d**

2 Why is it important not to overuse an aquifer? **3.d, 3.e**

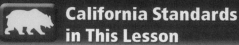

LESSON 3

Science Content

3.d *Students know* that the amount of fresh water located in rivers, lakes, underground sources, and glaciers is limited and that its availability can be extended by recycling and decreasing the use of water.

Investigation and Experimentation

6.d Identify the dependent and controlled variables in an investigation.

6.e Identify a single independent variable in a scientific investigation and explain how this variable can be used to collect information to answer a question about the results of the experiment.

Essential Question

How Can People Conserve Water?

California Fast Fact

Too Much Salt

California has several salty lakes. Mono Lake is one of them. In 1941, people started pumping water out of a stream that flows into Mono Lake. At that time, the lake had 50 g/L of salt (7 oz/gal). After many years of water removal, the lake's salt level has risen to 78 g/L (10 oz/gal). In comparison, ocean water has only about 32 g/L (4 oz/gal).

Mono Lake, California

pollution [puh•LOO•shuhn] Any change to a resource that makes the resource unhealthful to use (p. 254)

water quality [WAW•ter kwawl•uh•tee] How safe water is for use by humans, animals, and plants (p. 255)

conservation [kahn•ser•VAY•shuhn] The preserving and protecting of a resource (p. 256)

reclamation [rek•luh•MAY•shuhn] The recycling of used water (p. 257)

251

Filtering Water

Start with Questions

The water that comes out of your home's tap is clean. As you use it, though, it may become dirty with soap, oil, and other things. Clean water can also be made dirty by trash, chemicals, and animal waste.

- Can dirty water be cleaned?

- Can you clean water at home?

Investigate to find out. Then read to find out more.

Prepare to Investigate

Investigation Skill Tip
Changing variables can change the outcome of an investigation. Identify a single independent variable when you investigate, and explain how it can be used to collect information.

Materials

- spoon
- coffee filters
- water
- paper towels
- soil
- 3 clear plastic cups
- 2 funnels
- notebook paper

Make an Observation Chart

Filter System	Observations
1	
2	

Follow This Procedure

1. Stir one spoonful of soil into a cup of water until the water is cloudy.

2. Place a funnel in a clean cup. Then place two of the possible filters (coffee filters, paper towels, notebook paper) in layers inside the funnel.

3. Pour the dirty water through the funnel. **Observe** the water after it has passed through. **Record** your results.

4. Use the same dirty cup to prepare another batch of dirty water.

5. Place the second funnel in a clean cup, and add two clean filters. **Identify and control variables** by changing just one of the type of filters you used the first time. Pour the dirty water through the funnel. **Observe** the water, and **record** your results.

6. **Compare** how the two filter systems cleaned the dirty water.

Step 1

Step 3

Draw Conclusions

1. Based on what you **observed**, do you think dirty water can be filtered on a larger scale?

2. **Standards Link** Why do you think it is important to know how to filter drinking water? `3.d`

3. **Investigation Skill** Identify the independent variable you changed, and explain how it affected your outcome. `6.e`

Independent Inquiry

Identify Dependent and Controlled Variables

Plan and conduct an investigation to find the best system to clean water that has oil in it. Identify the dependent and controlled variables in the investigation. `6.d`

SCIENCE CONCEPTS
▶ what affects water quality
▶ how the supply of fresh water can be made to last

Focus Skill CAUSE AND EFFECT
Look for the ways water usage affects water quality.

cause ⟶ effect

Water Pollution

People need clean water to stay healthy, but some of Earth's water is already polluted. **Pollution** is any change to a resource that makes the resource unhealthful to use.

Water pollution comes from harmful substances that enter the water cycle. Some of those substances are there because some factories and mines dump wastes into rivers and lakes. The wastes can get into groundwater, too. Fertilizers and pesticides that farmers and homeowners use can also pollute groundwater.

Another water pollution source is sewage. *Sewage* is human waste that is usually

Some industries make wastes that seep into the ground. As shown in this diagram, the wastes can pollute the water supply.

Wastes can spill or leak.

The wastes seep into underground water.

If the polluted water joins larger bodies of water, it pollutes them, too.

Groundwater Pollution

flushed away by water. If sewage gets into the water supply that people use, people can get sick.

Pollution harms water quality. The term **water quality** refers to how safe a water source is for use by humans, animals, and plants. A water source with good water quality is safe. A water source with poor water quality may be dangerous to use.

Pollutants that soak into the ground affect the water quality of groundwater. The runoff from farms and city streets affects the quality of surface water. Land development in a watershed, such as the building of a new neighborhood, can also harm the quality of surface water. Finally, dams and other structures that are built to control a

Whatever you pour down a drain will end up in a body of water. To keep water clean, don't dump dangerous chemicals into a sink or toilet or down any other drain.

river's flow also affect water quality, because they change the river's ecosystem.

Many laws have been written to help maintain water quality. Some of these laws are local, state, and national laws. Other laws affect the entire world. The laws require industries and cities to clean surface water when they finish using it. The laws have improved water quality in many areas.

Focus Skill CAUSE AND EFFECT What factors affect a river's water quality?

Underground water supplies can be polluted by many different sources.

The polluted water reaches the ocean and pollutes it.

Insta-Lab

Traveling Pollution
Put 3 drops of red food coloring in a half-full glass of water. Observe the color of the water. Fill up the glass with clear water, and observe the color again. Then pour half of the water into another glass half-full of clear water. Observe the color. How does this process show how pollution spreads?

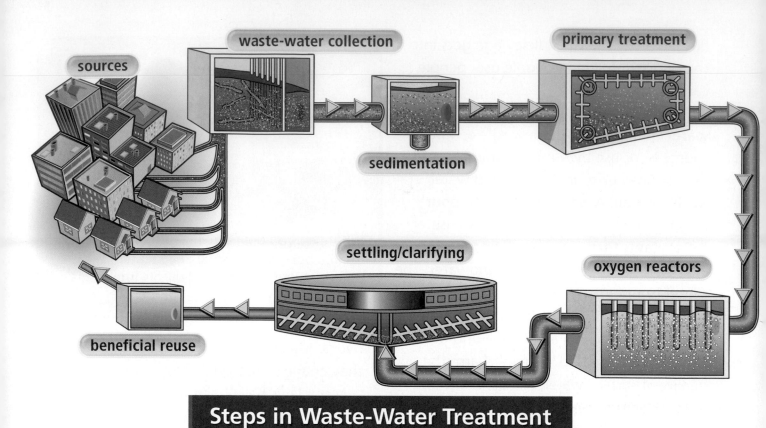

Steps in Waste-Water Treatment

sources

waste-water collection

primary treatment

sedimentation

settling/clarifying

oxygen reactors

beneficial reuse

Water Conservation

The amount of fresh water located in rivers, lakes, glaciers, and stored under the ground is limited. Water is a resource that must be conserved. The preserving and protecting of a resource is called **conservation**.

Water conservation is important in California because of *droughts* (DROWTZ), or long periods with little rain. Also, the population of California is growing. More people need water, but the water supply has stayed the same. These concerns have led many Californians to conclude that someday, there will not be enough water. As a result, government leaders, farmers, and others are looking for ways to extend water resources.

Recycling water and decreasing the amount of water used are two such ways.

Because many water sources are polluted, local governments may require water to be treated after it is used. At a water treatment plant, water is put in a holding tank. Chemicals that stick to solid particles are added so that the solids become heavy and sink. Next, smaller particles are filtered out of the water. Then, just enough chlorine is added to kill any organisms and germs in the water. The treated water can then enter a community's water system.

Some communities also practice water

RECLAIMED WATER USED FOR IRRIGATION DO NOT DRINK

NO BEBAN EL AGUA DE IRRIGACIÓN

Water reclamation is one way people recycle water resources.

Landscapes that conserve water usually include native plants that are well-adapted to the area's environment.

reclamation, or the recycling of used water. Water is reclaimed at special water treatment plants. Reclaimed water doesn't leave the treatment plant as clean as it once was. Because of that, people should not drink reclaimed water. Instead, they can use it for watering plants, flushing toilets, and washing cars. Farms and factories often use reclaimed water.

Some farmers no longer water their crops with sprinklers or sprayers. They conserve water by using drip irrigation. With this method, water slowly drips onto the ground, and less water is lost to evaporation.

Homeowners can conserve water by having a Xeriscape (ZIR•uh•skayp) instead of a lawn. Lawn grasses need great amounts of water. To conserve water, homeowners can plant native grasses, flowering plants, and shrubs that don't need as much water as lawns do.

People can conserve water in many other ways, too. They can take shorter showers. They can turn faucets off when water is not being used. What other ways can you think of to conserve water?

Focus Skill **CAUSE AND EFFECT** What has caused many Californians to start practicing water conservation?

How can people conserve water?

In this lesson, you learned that pollution can harm fresh water. You also learned that water conservation and reclamation can extend the supply of fresh water that people use.

 Science Content Standards in This Lesson

3.d *Students know* that the amount of fresh water located in rivers, lakes, underground sources, and glaciers is limited and that its availability can be extended by recycling and decreasing the use of water.

---

1. **CAUSE AND EFFECT** Draw and complete a graphic organizer to show some of the causes of poor water quality. **3.d**

2. **SUMMARIZE** Write three sentences that summarize this lesson. **3.d**

3. **DRAW CONCLUSIONS** How can a farmer and a factory owner conserve water? **3.d**

4. **VOCABULARY** Which is an example of pollution?
   A using less water
   B recycling sewage waste
   C a leakage of factory waste
   D a lake with high water quality **3.d**

5. **Critical Thinking** Which is not true of California's water?
   A Some is groundwater.
   B Some goes through treatment plants.
   C Some of it is reclaimed.
   D Some is cleaned by pollution. **3.d**

6. **Investigate and Experiment** Write a plan for an investigation to test the water quality in your community. In the plan, identify the dependent and controlled variables. **6.d**

7. Which of the following can help people conserve water?
   A using drip irrigation
   B recycling aluminum cans
   C closing water treatment plants
   D growing plants that need heavy watering **3.d**

8. How can the water cycle cause pollution to spread through different water resources? **3.d**

The Big Idea

Writing ELA–W 2.4

Write a Persuasive Letter

Research the conservation and reclamation methods your community uses. Write a letter to local government officials. Praise their conservation efforts or try to persuade them to find more ways to conserve water resources.

Math SDAP 1.4

Amount of Pollution (parts per million)	Estimated Number of Fish
20	3000
140	2000
220	1000
40	2500
60	2500
180	1500
200	1000

Display Data

Over the years, Crystal Lake has become polluted. The table shows data collected from Crystal Lake. Make a graph to show each row in the table as a point. Label your graph so the axis that goes across shows the number of fish. The axis that goes up should show the amount of pollution. What can you infer from your graph?

Health

Water Quality and Health

Research health problems caused by poor water quality. Make a checklist of things you can do to protect yourself from polluted water.

For more links and activities, go to **www.hspscience.com**

THE SALTON SEA

California's largest lake, the Salton Sea, formed because of an engineering accident. In 1905, engineers were working to move water from the Colorado River to farmland. But heavy rains that year caused the river to break through canal walls the engineers had built. For a year and a half, the entire flow of the Colorado River emptied into the Salton Sink, a large flood basin. When the engineers finally controlled the river again, the Salton Sink had become a huge lake, covering 376 square miles of land! The sink was renamed the Salton Sea.

A Lake with a Future?

The Salton Sea didn't dry up after the Colorado River was controlled. Instead, runoff from surrounding farmland kept the lake alive. Over time, the lake developed into a diverse ecosystem. Many kinds of fish, birds, and other wildlife were living in the newly formed wetlands.

But by 2002, the Salton Sea's future was threatened. As the population of southern California grows, so does the need for water. The legislature began to consider proposals to divert water from the lake's feeder streams to surrounding cities.

California's Shrinking Wetlands

At first glance, the idea seemed sensible. After all, humans had caused the lake's formation. And growing cities need new supplies of fresh water. However, many citizens raised concerns about the plan. Because of development, California has already lost 90 percent of its wetlands. The Salton Sea was one of the state's last refuges for wetland wildlife.

Besides being important environmentally, the lake was also important economically. It attracted tourists and fishers. The lake has also changed local weather patterns, making the climate milder, and better for farming.

 Think and Write

1 Why does a growing city need a source of fresh water?　3.e

2 Use the concept of watersheds to explain how the Salton Sea formed and has lasted.　3.e

The Salton Sea, located in southern California, has become a refuge for wetland wildlife.

Visual Summary

Tell how each picture helps explain the **Big Idea**.

The Big Idea Water on Earth moves between the oceans and land through the processes of evaporation and condensation.

3.a, 3.b

The Water Planet

Most of the water on Earth is found in the ocean. During the water cycle, water moves from the ocean to the air and to the land and then back to the ocean.

3.b, 3.c

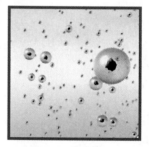

Condensation and Evaporation

Water vapor in the air can condense to form fog or clouds. The condensed water can then fall to Earth as rain, sleet, snow, or hail.

3.d, 3.e

Community Water Sources

Some communities don't have enough fresh water to meet their needs and must bring it in from other areas.

Show What You Know

Unit Writing Activity

Write an Essay

Write an essay about how a drop of water can change states from a gas to a liquid to a solid and back to a gas through the processes of evaporation, condensation, and freezing. Include specific information about the three processes. For example, discuss how temperature is related to these processes. Also, explain how these processes are related to the formation of rain, sleet, snow, and hail.

Unit Project

Plants and the Water Cycle

Plants, like people, need water to live. So how does water move through plants during the water cycle? Plan an investigation to find out. When planning your investigation, make sure you are able to control the amount of water being given to the plant. Also, be sure you are able to track the water that leaves the plant. (Hint: Enclose a plant in a plastic bag.) When your plan is finished, ask your teacher to approve it. Then conduct your experiment and report your results.

Vocabulary Review

Use the terms below to complete the sentences. The page numbers tell you where to look in the unit if you need help.

water cycle p. 228   **reservoir** p. 242

evaporation p. 230   **aqueduct** p. 242

condensation p. 231   **pollution** p. 254

watershed p. 242   **conservation** p. 256

1. Water changes from a gas to a liquid in the process of _____. **3.b**

2. Water changes from a liquid to a gas in the process of _____. **3.b**

3. The movement of water between the atmosphere, the land, and the ocean is known as the _____. **3.c**

4. The preserving or protecting of resources is _____. **3.d**

5. Sewage, such as human waste, is a form of _____. **3.d**

6. An area of land in which water runs off into a particular system of creeks and rivers is a _____. **3.e**

7. A pipe or channel used to transport water is an _____. **3.e**

8. A body of water stored for future use is a _____. **3.e**

Check Understanding

Choose the best answer.

9. In the water cycle, what happens just before water condenses in clouds? **3.c**
   A Water falls as rain.
   B Water evaporates.
   C Water vapor changes to a gas.
   D Water dissolves salt in the ocean.

10. **MAIN IDEA AND DETAILS** Where is most of Earth's water located? **3.a**
    A in lakes   C in the oceans
    B in rivers   D in the ground

11. Look at the diagram below. What is shown? **3.e**
    A river damming
    B aqueduct flow
    C saltwater evaporation
    D groundwater formation

12. What will most likely occur if water vapor in the air freezes into a solid without first becoming a liquid? **3.b**
    A It will snow.   C It will sleet.
    B It will rain.   D It will hail.

13. How can water be transported to a community? **3.b**

   A by building a dam

   B by using a reservoir

   C by building an aqueduct

   D by conserving groundwater

14. How can a community get to groundwater in order to use it? **3.e**

   A by digging a well

   B by building a dam

   C by using a reservoir

   D by building an aqueduct

15. What does this illustration show? **3.e**

   A how the water cycle works

   B how water can be polluted

   C how factories can be polluted

   D how businesses should landscape

16. CAUSE AND EFFECT What is the most likely effect of using native plants in a garden? **3.d**

   A Soil will be preserved.

   B Water will be conserved.

   C The garden won't need weeding.

   D The lawn will be lush and greener.

Investigation Skills

17. You observe clouds forming on a warm, sunny day. What can you infer is happening high up in the air? What may happen later in the day? **3.c**

18. Compare the amount of salt water on Earth with the amount of fresh water on Earth. **3.a**

Critical Thinking

19. Look at the picture below. How would the activities shown in the picture affect a community's water quality? Explain your answer. **3.d**

20. Suppose it is sunset on a warm, humid day. The temperature is predicted to get colder after dark. What will happen to the water vapor in the air if the temperature does get colder? Explain.

The Big Idea

UNIT 4 EARTH SCIENCE

Weather

California Standards in This Unit

4 Energy from the Sun heats Earth unevenly, causing air movements that result in changing weather patterns. As a basis for understanding this concept:

4.a *Students know* uneven heating of Earth causes air movements (convection currents).

4.b *Students know* the influence that the ocean has on the weather and the role that the water cycle plays in weather patterns.

4.c *Students know* the causes and effects of different types of severe weather.

4.d *Students know* how to use weather maps and data to predict local weather and know that weather forecasts depend on many variables.

4.e *Students know* that the Earth's atmosphere exerts a pressure that decreases with distance above Earth's surface and that at any point it exerts this pressure equally in all directions.

This unit also addresses these Investigation and Experimentation Standards: **6.b** **6.d** **6.f** **6.g**

What's the Big Idea?

Energy from the sun heats Earth unevenly. This causes air movements that result in changing weather patterns.

Essential Questions

266

San Fernando Valley

Dear Tony,

We had a great time hiking in the San Fernando Valley. The view down from the foothills is beautiful.

We had to be very careful, though. The fire danger was high. I guess it had to do with the hot, dry winds blowing down from the mountains.

We even got to walk through some of the area that was burned by the wildfires a couple years ago.

Nick

USA

What did Nick see that was related to weather? How do you think that relates to the **Big Idea?**

Unit Inquiry

Air Temperature and Surface Cover Color

If you have ever placed your hand on the hood of a car that has been parked in the sun, you know that sunlight can be changed into heat. Some colors, however, absorb or reflect heat better than others. Plan and conduct an experiment to find out why.

Science Content

4.a *Students know* uneven heating of Earth causes air movements (convection currents).

4.e *Students know* that the Earth's atmosphere exerts a pressure that decreases with distance above Earth's surface and that at any point it exerts this pressure equally in all directions.

Investigation and Experimentation

6.b Develop a testable question.

Essential Question

How Does Uneven Heating of Earth Affect Weather?

California Fast Fact

Snow Kidding!

This picture was taken on Mount Lassen in June. The area usually gets about 1 m (39 in.) of snow per month from December to March. Most of this snow melts during the spring and summer. But record snowfalls on the mountain one winter left these giant snowdrifts. This much snow takes a long time to melt!

Mount Lassen, California

atmosphere [AT•muhs•feer] The blanket of air surrounding Earth (p. 272)

weather [WETH•er] The condition of the atmosphere at a certain place and time (p. 272)

air pressure [AIR PRESH•er] The weight of the atmosphere pushing on a given square unit area of the Earth's surface (p. 272)

convection current [kuhn•VEK•shuhn KER•uhnt] The upward and downward movement of air in the atmosphere (p. 274)

local wind [LOH•kuhl WIND] Wind that results from local changes in temperature (p. 275)

prevailing wind [pree•VAYL•ing WIND] A global wind that blows constantly from the same direction (p. 276)

269

The Uneven Heating of Earth

Start with Questions

At the beach, the water is cool. But you may get hot feet on the way back to your towel.

- Which do you think heats faster, land or water?

- Which cools down faster? Why does this happen?

Investigate to find out. Then read to find out more.

Prepare to Investigate

Investigation Skill Tip
A prediction is based on previous observations. Before you predict, think about what you have already observed.

Materials
- 2 metal cans
- 2 thermometers
- water
- soil

Make a Data Table

Temperature (in °C)								
	Sun				Shade			
(min)	0	10	20	30	0	10	20	30
water								
soil								

Follow This Procedure

1. Fill one can about three-fourths full of water and the other can about three-fourths full of soil.

2. Place one thermometer in the can of water and the other in the can of soil. Put the cans in a shady place outside. Wait 10 minutes. Then **record** the temperature of the water and of the soil.

3. Put both cans in sunlight. **Predict** which can will heat faster. **Record** the temperature of each can every 10 minutes for 30 minutes.

4. Put the cans back in the shade. **Predict** which can will show the faster temperature drop. Again, **record** the temperature of each can every 10 minutes for 30 minutes.

5. Make line graphs to show how the temperatures of both materials changed as they heated and cooled.

Step 1

Step 2

Draw Conclusions

1. How did your results compare with your predictions?

2. **Standards Link** Which do you **predict** will heat faster—oceans or land? Which do you **predict** will cool faster? Explain.   4.a

3. **Investigation Skill** Scientists learn by **predicting** and then **experimenting** to test their predictions. How did you test your predictions in this Investigate?

Independent Inquiry   Develop Testable Questions

Think about your observations during this investigation. Develop another question that you could investigate.   6.b

Then write a plan for an investigation to test your question. Your plan should include the following details:

- **the materials you will need**
- **the variable you will change**
- **the procedure steps**
- **the variable you will measure**

VOCABULARY
atmosphere p. 272
weather p. 272
air pressure p. 272
convection current p. 274
local wind p. 275
prevailing wind p. 276

SCIENCE CONCEPTS
▶ what the atmosphere is like
▶ how uneven heating of Earth causes air to move

Focus Skill **MAIN IDEA AND DETAILS**
Look for details about the uneven heating of Earth.

Main Idea

detail   detail   detail

The Atmosphere

A blanket of air called the **atmosphere** surrounds Earth. The atmosphere is very thin compared to the size of Earth. In fact, if Earth were the size of a peach, the atmosphere would be thinner than the fuzz on the peach!

The atmosphere is made up of several layers. The layer closest to Earth's surface is the *troposphere* (TROH•puh•sfeer). The troposphere contains about 90 percent of the atmosphere's gases. Most of Earth's weather happens in the troposphere. **Weather** is the condition of the atmosphere at a certain place and time.

You can't see, taste, or touch the air in the atmosphere. So how do you know that air is even there? You know this because every time the wind blows, you feel the air. You can feel air blow against you because air has mass. Everything on Earth that has mass is pulled toward Earth's center by gravity. This pull causes air to have weight. Air particles closer to Earth's surface have more weight than the air higher in the atmosphere. This means that **air pressure**, or the weight of air in the atmosphere in one unit area, is greatest at sea level.

Another factor that causes air pressure to be greater at sea level is air density. Gravity pulls most of the air in the atmosphere down to the surface. Because of this, the air closer to Earth's surface is much denser than the air farther away from the surface.

Focus Skill **MAIN IDEA AND DETAILS** In which layer of the atmosphere does most weather occur?

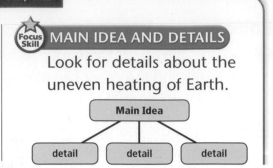

Atmosphere Layers

The stratosphere is the layer above the troposphere. It contains ozone. Ozone is a gas that protects Earth from the sun's harmful ultraviolet rays. Above the stratosphere, the air is very thin. The outermost layer of the atmosphere extends into space.

ozone

stratosphere

troposphere

Air Pressure

The higher you go into the atmosphere, the less air there is above you. On top of Mount Everest, the tallest mountain on Earth, air pressure is less than one-third of what it is at sea level. You can measure the air pressure around you to get a good idea of how far above sea level you are. Airplane pilots have instruments that do this so that they know how high they are flying.

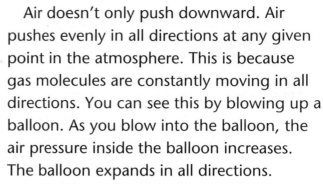

1

The particles in the upper atmosphere are far apart. Air in this part of the atmosphere is much less dense than air lower in Earth's atmosphere.

1 meter 1 meter

2

Air near the middle of the atmosphere is denser than air higher above it.

3

The weight of all the air above presses down on the air particles closest to Earth, forcing them close together. This makes air densest and air pressure greatest at Earth's surface.

Air doesn't only push downward. Air pushes evenly in all directions at any given point in the atmosphere. This is because gas molecules are constantly moving in all directions. You can see this by blowing up a balloon. As you blow into the balloon, the air pressure inside the balloon increases. The balloon expands in all directions.

Temperature also affects air pressure. Cold air is denser than warm air. Because of this, it sinks toward Earth's surface. As it does, it forces warmer, less dense air to rise. As warm air rises, it cools. The cooler air is now denser, so it sinks back to the surface. Throughout the troposphere, areas of high pressure—where dense, cold air is sinking—balance areas of low pressure—where warm, less dense air is rising.

Focus Skill **MAIN IDEA AND DETAILS** What factors affect air pressure?

How Strong Is Air Pressure?

Put one end of a straw in a plastic bag. Use tape to seal the bag. Put the bag on a table, and lay a book on the bottom half of the bag. Blow through the straw. Observe what happens. In what ways might you use air pressure?

Uneven Heating and Local Winds

When you left home this morning, how did the air feel? Was it hot or cold? Was it windy, or was it calm? If you were to go outside right now, would the air feel the same? It probably wouldn't. That's because air around you is always moving and changing. Why is this so?

When the sun's energy reaches Earth, some of the energy bounces off objects such as clouds. Earth absorbs the rest of the energy. However, different types of surfaces absorb different amounts of energy. For example, you learned in the Investigate that soil heats up faster and cools off faster than an equal amount of water. That means if you're spending the day at the beach and you want to cool off, your best bet is to get into the water. During the day, the sand is hotter than the water, so it gives off more heat. Because of this, the air over the beach will be hot, too. The water is cooler than the sand, so the air over the water will be cooler.

Remember, cool air is denser than warm air, so it sinks. Air that is warm is less dense, so it is pushed upward by the cooler, denser air. This upward and downward movement of air is called **convection currents** in the atmosphere. The movement of water in a

**Math in Science
Interpret Data**

Some energy from the sun is reflected or absorbed in the atmosphere. How much of the sun's energy reaches Earth?

20% absorbed and reflected by air.

25% absorbed and reflected by clouds.

50% absorbed by Earth's surface.

5% reflected by Earth's surface.

▲ During the day, the land heats up faster than the sea. Cooler sea air moves toward the land. This is called a sea breeze.

▲ At night, the [land] loses heat faster than the sea does. Coo[ler] air over the land moves toward the se[a]. This is called a land breeze.

pot that's heating on a stove is also due to convection.

Air in the troposphere moves horizontally, too. As cool, dense air sinks, it spreads out along the surface. Air at the surface moves from areas of higher pressure to areas of lower pressure. This horizontal movement of air is called wind.

Winds can be local, affecting small areas, or global, affecting large parts of the Earth. Sometimes, places in the same general area have slightly different temperatures. This produces **local wind**, or wind that results from a local difference in temperature.

Local winds often occur along lakeshores or seashores. During the day, the air over the land is warmer than the air over the water. The cooler air over the water has a higher pressure than the warmer air over the land. The result is a wind that blows from the water toward the land. This wind is called a sea breeze.

At night, the wind usually blows in the opposite direction. Land cools off more quickly than water does. Once the land becomes cooler than the water, a wind blows from the land toward the water. This wind is called a land breeze.

The arrows in this diagram show that in convection currents, air moves across the Earth's surface as well as up and down.

MAIN IDEA AND DETAILS Why is air always moving?

During summer in the Northern Hemisphere, the sun's rays hit Earth more directly than in winter. More direct rays cause more heating because they don't cover as large an area.

Global Winds

Local winds move short distances and can blow from any direction. But there are other, more constant winds. A **prevailing wind** is a global wind that almost always blows from the same direction. In the age of great sailing ships, sailors relied on prevailing winds to carry them across the oceans.

Prevailing winds are caused by the same thing as local winds—uneven heating of Earth's surface. However, unlike local winds, prevailing winds result from uneven heating of large parts of Earth.

An area's *latitude,* or distance from the equator, affects the amount of heat that

The global winds that blow over most of the United States are called the prevailing westerlies. They blow from west to east. ▼

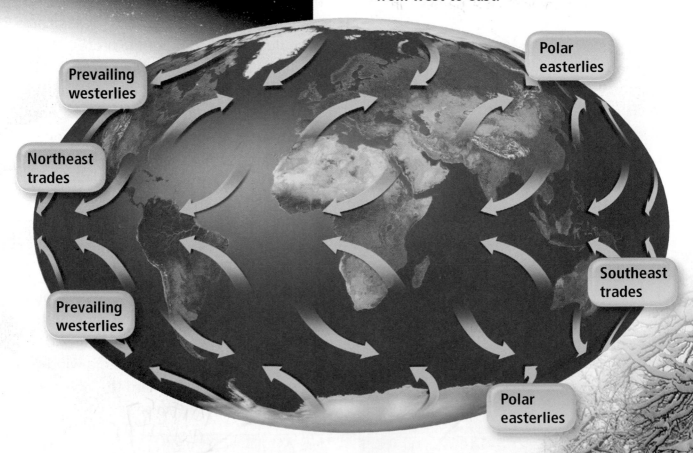

Prevailing westerlies

Polar easterlies

Northeast trades

Prevailing westerlies

Southeast trades

Polar easterlies

276

the area receives from the sun. Depending on the time of year, Earth's poles receive indirect sunlight or no sunlight at all, so they are always cold. In contrast, Earth's equator gets direct sunlight all year, so it's always warm. As a result, cold air above the poles sinks and moves toward the equator. As this happens, air at the equator is pushed up and moves toward the poles.

But air doesn't just move in one big circle. As warm air at the equator moves up, it begins to cool. Some of the cooling air sinks back to Earth before it reaches the poles. Air in the atmosphere travels in many circles as it continues to warm or cool.

You might expect air moving within these circles to move straight north and south. Instead, air moves in curved paths. This is because Earth's rotation causes prevailing winds. You can model this with a sheet of paper on a turntable. As the paper spins on the turntable counter clockwise, try to draw a straight line from the center of the turntable to its edge.

Winds moving north curve to the east. Winds moving south curve to the west. Around the equator, this curving causes the prevailing winds—called *trade winds*—to blow from the east. In the United States, this curving causes the prevailing winds—the *prevailing westerlies*—to blow from the west.

The prevailing westerlies cause most weather systems in the United States to move from west to east. This helps forecasters predict the weather, because weather in San Francisco today often moves toward Kansas City tomorrow and then toward Baltimore.

 **MAIN IDEA AND DETAILS** What two factors cause prevailing winds?

Since most weather systems in the United States move from west to east, this blizzard in Chicago may affect Buffalo tomorrow and Boston the next day. ▼

Standards Wrap-Up and Lesson Review

How does uneven heating of Earth affect weather?

In this lesson, you learned that the sun heats Earth's surface unevenly. This produces differences in air pressure, which result in local and global winds.

Science Content Standards in This Lesson

4.a *Students know* uneven heating of Earth causes air movements (convection currents).

4.e *Students know* that Earth's atmosphere exerts a pressure that decreases with distance above Earth's surface and that at any point it exerts this pressure equally in all directions.

1. 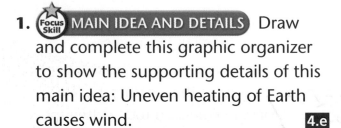 **MAIN IDEA AND DETAILS** Draw and complete this graphic organizer to show the supporting details of this main idea: Uneven heating of Earth causes wind. **4.e**

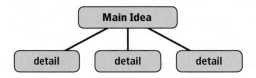

Main Idea

detail   detail   detail

2. **SUMMARIZE** Describe how local winds, such as sea breezes and land breezes, form. **4.a**

3. **DRAW CONCLUSIONS** Describe one way in which the atmosphere affects you every day. **4.e**

4. **VOCABULARY** Choose two vocabulary terms from this lesson that relate to wind. Draw a diagram to illustrate each term. **4.e**

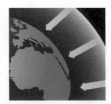

5. **Critical Thinking** Suppose you're going fishing on a lake. Describe the winds that might occur along the lakeshore. **4.a**

6. **Investigate and Experiment** Write a plan for an investigation to test the following question: Does dark-colored sand heat up faster than light-colored sand? **6.b**

7. In the United States, in which direction do weather systems usually move?

  A east to west   **C** north to south

  B west to east   **D** south to north **4.a**

8. How are prevailing winds and local winds similar?

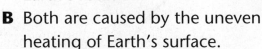
The **Big** Idea

  A Both are caused by Earth's rotation.

  B Both are caused by the uneven heating of Earth's surface.

  C Both are caused by the same season.

  D Both are caused by the latitude of an area. **4.e**

  Writing　ELA–W 1.1

Write a Composition

Suppose you want to fly your kite at the beach. Write a paragraph or two detailing the differences between flying your kite in the morning, in the afternoon, and in the evening.

  Math　NS 1.2

Solve Problems

About 20 percent of the sun's energy that reaches Earth's atmosphere is reflected back into space. Another 25 percent is absorbed or reflected by the clouds. What percent of the sun's energy never reaches Earth's surface?

  Health

Sunscreen

The sun's rays can be harmful to human skin. Make a brochure that explains how people can keep their skin healthy. Include details about proper sunscreen use. Also include details about when and where on Earth the sun's rays are most direct and, therefore, most dangerous.

 For more links and activities, go to **www.hspscience.com**

On the LOOKOUT

Weather forecasters have a tough job. Millions of people rely on weather forecasts to make their plans. When a weather forecast is wrong, you know that the weather experts will hear about it.

Weather forecasting isn't easy, though. Forecasters can't guess when they try to predict the weather. They have to rely on data from different sources and use computers to be as accurate as possible in their predictions.

Pictures from Space

Satellites are some of the most important tools that weather forecasters use. Satellites orbit about 35,000 kilometers (21,750 miles) above Earth. They give forecasters a view of clouds from above and how they are moving across land and water.

One pair of weather satellites, called GOES, is used by the National Weather Service. The satellites send weather data and pictures to forecasters on the ground. Using the images from the satellites, forecasters can track the movements of storms.

Doppler Radar

Doppler radar also helps forecasters figure out whether snow, sleet, hail, or rain is falling from clouds. The radar provides color-coded images that identify all the different types of precipitation. As you know, precipitation is any form of water that falls from the clouds.

The various colors show the intensity of the precipitation. Both light blue and dark blue colors usually indicate areas of light precipitation. Areas of red colors and pink colors usually indicate strong or severe thunderstorms. So if a radar image shows a broad band of pink moving toward an area, forecasters can warn people in the area of severe weather.

Reliable Technology

Weather balloons have been used by forecasters for many years. The balloons show forecasters what is happening high in the atmosphere.

Think and Write

❶ Why do you think the National Weather Service still uses weather balloons? **4.d**

❷ Why are accurate weather forecasts important to people and to businesses?

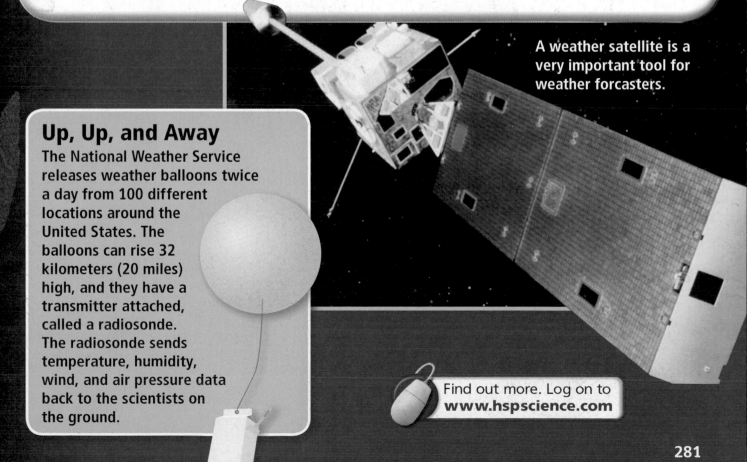

A weather satellite is a very important tool for weather forcasters.

Up, Up, and Away

The National Weather Service releases weather balloons twice a day from 100 different locations around the United States. The balloons can rise 32 kilometers (20 miles) high, and they have a transmitter attached, called a radiosonde. The radiosonde sends temperature, humidity, wind, and air pressure data back to the scientists on the ground.

Find out more. Log on to **www.hspscience.com**

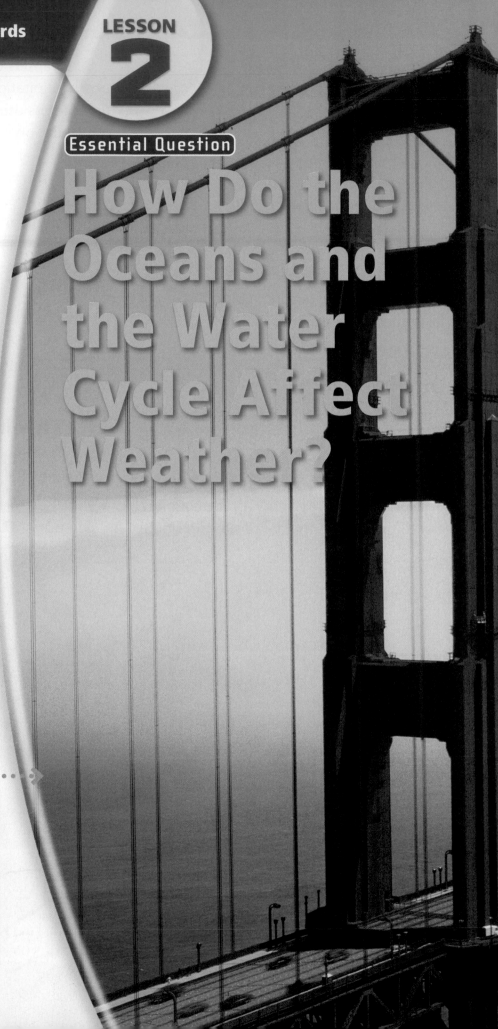

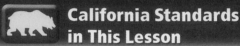
Science Content

4.b *Students know* the influence that the ocean has on the weather and the role that the water cycle plays in weather patterns.

Investigation and Experimentation

6.d Identify the dependent and controlled variables in an investigation.

LESSON 2

Essential Question

How Do the Oceans and the Water Cycle Affect Weather?

California Fast Fact

Blowing the Horn

During heavy fog, operators of the Golden Gate Bridge sound a horn. This helps ships avoid the bridge. From July through October, there's so much fog that the horn sounds for about five hours nearly every day!

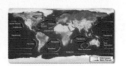

current [KUR•uhnt] A stream of water that flows like a river through the ocean (p. 286)

---

humidity [hyoo•MID•uh•tee] A measurement of the amount of water vapor in the air (p. 290)

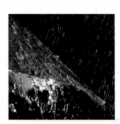

precipitation [pree•sip•uh•TAY•shuhn] Water that falls from clouds to the Earth (p. 290)

Golden Gate Bridge in San Francisco

The Water Cycle and Weather

Start with Questions

Sudden rainstorms happen all the time. You know to take an umbrella when the forecast says "rain today."

- Where does rain come from?

- What parts of the water cycle are involved?

Investigate to find out. Then read to find out more.

Prepare to Investigate

Investigation Skill Tip
When you infer, you use what you observe to explain what happened. Inferring is like using clues to solve a mystery. Observing carefully, like finding good clues, can help you infer correctly.

Materials

- graduate
- water
- small plastic cup
- zip-top plastic bag
- paper towels

Make an Observation Chart

Day	Observation
1	CUP: BAG:
2	CUP: BAG:
3	CUP: BAG:
4	CUP: BAG:

Follow This Procedure

1. Using the graduate, **measure** and pour 100 mL of water into the cup.

2. Open the plastic bag, and carefully put the cup inside. Then seal the bag. Be careful not to spill any water from the cup. If you do spill any, wipe it up with a towel.

3. Place the sealed bag near a sunny window. **Predict** what will happen to the water in the cup.

4. Leave the bag near the window for 3 to 4 days. **Observe** the cup and the bag each day. **Record** what you see. ·

5. Remove the cup from the bag. **Measure** the water in the cup by pouring it back into the graduate. By **using the numbers** you recorded, find any difference in the amount of water poured into the cup and the amount of water removed from the cup.

Step 1

Step 3

Draw Conclusions

1. What did you **observe** during the time the cup was inside the bag?

2. **Standards Link** What happened to the water in the cup? How does this relate to rain and clouds? `4.b`

3. **Investigation Skill** What can you **infer** about where the water in the bag came from?

Independent Inquiry ▶ Identify Variables

Think about the procedure for this Investigate. Which conditions do you think affected the results? How can you tell?

Assume you're going to plan an experiment based on this Investigate. List a variable that you could change. List the variable that you would observe or measure. Then tell which variables you would keep the same. `6.d`

VOCABULARY
current p. 286
humidity p. 290
precipitation p. 290

SCIENCE CONCEPTS
▶ how the ocean affects weather
▶ how the water cycle relates to weather

Focus Skill ★ **CAUSE AND EFFECT**

Look for effects of the water cycle on weather.

cause ⟶ effect

The Oceans Affect Weather

The oceans cover about 70 percent of Earth's surface. You learned in Lesson 1 that land heats up and cools off more quickly than water does. During the summer, the oceans absorb much heat from the sun. This absorption keeps the air over the oceans cooler than it would otherwise be. In the winter, the oceans release heat into the air above them, causing the planet to be warmer than it would otherwise be. In this way, the oceans help keep Earth's weather mild. Earth's temperatures would be much more extreme without oceans.

Although the oceans' overall temperature stays steady throughout the year, different parts of the oceans are heated unevenly by the sun. Water on the surface is pushed forward by winds. The result is a **current**, or stream of water, that flows like a river through the ocean. Currents distribute heat over great distances.

The Gulf Stream current flows across the Atlantic Ocean. It begins in the tropics and moves northeast. Part of it then becomes the North Atlantic Current, carrying warm

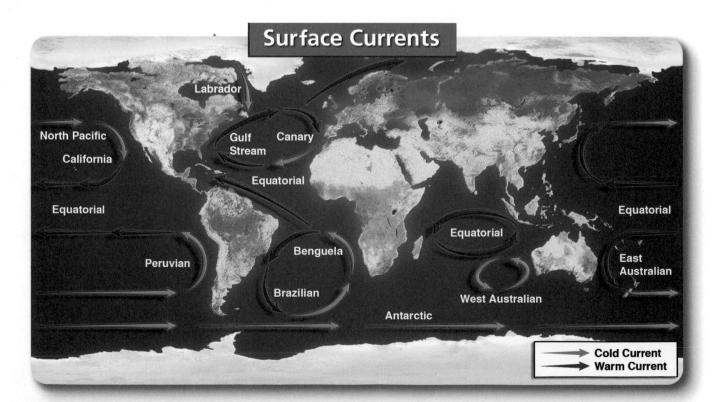

Surface Currents

Labrador
North Pacific
Gulf Stream
Canary
California
Equatorial
Equatorial
Equatorial
Equatorial
Peruvian
Benguela
East Australian
Brazilian
West Australian
Antarctic

⟶ Cold Current
⟶ Warm Current

▲ El Niño storms can contribute to problems along California's coast.

Insta-Lab

Kitchen El Niño

Fill a large container with very warm water. Fill a small cup with very cold water, and add a few drops of food coloring. Use tongs to gently lower the cup straight down into the warm water, below the surface. Observe what happens. How is this similar to what happens during El Niño?

water toward countries in northern Europe, such as Scotland and Norway. The warm current causes the weather in those places to be warmer than it would otherwise be.

Other currents carry cold water. The California Current flows from north to south. This cold current results in cool weather along California's coast.

Some currents are deep in the oceans. Off the west coast of South America, winds blow warm surface water away from the land. Deep currents then carry cooler water up toward the surface near the coast. Changing winds can affect these currents. If the winds don't blow the warm surface water away from the coast, the cooler

currents won't reach the surface. As a result, coastal water stays warm. This causes El Niño (EL NEEN•yoh), which changes many weather patterns over the Pacific Ocean.

How does this change affect the weather? The amount of rain depends a great deal on the surface temperature of the ocean. Warm water evaporates faster than cool water does. Where the ocean is warm, clouds form and it rains. In most years, the wind pushes the warm water to the west. As a result, Australia gets rain, and the west coast of North America stays dry. During El Niño, the weather pattern reverses. Australia has drier than normal weather. Western North America has wetter than normal weather, with huge amounts of rain on the coast and heavy snows in the mountains.

 **CAUSE AND EFFECT** How does the Gulf Stream affect Scotland's weather?

The Water Cycle

2 Water vapor condenses into cloud drops.

3 Water falls to Earth as rain, sleet, snow or hail.

4 Water soaks into the ground or falls into steams, rivers, lakes, and oceans.

1 Water evaporates from the oceans.

Weather Patterns and the Water Cycle

In Unit 3, you learned that water continuously moves from Earth's surface to the atmosphere and back to Earth in a process called the water cycle. Just as the sun's heat causes currents in the atmosphere and oceans, it also drives the movement of water in the water cycle.

During the water cycle, liquid water is heated and evaporates, becoming water vapor. Water vapor stays a gas as long as it

is warm. If the water vapor cools, much of it condenses back into liquid form.

Liquid water falls back to Earth. Some of the water soaks into the ground or runs into streams, rivers, lakes, and oceans. Rivers often carry the water back to the oceans. The cycle starts again as the sun heats the oceans' surface, causing water to again enter the atmosphere.

If the sun heated the atmosphere evenly, the air in the atmosphere would not move in convection currents. The water that evaporated over an ocean would eventually fall back down over that same area. More evaporation takes place in the tropics than in cooler regions. This means that if air did not move, almost all of the rain on Earth would fall near the equator.

But air in the atmosphere does move in convection currents. Because it does, water that evaporates from the oceans near the tropics moves long distances on global winds.

The water vapor carried by global winds contains heat. Warm air that flows toward the poles from places near the equator carries a lot of water vapor with it. As the air gradually cools and the vapor condenses, heat energy is released into the atmosphere. In this way, both heat and water are transported through the water cycle. This process helps balance temperatures in the atmosphere. The tropics lose some heat and water vapor while cooler regions gain heat and moisture.

Focus Skill **CAUSE AND EFFECT** Besides providing water for precipitation, what effect does the water cycle have on weather?

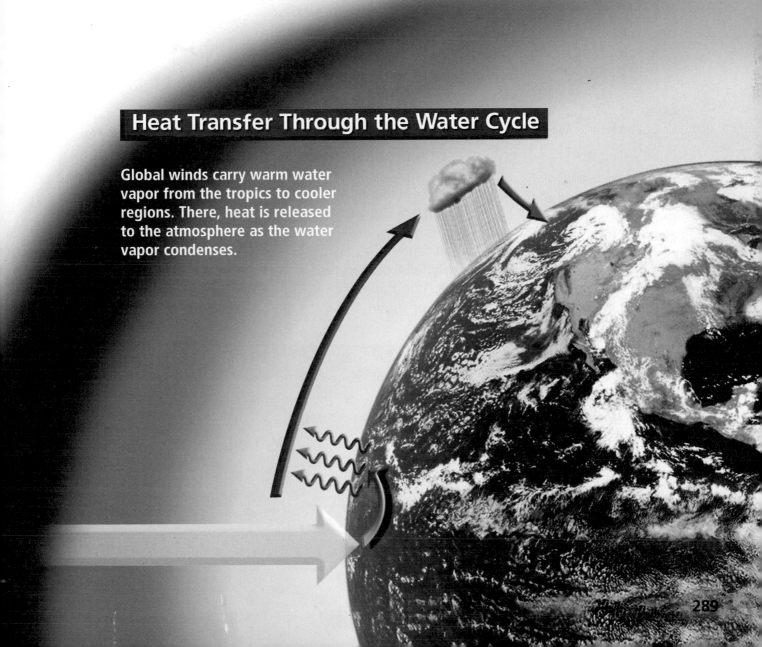

Heat Transfer Through the Water Cycle

Global winds carry warm water vapor from the tropics to cooler regions. There, heat is released to the atmosphere as the water vapor condenses.

Clouds

Much of what you may call weather is actually part of the water cycle. A large part of the water cycle occurs in the atmosphere. Water enters the atmosphere when it evaporates. Some areas of the atmosphere have more water vapor than other areas. The amount of water vapor in the air is called **humidity**. A large amount of water vapor in the air is high humidity. A small amount of water vapor in the air is low humidity.

Humidity depends partly on the air's temperature. Warm air can have more water vapor in it than cold air can. Suppose you're on an island near the equator. The air over the island is warm. The humidity is high because the air contains a lot of water that has evaporated from the ocean.

Clouds form in air that is relatively high in humidity. As warm air is forced up, it cools. Some of the water vapor begins to condense on dust and other particles in the air. As more and more water condenses, a cloud forms. A cloud is basically dust and condensed water.

The water that forms in clouds returns to Earth as precipitation. **Precipitation** (pree•sip•uh•TAY•shuhn) is water that falls from the atmosphere to Earth's surface.

Focus Skill **CAUSE AND EFFECT** What causes clouds to form?

Types of Clouds

CUMULUS CLOUDS
Cumulus (KYOO•myuh•luhs) clouds are puffy. They indicate fair weather, but as a cumulus cloud grows, rain can develop.

STRATUS CLOUDS
Stratus (STRAT•uhs) clouds form low in the atmosphere. They usually cover the sky. Heavy precipitation does not usually fall from stratus clouds, but moderate rainfall or snowfall is possible.

CIRRUS CLOUDS
Cirrus (SIR•uhs) clouds form high in the troposphere, where the air is very cold. They are made mostly of ice crystals.

290

How Precipitation Forms

Energy from the sun

Water Particles

Evaporation Heat from the sun causes evaporation. When water evaporates from the ocean, salts are left behind.

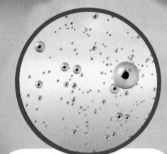

Condensation As water vapor rises into the air, it begins to lose heat. The water vapor turns back into a liquid, or condenses, on small pieces of dust in the air. This forms clouds.

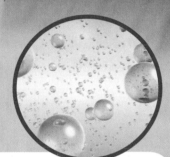

Precipitation Inside clouds, small water droplets form larger droplets. In time, these larger droplets become raindrops that fall to Earth. The water in raindrops is fresh water.

Precipitation

Precipitation falls only from certain types of clouds. Light drizzle may fall from *stratus* clouds. Rain as well as most other forms of precipitation fall from *cumulonimbus* clouds.

The other forms of precipitation—snow, sleet, and hail—are solid. Snow forms when water vapor turns directly into ice crystals. Sleet and hail form when liquid water passes through air that is cold enough to freeze water drops.

Water vapor doesn't always form precipitation as it condenses. Have you ever seen dew on the ground after a cool night? Car windows and other objects may also be covered with dew. Why does dew form? The ground loses heat more quickly than the air does. As the ground cools, water vapor in the air directly above the ground condenses. If the air is cold enough, frost forms.

A similar weather condition can form fog. Fog is water vapor that has condensed into small water droplets near ground level.

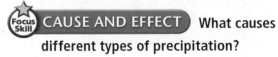

CAUSE AND EFFECT What causes different types of precipitation?

Standards Wrap-Up and Lesson Review

How do the oceans and the water cycle affect weather?

In this lesson, you learned that ocean currents can change weather patterns and that the water cycle provides moisture for precipitation.

 Science Content Standards in This Lesson

4.b *Students know* the influence that the ocean has on the weather and the role that the water cycle plays in weather patterns.

1. 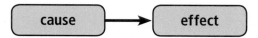 (Focus Skill) **CAUSE AND EFFECT** Draw and complete this graphic organizer to show the effects of ocean currents on weather. **4.b**

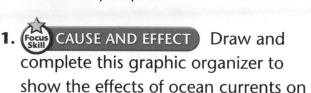

2. **SUMMARIZE** Fill in the blanks. The sun causes water to _____ from the ocean. Air containing water vapor is moved by _____. As air cools, water vapor _____, forming clouds. When cloud drops get too heavy, water falls as _____. **4.b**

3. **DRAW CONCLUSIONS** What would happen to the water cycle if the sun heated the Earth evenly? **4.b**

4. **VOCABULARY** Describe how the terms in each pair are related: *evaporation* and *condensation*; *cloud* and *fog*; *ocean current* and *convection current*. **4.b**

5. **Critical Thinking** You see cirrus clouds in the sky. Will it rain soon? Explain your answer. **4.b**

6. **Investigate and Experiment** In an investigation, why is it important to identify the variable that will change and the variables that will be controlled? **6.d**

7. You heat an ice cube, and it melts. What will happen to the water if you continue to apply heat?
   A It will condense.
   B It will freeze.
   C It will evaporate.
   D It will precipitate. **4.b**

8. Which two things form in similar ways?
   A frost and dew
   B snow and sleet
   C frost and sleet
   D rain and dew **4.b**

 The Big Idea

Write a Report

Suppose you're going to be on a sailing ship traveling along the coast of California. Research the types of weather you might encounter during different seasons. Write a report detailing the different types of weather you can expect on your trip.

Solve Problems

Use library resources to find the types and amounts of precipitation for 10 cities in different areas of the United States. Compare your data with a topographical map. How do you think geography affects the type of precipitation? How does it affect the amount of precipitation?

California Natives

Select an American Indian group from California. Find out how the water cycle and climate affected the group's culture. In particular, tell how these factors affected the buildings and the locations of the settlements.

 For more links and activities, go to **www.hspscience.com**

► **DR. CORT ANASTASIO**

► **Professor of Meteorolgy at the University of California at Davis**

► Knows about the tiniest pollution particles

Cort Anastasio

The mist from ocean waves helps cool you off at the beach. You probably never think of what else the mist can do. Dr. Cort Anastasio does. He studies how very small drops of ocean mist react with the atmosphere. Dr. Anastasio is Professor of Meteorology at the University of California at Davis. Besides doing research, he teaches about the chemistry of the atmosphere.

Dr. Anastasio also is interested in snow. Energy from the sun can cause tiny particles in snow to react with air. Over time, the reactions can cause small changes in the makeup of the atmosphere. This may not seem like much, but remember that most of the Arctic and Antarctica are covered with snow year-round.

Pollution also includes tiny particles. Dr. Anastasio studies possible dangers of certain metal pollution particles.

 Think and Write

❶ What is common to all of Dr. Anastasio's research?

❷ How can a small change affect large parts of the atmosphere?

4.a

Arctic camp

Joanne Simpson

Have you ever watched clouds change shape? As a child, Dr. Joanne Simpson loved to watch clouds. This led to a career as a weather scientist. She became the first woman to receive a Ph.D. degree in meteorology.

Dr. Simpson developed models of how clouds form and change. She began by filming clouds during long plane flights over the tropical Pacific Ocean. She analyzed the images. Over time, she built a mathematical model of cloud changes.

▶ **DR. JOANNE SIMPSON**

▶ **Weather Scientist**

▶ First woman to receive a Ph.D. degree in meteorology

Today, scientists know that heat from tropical oceans affects weather over all of Earth. Dr. Simpson was the first to hypothesize how clouds could transfer this heat to the upper atmosphere. She also explained the details of what keeps hurricanes from breaking up.

Until 2004, Dr. Simpson led the Tropical Rainfall Monitoring Mission at NASA. Data from their satellite has improved tropical weather forecasts. Scientists now know even more about how heat is transferred to the atmosphere.

✍️ Think and Write

❶ Which visible weather feature ties together Dr. Simpson's work? `4.a`

❷ What property of tropical oceans affects weather?

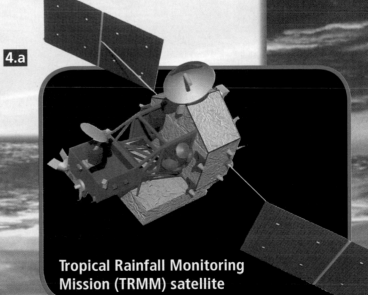

Tropical Rainfall Monitoring Mission (TRMM) satellite

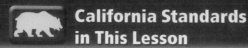
Science Content

4.d *Students know* how to use weather maps and data to predict local weather and know that weather forecasts depend on many variables.

Investigation and Experimentation

6.g Record data by using appropriate graphic representations (including charts, graphs, and labeled diagrams) and make inferences based on those data.

California Fast Fact

100-Year Bloom

Death Valley National Park is one of the hottest, driest places on Earth. The park usually gets less than 5 cm (2 in.) of rain each year. But in 2005, more than 15 cm (6 in.) of rain fell! Thousands of wildflowers sprouted across the park. This event is called a 100-year bloom because the area gets enough rain for it only about once a century.

LESSON 3

Essential Question

How Is Weather Predicted?

Death Valley National Park, California

meteorology [mee•tee•uh•RAHL•uh•jee] The study of weather (p. 300)

barometer [buh•RAHM•uht•er] An instrument for measuring air pressure (p. 300)

anemometer [an•uh•MAHM•uht•er] An instrument for measuring wind speed (p. 300)

hygrometer [hy•GRAHM•uht•er] An instrument for measuring humidity (p. 300)

air mass [AIR MAS] A large body of air that has similar temperature and humidity throughout (p. 302)

front [FRUHNT] A place where two air masses meet (p. 303)

Measuring Weather Conditions

Start with Questions

When you look out a window, you can see if it is sunny or cloudy or if the wind is blowing. But none of these observations are measurements of the weather.

- How do you think weather is measured?

- Is it hard to measure weather?

Investigate to find out. Then read to find out more.

Prepare to Investigate

Investigation Skill Tip
You gather data by making observations and measurements. You'll use the data table to record data on the weather each day for five days. Try to gather your data at the same time each day.

Materials

- weather station

Make an Observation Chart

Weather Station Daily Record					
Date					
Time					
Temperature					
Rainfall or snowfall					
Wind direction and speed					
Cloud conditions					

Follow This Procedure

1 Place the weather station in a shady spot, about 1 m above the ground. Be sure the rain gauge will not collect runoff from the buildings or trees. Put the wind vane where wind from any direction can reach it.

2 **Record** the amount of rain or snow, if any.

3 **Record** the wind direction and speed. Wind direction is the direction the wind is blowing from.

4 **Observe** and **record** the cloud conditions. Draw a circle, and shade part of it to show the fraction of the sky that's covered with clouds.

5 **Record** the temperature.

6 Repeat steps 2–5 each day for five days. Make a line graph showing how the temperature changes from day to day.

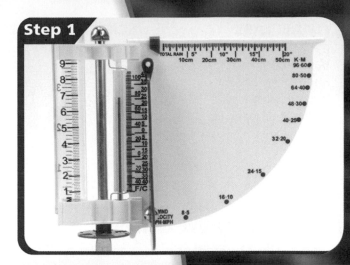

Step 1

Step 2

Draw Conclusions

1. **Compare** weather conditions you observed on two different days.

2. **Standards Link** What do you think caused changes in the weather? **4.d**

3. **Investigation Skill** Scientists learn about the weather by **gathering and recording data**. From the data you gathered, what might you **infer** about the weather for tomorrow? **6.g**

Independent Inquiry

Make Inferences from Data

Think about the data you recorded during this investigation. What inferences and predictions, if any, can you make about tomorrow's weather by using clues in today's weather data?

Plan and conduct an investigation to find out if specific observations can help you predict weather. You should search for patterns in the weather data you've already recorded. **6.g**

VOCABULARY	SCIENCE CONCEPTS	 MAIN IDEA AND DETAILS
meteorology p. 300 barometer p. 300 anemometer p. 300 hygrometer p. 300 air mass p. 302 front p. 303	▶ how weather can be predicted ▶ how to read weather maps	Look for details about how weather is measured and predicted.

Measuring Weather

The study of weather is **meteorology**. To study weather, scientists must first measure it. *Meteorologists,* scientists who study weather, use many different measuring instruments. Four important weather instruments are described below.

The measurements taken with weather instruments can be used to make weather *forecasts,* or predictions of future weather. Remember that air temperature and air pressure are related. A rising barometer reading shows increasing air pressure and often occurs just before the arrival of colder air. Since cold air usually has less water in it than warm air does, a rising barometer also means less humidity and a lower chance of rain. In contrast, a falling barometer reading often means more humidity and a higher chance of rain.

Wind is another weather factor that should be considered when making weather predictions. Several instruments can be used to measure wind. Anemometers measure

Weather Instrument	Measures
Thermometer	A thermometer measures air temperature. If the air cools down during the day or warms up in the evening, this change is a sign that rain may fall soon.
Barometer	A **barometer** measures the air pressure, which is also called *barometric pressure.* A change in the air pressure often means the weather is about to change.
Anemometer	An **anemometer** measures wind speed. Like a change in air pressure, a change in wind speed may mean that the weather is about to change.
Hygrometer	A **hygrometer** measures humidity. An increase in humidity often means it's about to rain.

In the past, people relied on simple observations to help them forecast the weather. Sayings such as "Red sky at night, sailors' delight" helped people remember what their observations might predict about the weather.

wind speed. Both *windsocks* and *wind vanes* measure wind direction. Information about wind speed and direction is important because wind often brings changes in the weather. Knowing which direction the wind is blowing from helps forecast the weather. For example, if it's winter and a wind starts blowing from the south, you can predict that the weather will soon be warmer.

People can also predict weather changes, although less accurately, just by observing the sky. For example, the clouds in the sky can tell you a lot about the weather. There's an old saying that goes "Red sky at night, sailors' delight. Red sky in the morning, sailors take warning." A red sky in the morning occurs when the rising sun reflects off clouds coming from the west. This often means it will rain later in the day. A red sunset means that no storms are approaching from the west, so the next day should be sunny.

Different cloud types are also associated with different types of weather. For example, cirrus clouds and small cumulus clouds mean fair weather is ahead. Large, gray cumulus clouds mean rain is probably on the way.

 MAIN IDEA AND DETAILS How can rising air pressure lead to a prediction about temperature?

Recording Raindrops

Tape a ruler to the inside of a jar. You have made a rain gauge. Put your rain gauge outside before a rain. When the rain stops, use the ruler to measure how much rain fell.

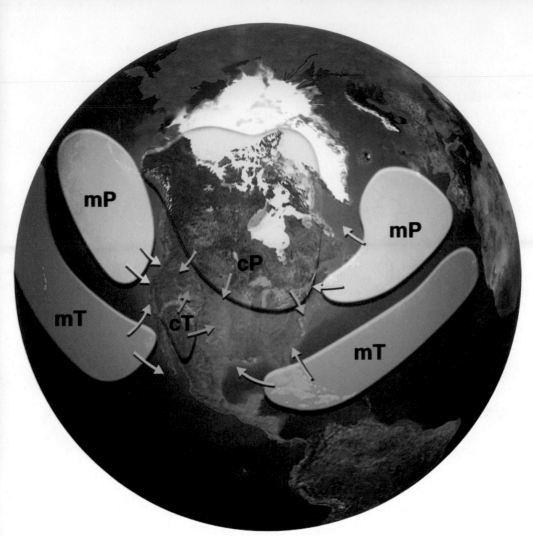

A continental air mass forms over land, so it is dry. A maritime air mass forms over water, so it is humid. A polar air mass forms over a cold area, so it is cold. A tropical air mass forms over a warm area, so it is warm.

Air Masses

You read in Lesson 1 that the sun heats Earth's atmosphere unevenly. The uneven heating causes the air to move. Air doesn't move around Earth randomly. Instead, air moves in regular, large air masses. An **air mass** is a large body of air that has the same temperature and humidity throughout.

Air masses can be warm or cold. They can also be humid or dry. What determines the characteristics of an air mass? An air mass takes on the characteristics of the region over which it forms. For example, an air mass that forms over the Pacific Ocean near the equator will be humid and warm. An air mass that forms over northern Canada will be dry and cold.

Look at the map above. Four kinds of air masses affect weather in the United States. Continental polar air masses (cP) bring cool, dry weather. Continental tropical air masses (cT) bring hot, dry weather. Maritime polar air masses (mP) bring cold, humid weather. Finally, maritime tropical air masses (mT) bring warm, humid weather.

When the weather changes in an area, the air mass over the area is changing. Because of pressure differences, changing air masses produce winds. A different air mass is replacing it. Air masses generally move from west to east across the United States.

 **MAIN IDEA AND DETAILS** What kind of air mass causes hot, humid weather?

302

Fronts

The border where two air masses meet is called a **front**. Most weather changes occur along fronts. For example, if a cold, dense air mass pushes into a warm, light air mass, the warm air is forced up. As that air moves up, it cools. Water vapor in the air condenses, and clouds form.

There are two main kinds of fronts, cold fronts and warm fronts. A cold front forms where a cold air mass moves under a warm air mass. The warm air mass is less dense, so it is pushed up and cooled. When a warm, moist air mass is suddenly cooled, much of the water vapor in the air mass condenses rapidly. This fast cooling and condensation causes heavy rain, thunderstorms, or snow. Cold fronts usually move quickly, so the storms they bring do not last long.

A warm front forms where a warm air mass moves over a cold air mass. As the warm air slowly slides up and over the cold air, stratus clouds form ahead of the front. They produce rain or snow that can last for hours.

 **MAIN IDEA AND DETAILS** What kind of weather does a cold front bring?

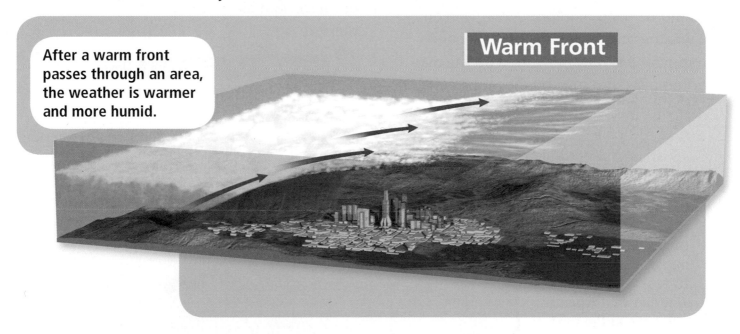

Warm Front

After a warm front passes through an area, the weather is warmer and more humid.

Cold Front

After a cold front passes through an area, the weather is cooler and drier.

Weather Maps

Have you ever used a street map to find someone's house? Another kind of map you can use is a weather map. A weather map gives information about what the weather is like in an area.

Weather maps use symbols to show the weather. A sun symbol means it's sunny in the area. The symbol of a cloud with rain means it's raining in the area. Fronts are also shown on weather maps. The symbol for a warm front is a red line with half circles on the side of the direction the front is moving. A blue line with triangles shows a cold front.

Another kind of information given on a weather map is temperature. Separate temperatures may be written on the map, or temperatures may be shown by colors.

The map's key explains what each of the symbols means.

Other information you may see on a weather map includes the high and low temperatures for that day, the wind speed and direction, and the air pressure. High- and low-pressure systems may be indicated on a weather map as well. A high-pressure system is symbolized by an *H*. High-pressure systems form where an area of cool, dense air is surrounded on all sides by lower-pressure air. A low-pressure system is symbolized on a weather map by an *L*. Low-pressure systems form where an area of warm, light air is surrounded by higher-pressure air.

Focus Skill **MAIN IDEA AND DETAILS** How is a warm front shown on a weather map?

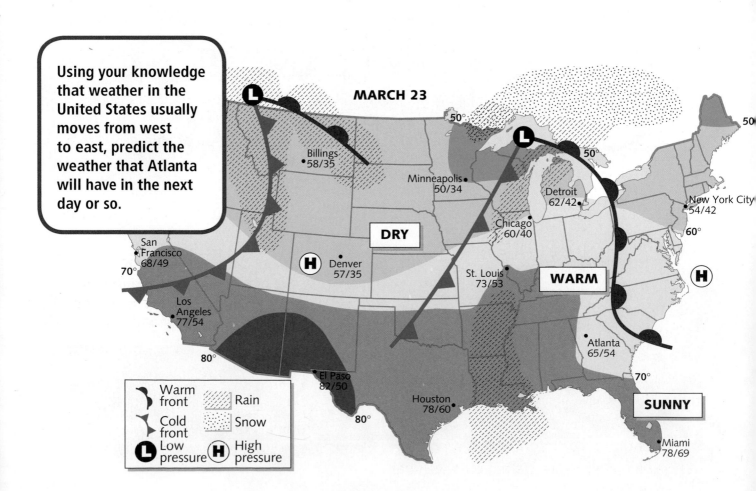

Using your knowledge that weather in the United States usually moves from west to east, predict the weather that Atlanta will have in the next day or so.

MARCH 23

Billings 58/35
Minneapolis 50/34
Detroit 62/42
New York City 54/42
Chicago 60/40
San Francisco 68/49
Denver 57/35
St. Louis 73/53
WARM
Los Angeles 77/54
Atlanta 65/54
El Paso 82/50
Houston 78/60
SUNNY
Miami 78/69
DRY

Warm front
Cold front
Low pressure
Rain
Snow
High pressure

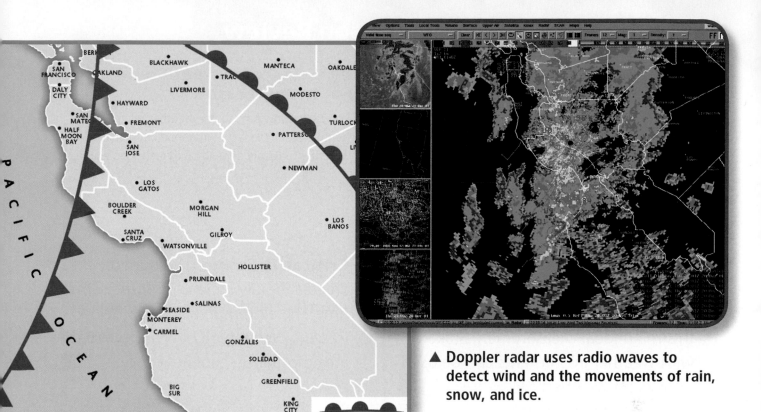

▲ Doppler radar uses radio waves to detect wind and the movements of rain, snow, and ice.

◄ This weather map shows the storm being tracked by Doppler radar.

WARM FRONT

COLD FRONT

Forecasting Weather

The information presented on a weather map is collected from different weather stations. A weather station is a place where many different instruments measure the weather. Meteorologists use weather-station data, along with data from weather satellites and other special weather instruments, to make forecasts.

Weather forecasts depend on many variables. One variable is wind direction. For example, if the wind is blowing from the north, look at a weather map to find what the weather is like just north of your location. Probably, your area will soon have the weather that's just north of you now.

Another variable to think about when forecasting the weather is air pressure. If you see a low-pressure system on a weather map, you can predict stormy weather in that area. A high-pressure system, on the other hand, usually means the weather will be fair.

Weather predictions for the near future are usually quite accurate. However, very small changes in temperature and air pressure can cause big changes in weather patterns over a few days. This effect is evidence for the *chaos theory*, the idea that very small changes can have great effects on a system. Because very small changes can affect weather systems, it still isn't possible to accurately predict the weather very far into the future.

Focus Skill **MAIN IDEA AND DETAILS** If a high-pressure system is moving into your area, what kind of weather can you expect?

Standards Wrap-Up and Lesson Review

Essential Question

How is weather predicted?

In this lesson, you learned how to use weather maps and weather data to predict weather. You also learned that weather forecasts depend on variables such as air masses and fronts.

Science Content Standards in This Lesson

4.d *Students know* how to use weather maps and data to predict local weather and know that weather forecasts depend on many variables.

1. **MAIN IDEA AND DETAILS** Draw and complete this graphic organizer to show three supporting details of this main idea: Measurements taken with weather instruments can be used to forecast weather. **4.d**

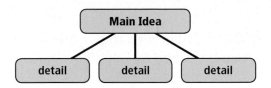

2. **SUMMARIZE** Make a list of the types of data shown on weather maps. Next to each type of data, list a weather instrument that could be used to gather that data. **4.d**

3. **DRAW CONCLUSIONS** You hear on the radio that a warm front is headed toward your town. What type of weather can you expect? **4.d**

4. **VOCABULARY** Write a paragraph explaining how the following terms are related: *air mass, front,* and *air pressure.* **4.d**

5. **Critical Thinking** The humidity in an area rapidly increases. At the same time, the air temperature falls below freezing. What type of weather will the area most likely experience soon? **4.d**

6. **Investigation Skill** Construct a table that you can use to record high and low temperatures from five different American cities. Use the weather map on page 304 to complete your table. **6.g**

7. On a weather map, cold fronts are indicated by
   A the letter H.
   B the letter L.
   C a blue line with triangles.
   D a red line with half circles. **4.d**

8. How are air masses related to the uneven heating of Earth's surface?

   The Big Idea

   A Air masses cause uneven heating.
   B Air masses are the result of uneven heating.
   C Air masses help uneven heating.
   D There is no relationship. **4.d**

Writing — ELA–W 1.1

Write a Report

Cut a weather map from a local newspaper. Use the weather map to write a report for the evening weather forecast on a local radio station. Be sure to use the correct vocabulary for the weather you are describing. Read your report aloud to the class.

Year	Total Rainfall in February	Year	Total Rainfall in February
1995	1.30	2000	5.54
1996	4.94	2001	8.87
1997	0.08	2002	0.29
1998	13.68	2003	4.64
1999	0.56	2004	4.89

9÷3 Math — SDAP 1.1

Find the Mean

Study the table, which gives the amounts of rainfall in Los Angeles during the month of February from 1995 through 2004. Find the mean, and use it to predict how much rainfall there was in Los Angeles during February 2005.

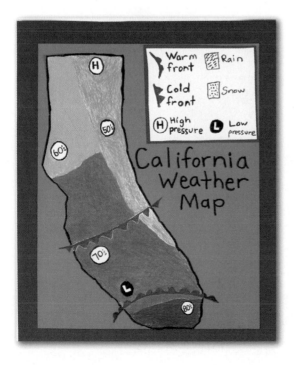

Art — VPA–VA 2.3

Draw a Weather Map

Find a weather report for your area of the state. Use the information in the weather report to make a weather map of this part of the state. Include fronts and high-pressure or low-pressure systems. Be sure to use the correct symbols when making your weather map.

For more links and activities, go to **www.hspscience.com**

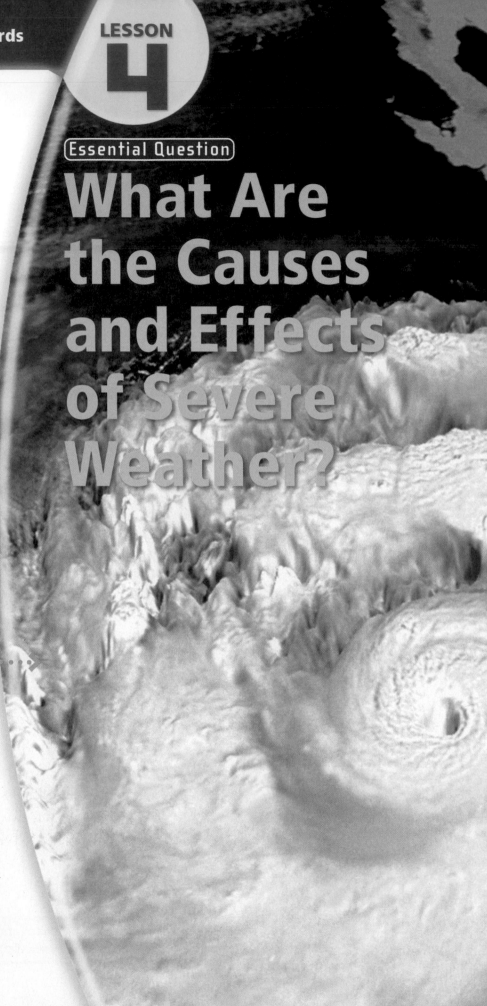

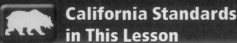
Science Content

4.c *Students know* the causes and effects of different types of severe weather.

Investigation and Experimentation

6.g Record data by using appropriate graphic representations (including charts, graphs, and labeled diagrams) and make inferences based on those data.

LESSON

4

[Essential Question]

What Are the Causes and Effects of Severe Weather?

California Fast Fact

Hurricane a-Comin'?

Plenty of hurricanes form in the eastern Pacific Ocean. But none of those hurricanes have ever actually hit California. This doesn't mean that hurricanes don't affect California's weather, however. Pacific hurricanes that slam into Mexico often move north into California, bringing heavy rains and, sometimes, strong winds with them.

Hurricane off Baja California

Vocabulary Preview

monsoon [mahn•SOON] A large wind system that reverses direction seasonally (p. 312)

hurricane [HUHR•ih•cayn] A large, rotating tropical storm system with wind speeds of at least 119 km/hr (74 mi/hr) (p. 314)

thunderstorm [THUHN•der•stawrm] A strong storm with rain, lightning, and thunder (p. 316)

tornado [tawr•NAY•doh] A violently spinning column of air that touches the ground (p. 317)

Tracking Hurricanes

Start with Questions

Severe storms are dangerous. They can damage property and injure, or even kill, people. Because of this, it is important for people to track storms.

- How can a storm be tracked?

- Have you ever tracked a storm?

After you do the Investigate, read to find out more about severe weather.

Prepare to Investigate

Investigation Skill Tip
A prediction is based on previous observations. Before you predict, think about the information you have already observed, gathered, and recorded.

Materials
- hurricane tracking map
- 3 different-colored pencils or markers
- history table for Hurricane Zelda
- current advisory for Hurricane Zelda

History of Hurricane Zelda			
Date and Time	Latitude	Longitude	Maximum Wind Speed
08/11 2:00 UT*	22.0°N	66.0°W	35 mi/hr
08/11 2:00 UT	22.5°N	67.0°W	35 mi/hr
08/11 14:00 UT	24.5°N	67.5°W	40 mi/hr
08/11 22:00 UT	25.0°N	68.0°W	45 mi/hr
08/12 1:00 UT	26.5°N	68.5°W	50 mi/hr
08/12 7:00 UT	28.5°N	70.5°W	60 mi/hr
08/12 3:00 UT	30.0°N	73.5°W	70 mi/hr
08/12 19:00 UT	31.0°N	75.0°W	75 mi/hr
08/13 1:00 UT	31.0°N	76.0°W	85 mi/hr

Forecast/ Advisory
BULLETIN

HURRICANE ZELDA FORECAST/ADVISORY NUMBER 12

NATIONAL WEATHER SERVICE MIAMI FL 13:00 UT

HURRICANE CENTER LOCATED NEAR 32°N, 78°W AT 13:00 UT AT 8/13
PRESENT MOVEMENT TOWARD THE NORTHWEST AT 20 MI PER HR

*UT means Universal Time and is the same as Greenwich Mean Time. In this 24-hour system, the time one hour after 12:00 noon is 13:00.

Follow This Procedure

1. Use the history table to plot Hurricane Zelda's path on the hurricane tracking chart. Draw a circle on the tracking chart for each location in the history table.

2. Your first circles show Zelda as a tropical depression. When the depression's winds exceed 39 mi/hr, it is **classified** as a tropical storm. Fill in the tropical-depression circles with one color. Write *Tropical Storm Zelda* under the place where the tropical depression becomes a tropical storm. Use a different color for the tropical-storm circles.

3. When winds exceed 74 mi/hr, a tropical storm becomes a hurricane. Write *Hurricane Zelda* under the place where Zelda reaches hurricane strength. Use a different color for the hurricane circles.

Step 1

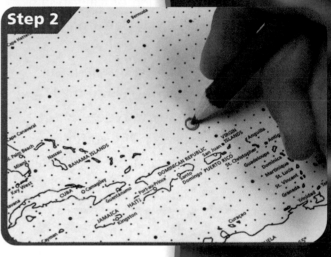

Step 2

Draw Conclusions

1. What can you **infer** from the storm's direction and wind speed?

2. **Standards Link** Use the tracking chart and the latest data on Zelda's speed and direction. **Predict** where and when the storm will strike the coast. **4.c**

3. **Investigation Skill** Scientists who track hurricanes **predict** by using probabilities. Which parts of the coastline would you give low, medium, and high probabilities of being hit by Hurricane Zelda?

Independent Inquiry > **Make Inferences from Data**

Collect data about what happens when hurricanes hit land. Make inferences about whether they continue as hurricanes. **6.g**

Research the wind speeds of a well-known hurricane before and after it struck land. Record in a chart the data you gather. Look for patterns in your data. Use these patterns to make inferences.

VOCABULARY
monsoon p. 312
hurricane p. 314
thunderstorm p. 316
tornado p. 317

SCIENCE CONCEPTS
▶ what some causes of severe weather are
▶ what some effects of severe weather are

CAUSE AND EFFECT
Look for the causes and effects of severe weather.

cause → effect

Pacific Storms

In North America, weather typically moves from the west to the east. The Pacific Ocean is west of California. Because it is to the west, it affects much of California's weather. One result is that California's weather has a monsoon pattern. A **monsoon** is a wind system that reverses its direction seasonally. You can think of a monsoon as being a land breeze in the winter and a sea breeze in the summer.

During winter, as the land cools, the air over the land cools as well. This cooler air is denser than the air above the Pacific Ocean. The dense air over the land moves toward the Pacific, forcing the warm, less dense air above the ocean to rise. Because the wind comes from the land, it is very dry. The Santa Ana winds are part of the dry phase of southern California's monsoon.

During the summer, the opposite effect occurs. The air that moves toward the land from the Pacific is very humid. When the air reaches land, it warms up, becomes

The Pacific Ocean absorbs a lot of energy from sunlight that reaches Earth. This energy can produce storms when it becomes part of the water cycle and moves into the atmosphere.

Storms coming in from the Pacific Ocean bring more than just rain. In the winter, storms that move inland are forced upward by mountains. This causes the water vapor in the air to turn into snow. *Blizzards*, or severe snowstorms, may occur.

less dense, and is forced upward. The rising air cools, and clouds form. In some places, monsoons cause huge amounts of rain to fall daily for months. In California in the summer, the monsoon leads to the formation of a marine layer—a layer of low clouds that hangs over the coast for much of the day.

Another type of Pacific weather that affects California is known as a cyclone. A *cyclone* is an air mass that is turning rapidly. There are many different kinds of cyclones, but all cyclones form in similar ways.

In Lesson 3, you learned that a low-pressure system forms where an air mass with low pressure is surrounded by air masses with higher pressure. The air with low pressure tends to rise as it is forced up by denser air that flows in. This movement forms a convection current.

Because Earth rotates, winds do not blow in straight lines. Instead, they blow in curved paths. Therefore, air blowing into a low-pressure area curves. It forms a circular wind around the low-pressure area. As the air rotates and rises, a storm forms. Winter storms can bring heavy rains to the coast and heavy snows in the mountains. On the next two pages, you will learn about different types of cyclones.

 **CAUSE AND EFFECT** What causes a cyclone to form?

313

Hurricanes and Other Cyclones

If you have ever seen a picture of a strong wind bending tall palm trees, you have an idea of the power of a hurricane. A **hurricane** is a large, rotating tropical storm system with wind speeds of at least 119 km/hr (74 mi/hr).

A hurricane might start as a cyclone over a warm ocean. The storm is first called a tropical depression, because the air pressure is low, or depressed. The winds rotate around the low-pressure center of the depression. If the winds reach a constant speed of 63 km/hr (39 mi/hr), the tropical depression is called a *tropical storm* and is given a name. As the storm grows stronger, it becomes a hurricane. About half of the tropical storms that form each year develop into hurricanes.

The eye of a hurricane is a calm center, caused by dry, cool air that is pulled down from above. Around the eye is the eye wall, the most intense part of the storm. The warm, wet air that rushes into the center of a hurricane is pulled upward in the eye wall. As the air travels upward, it causes low pressure at Earth's surface. This pulls in more air.

Water vapor that is carried up condenses into rain, releasing heat that strengthens the storm. Heat and moisture from below increase the energy of both the upward-moving and the downward-moving air.

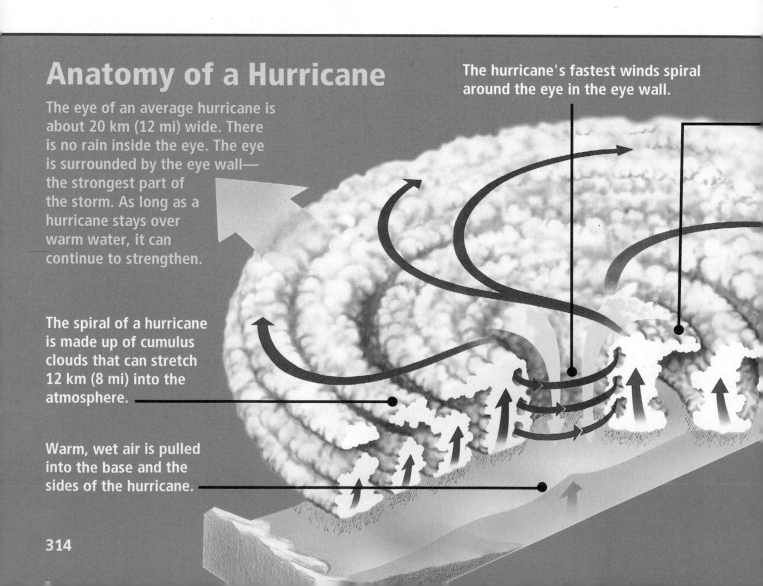

Anatomy of a Hurricane

The eye of an average hurricane is about 20 km (12 mi) wide. There is no rain inside the eye. The eye is surrounded by the eye wall— the strongest part of the storm. As long as a hurricane stays over warm water, it can continue to strengthen.

The spiral of a hurricane is made up of cumulus clouds that can stretch 12 km (8 mi) into the atmosphere.

Warm, wet air is pulled into the base and the sides of the hurricane.

The hurricane's fastest winds spiral around the eye in the eye wall.

Pushed ahead of the storm, the ocean's surface can rise by as much as 10 m (33 ft). These rises are called *storm surges*. They can be as wide as 80 to 161 km (50 to 100 mi). Storm surges can smash into coastlines with tremendous force, causing great harm to people, farm animals, and property. Other hurricane dangers include high winds, heavy rain, flooding, and tornadoes.

A typical hurricane may be as wide as 485 km (about 300 mi). It can travel for thousands of kilometers and last for more than a week. In time, it will reach cooler seas or move across land. Because the air above land is cooler and less humid, the hurricane will lose its energy source. This will cause the hurricane to weaken.

Insta-Lab

Spin the Cyclone

Place a pencil horizontally between the palms of your hands. The pencil represents a low-pressure air mass. Your hands are high-pressure air masses surrounding it. Pressing the pencil between your hands, move your right hand away from you. What happens to the pencil? How is this related to how a hurricane forms?

Hurricane is the name given to a tropical cyclone in the North Atlantic Ocean, the North Pacific Ocean east of the International Date Line, and the South Pacific Ocean east of 160°E. In the North Pacific, west of the International Date Line, a tropical cyclone is called a *typhoon.* When you hear or read about a typhoon hitting Japan or China, you will know that it is the same kind of storm we call a hurricane.

Because meteorologists can track hurricanes for a long time, people who may be in the storm's path can usually be given plenty of warning. People living near the coast may have to evacuate their homes until the danger of a storm surge has passed. People must leave mobile homes and manufactured housing, which can be severely damaged by hurricane winds. Hurricane shelters are often opened for those who have no safe place to wait for the storm to pass or who can't safely leave.

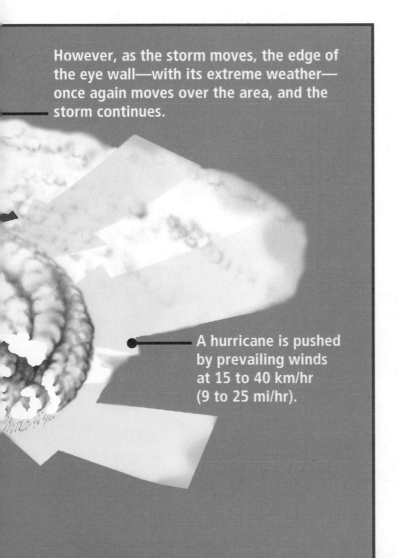

However, as the storm moves, the edge of the eye wall—with its extreme weather—once again moves over the area, and the storm continues.

A hurricane is pushed by prevailing winds at 15 to 40 km/hr (9 to 25 mi/hr).

CAUSE AND EFFECT What are three ways hurricanes cause damage?

Thunderstorms and Tornadoes

About 45,000 thunderstorms occur on Earth every day. A **thunderstorm** is a storm with rain, wind, lightning and thunder, and sometimes hail. This type of storm begins to form when warm, humid air moves upward rapidly. The sun heats an area on Earth's surface, which then warms the air mass above it. Then a cold front may push under the warm air mass, or wind may force it up.

As the warm air cools, the water vapor in it condenses and forms clouds. Soon rain begins to fall. The falling rain pulls cool air down with it. Winds blow both upward and downward in the cloud.

Electric charges build up in the bottom of the cloud. The charges travel through the air in a lightning discharge. The air along the path of a lightning bolt is so hot that the heat makes the air expand rapidly. The expansion produces sound waves, which you hear as thunder.

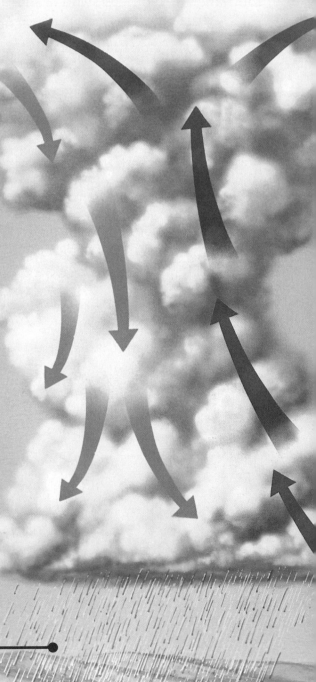

Thunderstorm updrafts can carry moisture all the way to the edge of the stratosphere. There, the storm forms a flat-topped, anvil-shaped cloud.

The large volumes of warm air being pushed upward add height to the cloud that forms. These upward movements of air, called updrafts, can reach speeds of 100 km/hr (62 mi/hr).

Falling ice crystals gather water droplets that freeze to form a coating around them. The lumps of ice—called hailstones—are carried upward by updrafts and then fall again. Each time this happens, the hailstones get bigger.

The wind speed in a tornado can reach 400 km/hr (250 mi/hr) or more. The force of a tornado's winds destroys houses, cars, and anything else in the tornado's path. The greatest danger is flying debris, or wreckage.

Most thunderstorms are over within an hour. The rain and cool air moving down through the clouds prevent more warm air from moving up into the clouds. Sometimes, however, the cool air rushing down to Earth's surface pushes more warm air up, causing another cloud to form.

Whenever meteorologists detect a strong thunderstorm, they look for another severe weather event—a tornado. A **tornado** is a violently rotating column of air that extends down from thunderstorm clouds and touches the ground. Tornadoes form in fewer than 1 percent of all thunderstorms.

A tornado forms where winds spin a column of air that bulges from the bottom of a cloud. Strong updrafts, or rising air, are already present inside this bulge. Next, warm, humid air is pulled into the often funnel-shaped column. The air spins so fast that an area of very low pressure forms in the center. The swirling funnel starts to descend. Because of the low pressure in the center of the funnel, nearby air on the ground rushes into the funnel. The air in the funnel rotates upward around the center, joining the storm above.

These violent storms can last from a few minutes to a few hours. Their paths are usually very narrow. Tornadoes are more difficult to predict than other storms are. However, meteorologists usually issue warnings that give people time to take cover.

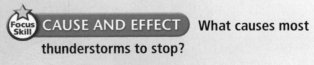

CAUSE AND EFFECT What causes most thunderstorms to stop?

317

Standards Wrap-Up and Lesson Review

Essential Question

What are the causes and effects of severe weather?

In this lesson, you learned about the causes and the effects of severe weather, such as Pacific storms, hurricanes and other cyclones, thunderstorms, and tornados.

Science Content Standards in This Lesson

4.c *Students know* the causes and effects of different types of severe weather.

---

1. **(Focus Skill) CAUSE AND EFFECT** Draw and complete this graphic organizer to show the effects of hurricanes and other cyclones. **4.c**

cause ➞ effect

2. **SUMMARIZE** Write a summary describing three different types of severe weather that affect California. **4.c**

3. **DRAW CONCLUSIONS** Why is a wooden house an unsafe place to be during a tornado? **4.c**

4. **VOCABULARY** Write four sentences briefly describing *thunderstorms*, *monsoons, hurricanes,* and *tornadoes.* **4.c**

5. **Critical Thinking** Why do most thunderstorms form in the afternoon? **4.c**

6. **Investigation Skill** Make a table or graph that shows the differences between a tropical depression, a tropical storm, and a hurricane. **6.g**

7. The most violent weather in a hurricane is in the
   A eye.
   B spiral.
   C eye wall.
   D downdraft. **4.c**

8. How does uneven heating of Earth's surface help produce hurricanes and other cyclones?

   The Big Idea

   A Hurricanes form over warm, tropical oceans.
   B Hurricanes need cold land masses to form.
   C Hurricanes are nothing more than strong sea breezes.
   D Uneven heating has nothing to do with hurricane formation. **4.c**

Hurricane	Cost of damage in dollars
Charley	14 billion
Frances	9 billion
Ivan	14.2 billion
Jeanne	6.9 billion
Dennis	4.5 billion
Katrina	80 billion

 Writing ELA–W 1.1

Narrative Writing

Write a description of a severe weather event that you have experienced. If you have never lived through severe weather, interview a family member about a weather event he or she has seen. When you write the description, be sure to include information about the effects of the storm.

 Math NS 2.1

Adding Decimals

The 2004 and 2005 hurricane seasons were among the worst on record. A total of six major hurricanes struck the southeastern United States. The chart at the right shows the cost of the damage done by each of the hurricanes. What is the total cost of the damage done by the six hurricanes?

 Health

Storm Safety Steps

Research the steps that people can take to protect themselves during severe storms. Make a pamphlet that lists tips for each type of storm. Illustrate the pamphlet, and share it with your family.

 For more links and activities, go to **www.hspscience.com**

Santa Ana Winds

Hot, dry winds blow into the Los Angeles area each year. They're called Santa Ana winds, or just the Santa Anas. Some people blame them on hot air from the Mojave desert. However, these winds occur during late fall and winter, when the desert is cooler. So what could be the real cause?

Los Angeles

This satellite photo shows smoke from wildfires being blown out to sea by Santa Ana winds.

Air Pressure and Geography

Santa Ana winds do begin in the Mojave desert. They actually start with colder air. The lower temperatures cause dense, high-pressure air masses. The high-pressure air flows toward areas of lower pressure. The air flows out toward the coast, through valleys in the San Gabriel and Santa Ana Mountains.

When the Santa Ana winds begin, they are cool, dry, and gentle flows of air. As they move toward the coast, they are changed. These changes are what make the winds unpleasant and dangerous.

Cool, dry air

Santa Ana winds

Squeezing and Drying Out

When air flows through a narrow opening, it speeds up. When the winds from the Mojave move into valleys, they speed up. To be called a Santa Ana wind, the speed must be at least 45 kilometers (28 miles) per hour. Santa Ana winds have gusts of 90 kilometers (56 miles) per hour or more. Air pressure increases as you move closer to sea level. As air flows downhill, it's squeezed by this higher pressure. Squeezing warms the air. Santa Ana winds get about 10°C warmer with each kilometer they move downward. By the time they reach the coast, they are hot, fast, and rough!

Think and Write

❶ How does this article relate to what you've learned about air pressure and causes of weather? **4.a**

❷ What two properties make Santa Ana winds dangerous?

▶ Visual Summary

Tell how each picture helps explain the **Big Idea**.

The Big Idea Energy from the sun heats Earth unevenly. This causes air movements that result in changing weather.

4.a, 4.e

Air Pressure and Convection
Water and land warm up and cool down differently. This causes convection currents and wind. It also affects air pressure.

4.b, 4.d

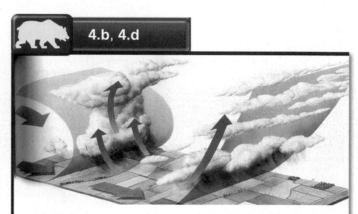

Air Masses and the Water Cycle
Tracking air masses helps predict weather. Temperature and pressure changes indicate moving air masses. Precipitation usually happens along fronts.

4.c

Severe Weather
Fronts can produce severe weather such as tornadoes, thunderstorms, and blizzards. Hurricanes are also severe storms.

Show What You Know

Unit Writing Activity

Write a Persuasive Letter

Energy from the sun heats Earth unevenly, resulting in changing weather patterns. Learning more about the sun might allow us to better predict severe weather events. Write a persuasive letter to your local representative in Congress, asking for greater funding for weather research. Include specific information about what you know about uneven heating of the earth's surface. Explain how more weather research might benefit people in your community.

Unit Project

Forecast Broadcast

Plan, write, and produce a weather forecast. You will need a script, maps, current weather data, and a place to perform the forecast. If possible, videotape the forecast. Be sure to share the responsibilities fairly.

323

Vocabulary Review

Use the terms below to complete the sentences. The page numbers tell you where to look in the unit if you need help.

air pressure p. 272

prevailing wind p. 276

precipitation p. 290

barometer p. 300

hygrometer p. 300

air mass p. 302

front p. 303

hurricane p. 314

1. Water that falls from the air to Earth is _____. **4.b**

2. A global wind that blows constantly in the same direction is a _____. **4.a**

3. The weight of the atmosphere due to gravity is called _____. **4.e**

4. A large body of air that has the same temperature and humidity is an _____. **4.c**

5. The border between two air masses is a _____. **4.c**

6. A tropical storm with winds greater than 119 km/hr is a _____. **4.c**

7. Air pressure is measured with a ____. **4.d**

8. Humidity is measured with a _____. **4.d**

Check Understanding

Choose the best answer.

9. **MAIN IDEA AND DETAILS** Which statement is **true** about air pressure? **4.e**
   A It is the same throughout an air mass.
   B It is the same everywhere on Earth.
   C It is lower in cold air than in warm air.
   D It increases with height above Earth.

10. What causes winds? **4.a**
    A the rotation of Earth on its axis
    B the movement of ocean currents
    C the evaporation of surface water
    D the uneven heating of the atmosphere

11. How does the process occurring on the outside of the glass in the picture below relate to weather? **4.b**
    A Water freezes along fronts.
    B Water evaporates to form winds.
    C Water flows in ocean currents.
    D Water condenses to form precipitation.

12. What type of weather does the California Current bring to California? **4.b**

A dry weather   C warm weather

B cool weather   D windy weather

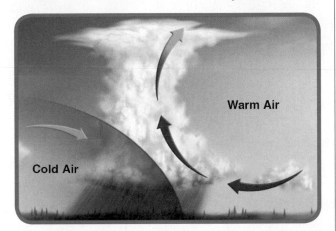

Warm Air

Cold Air

13. What is shown in the picture above? **4.d**

A tornado   C cold front

B hurricane   D warm front

14. What type of weather would most likely occur if a cold front moved into your area? **4.d**

A stormy weather   C sunny weather

B warm weather   D cloudy weather

15. CAUSE AND EFFECT What is the cause of a hurricane? **4.c**

A Electric charges in the air build up.

B Air masses collide along a cold front.

C Ocean currents push volatile winds in a circle.

D Air around a low-pressure system begins rotating.

16. Which of the following types of weather can cause rain to fall for months at a time? **4.c**

A a hurricane   C a thunderstorm

B a monsoon   D a tornado

Investigation Skills

17. Which do you infer will heat up faster on a sunny day—a pond or a meadow? Explain your answer. **6.g**

18. What two instruments are most important for measuring a region's weather? Explain your answer. **6.f**

Critical Thinking

19. Draw a picture of the type of cloud that may cause drizzle and a picture of the type that may cause thunderstorms. Label your drawings. **4.d**

20. Weather never stays the same for very long. Several factors affect weather changes. Explain what causes air pressure in an area to change.

The **Big** Idea

UNIT 5
EARTH SCIENCE

The Solar System

California Standards in This Unit

5 The solar system consists of planets and other bodies that orbit the Sun in predictable paths. As a basis for understanding this concept:

5.a *Students know* the Sun, an average star, is the central and largest body in the solar system and is composed primarily of hydrogen and helium.

5.b *Students know* the solar system includes the planet Earth, the Moon, the Sun, eight other planets and their satellites, and smaller objects, such as asteroids and comets.

5.c *Students know* the path of a planet around the Sun is due to the gravitational attraction between the Sun and the planet.

This unit also includes these Investigation and Experimentation Standards: **6.b 6.g 6.i**

What's the Big Idea?

The solar system consists of planets and other bodies that orbit the sun in predictable paths.

Essential Questions

Dear Chase,

We just got home from our trip to Edwards Air Force Base. We took a tour of the base and saw an Air Force show. The best part of the day was seeing a space shuttle landing. It was awesome! I'd like to be an astronaut someday. I can imagine all the amazing things I could see from the space shuttle.

I'll see you soon!

Chandler

What objects in space might an astronaut be able to observe from a space shuttle? How does this relate to the **Big Idea?**

Unit Inquiry

Model of the Solar System

Our solar system is made up of nine unique planets. It takes Earth 365.26 days, which we round off to 365 and call one year, to travel around the sun. Do the other planets take the same amount of time to orbit the sun? Build a model of the solar system. Plan and conduct an investigation to find out.

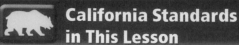

California Standards in This Lesson

Science Content

5.a *Students know* the Sun, an average star, is the central and largest body in the solar system and is composed primarily of hydrogen and helium.

Investigation and Experimentation

6.b Develop a testable question

LESSON

1

Essential Question

What Is the Sun?

A solar eclipse in San Diego, California

star [STAR] A huge ball of very hot gases in space (p. 332)

sun [SUHN] The star at the center of the solar system (p. 332)

fusion [FYOO•zhuhn] The energy-producing reaction that occurs inside stars (p. 336)

Sunspots

Directed Inquiry

Start with Questions

From Earth, the sun always seems to be the same.

- Is the sun really always the same?

- What changes might take place on the sun?

Investigate to find out. Then read to discover more.

Prepare to Investigate

> **Investigation Skill Tip**
> A prediction is based on previous observations. Before you predict, think about what you observed.

Materials

- white paper
- tape
- clipboard
- scissors
- small telescope or binoculars
- large piece of cardboard

Make an Observation Chart

Date	Time	Observations

Follow This Procedure

CAUTION: Never look directly at the sun.

1. Tape the paper to the clipboard.

2. Center the eyepiece of the telescope on the cardboard. Trace a circle around the eyepiece. Cut out the circle. Fit the eyepiece into the hole.

3. Point the telescope or binoculars at the sun, and focus the sun's image on the white paper. **Observe** the image of the sun on the paper.

4. On the observation chart, outline the image of the sun. Shade any dark spots you see; these are sunspots. **Record** the date and time.

5. Repeat Step 4 on each sunny day for several days. **Record** the date, the time, and the positions of the sunspots each day.

Step 3

Step 5

Draw Conclusions

1. How did the positions of the sunspots change over several days?

2. **Standards Link** What can you **infer** from the movement of sunspots? **5.a**

3. **Investigation Skill** Scientists make **predictions** from what they observe. How can you use the movement of sunspots to **predict** the time it takes the sun to make one complete rotation?

Independent Inquiry

Develop a Testable Question

Think about your observations during this investigation. Hypothesize whether sunspots change in size. Plan and conduct a simple investigation to test this hypothesis. **6.b**

Write a plan to test your question. Your plan should include the materials you will need and the procedure steps.

VOCABULARY
star p. 332
sun p. 332
fusion p. 336

SCIENCE CONCEPTS
▶ what the sun is like
▶ how the sun produces energy

Focus Skill **MAIN IDEA AND DETAILS**
Look for details about the sun and how it produces energy.

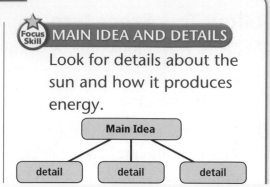

Stars

You've probably looked up at the stars in the night sky and noticed some of their features. You may know that a **star** is a huge sphere, or ball of very hot gases. The **sun** is the star at the center of the solar system. From Earth, the sun looks like a large ball of light.

The sun is the source of most energy on Earth. Without it, life on Earth could not exist. The sun is also responsible for wind and other weather on Earth. Recall that as the sun's rays strike Earth's surface, land heats up faster than water. This uneven heating causes wind by producing differences in air pressure.

The sun is important to us on Earth, but it is just one of billions of stars in the universe. Among stars, the sun is average—it's a yellow star of medium size. Like other stars, the sun is made up of gases, mostly hydrogen and helium.

One way scientists classify stars is by color. Star colors range from blue, white, and yellow to orange and red. Color is a clue to a star's surface temperature. Blue stars are the hottest, and red stars are the coolest. Compared to other stars, the sun has a medium surface temperature.

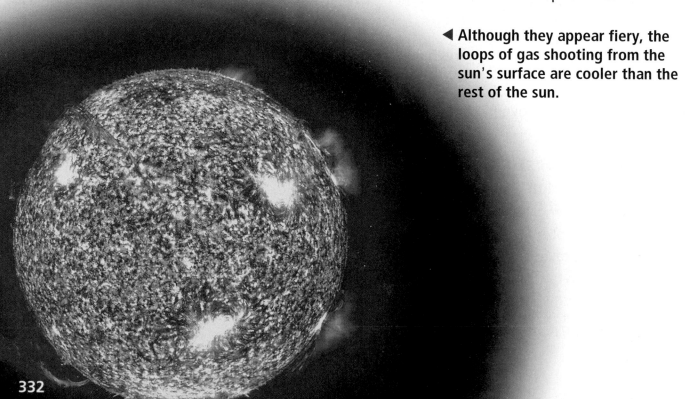

◀ **Although they appear fiery, the loops of gas shooting from the sun's surface are cooler than the rest of the sun.**

▲ Stars are classified by their
size, temperature, and color.

Another way scientists classify stars is
by brightness. How bright a star appears
depends on two factors. One is how far it is
from Earth. Being the closest star to Earth,
the sun is the brightest object in the sky.
The other factor that determines brightness
is the size of the star. Compared with other
stars, the sun's brightness is about average.

The sun is larger than everything else in
the solar system. It has a diameter of about
1.4 million km (860,000 mi), more than
100 times Earth's. The sun's volume is so
great, it could hold one million Earths.

Focus Skill **MAIN IDEA AND DETAILS** What are two
ways that scientists classify stars?

The sun is huge. Suppose 333,000
marbles fit in this container. If one
marble represents the mass of Earth,
the container of marbles represents
the mass of the sun. ▼

333

Features of the Sun

Since the sun is so much closer to Earth than other stars are, astronomers study it in detail to try to understand all stars. They have discovered that the sun has several layers. The layers don't have definite boundaries. Instead, each layer blends into the next.

At the center of the sun is the core. As you can see below, the core is small compared to the entire sun. However, most of the sun's mass is in its core. As energy from the sun's core moves outward, it passes through the *radiation zone*. The energy heats this layer in the same way a radiator warms the air in a room. Energy then moves to the sun's outer layer, the *convection zone*. From here, energy moves to the sun's surface by a process called convection. In convection, cooler, denser matter is pulled down by gravity, pushing warmer, less dense matter up.

The surface of the sun is known as the *photosphere,* or "sphere of light." This is

Science Up Close

For more links and animations, go to **www.hspscience.com**

The Sun's Structure

The photosphere has a grainy look. Its surface is made up of hot, bright areas called granules, surrounded by cooler, darker areas. A solar flare, at the far right, is a brief burst of energy and matter from the sun's photosphere.

The sun's corona, or atmosphere, is visible only during an eclipse. Streams of tiny particles, called the solar wind, travel outward from the corona throught hte solar system.

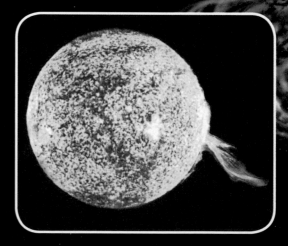

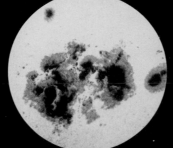

A sunspot is a dark area on the photosphere. Sunspots appear dark because they are cooler than the rest of the sun. Many sunspots are larger than Earth.

mostly what we see from Earth. Above the photosphere is the sun's atmosphere. This area of hot gases extends about 1 million km (600,000 mi) from the photosphere.

The sun has several features at or near its surface. Bright spots on the photosphere are called granules. They are the tops of columns of rising gases in the convection layer. Darker areas between granules contain cooler gases.

Sunspots, like the ones you observed in the Investigate, are dark, cooler areas of the sun. For the past few hundred years, scientists have recorded the number of sunspots they observe each year. They have noticed that the number increases and decreases over a period of about 11 years. This is called the sunspot cycle. Sunspots can produce brief bursts of energy and matter from the photosphere. These bursts are called solar flares.

 **MAIN IDEA AND DETAILS** What are the layers of the sun?

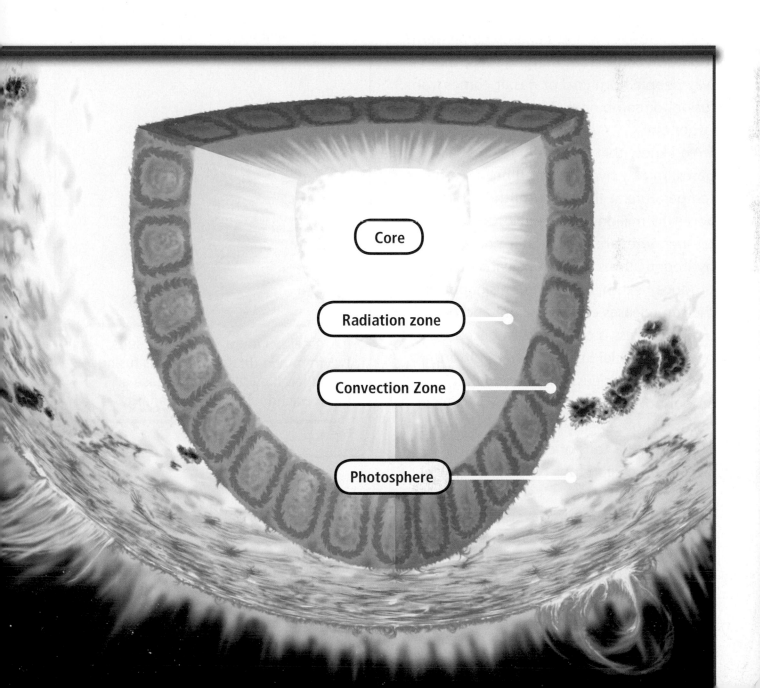

Core

Radiation zone

Convection Zone

Photosphere

How the Sun Produces Energy

The sun is the source of energy for most life on Earth. Plants use the sun's energy to make food energy through the process of photosynthesis. When an animal eats plants, it gets food energy that came from the sun. If the animal is eaten, the sun's energy is passed along again.

When organisms die, they decay. Some organisms that died long ago became fossil fuels, which are used today to light and heat homes and to run cars. That energy, too, originally came from the sun.

Where does the sun's energy come from? It doesn't come from burning fuels, the way people burn coal or gas. It comes from fusing, or combining, small particles into larger ones.

You know that the sun is a huge ball of gases, mostly hydrogen and helium. The temperature at the center of the sun is about 15 million °C (27 million °F). At that temperature, and under enormous pressure, hydrogen atoms smash into each other and produce helium. Every time this happens, the sun releases energy as light and heat.

This process is called **fusion** because two hydrogen nuclei fuse, or join, to produce one helium nucleus. The fusion of an amount of hydrogen the size of a pinhead releases more energy than the burning of about 1000 tons of coal. The sun fuses about 600 million tons of hydrogen every second.

Energy from the sun travels in waves, as shown in the illustration. The amount of energy in waves varies. Some waves have more energy than others. This range of energy is called the *electromagnetic*

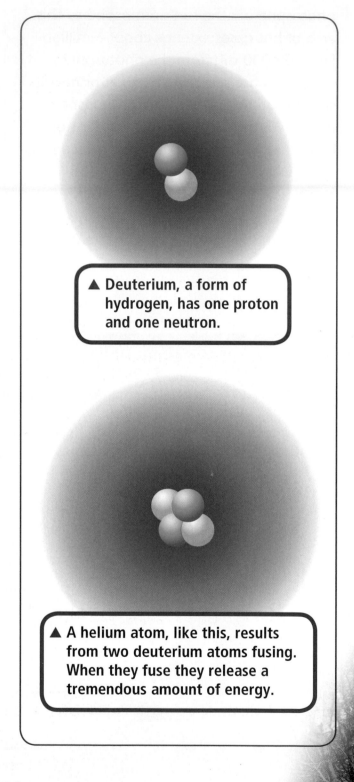

▲ Deuterium, a form of hydrogen, has one proton and one neutron.

▲ A helium atom, like this, results from two deuterium atoms fusing. When they fuse they release a tremendous amount of energy.

spectrum. We see some of the energy as visible light. We feel infrared waves as heat. The sun also produces radio waves, which are picked up as static on radios and TVs. Some of the sun's energy, such as X rays, can be harmful to life on Earth. However, the atmosphere keeps most harmful rays from reaching Earth's surface.

 **MAIN IDEA AND DETAILS** How does the sun produce energy?

Insta-Lab

Distance and Heat

Hold a thermometer 40 cm from a light bulb. (Don't use a fluorescent light.) After two minutes, record the temperature. Repeat, holding the thermometer 30, 20, and 10 cm from the bulb. How does distance from the source affect the amount of heat that reaches an object?

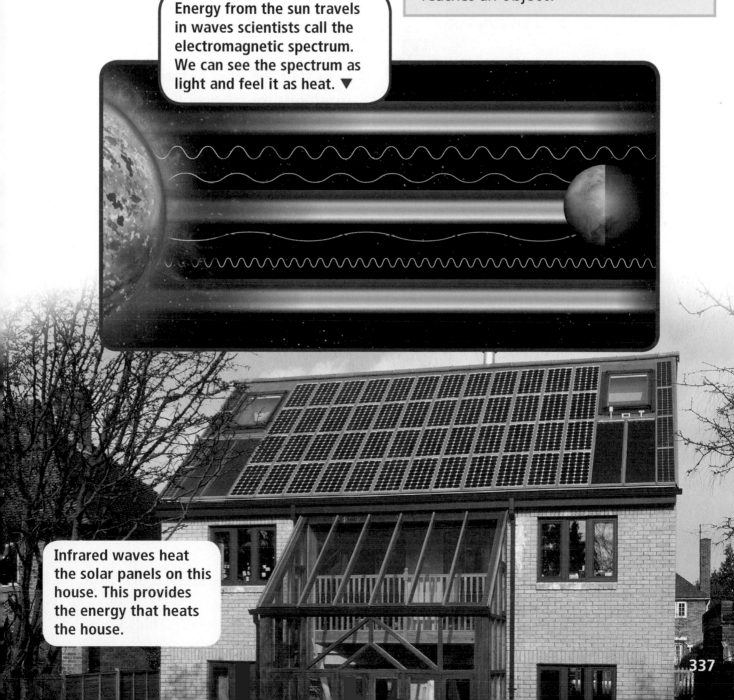

Energy from the sun travels in waves scientists call the electromagnetic spectrum. We can see the spectrum as light and feel it as heat. ▼

Infrared waves heat the solar panels on this house. This provides the energy that heats the house.

Standards Wrap-Up and Lesson Review

What is the sun?

In this lesson, you learned that the sun is an average star that is made up mostly of hydrogen and helium. The fusion of hydrogen into helium produces most of the sun's energy.

 Science Content Standards in This Lesson

5.a *Students know* the Sun, an average star, is the central and largest body in the solar system and is composed primarily of hydrogen and helium.

1. **MAIN IDEA AND DETAILS** Draw and complete a graphic organizer to show the supporting details for this main idea: The sun is an average star. **5.a**

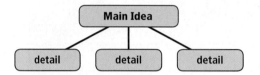

```
        Main Idea
    ┌───────┼───────┐
  detail  detail  detail
```

2. **SUMMARIZE** Write two or three sentences to summarize the main ideas of the lesson. **5.a**

3. **DRAW CONCLUSIONS** If the sun were a red star or a blue star, how would it be different? **5.a**

4. **VOCABULARY** How are the terms *sun* and *star* related? **5.a**

5. **Critical Thinking** The energy in solar flares consists of radio waves as well as other waves. How might a huge solar flare affect Earth? **5.a**

6. **Investigate and Experiment** What questions might scientists ask when studying features of the sun? **6.b**

7. Solar flares are loops of gas from the sun's _____.
   A core
   B photosphere
   C convection zone
   D radiation zone **5.a**

8. How is the sun different from other stars?
   A It is the center of our solar system.
   B It is made up of gases.
   C It gives off energy.
   D It gives off light. **5.a**

 The **Big Idea**

  Writing   ELA–W 5.2

Write a Report

What more would you like to know about the sun? Write a question you would like to answer. Do research to find the answer, and then write a report about your findings.

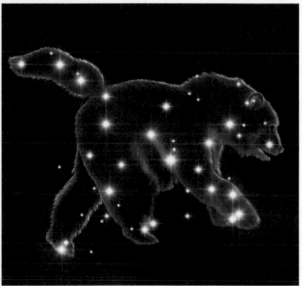

  Math   NS 5.1

Calculate Distance

Find out the name of a star in the constellation Ursa Major. Then find out the star's distance from Earth in light-years. One light-year is equal to about 9.5 trillion km. Calculate the distance of your star in kilometers. Write the distance in scientific notation.

  Art   VPA–VA 5.2

Energy Art

Make a work of art that shows how the sun produces energy. The art does not have to show how things actually happen or look. Instead, you can use shapes, forms, and colors to represent the process. The ideas in the art should be correct, however.

 For more links and activities, go to **www.hspscience.com**

Catching Some Rays

For most people, "catching some rays" means putting on some sunscreen and working on your tan. To a group of NASA scientists, catching some rays meant sending a robot spacecraft named *Genesis* around the sun to collect and bring home tiny bits of solar dust. By studying those dust particles, scientists hope to be able to find out more about how our solar system formed.

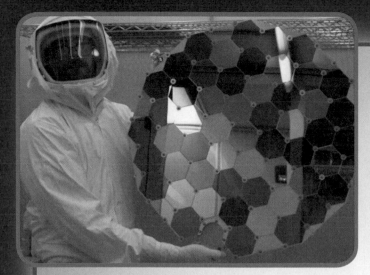

Although scientists are not sure what the solar nebula was like, they hope that samples from the sun's solar wind will give them some clues. For example, scientists believe the solar wind contains the same kinds of elements as the solar nebula. By capturing the elements from the solar wind, scientists hope to learn how those elements formed the canyons on Mars, Earth's oceans, and the moons of Jupiter.

An Unfortunate Ending

The *Genesis* mission, however, did not go entirely as planned. The spacecraft, which was launched August 8, 2001, returned to Earth's atmosphere on September 8, 2004.

Upon arrival, the spacecraft was to deploy parachutes that would allow it to descend slowly to the ground. At the same time, helicopters were in position to snatch the craft before it landed. Unfortunately, the parachutes did not deploy, and the craft slammed into the ground in Utah.

Although the craft was badly damaged, scientists were able to retrieve many of the samples collected during the three-year mission. They are confident they will learn something from the materials collected.

A Dusty Wind

The *solar wind* that *Genesis* passed through is a high-speed stream of tiny particles given off by the sun. Those particles rush through the solar system at about 1.6 million km (1 million mi) per hour. Astronomers hypothesize that everything in the solar system, including the sun, planets, moons, comets, and asteroids, formed about 4.5 billion years ago from a large, swirling cloud of gas and dust called the *solar nebula*.

Like a Flytrap

How did the craft collect its samples? When *Genesis* was passing through the solar wind about 1.6 million km (1 million mi) from Earth, scientists signaled the probe to flip its lid. Once the probe's top was open, five collector plates—the size of bicycle tires—swung out and acted like giant flytraps, collecting stray bits of solar dust. Once through the solar wind, the traps were lowered.

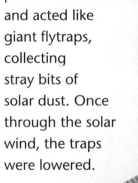

 ## Think and Write

① Why is it important for scientists to study the origins of the solar system? **5.b**

② From which materials do scientists think the solar system was created? **5.b**

 Find out more. Log on to **www.hspscience.com**

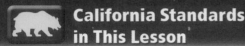

Science Content

5.b *Students know* the solar system includes the planet Earth, the Moon, the Sun, eight other planets and their satellites, and smaller objects such as asteroids and comets.

Investigation and Experimentation

6.g Record data by using appropriate graphic representations (including charts, graphs, and labeled diagrams) and make inferences based on those data

California Fast Fact

Planetariums

Long ago, most planetariums were small models of our solar system. Today, the planetarium at the Griffith Observatory in California allows visitors to view on a large indoor dome the positions of the sun, the moon, the planets, and distant stars.

LESSON 2

Essential Question

What Makes Up the Solar System?

solar system [SOH•ler SIS•tuhm] A star and all the planets and other objects that revolve around it (p. 346)

planet [PLAN•it] A body that revolves around a star (p. 346)

satellite [SAT•uh•lyt] A body in space that orbits a larger body (p. 346)

asteroid [AS•ter•oyd] A piece of rock and metal that orbits the sun (p. 350)

comet [KAHM•it] A ball of ice, rock, and frozen gases that orbits the sun (p. 350)

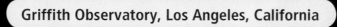

Griffith Observatory, Los Angeles, California

The Solar System

Directed Inquiry

Start with Questions

At night, you can see bright points of light in the sky. A few of these are the planets that are closest to Earth. From Earth, they look tiny.

- How big are the planets?

- What is the order of the planets from the sun?

Investigate to find out. Then read to find out more.

Prepare to Investigate

Investigation Skill Tip
Inferences are ideas that come from data you gather and record using a graphic representation.

Materials

- 10 balloons
- marker
- tape
- meterstick
- 10 straws

Planetary Information		
Planet	Diameter (km)	Distance from Sun (km)
Mercury	4,878	58 million
Venus	12,100	108 million
Earth	12,756	150 million
Mars	6,786	228 million
Jupiter	142,984	778 million
Saturn	120,536	1,424 million
Uranus	51,108	2,867 million
Neptune	49,538	4,488 million
Pluto*	2,350	5,909 million

*In 2006, the International Astronomical Union classified Pluto as a "dwarf planet."

Follow This Procedure

1. Choose a safe area outside your school for your "solar system."

2. Study the table on page 344. Then, **use numbers** to decide on a scale for the distances in your solar system. For example, you might have 1 cm equal 1 million km.

3. Calculate the distances you will use. Write them down.

4. Blow up 10 balloons, and tape each balloon to a straw. Use the marker to label one balloon as the sun and the others as the planets.

5. Push the straw with the sun balloon into the ground at one end of your solar system. Use the meterstick to measure the distance from the sun to each planet. Push each planet's straw into the ground at the correct position.

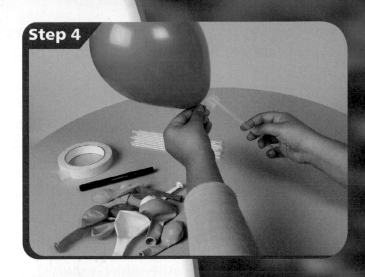

Step 4

Step 5

Draw Conclusions

1. How did you choose a scale for your solar system?

2. **Standards Link** In your solar system, which two planets are closest to each other? `5.b`

3. **Investigation Skill** How did your data help you make **inferences** in this Investigate? `6.g`

Independent Inquiry ▸

Record Data and Make Inferences

Think about the data you gathered. What other data could you gather about the planets? What inferences could you make from that data? `6.g`

Write a plan for an investigation in which you gather data and make inferences. Include the materials you will need, the procedure steps, and the data you will need to gather.

VOCABULARY
solar system p. 346
planet p. 346
satellite p. 346
asteroid p. 350
comet p. 350

SCIENCE CONCEPTS
▶ what objects make up the solar system
▶ what the planets are like

Focus Skill **MAIN IDEA AND DETAILS**
Look for main ideas about the planets and other objects in the solar system.

Main Idea

detail   detail   detail

The Inner Planets

A **solar system** is made up of a star and all the planets and other objects that revolve around that star. Our solar system includes nine planets. A **planet** is a body that revolves around a star. The force of gravity between the star and the planet holds the planet in orbit. Most planets in the solar system have moons, or satellites. A **satellite** is a body that revolves around a planet. Scientists classify the planets that orbit the sun as either inner planets or outer planets.

The four inner planets are Mercury, Venus, Earth, and Mars. All the inner planets are rocky and dense. Mercury, which is closest to the sun, is about the size of Earth's moon. Like the moon, Mercury has no atmosphere and a surface covered with craters and dust. The side of Mercury that faces the sun is hot—about 430°C (810°F). The side not facing the sun can become very cold, however—about –180°C (–290°F).

Venus is the brightest object in the night sky, after the moon. This planet is about the same size as Earth. Venus can become very hot, reaching about 460°C (860°F). It's even hotter than Mercury because Venus's thick atmosphere keeps heat from escaping.

Earth's atmosphere and its liquid water make it the only planet known to support

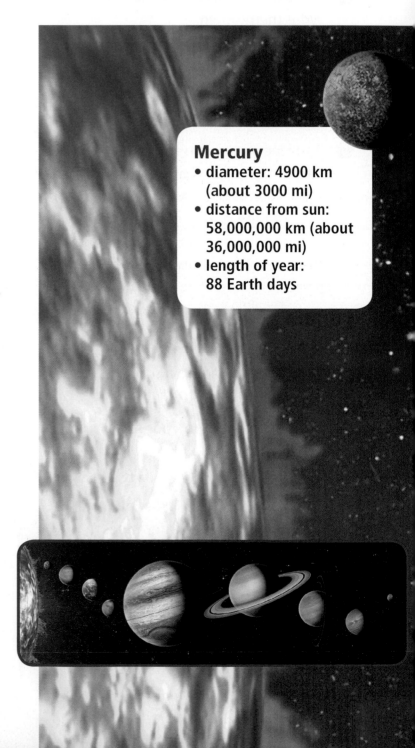

Mercury
- diameter: 4900 km (about 3000 mi)
- distance from sun: 58,000,000 km (about 36,000,000 mi)
- length of year: 88 Earth days

life. Earth's atmosphere keeps the planet at temperatures at which living things can survive.

Mars is called the red planet because of its reddish soil. Its atmosphere is mostly carbon dioxide. Its "river" valleys are evidence that Mars once had liquid water. Mars has the largest volcano in the solar system, and it has dust storms that can last for months.

Focus Skill **MAIN IDEA AND DETAILS** What do all of the inner planets have in common?

Math in Science
Interpret Data

Weight on Different Planets

The pull of gravity at a planet's surface depends on the planet's diameter and on how much mass the planet has. The greater the planet's pull of gravity, the more you would weigh on its surface. Here are the weights on different planets for a person who weighs 100 pounds on Earth.

Planet	Weight (lb)
Mercury	37.8
Earth	100.0
Venus	90.7
Mars	37.7

■ Does Venus have a stronger or weaker pull of gravity than Earth?

Venus
- diameter: 12,100 km (about 7520 mi)
- distance from sun: 108,000,000 km (about 67,000,000 mi)
- length of year: 225 Earth days

Earth
- diameter: 12,700 km (about 7900 mi)
- distance from sun: 150,000,000 km (about 93,000,000 mi)
- length of year: 365.25 Earth days

Mars
- diameter: 6800 km (about 4200 mi)
- distance from sun: 228,000,000 km (about 142,000,000 mi)
- length of year: 687 Earth days

The Outer Planets

Beyond the inner planets are the five outer planets. In order from the sun, they are Jupiter, Saturn, Uranus, Neptune, and Pluto. The first four of these planets are called gas giants, because they are very large and made up mostly of the gases hydrogen and helium.

Jupiter is the largest planet in the solar system. It has a ring, and dozens of moons, including Ganymede [GAN•ih•meed], the largest moon in the solar system. There is a huge storm on Jupiter that has lasted for 400 years. This storm has been named the Great Red Spot, which describes how it looks from Earth.

Saturn is best known for its rings, which are made of ice, dust, boulders, and frozen gases. The rings stretch about 136,200 km (84,650 mi) from the center of the planet. Like Jupiter, Saturn has dozens of moons. Jupiter and Saturn are the only outer planets that can be seen without a telescope.

Uranus also has many moons and rings. This planet rotates on an axis that is tilted much more than those of the other planets. Compared with other planets, Uranus seems to be rolling around its orbit rather than spinning.

Neptune has several rings and moons and the strongest winds in the solar system. The winds can reach 2000 km/hr (1200 mi/hr)! Both Neptune and Uranus are similar in size.

Pluto is small and rocky, unlike the other outer planets. It also has an unusual orbit. Part of its orbit passes inside the orbit of Neptune, so sometimes Neptune is the farthest planet from the sun. Pluto's moon, Charon [KER•uhn], is nearly as big as the planet itself. Some scientists claim that Pluto does not qualify as a planet because it is

Jupiter
- diameter: 143,000 km (about 89,000 mi)
- distance from sun: 778,000,000 km (about 483,000,000 mi)
- length of year: 11.9 Earth years

unlike the other planets in the solar system. Other scientists say that Pluto and Charon form a double planet. They are about the same size, and they are made of very similar materials.

Scientists recently gathered data that shows there may even be more planets in the solar system. One object, called Sedna, is the most distant object in the solar system. It is almost 10 billion miles from the sun. Some scientists hypothesize that the surface of Sedna is similar to that of Pluto—cold and very icy. Sedna is three-quarters the size of Pluto, so some scientists argue

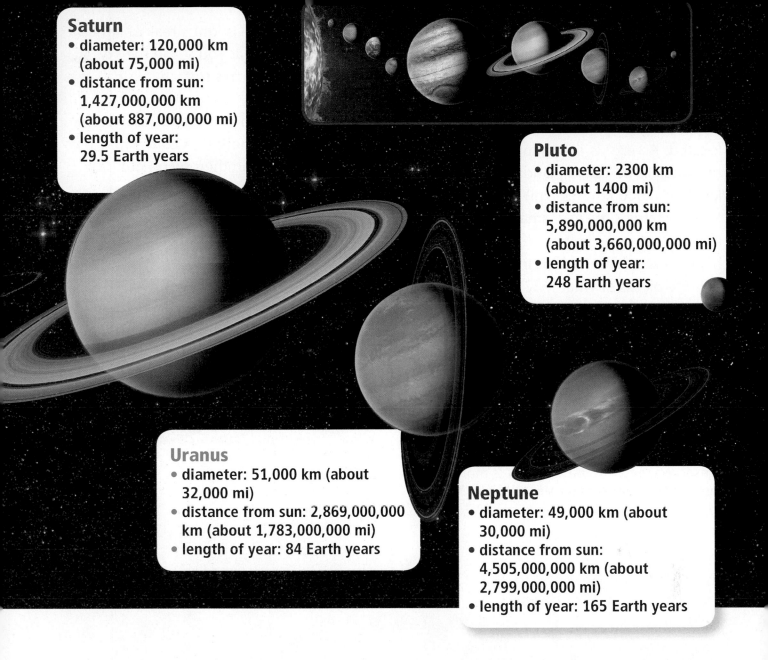

Saturn

- diameter: 120,000 km (about 75,000 mi)
- distance from sun: 1,427,000,000 km (about 887,000,000 mi)
- length of year: 29.5 Earth years

Pluto

- diameter: 2300 km (about 1400 mi)
- distance from sun: 5,890,000,000 km (about 3,660,000,000 mi)
- length of year: 248 Earth years

Uranus

- diameter: 51,000 km (about 32,000 mi)
- distance from sun: 2,869,000,000 km (about 1,783,000,000 mi)
- length of year: 84 Earth years

Neptune

- diameter: 49,000 km (about 30,000 mi)
- distance from sun: 4,505,000,000 km (about 2,799,000,000 mi)
- length of year: 165 Earth years

that it is big enough to count as a planet. Others aren't so sure, since they question whether *Pluto* is really a planet!*

Focus Skill MAIN IDEA AND DETAILS What are some characteristics of the gas giants?

*In 2006, the International Astronomical Union defined a planet as a body that orbits the sun, is spherical, and is large enough to clear its orbit. They reclassified Pluto as a "dwarf planet," because it is not large enough to clear its orbit.

Insta-Lab

Planet Sizes

Compare the approximate sizes of planets. Use a marble to represent Pluto, a table-tennis ball to represent Earth, and a basketball to represent Jupiter. Which of these would best represent the size of Venus?

Asteroids and Comets

Between Mars and Jupiter is a huge area of space called the asteroid belt. This is a ring-shaped region where thousands of small, rocky bodies called asteroids are located. **Asteroids** are chunks of rock too small to be called planets. They are less than 1000 km (621 mi) in diameter. Some asteroids are very small—only a few kilometers wide. Some scientists hypothesize that asteroids in the asteroid belt are pieces of what may have been a planet orbiting between Mars and Jupiter.

Other pieces of rock that travel through space are called *meteors*. When a meteor hits Earth's atmosphere, it usually burns up. This causes the bright streak of light, or "shooting star," that you see in the sky. If a meteor reaches Earth's surface, it is called a *meteorite*.

A **comet** is a ball of ice, rock, and frozen gases that orbits the sun. A comet may pass close to the sun and then swing out past the orbit of Pluto, to the edge of the solar system. Each time a comet approaches the sun, it changes. The center, or core, of the comet begins

Asteroid Ida actually has a tiny moon, called Dactyl, that orbits it.

Meteor Crater, in Arizona, is the best-preserved crater in the world. It is more than a kilometer (nearly a mile) wide. ▼

350

Comet Close-Up

head

tails

A comet can have two or more visible tails. They are made of different materials. One of the tails always points away from the sun.

to melt. This forms a cloud of gas that is pushed into a long tail by energy from the sun. A comet's tail can be tens of millions of kilometers long.

Many comets have been named for the people who discovered them. One is Halley's comet, which was last seen from Earth in 1986. It will appear again in 2061–

2062 as part of its 76-year orbit around the sun. People discover comets as these bodies get close to Earth and become visible. One comet, named Machholz, was discovered in 2004.

 **MAIN IDEA AND DETAILS** What are comets made of?

Standards Wrap-Up and Lesson Review

What makes up the solar system?

In this lesson, you learned about the different objects that make up the solar system. You also learned about the characteristics of each planet.

Science Content Standards in This Lesson

5.b *Students know* the solar system includes the planet Earth, the Moon, the Sun, eight other planets and their satellites, and smaller objects such as asteroids and comets.

1. (Focus Skill) **MAIN IDEA AND DETAILS** Copy and complete this graphic organizer to show the supporting details of this main idea: The sun is the center of our solar system. **5.b**

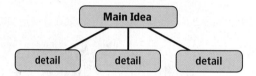

```
        Main Idea
   /       |       \
detail   detail   detail
```

2. **SUMMARIZE** Using the graphic organizer, write a lesson summary. **5.b**

3. **DRAW CONCLUSIONS** Why is Pluto considered an unusual planet? **5.b**

4. **VOCABULARY** How are asteroids and comets similar? How are they different? **5.b**

5. **Critical Thinking** Why is it difficult for scientists to observe planets in space beyond the solar system? **5.b**

6. **Investigate and Experiment** How can the data gathered from studying the planets help scientists make inferences about the solar system? **6.g**

7. Asteroids can be found
   A near the sun.
   B between Mars and Jupiter.
   C outside the orbit of Pluto.
   D between Earth and Mars. **5.b**

8. What makes Earth different from other planets in the solar system?

The Big Idea

   A It has an atmosphere.
   B It is very rocky.
   C It has liquid water.
   D It has only one moon. **5.b**

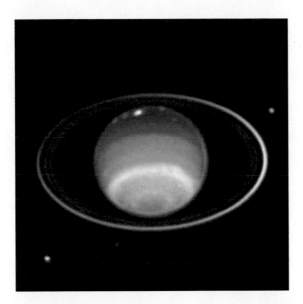

 Writing ELA–W 5.2

Narrative Writing

Research a planet other than Earth. Write a travel guide that people from Earth could use when visiting that planet. Tell about the sights they would see or what a typical day might be like.

 Math NS 5.1

Computing Distance

Astronomers measure distance in astronomical units (AU). One AU is the distance of Earth from the sun, about 150,000,000 km. Choose a planet and find out how many AUs it is from Earth and from the sun. Then calculate the distance in kilometers.

 Social Studies HSS 5.2

Exploration

Find out about the early exploration of space by humans. How is this similar to Europeans' early explorations of the Americas? How is it different? Create a poster to display your findings.

 For more links and activities, go to **www.hspscience.com**

Jet Propulsion Laboratory

In 1958, the Jet Propulsion Laboratory (JPL) received an assignment. It was to build and operate NASA's first satellite in space, *Explorer 1*. Since then, the lab's Mission Control center in Pasadena has built, launched, and operated hundreds of spacecraft.

From satellites to space probes, the missions at JPL have reached millions of miles to the edge of our solar system and beyond. Some, like the Mars rovers in 2004, explore the surface of planets. Some probes collect samples. On the *Stardust* probe's seven-year mission, it collected cosmic dust from space to return it to Earth for study.

An artist made this drawing of what the *Cassini* spacecraft may have looked like as it sped toward Saturn.

Planning Is the Key

The engineers at Mission Control in Pasadena have a huge job anytime a spacecraft is launched from Earth. For months before, the specialists at the center plan and build the spacecraft. They must also figure out the best time to launch the spacecraft and where to aim it. How do the engineers aim a spacecraft to head for a certain planet?

Earth travels around the sun at about 107,000 km/hr (66,000 mi/hr). Launching a rocket in the same direction in which Earth is moving will give the rocket a huge boost. Launching it in the same direction in which Earth spins also helps. Once the spacecraft is launched, its rockets power it to move through space. On the ground at the JPL are computers and engineers that analyze signals from the spacecraft. They monitor the progress of the craft as it sends photos and other data back to Earth.

Flybys in Space

Missions on which probes speed past planets or other bodies in space are called flybys. A spacecraft is pulled toward a planet by the planet's gravitational force. Gravity acts likes a slingshot, propelling the craft past the planet. If a space probe is sent close enough to the planet, the gravitational force pulls the probe toward the planet. Examples of flybys conducted by the JPL are the *Voyager* missions that flew past the outer planets of the solar system. Another mission sent the *Cassini* spacecraft into orbit around Saturn and on flybys of Saturn's moon Titan. *Cassini* also released a probe that collected data about Titan and landed on its surface.

Think and Write

1 What have been some of the missions at the JPL? **5.b**

2 How do engineers at JPL keep track of spacecraft once they are launched? **5.b**

355

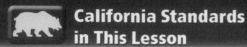

Science Content

5.c *Students know* the path of a planet around the Sun is due to gravitational attraction between the Sun and the planet.

Investigation and Experimentation

6.i Write a report of an investigation that includes conducting tests, collecting data or examining evidence, and drawing conclusions

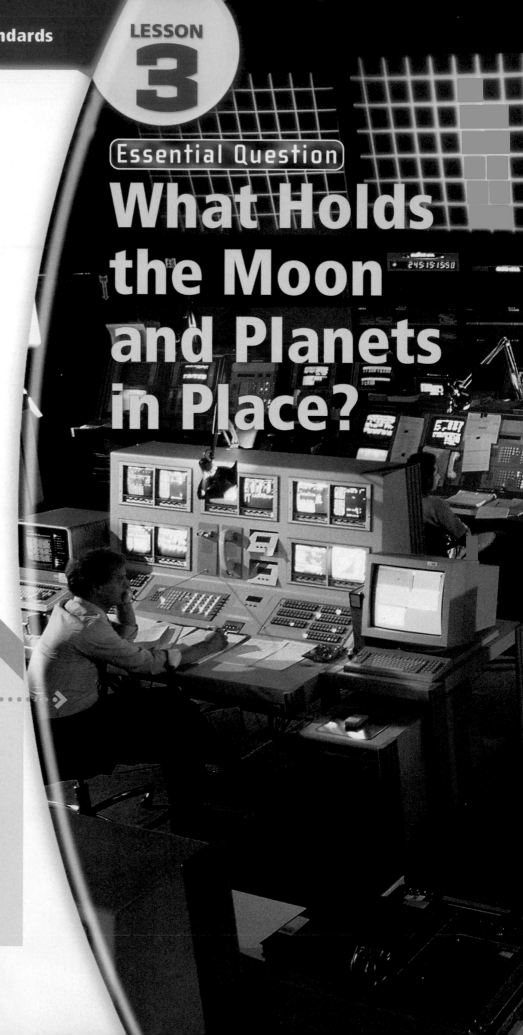

LESSON

3

Essential Question

What Holds the Moon and Planets in Place?

California Fast Fact

Launch Window

Earth spins at 1600 km (about 1000 mi) per hour and travels through space at 107,000 km (66,000 mi) per hour! At the Jet Propulsion Laboratory in Pasadena, mission control specialists must calculate the best time to launch a vehicle into space. This is called the launch window.

Mission Control, Jet Propulsion
Laboratory, Pasadena, California

orbit [OR•bit] The path that one body takes in space as it revolves around another body (p. 360)

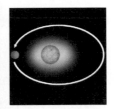

elliptical [ee•LIP•tih•kuhl] Oval-shaped (p. 360)

inertia [in•ER•shuh] The property of matter that keeps an object at rest or moving in a straight line (p. 362)

gravity [GRAV•uh•tee] The attraction that pulls objects toward Earth (p. 362)

357

Moving Through Space

Start with Questions

You know that Earth moves through space. So do the planets, the moon, and other bodies in space.

- How do the planets move through space?

- How are the movements of the planets and the sun related?

Investigate to find out. Then read to find out more.

Prepare to Investigate

Investigation Skill Tip
A model helps you understand a science process or structure. Be sure to use appropriate materials when you make a model.

Materials

- beach ball
- baseball
- table-tennis ball

Make an Observation Chart

Observations of Movements	
Sun	
Earth	
Moon	

Follow This Procedure

① You will **use a model** to show the **time and space relationships** between Earth, the moon, and the sun. One person should hold the beach ball (the sun). Another should stand far away and hold the baseball (Earth). A third person should hold the table-tennis ball (the moon) near the baseball. The fourth person should record the movements.

② For the model, Earth should move around the sun in a circle and spin at the same time. The real Earth spins about 365 times during one complete path around the sun.

③ While the model Earth moves, the model moon should move around Earth in a nearly circular path. The real moon spins once during each complete path around Earth.

Step 1

Step 3

Draw Conclusions

1. One movement of this model represented a year. Which movement was that?

2. **Standards Link** Why do you think Earth moves in a curved path instead of a straight path? **5.c**

3. **Investigation Skill** Use the **model** and your understanding of **time and space relationships** to write a paragraph about the movements of the moon and Earth.

Independent Inquiry ▸ **Write a Report**

Investigate to find out about the paths of the planets and their moons.

Find out how many moons each planet has. Which planet has the most moons? Are they all like Earth's moon? Write a report sharing your findings. Be sure to include pictures or drawings of the different planets and moons. **6.i**

VOCABULARY
orbit p. 360
elliptical p. 360
inertia p. 362
gravity p. 362

SCIENCE CONCEPTS
▶ the paths of planets around the sun
▶ how planets are held in their orbits

Focus Skill CAUSE AND EFFECT
Look for causes and effects of gravity and inertia on the planets.

cause → effect

The Path of a Planet Around the Sun

It has taken astronomers hundreds of years to understand how the planets move through space. Around A.D. 140, astronomer Claudius Ptolemy, of Egypt, wrote an explanation of how objects move in space. He hypothesized that the moon, the sun, and the planets revolved in circular orbits around Earth. An **orbit** is the path that a body follows as it revolves around another body. Now we know that Ptolemy's model was wrong, but for many years astronomers thought it was correct.

Centuries later, Polish astronomer Nicolaus Copernicus came up with a different model. He placed the sun at the center of the solar system, with the planets moving in circular orbits around it. Most people at the time, however, did not accept this idea. Later, it turned out that Copernicus was correct about the path of the planets around the sun, but he was wrong about the shape of their orbits.

In the early 1600s, German astronomer Johannes Kepler discovered that Mars does not have a circular orbit. Its orbit is slightly elliptical. An **elliptical** orbit is shaped like a flattened circle. Kepler inferred that if Mars has an elliptical orbit, then the other planets must also have elliptical orbits.

During that time, Italian astronomer Galileo Galilei was studying the planets with the newly invented *telescope*. A telescope is a tool that scientists use to study parts of the universe not visible to the human eye by itself. Galileo's observations supported

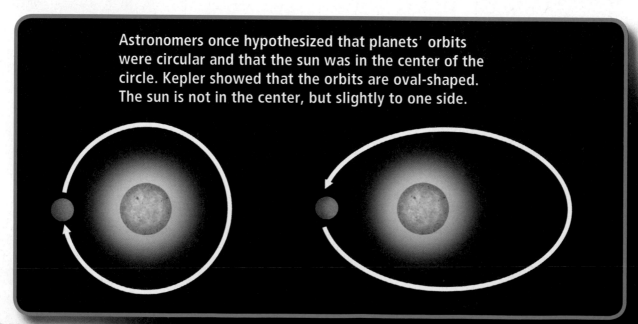

Astronomers once hypothesized that planets' orbits were circular and that the sun was in the center of the circle. Kepler showed that the orbits are oval-shaped. The sun is not in the center, but slightly to one side.

Copernicus's model. The sun is the center of the solar system, and the planets move in elliptical orbits around it. Likewise, the moon moves in a slightly elliptical orbit around Earth.

If you looked at a planet's orbit from above, you would see that the sun is not at the center of the planets' orbits. It is slightly away from the center. Because the planetary orbits are elliptical, each planet is closer to the sun at certain times during its orbit than at others.

CAUSE AND EFFECT What effect does the shape of a planet's orbit have on the planet's distance from the sun?

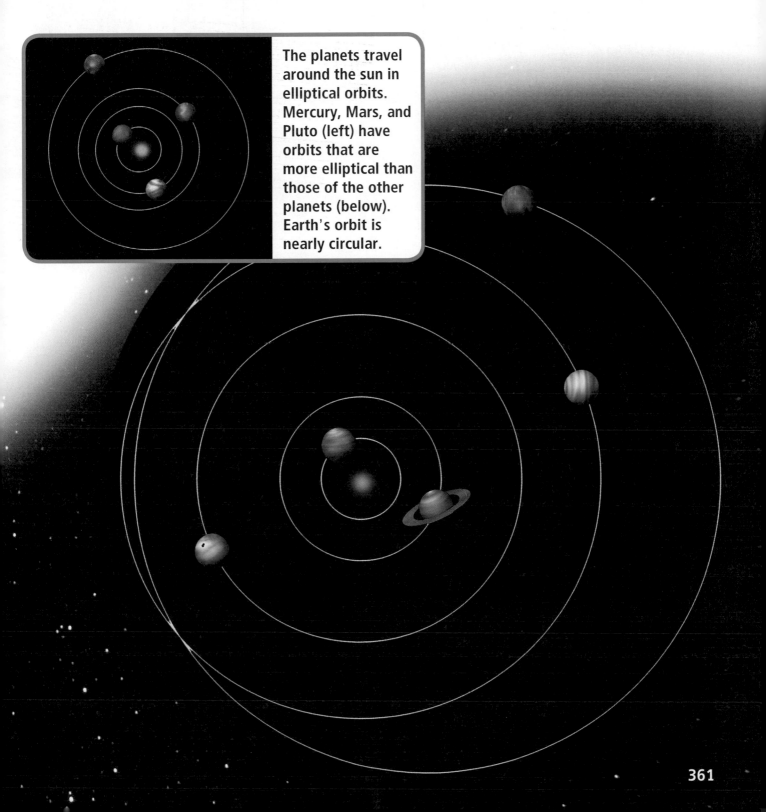

The planets travel around the sun in elliptical orbits. Mercury, Mars, and Pluto (left) have orbits that are more elliptical than those of the other planets (below). Earth's orbit is nearly circular.

American astronaut on the moon

What Holds the Moon and Planets in Orbit?

What keeps the planets moving in their orbits? Why don't they just fall into the sun or shoot off into space? Why doesn't the moon crash into Earth? Two properties can explain this. The first is called inertia. **Inertia** is a property of matter that keeps objects moving in a straight line and at a constant speed unless they are pushed or pulled by some force.

Suppose you throw a baseball to a friend. If no outside force pushed or pulled on it, the baseball would travel in a straight line forever. Instead, the baseball is slowed down by air resistance, or friction, and pulled down by another force, Earth's gravitational force, or gravity. **Gravity** is the attraction that pulls objects toward Earth.

A planet moves in space, where there is no air. A planet, such as Earth, would travel forever in a straight line if gravitational force did not change its motion. Gravitational force causes a pull between the mass of a planet and the mass of the sun. Gravitational force, combined with inertia, produces a planet's orbit. Instead of following a straight line, the planet follows a curved path. The sun's constant pull on a planet changes the direction in which the planet is moving. As a result, the planets "fall" constantly in a curved path around the sun.

In the same way, the moon is held in its orbit around Earth. As the moon is pulled toward Earth, inertia causes it to move forward. This results in its curved path around Earth. The moon, like the planets, is constantly falling through space. The gravitational force and inertia are balanced. Because of this, the average distance of any planet from the sun, or of the moon from Earth, never changes.

Focus Skill **CAUSE AND EFFECT** What causes planets to stay in their orbits?

The Earth and the Moon

Inertia and gravity keep the moon in a nearly circular orbit around Earth.

Earth and its moon move together around the sun. Because the moon is always orbiting Earth while the Earth-moon system orbits the sun, the moon's path around the sun is a series of loops.

Phases of the Moon

On some nights, you may notice that the moon seems to have disappeared. On other nights, you see a large, white moon shining brightly. The moon, though, has not changed at all. Instead, the moon and Earth have moved.

In the Investigate, you learned how Earth travels around the sun and how, at the same time, the moon travels around Earth. Earth's path around the sun is slightly elliptical. The moon's orbit around Earth is also slightly elliptical. When the moon is closest to Earth, it is about 356,400 km (221,000 mi) away.

Both Earth and the moon rotate as they revolve, though at different speeds. The moon rotates more slowly. It completes a rotation every $29\frac{1}{2}$ Earth days. So a day on the moon is $29\frac{1}{2}$ Earth days long.

The moon rotates as it orbits Earth, but the same side of the moon always faces Earth. That's because one lunar cycle, from new moon to new moon, takes $29\frac{1}{2}$ days, the same amount of time the moon takes to complete one rotation.

The side of the moon we can't see from Earth was once called the dark side of the moon. A better name is the far side of the moon. Although we can't see the far side of the moon, the sun shines on that side as brightly as on the side we see.

The moon is often bright at night, but it doesn't give off its own light. The part of the moon that is exposed to the sun reflects the sun's light.

The *Apollo 8* mission, in 1968, was the first mission to carry people in orbit around the moon. While in orbit, the crew took pictures like this one of the moon's far side.

Science Up Close

For more links and animations, go to **www.hspscience.com**

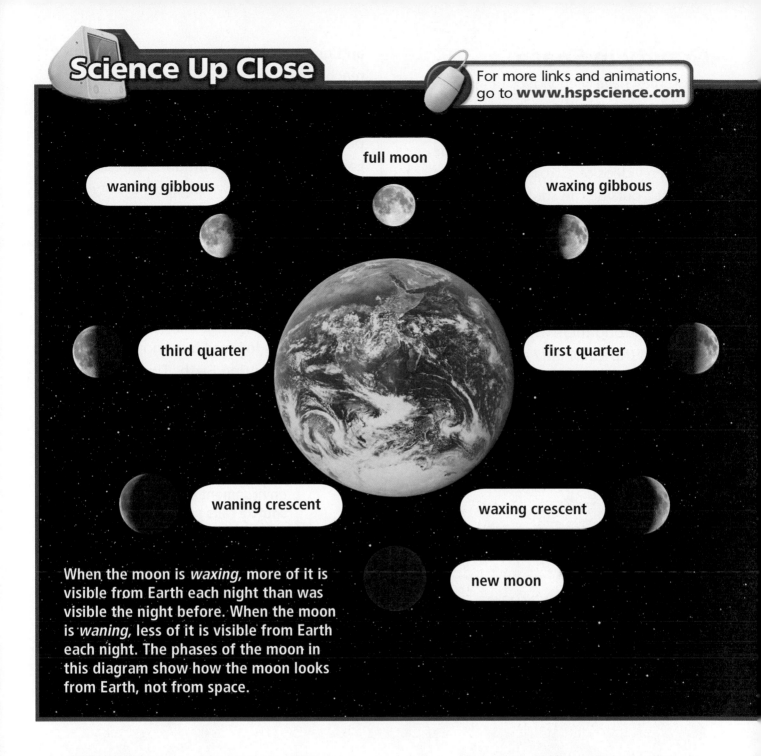

full moon

waning gibbous

waxing gibbous

third quarter

first quarter

waning crescent

waxing crescent

new moon

When the moon is *waxing*, more of it is visible from Earth each night than was visible the night before. When the moon is *waning*, less of it is visible from Earth each night. The phases of the moon in this diagram show how the moon looks from Earth, not from space.

The way the moon looks from Earth changes daily. At any time, half of the moon is lit by the sun. How much of it you see depends on the moon's phase. A *moon phase* is one of the shapes the moon seems to have as it orbits Earth. When Earth is between the moon and the sun, you see a full moon. When the moon is between Earth and the sun, you can't see the moon at all. This is called a new moon.

During the moon's cycle, the visible portion of the moon changes a little at a time. Starting with a new moon, you see more and more of the moon each day until you see the full moon. Then you see less and less each day, until the next new moon.

Focus Skill **CAUSE AND EFFECT** What do we see from Earth when the moon is between Earth and the sun?

365

Gravity in Space

You may have seen videos of astronauts aboard a space shuttle or in a space station. Most likely, the astronauts you saw were floating inside the cabin. You may have also seen videos of astronauts "walking in space" outside the shuttle. Again, the astronauts appeared to float in space. It looked as though gravity was not acting on them. Earth's gravity on the shuttle isn't zero or even near zero, though. The shuttle orbits close enough to Earth that gravity is almost as strong there as it is on Earth.

Why do the astronauts appear to be weightless? This happens because inertia and gravity are balanced. After the shuttle reaches its orbit, its engines shut down. Inertia keeps the shuttle moving forward. This is the same property that carries the planets forward through space. Space near Earth has only a small amount of resistance, or drag, to slow down objects. Gravity causes the shuttle to "fall" toward Earth. This is like the gravitational force of the sun causing the planets to "fall" toward it.

The downward and sideways motions of the shuttle are balanced. That is, the shuttle falls continuously toward Earth. At the same time, it moves forward fast enough to keep from actually hitting Earth. The curve of the shuttle's path as it moves forward and toward Earth is the same as the curve of

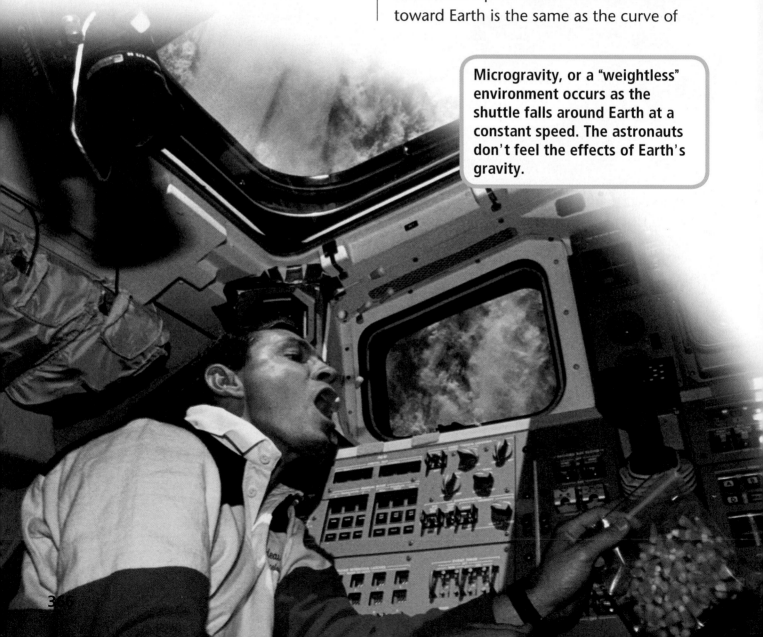

Microgravity, or a "weightless" environment occurs as the shuttle falls around Earth at a constant speed. The astronauts don't feel the effects of Earth's gravity.

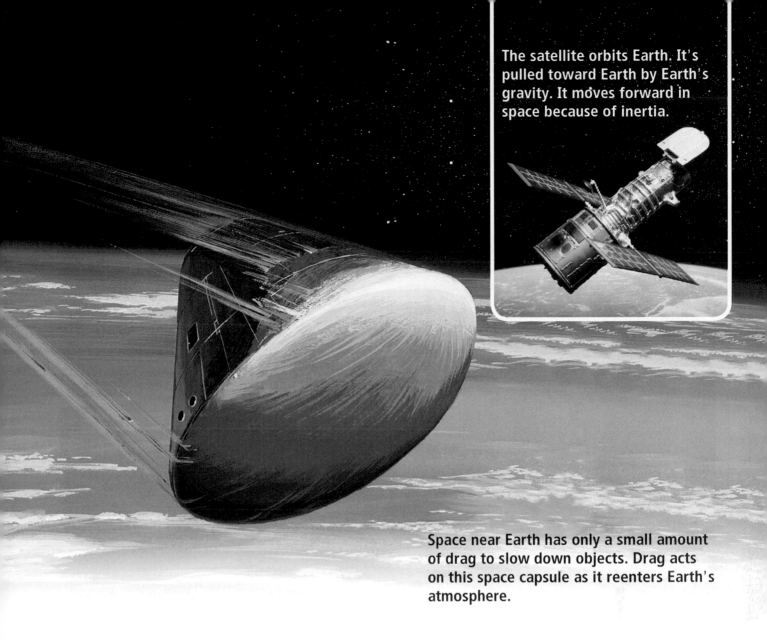

The satellite orbits Earth. It's pulled toward Earth by Earth's gravity. It moves forward in space because of inertia.

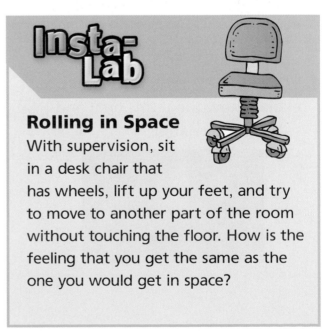

Space near Earth has only a small amount of drag to slow down objects. Drag acts on this space capsule as it reenters Earth's atmosphere.

Earth. As a result, the shuttle doesn't get any closer to Earth's surface or any farther away from it.

Gravity acting on the space shuttle explains why the astronauts appear to be weightless. Gravity actually exists in space. The astronauts appear weightless, however, because they are basically free-falling. As with the moon, inertia and gravity are balanced. The astronauts "fall" toward Earth as they move forward through space.

Focus Skill **MAIN IDEA AND DETAILS** What causes astronauts to appear weightless in space?

Insta-Lab

Rolling in Space
With supervision, sit in a desk chair that has wheels, lift up your feet, and try to move to another part of the room without touching the floor. How is the feeling that you get the same as the one you would get in space?

Standards Wrap-Up and Lesson Review

Essential Question

What holds the moon and the planets in space?

In this lesson, you learned about the paths of the planets around the sun. You also learned how planets stay in their orbits around the sun.

 Science Content Standards in This Lesson

5.c *Students know* the path of a planet around the Sun is due to gravitational attraction between the Sun and the planet.

1. (Focus Skill) **CAUSE AND EFFECT** Copy and complete a graphic organizer to identify the cause of this effect: *A planet orbits the sun.* **5.c**

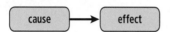

2. **SUMMARIZE** Use the graphic organizer to write two sentences that summarize the main points of the lesson. **5.c**

3. **DRAW CONCLUSIONS** Suppose the paths of the planets were perfectly circular. Would each planet's distance from the sun always be the same? Explain. **5.c**

4. **VOCABULARY** Write a sentence to explain how the terms *orbit* and *elliptical* are related.

5. **Critical Thinking** What is the difference between the solar system models of Ptolemy and Copernicus? **5.c**

6. **Investigation Skill** What information should you include in a report about how the planets stay in their orbits around the sun? **6.i**

7. Which of the following explains why an object moves forward at a constant speed in a straight line?
   A drag
   B gravity
   C inertia
   D weightlessness **5.c**

8. What causes the moon to "fall" toward Earth?
   A Earth's gravity
   B the sun's gravity
   C the moon's gravity
   D the moon's inertia **5.c**

The Big Idea

 Writing ELA–W 5.2

Write a Report

Research the life of an astronaut aboard the International Space Station. Describe how the space station is able to stay in its orbit around Earth.

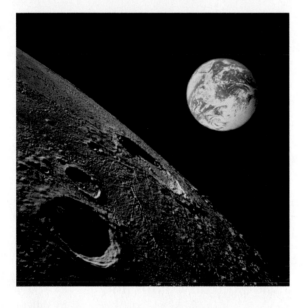

 Math NS 5.5

Calculate Distance

Earth travels through space at 107,000 km (66,000 mi) per hour! Calculate how many kilometers Earth travels in one day, one week, and one year.

 Literature ELA–W 5.3

Space Poetry

Myra Cohn Livingston writes poetry about space. Read a book of her poetry, and choose your favorite poem. Write a paragraph telling why you like that poem best.

 For more links and activities, go to **www.hspscience.com**

Ellen Ochoa

▶ **DR. ELLEN OCHOA**

▶ **Astronaut**

▶ Has spent nearly 1000 hours in space

Ellen Ochoa puts no limits on herself. In 1991 she became the first Hispanic woman in space. Ochoa was a mission specialist on her first flight. On that nine-day mission aboard the *Discovery* space shuttle, she studied the sun and Earth's atmosphere to learn about the sun's effects on Earth's climate. On an 11-day mission in November 1994, she studied the energy of the sun during an 11-year solar cycle. Dr. Ochoa also flew on the shuttle *Discovery* in 1999 and on the *Atlantis* in 2002. During those two missions, the shuttles docked with the International Space Station to deliver supplies.

One of the most challenging parts of space travel is remembering details. Every astronaut is trained to run all the shuttle systems, such as computer and communication systems, air and water systems, and other equipment. All astronauts also learn about the experiments and the other jobs that are a part of each shuttle mission. Dr. Ochoa says that astronauts must work very hard in space because they have little time.

Dr. Ochoa believes that education is the key to success in life. She also believes that students, especially girls, should study math and science. One of her role models is Sally Ride, the first woman in space.

✍ Think and Write

❶ How do astronauts like Dr. Ochoa help other scientists learn about Earth? **5.b**

❷ How can studying math and science help a person succeed as an astronaut?

"Only you put limitations on yourself about what you can achieve, so don't be afraid to reach out for the stars."
—Ellen Ochoa

Carolyn Shoemaker

▶ **DR. CAROLYN SHOEMAKER**

▶ **Astronomer**

▶ Discovered more comets than any other living person

Carolyn Shoemaker likes to watch the night sky. She has been doing it for more than 25 years. So far, she has discovered 32 comets—more than any other person now living. She has also discovered hundreds of asteroids. For many years, Dr. Shoemaker worked with her husband, Gene Levy, studying meteorite craters. She is best known for their co-discovery of a comet that crashed into Jupiter in 1993. The comet was named Shoemaker-Levy in their honor.

Dr. Shoemaker does her sky-watching by taking photographs through one of the telescopes at Mount Palomar, in California. Later, she examines the photographs carefully, looking for comets and asteroids. She has developed efficient ways to do this. They include the use of a stereo microscope, which cuts in half the time needed to scan the whole sky.

Dr. Shoemaker originally did not intend to be a scientist. In college, she studied history and politics. Her career change began when she was 51. At that time, her husband asked her to help him with some of his projects on asteroids. She became interested in the study of space and soon knew that she had found her field.

Today, she says that she could spend 24 hours a day "pointing the big telescope at the sky and looking for comets and asteroids."

✍ Think and Write

❶ What discoveries has Carolyn Shoemaker made?

❷ How does technology help Dr. Shoemaker make these discoveries?

Dr. Shoemaker and her husband, Gene Levy, improved ways in which scientists find and study meteors, asteroids, and comets.

371

Wrap-Up

▶ Visual Summary

Tell how each picture helps explain the **Big Idea**.

The Big Idea The solar system is made up of planets and other bodies that orbit the sun in predictable paths.

5.a

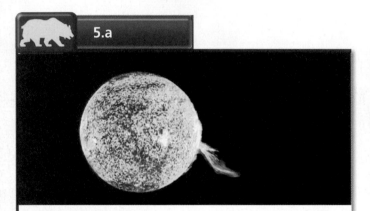

The Sun
The sun is an average star at the center of our solar system. It is made up almost entirely of hydrogen and helium. It is the fusion of these gases that produces the sun's energy.

5.b

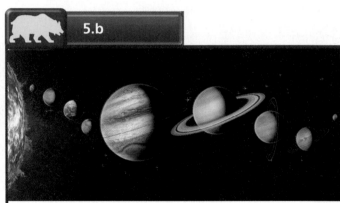

The Solar System
The solar system is made up of the sun, Earth, eight other planets, and their moons. Smaller objects such as asteroids and comets are also part of the solar system.

5.c

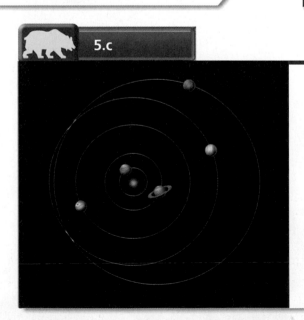

Paths of the Planets
The planets are held in their orbits by inertia and the sun's gravitational force. All planets move around the sun in slightly elliptical orbits.

Show What You Know

Unit Writing Activity

Write a Description

Imagine you are a photographer. NASA has hired you to study images taken by cameras that can operate in extreme temperatures. The cameras were placed on the sun, the planets, and the moon. They also were carried on satellites throughout the solar system. Write descriptions of the various objects you see. Include the features you see on the sun and on some of the planets of your choice. Also include descriptions of other bodies in space, such as asteroids, comets, and planets' moons.

Unit Project

Science Show

Plan and produce a science show about the planets, the sun, and other bodies in the solar system. You will need to prepare posters or diagrams illustrating the main ideas in this unit. Be sure to include displays about the solar system and the sun, its features, and how it produces energy. Use a variety of media such as posters, diagrams, models, and videotapes to present the information. Invite younger students in your school to attend the show.

Vocabulary Review

Use the terms below to complete the sentences. The page numbers tell you where to look in the unit if you need help.

star p. 332   **asteroid** p. 350

fusion p. 336   **comet** p. 350

planet p. 346   **orbit** p. 360

satellite p. 346   **elliptical** p. 360

1. A body that revolves around a star is a _____.   `5.a`

2. The path of a body in space around another body is an _____.   `5.b`

3. A huge sphere of hot gas that gives off energy is a _____.   `5.a`

4. A chunk of ice with a long tail that orbits the sun is a _____.   `5.b`

5. A chunk of rock found between Mars and Jupiter is an _____.   `5.b`

6. A body in space that revolves around a planet is called a _____.   `5.b`

7. The joining of particles to produce energy is called _____.   `5.c`

8. The oval-shaped path of a planet is an _____ orbit.   `5.c`

Check Understanding

Choose the letter of the correct response.

9. **CAUSE AND EFFECT** Which of these causes a change in distance between a planet and the sun?   `5.c`
   A inertia   C orbit
   B fusion   D gravity

10. **MAIN IDEA AND DETAILS** Which details **best** describe the sun?   `5.a`
    A medium-size yellow star
    B large, bright red star
    C small blue star
    D dim yellow star

11. Which planet below is labeled X?   `5.b`
    A Earth   C Mars
    B Mercury   D Venus

12. Gail observes a bright light in the sky with a long streak behind it. The light disappears after a few seconds. Gail most likely observed which of the following?   `5.b`
    A asteroid   C comet
    B meteoroid   D sunspot

Use the image below to answer questions 13 and 14.

13. What effect do inertia and gravity have on Earth's path through space? `5.c`

　A They hold Earth in its orbit.

　B They cause Earth to spin on its axis.

　C They force Earth to travel in a straight line.

　D They keep Earth traveling at a constant speed.

14. What does the diagram show? `5.b`

　A the inner planets

　B the outer planets

　C the asteroid belt

　D the solar system

15. Which other planet is most like Earth? `5.b`

　A Mars 　　　**C** Mercury

　B Pluto 　　　**D** Venus

16. A scientist observes a red star that is very bright. What might the scientist conclude about the star? `5.a`

　A It is cold star very far from Earth.

　B It is a very hot star.

　C It is larger than the sun.

　D It is a hot star close to Earth.

Investigation Skills

17. What kind of data did scientists need to gather and record in order to predict the 11-year sunspot cycles? `6.g`

18. What inferences might scientists make about the sun by studying its layers and what it is made of? `6.g`

Critical Thinking

19. What is the main difference between the planets known as gas giants and the inner planets? `5.b`

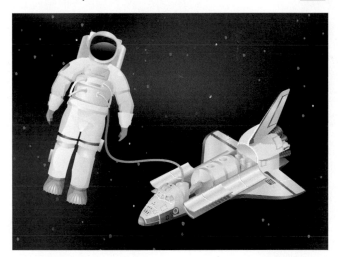

20. The solar system consists of planets and other bodies that orbit the sun in predictable paths. Explain what an orbit is.

The **Big Idea**

References

Contents

Health Handbook

Reading in Science Handbook

Math in Science Handbook   R28

Your Skin

Your skin is your body's largest organ. It provides your body with a tough protective covering. It produces sweat to help control your body temperature. It protects you from disease. Your skin also provides your sense of touch that allows you to feel pressure, textures, temperature, and pain.

When you play hard or exercise, your body produces sweat, which cools you as it evaporates. The sweat from your skin also helps your body eliminate excess salts and other wastes.

The skin is the body's largest organ. ▼

Epidermis
Many layers of dead skin cells form the top of the epidermis. Cells in the lower part of the epidermis are always making new cells.

Dermis
The dermis is much thicker than the epidermis. It is made up of tough, flexible fibers.

Hair Follicle
Each hair follicle has a muscle that can contract and make the hair "stand on end."

Pore
These tiny holes on the surface of your skin lead to your dermis.

Oil Gland
Oil glands produce oil that keeps your skin soft and smooth.

Sweat Gland
Sweat glands produce sweat, which contains water, salt, and various wastes.

Fatty Tissue
This tissue layer beneath the dermis stores food, provides warmth, and attaches your skin to underlying bone and muscle.

Caring for Your Skin

- To protect your skin and to keep it healthy, you should wash your body, including your hair and your nails, every day. This helps remove germs, excess oils and sweat, and dead cells from the epidermis, the outer layer of your skin. Because you touch many things during the day, you should wash your hands with soap and water frequently.

- If you get a cut or scratch, you should wash it right away and cover it with a sterile bandage to prevent infection and promote healing.

- Protect your skin from cuts and scrapes by wearing proper safety equipment when you play sports or skate, or when you're riding your bike or scooter.

- Always protect your skin from sunburn by wearing protective clothing and sunscreen when you are outdoors in bright sun.

Your Senses

Eyes

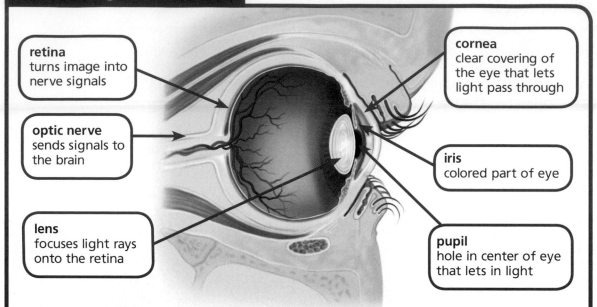

retina
turns image into
nerve signals

optic nerve
sends signals to
the brain

lens
focuses light rays
onto the retina

cornea
clear covering of
the eye that lets
light pass through

iris
colored part of eye

pupil
hole in center of eye
that lets in light

Light rays bounce off objects and enter the eye through the pupil. A lens inside the eye focuses the light rays, and the image of the object is projected onto the retina at the back of the eye. In the retina the image is turned into nerve signals. Your brain analyzes these signals to "tell" you what you're seeing.

Ears

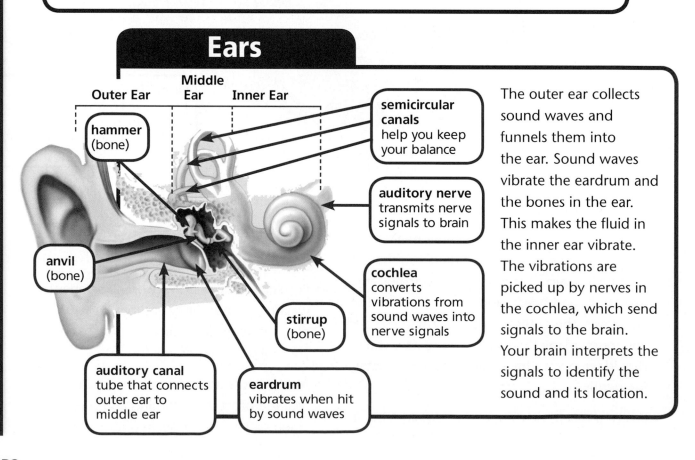

Outer Ear

Middle Ear

Inner Ear

hammer
(bone)

anvil
(bone)

auditory canal
tube that connects
outer ear to
middle ear

stirrup
(bone)

eardrum
vibrates when hit
by sound waves

semicircular canals
help you keep
your balance

auditory nerve
transmits nerve
signals to brain

cochlea
converts
vibrations from
sound waves into
nerve signals

The outer ear collects sound waves and funnels them into the ear. Sound waves vibrate the eardrum and the bones in the ear. This makes the fluid in the inner ear vibrate. The vibrations are picked up by nerves in the cochlea, which send signals to the brain. Your brain interprets the signals to identify the sound and its location.

Nose

When you breathe in, air is swept upward to nerve cells in the nasal cavity. The nasal cavity is the upper part of the nose, inside the skull. Different nerve cells respond to different chemicals in the air and send signals to your brain.

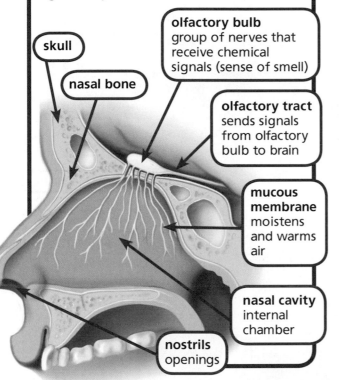

skull

nasal bone

olfactory bulb group of nerves that receive chemical signals (sense of smell)

olfactory tract sends signals from olfactory bulb to brain

mucous membrane moistens and warms air

nasal cavity internal chamber

nostrils openings

Skin

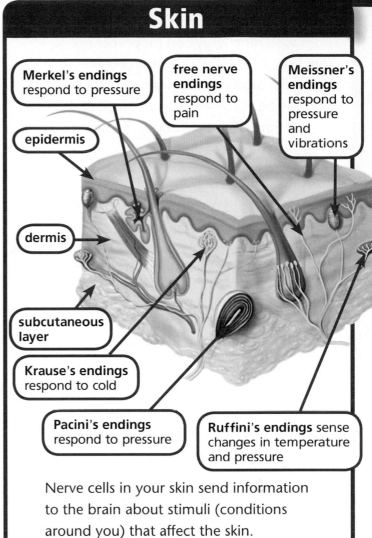

Merkel's endings respond to pressure

free nerve endings respond to pain

Meissner's endings respond to pressure and vibrations

epidermis

dermis

subcutaneous layer

Krause's endings respond to cold

Pacini's endings respond to pressure

Ruffini's endings sense changes in temperature and pressure

Nerve cells in your skin send information to the brain about stimuli (conditions around you) that affect the skin.

Caring for Your Senses

- Injuries to these organs can affect your senses.

- Protect your skin and eyes by wearing sunscreen and sunglasses. Protect your ears from loud sounds. Protect your nose from harsh chemicals and your tongue from hot foods and drinks.

Tongue

The tongue is covered with about 10,000 tiny nerve cells, or taste buds, that detect basic tastes in things you eat and drink. Different taste buds respond to different chemicals and send signals to your brain.

taste buds

Your Digestive System

Your body systems need nutrients from food for energy and for proper cell function. Your digestive system breaks down the food you eat into tiny particles that can be absorbed by your blood and carried throughout your body, so various cells and tissues can use the nutrients.

Digestion begins in your mouth when food is chewed, mixed with saliva, and swallowed. Your tongue pushes the food into your esophagus, which pushes the food down to your stomach with a muscular action, much like the one you use to squeeze toothpaste from a tube.

Your stomach produces gastric juices and mixes them with your food to begin breaking down proteins. Partially digested food leaves your stomach and moves to your small intestine.

Most of the digestive process occurs in your small intestine, where partially digested food is mixed with bile from your liver. This helps break down fats. Your pancreas also produces digestive juices that continue the process of digesting fats and proteins in the small intestine. Your pancreas also produces a special substance called insulin, which helps your body move sugar from your blood into your cells.

As food moves through your small intestine, nutrients are absorbed by the villi and pass into your blood.

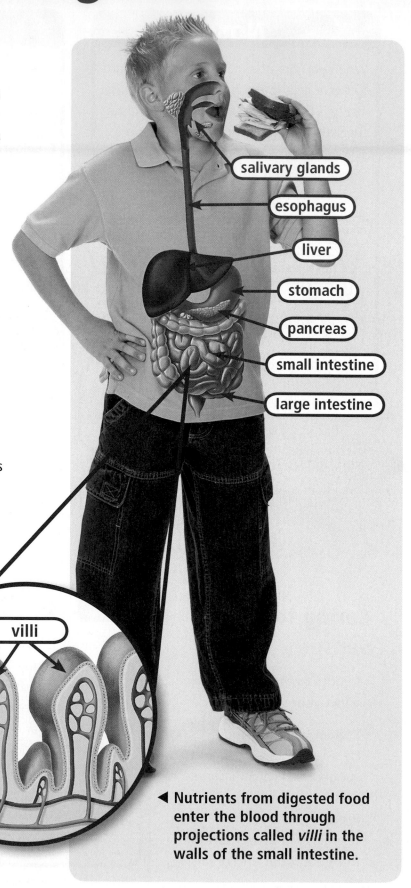

salivary glands

esophagus

liver

stomach

pancreas

small intestine

large intestine

villi

◀ Nutrients from digested food enter the blood through projections called *villi* in the walls of the small intestine.

Specialized Digestive Organs

Your liver produces a fluid called bile that helps break down fats. Bile is stored in your gallbladder. During digestion, the stored bile flows through the bile duct into your small intestine, to help with the digestive process.

Material that is not absorbed by your small intestine passes into your large intestine. This organ absorbs water and vitamins from the undigested materials. The remaining solid wastes are stored by your large intestine until they leave your body.

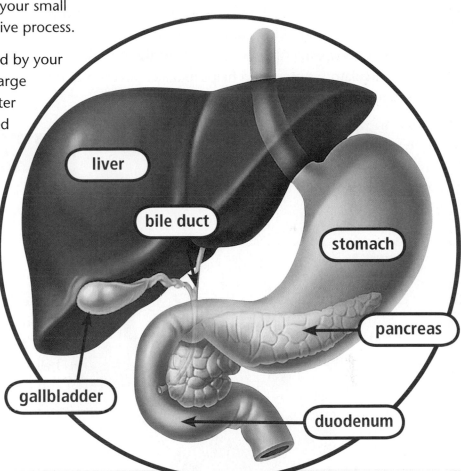

liver

bile duct

stomach

pancreas

gallbladder

duodenum

Caring for Your Digestive System

- Drink plenty of water every day. Water helps move food through your digestive system and helps your body replenish saliva, gastric juices, and bile consumed during digestion.

- Eat a variety of foods, choose a well-balanced diet, and maintain a healthy weight.

- Eat plenty of fruits and vegetables. These foods contain essential nutrients and help your digestive system function effectively.

- Chew your food thoroughly before swallowing.

Your Circulatory System

Your body relies on your circulatory system to deliver essential nutrients and oxygen to your organs, tissues, and cells. These materials are carried by your blood. As it circulates, your blood also removes wastes from your tissues. Your circulatory system includes your heart, arteries that carry oxygen and nutrient-rich blood away from your heart, tiny capillaries that exchange gases and nutrients between your blood and your body's tissues, and veins that carry blood and wastes back to your heart. Your veins have a system of one-way valves that maintains the direction of blood flow within your circulatory system and helps maintain an even distribution of oxygen and nutrients to all parts of your body.

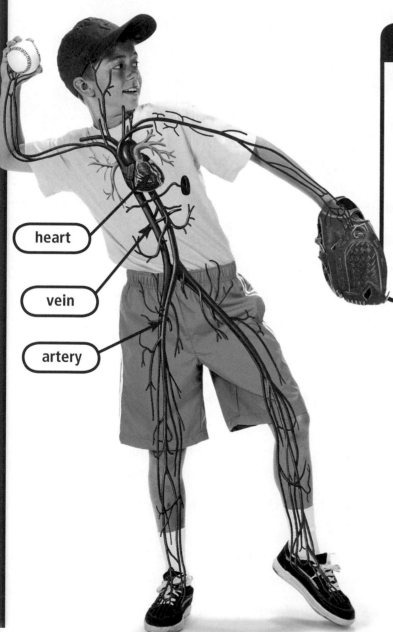

heart

vein

artery

Your Heart

Your heart is a strong, muscular organ that contracts rhythmically to pump blood throughout your circulatory system. When you exercise or work your muscles hard, your heart beats faster to deliver more oxygen and nutrient-rich blood to your muscles. When you rest, your heartbeat slows. Regular exercise helps keep your heart muscle and the rest of your circulatory system strong.

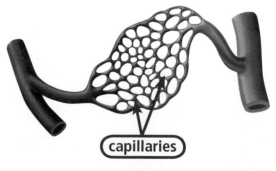

capillaries

▲ Oxygen and nutrients pass from the blood, through capillary walls, and into the cells. Cell wastes pass through capillary walls and into the blood.

Blood Flow and Your Excretory System

Your veins carry blood from your tissues back to your lungs, where carbon dioxide and other waste gases are removed from your red blood cells and expelled when you exhale. Your blood also travels through your kidneys, where small structures called nephrons remove salts and liquid wastes. Urine formed in your kidneys is held in your bladder until it is eliminated. Your liver removes other wastes from your blood, including blood cells. Red blood cells live for only 120 days. Specialized cells in your spleen and liver destroy damaged or dead red blood cells.

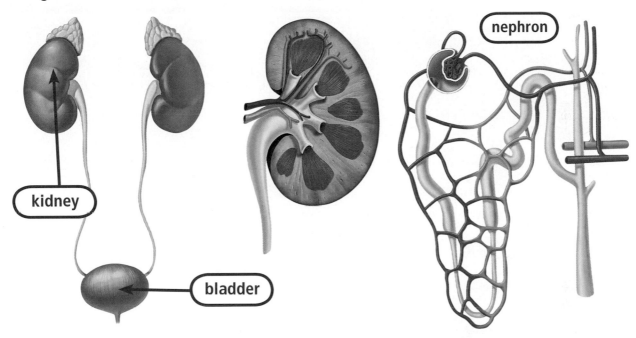

kidney

bladder

nephron

Caring for Your Circulatory System

- Eat foods that are low in fat and high in fiber. Fiber helps take away substances that can lead to fatty buildup in your blood vessels. Eat foods high in iron to help your red blood cells carry oxygen.

- Drink plenty of water to help your body replenish your blood fluid.

- Avoid contact with another person's blood.

- Exercise regularly to keep your heart and blood vessels strong.

- Never smoke or use tobacco. It can strain your heart and damage your blood vessels.

- Don't use illegal drugs or alcohol. They can damage your liver and your heart.

- Follow directions for all medicines carefully. Misuse of medicine can damage your blood's ability to clot after a cut, and can damage your liver and heart.

Your Immune System

A pathogen is an organism or virus that causes illness. An infection is the growth of pathogens in the body. Some pathogens weaken or kill body cells. A disease is an illness that damages or weakens the body, so you are not able to do the things you normally do. You may have a sore throat, or you may feel achy or tired, or you may have an unusually high body temperature, or fever. These are signs that your body is fighting an infection.

Infectious diseases have different symptoms because they are caused by different pathogens. There are four main types of pathogens: viruses, bacteria, fungi, and protozoa.

Diseases Caused by Pathogens

Pathogen	Characteristics	Diseases
Viruses	The smallest pathogens; the ones that cause most infectious diseases	Colds, chicken pox, HIV, infectious hepatitis, influenza (flu), measles, mumps, polio, rabies, rubella (German measles)
Bacteria	One-celled organisms that can—but do not always—cause disease; they make people ill by producing harmful wastes	Strep throat, pertussis (whooping cough), some kinds of pneumonia, Salmonella food poisoning, tetanus, tuberculosis (TB), Lyme disease
Fungi	Small, simple organisms like yeasts and molds; they most often invade the skin or respiratory system	Ringworm, athlete's foot, allergies
Protozoa	One-celled organisms somewhat larger than bacteria; they can cause serious diseases	Amoebic dysentery, giardiasis, malaria

There are pathogens all around you. You don't become ill often because your body has a complex system of defenses that prevents most pathogens from entering your body and destroys the ones that get through.

Sometimes pathogens do manage to overcome your body's defenses. When they do, your body's next line of defense is in your blood. Your blood contains white blood cells that have their own role to play in fighting infection.

Some white blood cells manufacture substances called antibodies. Each antibody is designed to fight a specific kind of pathogen. The antibodies attach themselves to the pathogen and either kill it or mark it to be killed by another kind of white blood cell. When a pathogen enters your body, your immune system produces antibodies to fight it. This process may take several days, during which you may have a fever and feel some other symptoms of the disease. When you have recovered from an illness, your white blood cells "remember" how to make the antibody needed to fight the pathogen that made you ill. The ability to recognize pathogens and "remember" how to make antibodies to fight disease is called *immunity*.

You can also develop immunity to certain diseases by getting vaccinations from your doctor that prevent the disease. A vaccine is usually a killed or weakened form of the pathogen that causes a particular disease.

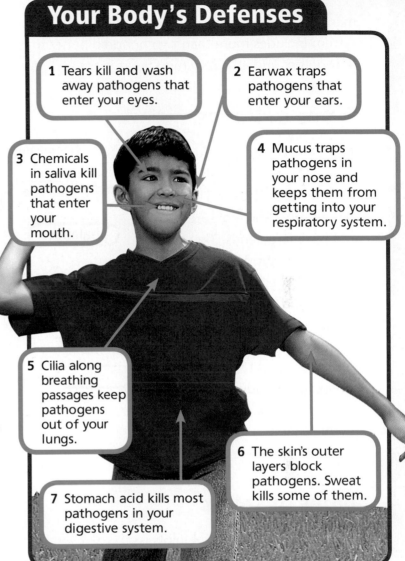

Your Body's Defenses

1 Tears kill and wash away pathogens that enter your eyes.

2 Earwax traps pathogens that enter your ears.

3 Chemicals in saliva kill pathogens that enter your mouth.

4 Mucus traps pathogens in your nose and keeps them from getting into your respiratory system.

5 Cilia along breathing passages keep pathogens out of your lungs.

6 The skin's outer layers block pathogens. Sweat kills some of them.

7 Stomach acid kills most pathogens in your digestive system.

Caring for Your Immune System

- Exercise regularly and get plenty of rest. This helps your body rebuild damaged tissues and cells.

- Eat a healthful, balanced diet. Good nutrition keeps your immune system strong.

- Avoid substances like illegal drugs, tobacco, and alcohol, that can weaken your immune system.

- Wash your hands frequently and avoid touching your eyes, nose, and mouth.

Your Skeletal System

All of the bones in your body form your skeletal system. Your bones protect many vital organs and support the soft tissues of your body. Your skeletal system includes more than two hundred bones that fit together and attach to muscles at joints.

Types of Bones

Your skeleton includes four basic types of bones: long, short, flat, and irregular. Long bones, like the ones in your arms and legs, are narrow and have large ends. These bones support weight. Short bones, found in your wrists and ankles, are chunky and wide. They allow maximum movement around a joint. Flat bones, like the ones in your skull and ribs, protect your body. Irregular bones, like your vertebrae, have unique shapes and fall outside of the other categories.

Types of Joints

Each of the three types of joints is designed to do a certain job.

Ball-and-Socket Joints like your hips and shoulders allow rotation and movement in many directions.

Hinge Joints like your elbow and knees only move back and forth.

Gliding Joints like the vertebrae in your spine or the bones in your wrists and feet allow side-to-side and back-and-forth movement.

Some joints, like the ones in your skull do not allow any movement. These flat bones fit tightly together to protect your brain.

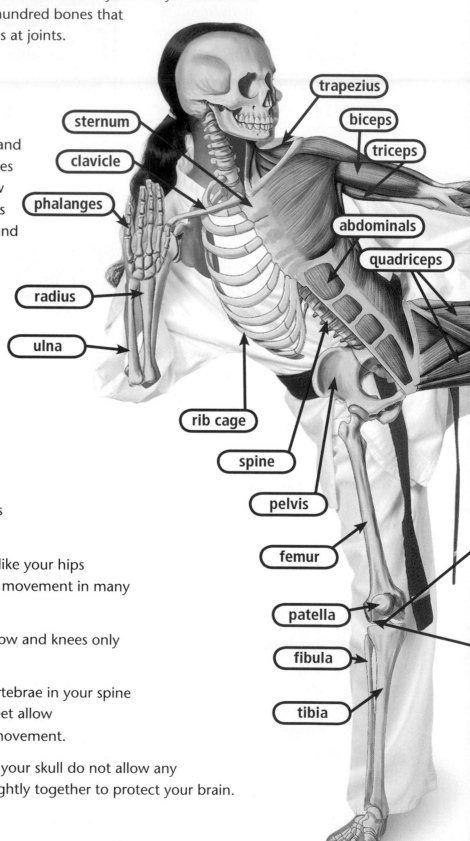

sternum
clavicle
phalanges
radius
ulna
trapezius
biceps
triceps
abdominals
quadriceps
rib cage
spine
pelvis
femur
patella
fibula
tibia

Parts of a Joint

Your bones attach to your muscles and to each other at joints. Your muscles and bones work together to allow your body to move. Joints are made up of ligaments and cartilage. Ligaments are tough, elastic tissues that attach one bone to another. Cartilage is a soft cushioning material at the ends of bones that helps bones move smoothly and absorbs some of the impact when you move. Tendons are dense, cordlike material that joins muscles to bones.

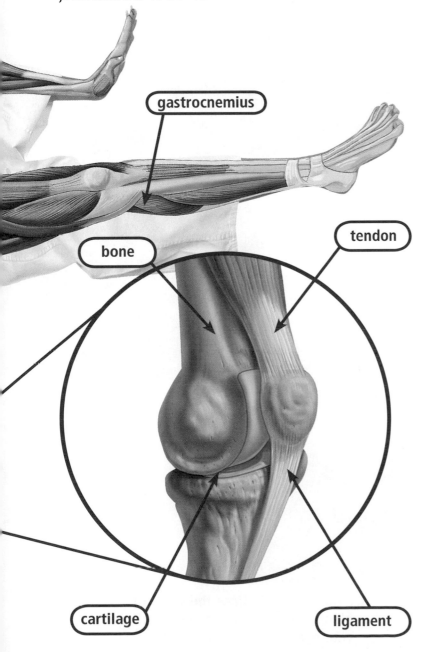

gastrocnemius

bone

tendon

cartilage

ligament

Caring for Your Skeletal System

- Always wear a helmet and proper safety gear when you play sports, skate, or ride a bike or a scooter.
- Your bones are made mostly of calcium and other minerals. To keep your skeletal system strong and to help it grow, you should eat foods that are high in calcium like milk, cheese, and yogurt. Dark green, leafy vegetables like broccoli, spinach, and collard greens are also good sources of calcium.
- Exercise to help your bones stay strong and healthy.
- Always warm up before you exercise.
- Get plenty of rest to help your bones grow.
- Stand and sit with good posture. Sitting slumped over puts strain on your muscles and on your bones.

Your Muscular System

A muscle is a body part that produces movement by contracting and relaxing. All of the muscles in your body make up the muscular system.

Types of Muscle

Your muscular system is made up of three types of muscle. The muscles that make your body move are attached to the bones of your skeletal system. These muscles are called skeletal muscles. A skeletal muscle has a bulging middle and narrow tendons at each end. Tendons are strong flat bands of tissue that attach muscles to bones near your joints. Skeletal muscles are usually under your control, so they are also called voluntary muscles.

Your muscular system includes two other types of muscle. The first of these is called smooth muscle. This specialized muscle lines most of your digestive organs. As these muscles contract and relax, they move food through your digestive system.

Your heart is made of another specialized muscle called cardiac muscle. Your heart's muscle tissue squeezes and relaxes every second of every day to pump blood through your circulatory system. Smooth muscle and cardiac muscle operate automatically. Their contraction is not under your control, so they are also called involuntary muscles.

▼ Skeletal muscle appears striped. It is the kind of muscle that moves bones.

Cardiac muscle forms the walls of the heart. It contracts and relaxes to pump blood through your body. ▶

▲ Smooth muscle lines the walls of blood vessels and of organs such as your esophagus and stomach.

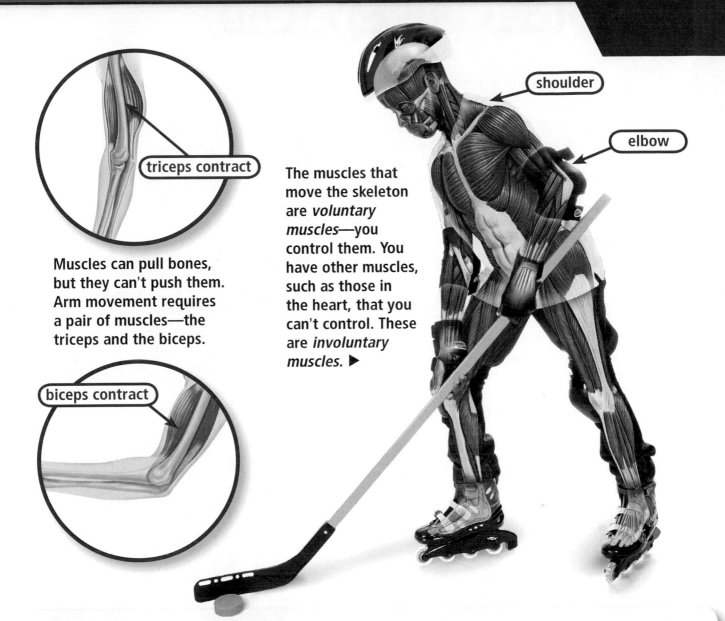

triceps contract

Muscles can pull bones, but they can't push them. Arm movement requires a pair of muscles—the triceps and the biceps.

biceps contract

The muscles that move the skeleton are *voluntary muscles*—you control them. You have other muscles, such as those in the heart, that you can't control. These are *involuntary muscles.* ▶

shoulder

elbow

Caring for Your Muscular System

- Always stretch and warm up your muscles before exercising or playing sports. Do this by jogging slowly or walking for at least ten minutes. This brings fresh blood and oxygen to your muscles, and helps prevent injury or pain.

- Eat a balanced diet of foods to be sure your muscles have the nutrients they need to grow and remain strong.

- Drink plenty of water when you exercise or play sports. This helps your blood remove wastes from your muscles and helps you build endurance.

- Always cool down after you exercise. Walk or jog slowly for five or ten minutes to let your heartbeat slow and your breathing return to normal. This helps you avoid pain and stiffness after your muscles work hard.

- Stop exercising if you feel pain in your muscles.

- Get plenty of rest before and after you work your muscles hard. They need time to repair themselves and to recover from working hard.

Your Nervous System

Your body consists of a number of different systems. Each of your body's systems plays a different role. The different systems of your body work together to keep you alive and healthy.

Just as a leader directs the work of a group, your nervous system controls your body's activities. Some activities, like the beating of your heart and breathing, are controlled automatically by your nervous system.

Your nervous system allows you to move and to see, hear, taste, touch, and smell the world around you. Your brain also allows you to learn, remember, and feel emotions.

Your nervous system is made up of your brain, your spinal cord, and your nerves.

Your spinal cord is a thick bundle of nerves inside the column of bone formed by your vertebrae. Your nerves are bundles of specialized cells branching from your spinal cord. They send messages about your environment to your brain and send signals to your muscles.

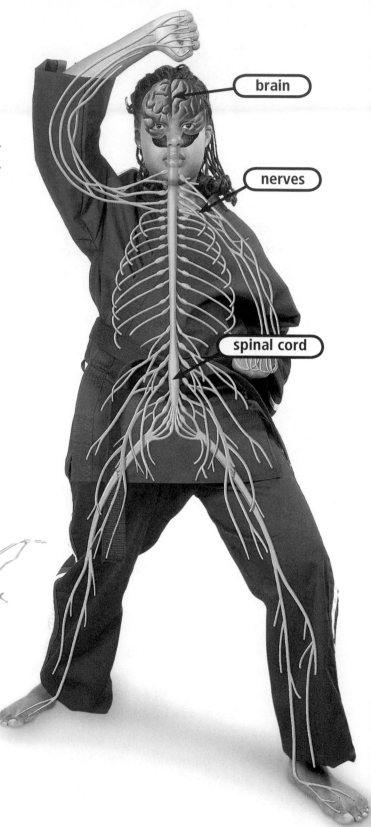

brain

nerves

spinal cord

A nerve cell is called a neuron. Signals travel to and from your brain along branching fibers of one neuron to branching fibers of other neurons.

Your brain contains about 100 billion neurons.
Different areas of your brain control different activities.

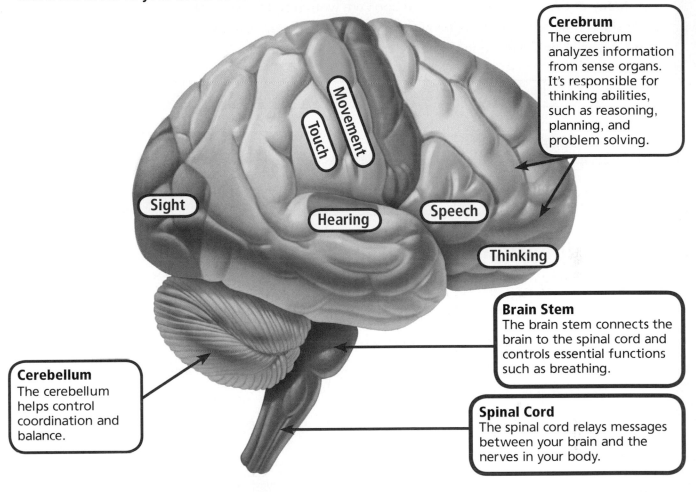

Cerebrum
The cerebrum analyzes information from sense organs. It's responsible for thinking abilities, such as reasoning, planning, and problem solving.

Movement

Touch

Sight

Hearing

Speech

Thinking

Brain Stem
The brain stem connects the brain to the spinal cord and controls essential functions such as breathing.

Cerebellum
The cerebellum helps control coordination and balance.

Spinal Cord
The spinal cord relays messages between your brain and the nerves in your body.

Caring for Your Nervous System

• Don't take illegal drugs, and avoid alcohol. These substances can impair your judgment, which may cause you to react slowly or improperly to danger. They can also damage your nervous system.

• When your doctor prescribes medicines, follow the instructions your doctor gives you. Too much medicine can affect your nervous system. Never take medicine prescribed for someone else.

• Eat a well-balanced diet to be sure your nervous system receives the nutrients it needs.

• Protect your brain and spine from injury by wearing proper safety equipment when you play sports, ride a bike or scooter, or skate.

• Get plenty of rest. Sleep helps keep your mind sharp. Like all of your body's systems, your nervous system requires rest to stay healthy.

Identify the Main Idea and Details

Many of the lessons in this science book are written so that you can understand main ideas and the details that support them. You can use a graphic organizer like this one to show a main idea and details.

Main Idea: The most important idea of a selection

| **Detail:** Information that tells more about the main idea | **Detail:** Information that tells more about the main idea | **Detail:** Information that tells more about the main idea |

Tips for Identifying the Main Idea and Details

- To find the main idea, ask—*What is this mostly about?*

- Remember that the main idea is not always stated in the first sentence.

- Be sure to look for details that help you answer questions such as *Who?, What?, Where?, When?, Why?* and *How?*

- Use pictures as clues to help you figure out the main idea.

Here is an example.

Main Idea

All living things are made up of one or more cells. Cells that work together to perform a specific function form tissues. Tissues that work together make up an organ. Each organ in an animal's body is made up of several kinds of tissues. Organs working together form a body system.

Detail

You could record this in the graphic organizer.

Main Idea: All living things are made up of one or more cells.

| **Detail:** Cells that work together form tissues. | **Detail:** Tissues that work together make up an organ. | **Detail:** Organs that work together form a body system. |

More About Main Idea and Details

Sometimes the main idea of a passage is at the end instead of the beginning. The main idea may not be stated. However, it can be understood from the details. Look at the following graphic organizer. What do you think the main idea is?

Main Idea:

Detail:
Bones make up the skeletal system.

Detail:
The muscular system is made up of voluntary muscles, smooth muscles, and cardiac muscles.

Detail:
Muscles are controlled by the central nervous system.

A passage can contain details of different types. In the following paragraph, identify each detail as a reason, an example, a fact, a step, or a description.

> Digestion begins as you chew food. When you swallow, food passes through the esophagus. Gastric juice breaks down proteins. After several hours in the stomach, partly digested food moves into the small intestine. Digestion of food into nutrients is completed in the small intestine. From the small intestine, undigested food passes into the large intestine. In the large intestine, water and minerals pass into the blood and wastes are removed from the body.

Skill Practice

Read the following paragraph. Use the Tips for Identifying Main Idea and Details to answer the questions.

> The circulatory, respiratory, digestive, and excretory systems work together to keep the body alive. The circulatory system transports oxygen, nutrients, and wastes through the body. In the respiratory system, oxygen diffuses into the blood and carbon dioxide diffuses out of the blood. The digestive system provides the nutrients your cells need to produce energy. The excretory system removes cell wastes from the blood.

1. What is the main idea of the paragraph?

2. What supporting details give more information?

3. What details answer any of the questions *Who?, What?, Where?, When?, Why?* and *How?*

Compare and Contrast

Some lessons are written to help you see how things are alike or different. You can use a graphic organizer like this one to compare and contrast.

Topic: Name the topic—the two things you are comparing and contrasting.

Alike
List ways the things are alike.

Different
List ways the things are different.

Tips for Comparing and Contrasting

- To compare, ask—*How are people, places, objects, ideas, or events alike?*

- To contrast, ask—*How are people, places, objects, ideas, or events different?*

- When you compare, look for signal words and phrases such as *similar, both, too,* and *also.*

- When you contrast, look for signal words and phrases such as *unlike, however, yet,* and *but.*

Here is an example.

Compare

The two basic kinds of energy are kinetic energy and potential energy. Kinetic energy is the energy of motion. Any matter in motion has kinetic energy. However, potential energy is the energy of position or condition. Transformation of energy is the change between kinetic energy and potential energy. The total amount of energy does not change when energy is transformed.

Contrast

Here is what you could record in the graphic organizer.

Topic: Kinetic and Potential Energy

Alike
Both are basic kinds of energy.
The total amount of energy stays the same when it changes forms.

Different
Kinetic energy is the energy of motion.
Potential energy is the energy of position or condition.

More About Comparing and Contrasting

Identifying how things are alike and how they're different can help you understand new information. Use a graphic organizer to sort the following information about kinetic energy and potential energy.

kinetic energy	electric energy	thermal energy	mechanical energy	light energy

potential energy	elastic potential energy	gravitational potential energy	chemical energy

Sometimes a paragraph compares and contrasts more than one topic. In the following paragraph, one topic of comparison is underlined. Find a second topic for comparison or contrast.

> Material that conducts electrons easily is called a conductor. An insulator is a material that does not carry electrons. An electric circuit is any path along which electrons can flow. Some circuits are series circuits. They have only one path for the electrons. Other circuits are parallel circuits, where each device is on a separate path.

Skill Practice

Read the following paragraph. Use the Tips for Comparing and Contrasting to answer the questions.

> Within an atom, electrons have a negative charge and protons have a positive charge. Most objects have equal numbers of protons and electrons. Both protons and electrons attract each other. Sometimes, however, electrons are attracted to the protons of another object and rub off. These objects become negatively charged.

1. What are two ways protons and electrons are alike?

2. Explain a difference between protons and electrons.

3. Name two signal words that helped you identify likenesses or differences in this paragraph.

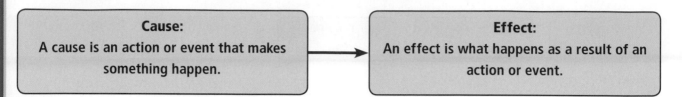

Cause and Effect

Some of the lessons in this science book are written to help you understand why things happen. You can use a graphic organizer like this one to show cause and effect.

Cause:	Effect:
A cause is an action or event that makes something happen.	An effect is what happens as a result of an action or event.

Tips for Identifying Cause and Effect

- To find an effect, ask—*What happened?*
- To find a cause, ask—*Why did this happen?*
- Remember that events can have more than one cause or effect.
- Look for signal words and phrases, such as *because* and *as a result,* to help you identify causes and effects.

Here is an example.

Earth's surface is made up of many plates. Plates are rigid blocks of crust and upper mantle rock. Earth's plates fit together like the pieces of a puzzle. Plate movement is very slow. As plates move around, they cause great changes in Earth's landforms. Where plates collide, energy is released, and new landforms are produced. On land, mountains rise and volcanoes erupt.

Here is what you could record in the graphic organizer.

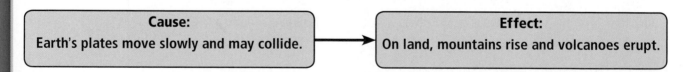

Cause:	Effect:
Earth's plates move slowly and may collide.	On land, mountains rise and volcanoes erupt.

More About Cause and Effect

Events can have more than one cause or effect. For example, suppose a paragraph included a sentence that said "On the ocean floor, deep trenches form." You could then identify two effects of Earth's plates colliding.

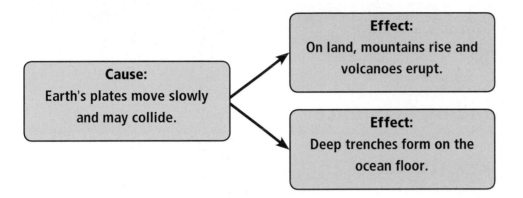

Cause:
Earth's plates move slowly and may collide.

Effect:
On land, mountains rise and volcanoes erupt.

Effect:
Deep trenches form on the ocean floor.

Some paragraphs contain more than one cause and effect. In the paragraph below, one cause and its effect are underlined. Find the second cause and its effect.

> As Earth's plates pull apart on land, valleys with volcanoes develop. Africa's Great Rift Valley was formed by the African and Arabian plates pulling apart. When plates pull apart under the sea, ridges and volcanoes form. New sea floor is formed at the ridges.

Skill Practice

Read the following paragraph. Use the Tips for Identifying Cause and Effect to help you answer the questions.

> When energy is suddenly released in Earth's crust, the ground shakes and an earthquake occurs. The earthquake is a result of plates crushing together, scraping past each other, or bending along jagged boundaries. Because Earth shakes in an earthquake, great damage can occur, such as streets splitting open and bridges collapsing.

1. What causes an earthquake to occur?

2. What are some effects of an earthquake?

3. What two signal words or phrases helped you identify the causes and effects in this paragraph?

Sequence

Some lessons in this science book are written to help you understand the order in which things happen. You can use a graphic organizer like this one to show sequence.

I. The first thing that happened	→	2. The next thing that happened	→	3. The last thing that happened

Tips for Understanding Sequence

- Pay attention to the order in which events happen.

- Remember dates and times to help you understand the sequence.

- Look for signal words such as *first, next, then, last,* and *finally.*

- Sometimes it's helpful to add your own time-order words to help you understand the sequence.

Here is an example.

Time-order words

A substance is buoyant, or will float in a liquid, if its density is less than that of the liquid. Here is a procedure that will show you what it takes for an egg to float in water. First, place an egg in a cup of water. Observe whether or not it floats. Next, remove the egg and stir several spoonfuls of salt into the water. Finally, replace the egg in the water and observe whether or not it floats. By changing the density of the water, you allow its density to become greater than the density of the egg.

You could record this in the graphic organizer.

I. First, place an egg in a cup of water and observe.	→	2. Next, remove the egg and stir salt into the water.	→	3. Finally, replace the egg in the water and observe.

More About Sequence

Sometimes information is sequenced by dates. For example, models of the atom have changed since the late 1800s. Use the graphic organizer to sequence the order of how the model of an atom has changed over time.

1. Near the end of the 1800s, Thomson's model of an atom was the first to include subatomic particles.	**2.** In the early 1900s, Rutherford's model suggested that the atom was made up mostly of empty space. Bohr's model showed different orbits for electrons.	**3.** Today, the modern model of an atom includes a cloud of electrons around the central positive nucleus.

When time-order words are not given, add your own words to help you understand the sequence. In the paragraph below, one time-order word has been included and underlined. What other time-order words can you add to help you understand the paragraph's sequence?

A person riding a bicycle changes the chemical energy in his or her cells to mechanical energy in order to push the pedals. The energy is transferred from the pedals through the chain to the rear wheel. <u>Finally</u>, the kinetic energy of the turning of the wheel is transferred to the whole bicycle.

Skill Practice

Read the following paragraph. Use the Tips for Understanding Sequence to answer the questions.

First, a flashlight is switched on. Then, the chemical energy stored in the battery is changed into electric energy. Next, the circuit is closed. Finally, the electric energy is changed to light energy in the flashlight bulb.

1. What is the first thing that happened in this sequence?

2. About how long did the process take?

3. What signal words helped you identify the sequence in this paragraph?

Draw Conclusions

At the end of each lesson in this science book, you will be asked to draw conclusions. To draw conclusions, use information from the text you are reading and what you already know. Drawing conclusions can help you understand what you read. You can use a graphic organizer like this.

| **What I Read** List facts from the text. | + | **What I Know** List related ideas from your own experience. | = | **Conclusion:** Combine facts from the text with your own experience. |

Tips for Drawing Conclusions

- Ask—*What text information do I need to think about?*

- Ask—*What do I know from my own experience that could help me draw a conclusion?*

- Pay close attention to the information in the text and to your experience to be sure the conclusion is valid, or makes sense.

Here is an example.

> The shore is the area where the ocean and land meet and interact. Waves grind pebbles and rocks against the shore which can cause erosion. The water pressure from a wave can loosen pebbles and small rocks, which outgoing waves carry into the ocean. Long shore currents move sand, pebbles, and shells along the shore.

Here is what you could record in the graphic organizer.

Text information

Your own experience

| **What I Read** The shore is where the ocean and land meet and interact. | + | **What I Know** I have seen waves and currents move rocks, sand, and shells on the shore. | = | **Conclusion:** Waves and currents can change the shore. |

More About Drawing Conclusions

Sensible conclusions based on your experience and the facts you read are valid. For example, suppose a paragraph had ended with the sentence "Human activities can also change the shore." You might have come to a different conclusion about what changes the shore.

What I Read		**What I Know**		**Conclusion:**
The shore is where the ocean and land meet and interact.	**+**	Waves loosen rocks and pebbles. Currents move sand, pebbles, and shells. Structures can be built to prevent erosion.	**=**	Waves, currents, and human activities can change the shore.

Sometimes a paragraph might not contain enough information for drawing a valid conclusion. Read the paragraph below. Think of one valid conclusion you could draw. Then think of one invalid conclusion someone might draw from the given information.

A jetty is a wall-like structure made of rocks that sticks out into the ocean. Jetties are usually built on either side of an opening to a harbor. Jetties catch sand and pebbles that normally flow down the coast with the current. Jetties can change the shore by building up the beach.

Skill Practice

Read the following paragraph. Use the Tips for Drawing Conclusions to answer the questions.

Most of the movement of water on the ocean's surface is due to waves. A wave is the up-and-down movement of surface water. On a calm day, ocean waves may only be 1.5 meters high or less. However, during a storm, waves can reach heights of 30 meters.

1. What conclusion did you draw about the height of a wave?

2. What information from your personal experience did you use to draw the conclusion?

3. What text information did you use?

Summarize

At the end of every lesson in this science book, you will be asked to summarize. When you summarize, you use your own words to tell what something is about. In the lesson, you will be given ideas for writing your summary. You can also use a graphic organizer like this one to summarize.

Main Idea:		Details:		Summary:
Tell about the most important information you have read.	**+**	Add details that answer important questions *Who?*, *What?*, *Where?*, *When?*, *Why?*, and *How?*	**=**	Retell what you have just read, including only the most important details.

Tips for Summarizing

- To write a summary, ask—*What is the most important idea of the paragraph?*

- To include details with your summary, ask—*Who?, What?, When?, Where?, Why?* and *How?*

- Remember to use fewer words than the original has.

- Don't forget to use your own words when you summarize.

Here is an example.

Main Idea

Sound waves are carried by vibrating matter. Most sound waves travel through air, but they may also travel through liquids and even some solids. As the sound waves travel, the energy of the wave decreases. The frequency at which the sound wave moves determines the pitch of the sound. The greater the frequency, the higher the pitch. The strength of a sound wave can also be measured. The more energy a sound has, the louder it is.

Details

Here's what you could record in your graphic organizer.

Main Idea:		Details:		Summary:
Sound waves are carried by vibrating matter.	**+**	Pitch is determined by the frequency at which the sound wave moves. The more energy a sound has, the louder it is.	**=**	Sound waves are carried by vibrating matter. Pitch is determined by the frequency at which the sound wave moves. The loudness of a sound is determined by how much energy it has.

More About Summarizing

Sometimes a paragraph includes information that should not be included in a summary. For example, suppose a paragraph included a sentence that said "High musical notes have high pitch and high frequency, and low musical notes have low pitch and low frequency." The graphic organizer would remain the same, because that detail is not important to understanding the paragraph's main idea.

Sometimes the main idea of a paragraph is not in the first sentence. In the following paragraph, two important details are underlined. What is the main idea?

> <u>Air, water, clear glass, and clear plastic are substances which objects can clearly be seen through.</u> Substances that light can travel through are transparent. <u>Substances that are transparent are used to make things like windows and eyeglasses.</u> Some substances are transparent only to certain colors of light. They are described as clear since you can see objects through them, but they have a color.

Skill Practice

Read the following paragraph. Use the Tips for Summarizing to answer the questions.

> Light can be absorbed, reflected, or refracted. Sometimes light waves are absorbed when they strike an object. Most objects absorb some colors of light. Other colors of light bounce off objects, or are reflected. These are the colors we see. The change in speed of light causes it to bend. This bending of light waves is called refraction.

1. If a friend asked you what this paragraph was about, what information would you include? What would you leave out?

2. What is the main idea of the paragraph?

3. What two details would you include in a summary?

Using Tables, Charts, and Graphs

As you do investigations in science, you collect, organize, display, and interpret data. Tables, charts, and graphs are good ways to organize and display data so that others can understand and interpret your data.

The tables, charts, and graphs in this Handbook will help you read and understand data. You can also use the information to choose the best ways to display data so that you can use it to draw conclusions and make predictions.

Reading a Table

A bird-watching group is studying the wingspans of different birds. They want to find out the birds with the greatest wingspans. The table shows the data the group has collected.

Largest Wingspans	
Type of Bird	Wingspan (in feet)
Albatross	12
Trumpeter Swan	11
California Condor	10
Marabou Stork	10

Title
Headings
Data

How to Read a Table

1. **Read the title** to find out what the table is about.

2. **Read the headings** to find out what information is given.

3. **Study the data.** Look for patterns.

4. **Draw conclusions.** If you display the data in a graph, you might be able to see patterns easily.

By studying the table, you can see the birds with the greatest wingspans. However, suppose the group wants to look for patterns in the data. They might choose to display the data in a different way, such as in a bar graph.

Reading a Bar Graph

The data in this bar graph is the same as in the table. A bar graph can be used to compare the data about different events or groups.

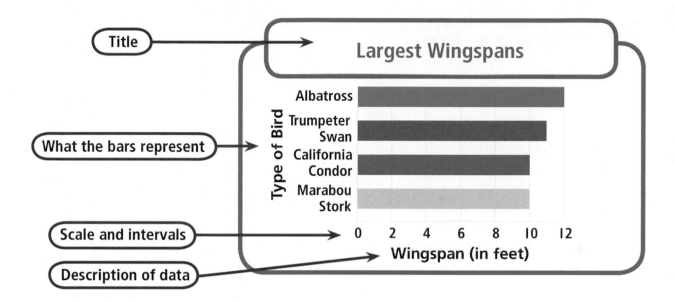

How to Read a Bar Graph

1. **Look** at the graph to determine what kind of graph it is.

2. **Read** the graph. Use the labels to guide you.

3. **Analyze** the data. Study the bars to compare the measurements. Look for patterns.

4. **Draw conclusions.** Ask yourself questions, like the ones in the Skills Practice.

Skills Practice

1. Which two birds have the same wingspan?

2. How much greater is the wingspan of an albatross than the wingspan of a California condor?

3. A red-tailed hawk has a wingspan of 4 feet. Which type of bird has a wingspan that is three times that of the hawk?

4. **Predict** A fifth-grade student saw a bird that had a wingspan that was about the same as her height. Could the bird have been an albatross?

5. Was the bar graph a good choice for displaying this data? Explain your answer.

Reading a Line Graph

A scientist collected this data about how the amount of ice in the Nordic Sea area of the Arctic Ocean has changed over the years.

Nordic Sea Area Ice

Year	Number of Square Kilometers (in millions)
1860	2.8
1880	2.7
1900	2.2
1920	2.4
1940	2.0
1960	1.8
1980	1.5
2000	1.6

Here is the same data displayed in a line graph. A line graph is used to show changes over time.

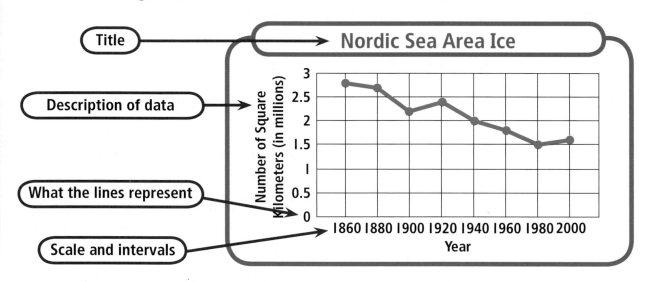

How to Read a Line Graph

1. **Look** at the graph to determine what kind of graph it is.

2. **Read** the graph. Use the labels to guide you.

3. **Analyze** the data. Study the points along the lines. Look for patterns.

4. **Draw conclusions.** Ask yourself questions, like the ones in the Skills Practice to help you draw conclusions.

Skills Practice

1. By how much did the ice in the Nordic Sea area change from 1940 to 1980?

2. **Predict** Will there be more or less than 2.5 million square kilometers of ice in the Nordic Sea area in 2020?

3. Was the line graph a good choice for displaying this data? Explain why.

Reading a Circle Graph

A fifth-grade class is studying U.S. energy sources. They want to know which energy sources are used in the U.S. They classified the different sources by making a table. Here is the data they gathered.

U.S. Energy Sources	
Source of Energy	**Percent Used**
Petroleum	38
Natural Gas	24
Coal	22
Hydroelectric and Nuclear Power	12
Other	4

The circle graph shows the same data as the table. A circle graph can be used to show data as a whole made up of different parts.

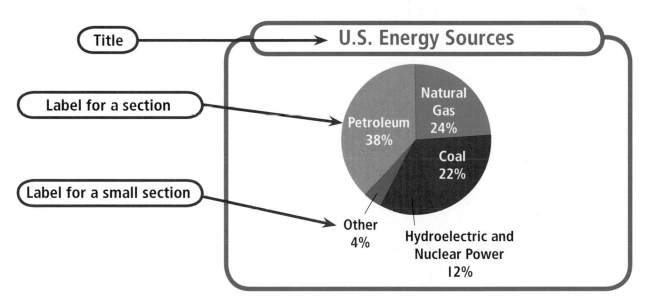

How to Read a Circle Graph

1. **Look** at the title of the graph to learn what kind of information is shown.

2. **Read** the graph. Look at the label of each section to find out what information is shown.

3. **Analyze** the data. Compare the sizes of the sections to determine how they are related.

4. **Draw conclusions.** Ask yourself questions, like the ones in the Skills Practice.

Skills Practice

1. Which source of energy is used most?

2. **Predict** If wind, geothermal, and solar make up some of the other energy sources, will they be a greater or lesser part of U.S. energy sources in the future?

3. Was the circle graph a good choice for displaying this data? Explain why.

Using Metric Measurements

A measurement is a number that represents a comparison of something being measured to a unit of measurement. Scientists use many different tools to measure objects and substances as they work. Scientists almost always use the metric system for their measurements.

Measuring Length and Capacity

When you measure length, you find the distance between two points. The distance may be in a straight line, along a curved path, or around a circle. The table shows the metric units of **length** and how they are related.

Equivalent Measures
1 centimeter (cm) = 10 millimeters (mm)
1 decimeter (dm) = 10 centimeters (cm)
1 meter (m) = 1,000 millimeters
1 meter = 10 decimeters
1 kilometer (km) = 1,000 meters

You can use these comparisons to help you understand the size of each metric unit of length.

A **millimeter (mm)** is about the thickness of a dime.

A **centimeter (cm)** is about the width of your index finger.

A **decimeter (dm)** is about the width of an adult's hand.

A **meter (m)** is about the width of a door.

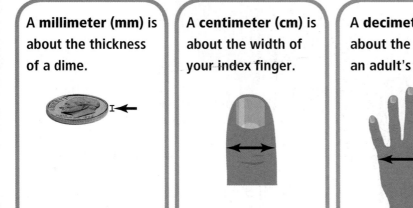
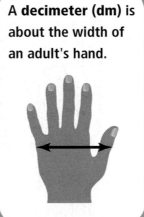

Sometimes you may need to change units of length. The following diagram shows how to multiply and divide to change to larger and smaller units.

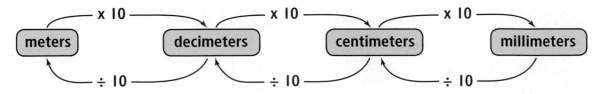

The photos below show the metric units of **capacity** and common comparisons. The metric units of volume are the milliliter (mL) and the liter (L). You can use multiplication to change liters to milliliters. You can use division to change milliliters to liters.

A **milliliter (mL)** is the amount of liquid that can fill part of a medicine dropper.

1 mL

A **liter (L)** is the amount of liquid that can fill a plastic bottle of the size shown here.

1 L

1 L = 1000 mL

To change *larger* units to *smaller* units, you need more of the *smaller units*. So, **multiply** by 10, 100, or 1,000. To change *smaller* units to *larger* units, you need *fewer of the larger units*. So, **divide** by 10, 100, or 1,000.

500 dm = ____ cm

Think: There are 10 cm in 1 dm.

500 dm = 500 x 10 = 5,000

So, 500 dm = 5,000 cm.

4,000 mL = ____ L

Think: There are 1,000 mL in 1 L.

4,000 ÷ 1,000 = 4

So, 4,000 mL = 4 L.

Skills Practice

Complete. Tell whether you multiply or divide by 10, 100, or 1,000.

1. 7 m = _____ cm

2. 4 m = _____ dm

3. 800 _____ = 8 m

4. 9,000 mm = _____ m

5. 9 L = _____ mL

6. 6,000 mL = _____ L

7. 3,000 mL = _____ L

8. 8 _____ = 8,000 mL

Measuring Mass

Matter is what all objects are made of. Mass is the amount of matter that is in an object. The metric units of mass are the gram (g) and the kilogram (kg).

You can use these comparisons to help you understand the masses of some everyday objects.

A paper clip is about **1 gram (g)**. 	A slice of wheat bread is about **20 g**. 	A box of 12 crayons is about **100 g**. 	A large wedge of cheese is about **1 kilogram** (kg). 

You can use multiplication to change kilograms to grams.

You can use division to change grams to kilograms.

2 kg = ___ g	4,000 g = ____ kg
Think: There are 1,000 g in 1 kg.	Think: There are 1,000 g in 1 kg.
2 kg = 2 x 1,000 = 2,000 g	4,000 ÷ 1,000 = 4
So, 2 kg = 2,000 g.	So, 4,000 g = 4 kg.

Skills Practice

Complete. Tell whether you multiply or divide by 1,000.

1. 4,000 g = _____ kg

2. 3,000 g = _____ kg

3. 7 kg = _____ g

4. 8 _____ = 8,000 g

Measurement Systems

SI Measures (Metric)

Temperature
Ice melts at 0 degrees Celsius (°C)
Water freezes at 0°C
Water boils at 100°C

Length and Distance
1000 meters (m) = 1 kilometer (km)
100 centimeters (cm) = 1 m
10 millimeters (mm) = 1 cm

Force
1 newton (N) = 1 kilogram x
    1 meter/second/second (kg-m/sec^2)

Volume
1 cubic meter (m^3) = 1 m x 1 m x 1 m
1 cubic centimeter (cm^3) =
    1 cm x 1 cm x 1 cm
1 liter (L) = 1000 millimeters (mL)
1 cm^3 = 1 mL

Area
1 square kilometer (km^2) =
    1 km x 1 km
1 hectare = 10 000 m^2

Mass
1000 grams (g) = 1 kilogram (kg)
1000 milligrams (mg) = 1 g

Rates (Metric and Customary)
km/hr = kilometers per hour
m/sec = meters per second
mi/hr = miles per hour

Customary Measures

Volume of Fluids
2 c = 1 pint (pt)
2 pt = 1 quart (qt)
4 qt = 1 gallon (gal)

Temperature
Ice melts at 32 degrees
    Fahrenheit (°F)
Water freezes at 32°F
Water boils at 212°F

Length and Distance
12 inches (in.) = 1 foot (ft)
3 ft = 1 yard (yd)
5,280 ft = 1 mile (mi)

Weight
16 ounces (oz) = 1 pound (lb)
2,000 pounds = 1 ton (T)

Safety in Science

Doing investigations in science can be fun, but you need to be sure you do them safely. Here are some rules to follow.

1. **Think ahead.** Study the steps of the investigation so you know what to expect. If you have any questions, ask your teacher. Be sure you understand any caution statements or safety reminders.

2. **Be neat.** Keep your work area clean. If you have long hair, pull it back so it doesn't get in the way. Roll or push up long sleeves to keep them away from your activity.

3. **Oops!** If you should spill or break something, or get cut, tell your teacher right away.

4. **Watch your eyes.** Wear safety goggles anytime you are directed to do so. If you get anything in your eyes, tell your teacher right away.

5. **Yuck!** Never eat or drink anything during a science activity.

6. **Don't get shocked.** Be especially careful if an electric appliance is used. Be sure that electric cords are in a safe place where you can't trip over them. Don't ever pull a plug out of an outlet by pulling on the cord.

7. **Keep it clean.** Always clean up when you have finished. Put everything away and wipe your work area. Wash your hands.

Visit the Multimedia Science Glossary to see illustrations of these words and to hear them pronounced.
www.hspscience.com

Every entry in the glossary begins with a term and a *phonetic respelling*. A phonetic respelling writes the word the way it sounds, which can help you pronounce new or unfamiliar words. The definition of the term follows the respelling. An example of how to use the term in a sentence follows the definition.

The page number in ( ) at the end of the entry tells you where to find the term in your textbook. Many of the glossary terms are highlighted in yellow in a lesson.

Most glossary entries have an illustration to help you understand the term. The Pronunciation Key below will help you understand the respellings. Syllables are separated by a bullet (•). Small capital letters show stressed syllables.

Pronunciation Key

Sound	As in	Phonetic Respelling	Sound	As in	Phonetic Respelling
a	bat	(BAT)	oh	over	(OH•ver)
ah	lock	(LAHK)	oo	pool	(POOL)
air	rare	(RAIR)	ow	out	(OWT)
ar	argue	(AR•gyoo)	oy	foil	(FOYL)
aw	law	(LAW)	s	cell	(SEL)
ay	face	(FAYS)		sit	(SIT)
ch	chapel	(CHAP•uhl)	sh	sheep	(SHEEP)
e	test	(TEST)	th	that	(THAT)
	metric	(MEH•trik)		thin	(THIN)
ee	eat	(EET)	u	pull	(PUL)
	feet	(FEET)	uh	medal	(MED•uhl)
	ski	(SKEE)		talent	(TAL•uhnt)
er	paper	(PAY•per)		pencil	(PEN•suhl)
	fern	(FERN)		onion	(UHN•yuhn)
eye	idea	(eye•DEE•uh)		playful	(PLAY•fuhl)
i	bit	(BIT)		dull	(DUHL)
ing	going	(GOH•ing)	y	yes	(YES)
k	card	(KARD)		ripe	(RYP)
	kite	(KYT)	z	bags	(BAGZ)
ngk	bank	(BANGK)	zh	treasure	(TREZH•er)

Multimedia Science Glossary: www.hspscience.com

A

absorb [ab•ZAWRB]
To take in: Sponges
absorb liquid easily.
(194)

acid [AS•id] **A**
chemical compound
that turns blue
litmus paper red
and has a pH of less
than 7: The juice
from an orange is a
mild *acid*. (110)

adaptation
[ad•uhp•TAY•shuhn] **A**
trait or characteristic
that helps an
organism survive:
The dolphin's flippers
are an *adaptation* that
helps it swim. (190)

air mass [AIR MAS]
A large body of
air that has similar
temperature
and humidity
throughout: The
blue arrows represent
cool *air masses*. (302)

air pressure [AIR
PRESH•er] **The weight**
of the atmosphere
pressing down on
Earth: *Air pressure*
changes with
altitude. (272)

alloy [AL•oy] **A solid**
solution in which a
metal or a nonmetal
is dissolved in a
metal: This statue
is made of an *alloy*
called bronze. (84)

anemometer
[an•uh•MAHM•uht•er]
An instrument for
measuring wind
speed: Wind makes
an *anemometer* spin.
(300)

aqueduct
[AK•wuh•duhkt] **A**
pipe or channel that
is used to transport
water: You can see
aqueducts built by
ancient Romans
throughout western
Europe. (242)

array [uh•RAY] **A pattern of atoms:** This *array* of atoms can be seen only through a very powerful microscope. (83)

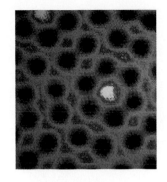

artery [ART•er•ee] **A blood vessel that carries blood from the heart to the rest of the body:** *Arteries* (red) carry blood from the heart to the body. (158)

asteroid [AS•ter•oyd] **A piece of rock and metal that orbits the sun:** Some *asteroids* are pieces of rock from collisions of larger objects in space. (350)

atmosphere [AT•muhs•fir] **The blanket of air surrounding Earth:** Earth's *atmosphere* has several layers. (270)

atom [AT•uhm] **The smallest unit of an element, that has the properties of that element:** Nearly all *atoms* have neutrons. (62)

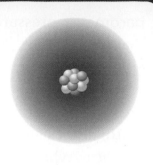

atomic number [uh•TAHM•ik NUHM•ber] **The number of protons in an atom:** The *atomic number* of carbon is 6. (64)

B

balance [BAL•uhns] **A tool that measures an object's mass:** The *balance* shows that the masses of these objects are equal. (11)

barometer [buh•RAHM•uht•er] **An instrument for measuring air pressure:** The original *barometer* used mercury in a glass tube to measure air pressure. (300)

barometric pressure [bair•uh•MEH•trik PRESH•er] **The weight of the atmosphere pressing down on Earth; also called air pressure:** When the *barometric pressure* drops quickly, you can expect a storm. (300)

base [BAYS] **A chemical compound that turns red litmus paper blue and has a pH of more than 7:** Soap is a mild *base*. (110)

binoculars [by•NAHK•yuh•lerz] **A device for looking at distant objects that magnifies what is seen, using a lens for each eye:** You can use *binoculars* to see things that are far away. (331)

bladder [BLAD•er] **A saclike muscular organ where urine is stored until it is released from the body:** The *bladder* is connected to the kidneys. (183)

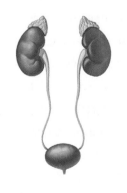

blizzard [BLIZ•erd] **A severe snowstorm:** It is hard to see in a *blizzard*. (313)

blood circulation [BLUHD ser•kyoo•LAY•shuhn] **The movement of blood through the body, taking oxygen and nutrients to the cells and wastes away from the cells:** The heart provides the force for *blood circulation*. (158)

boil [BOYL] **To change from a liquid to a gas:** Water *boils* at 100°C (212°F). (68)

brittle [BRIT•uhl] **Able to be broken or crushed easily:** Chalk is *brittle*. (111)

C

capillary
[KAP•uh•lair•ee]
One of the tiny blood vessels that exchange materials between the blood and body cells: You have many *capillaries* in your skin. (158)

carbon dioxide
[KAR•buhn dy•AHK•syd]
A molecule formed from one atom of carbon and two atoms of oxygen: *Carbon dioxide* is the compound in dry ice. (95)

cardiovascular
[kar•dee•oh•VAS•kyoo•ler]
Having to do with the heart and the circulatory system: The condition of your heart is important to your *cardiovascular* health. (158)

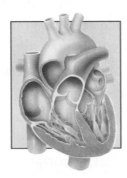

cell
[SEL] **The basic unit of structure and function in all living things:** Plants *cells* have a cell wall. (142)

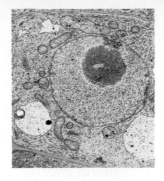

cellular respiration
[SEL•yoo•ler res•puh•RAY•shuhn]
The process by which cells use oxygen to break down sugar to release energy: *Cellular respiration* takes place in the mitochondria. (208)

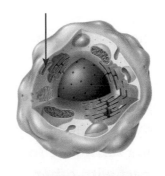

cellular waste
[SEL•yoo•ler WAYST]
A product of cell functions: Vesicles store *cellular waste*. (182)

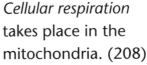

chaos theory
[KAY•ahs THEE•uh•ree]
The idea that very small changes can have major effects on a system: An illustration of *chaos theory* is the effect that one falling domino has on the others in a row. (305)

chemical change
[KEM•ih•kuhl CHAYNJ]
**A change in which
a substance or two
becomes a new
substance or two:**
Burning is one kind
of *chemical change*.
(118)

chemical compound
[KEM•ih•kuhl
KAHM•pownd] **A
substance made
of two or more
different elements:**
Water is a *chemical
compound* because it
is made of hydrogen
and oxygen. (66)

chemical property
[KEM•ih•kuhl
PRAHP•er•tee] **A
property that
involves the ability
of a substance to
react with other
materials and form
new substances:**
Flammability is one
kind of *chemical
property*. (108)

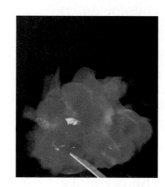

chemical reaction
[KEM•ih•kuhl
ree•AK•shuhn] **A
change in which
one or more new
substances are
formed:** Rusting is
one kind of *chemical
reaction*. (118)

chlorophyll
[KLAWR•uh•fil] **A green
pigment that allows
a plant cell to use
light to make food:**
Chlorophyll is what
makes leaves green.
(206)

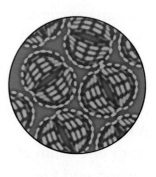

circulation
[ser•kyoo•LAY•shuhn]
**The movement of
something from
place to place (such
as water and air
around Earth):** The
water cycle is the
circulation of water
from the atmosphere
to Earth's surface
and back to the
atmosphere. (288)

circulatory system
[SER•kyoo•luh•tawr•ee SIS•tuhm]
A group of organs that transports needed materials throughout the body: The *circulatory system* moves blood throughout the body. (158)

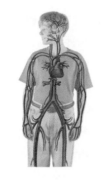

classify [KLAS•uh•fy] To group or organize objects or events into categories based on certain criteria: This student is *classifying* objects. (32)

cloud [KLOWD] Water that has either condensed on dust particles in the air or frozen at a high altitude: The types of *clouds* are related to different kinds of weather. (290)

colon [KOH•luhn] An organ that produces solid waste from undigested food: The *colon* is part of the digestive system. (175)

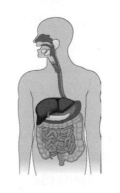

comet [KAHM•it] A ball of ice, rock, and frozen gases that orbits the sun: A *comet's* orbit around the sun is usually irregular. (350)

compound [KAHM•pownd] A substance made of two or more different elements: Baking soda and vinegar are *compounds*. (66)

conclusion [kuhn•KLOO•zhuhn] A decision you make based on information: These students are using information from an experiment to draw a *conclusion*. (33)

condensation [kahn•duhn•SAY•shuhn] The process by which a gas changes into a liquid: Rain results from *condensation*. (231)

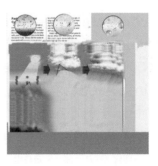

conductivity
[kahn•duhk•TIV•uh•tee]
The ability of a metal to transfer energy easily: These wires are made of metal that has very high *conductivity*. (80)

conservation
[kahn•ser•VAY•shuhn]
The preserving and protecting of a resource: Protecting resources is a part of *conservation*. (256)

control variable
[kuhn•TROHL VAIR•ee•uh•buhl] **One of the parts of an investigation that you can control:** It is important to keep track of your *control variables*. (22)

convection
[kuhn•VEK•shuhn]
Circular movement in a liquid or gas, resulting from regions of different temperatures and different densities: *Convection* in the atmosphere produces rain clouds. (275)

convection currents
[kuhn•VEK•shuhn KER•uhnts] **The upward and downward movements of a gas or a liquid:** These candles heat the air and cause it to move in a *convection current*. (274)

creek [KREEK] **A narrow and shallow river:** Water can move quickly, even in a small *creek*. (242)

crescent moon
[KRES•uhnt MOON] **The moon phase just after or just before a new moon:** There are two *crescent moons* in a month. (365)

criteria
[kry•TIR•ee•uh] **The specific qualities that allow you to group items:** The students are classifying the objects according to the *criteria* they discussed. (32)

current [KER•uhnt] **A stream of water that flows like a river through the ocean:** Ocean *currents* flow in only one direction. (286)

cyclone [SY•klohn] **A rapidly turning air mass:** The air in a *cyclone* turns counterclockwise in the Northern Hemisphere. (313)

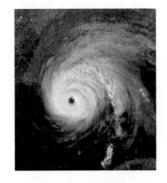

cytoplasm [SYT•oh•plaz•uhm] **The jellylike substance between a cell membrane and the nucleus, containing most organelles:** *Cytoplasm* helps protect organelles. (144)

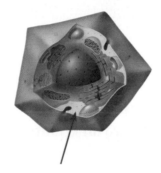

D

dam [DAM] **A barrier across a river, controlling its flow:** *Dams* can be natural, animal-made, or human-made. (242)

deflect [dee•FLEKT] **To turn something from its path, as when winds are deflected by a mountain range:** The windshield of a car *deflects* the air. (277)

dependent variable [dee•PEN•duhnt VAIR•ee•uh•buhl] **The part of an investigation that is out of your control:** The results of your investigation are shown by a *dependent variable*. (22)

diagram [DY•uh•gram] **A drawing, sketch, or other visual representation that explains an idea or object:** This *diagram* shows the parts of a flower. (36)

diffusion
[dih•FYOO•zhuhn]
The movement of materials from an area of higher concentration to an area of lower concentration: Nephrons in the kidneys remove liquid waste through *diffusion*. (183)

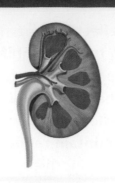

digestion
[dih•JES•chuhn] **The process of breaking food down into nutrients the body's cells need for energy, growth, and repair:** Several organs are involved in *digestion*. (173)

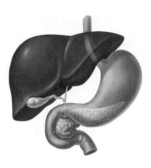

digestive system
[dih•JES•tive SIS•tuhm]
The organ system that breaks food down into chemical nutrients the body can use: The *digestive system* includes the stomach and the intestines. (172)

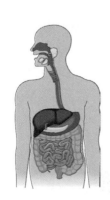

ductile [DUHK•tuhl]
Able to be pulled into thin strands: *Ductile* metal is used to make wire. (79)

E

Earth [ERTH] **The planet we live on:** *Earth* looks mostly blue from space. (346)

El Niño [el NEEN•yoh]
Warming of South American equatorial ocean waters that leads to changing weather patterns: On this colored satellite map, you can see the warm water that causes *el Niño*. (287)

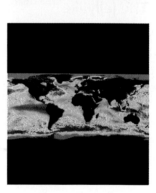

electrical conductivity
[ee•LEK•trih•kuhl kahn•duhk•TIV•uh•tee]
The ability of a metal to transfer electrons: Silver has *electrical conductivity*. (80)

electron
[ee•LEK•trahn] **One of the particles in an atom:** An *electron* has a negative charge. (62)

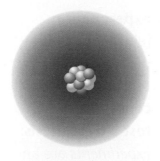

electron microscope
[ee•LEK•trahn MY•kruh•skohp] **A microscope that uses a stream of electrons to produce images of objects:** The *electron microscope* is very powerful. (82)

element
[EL•uh•muhnt] **A substance made of only one kind of atom:** Gold is an *element* because it is made of only gold atoms. (62)

elliptical
[eh•LIP•tuh•kuhl] **Oval-shaped:** The orbits of most planets are *elliptical*. (360)

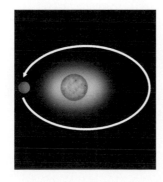

Equator [ee•KWAYT•er] **An imaginary line around Earth, equally distant from the North and South Poles:** The *equator* divides Earth into the Northern and Southern Hemispheres. (276)

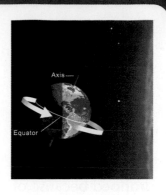

erosion
[ee•ROH•zhuhn] **The process of moving sediment by wind, moving water, or ice:** This gully was formed by *erosion*. (242)

esophagus
[ih•SAHF•uh•guhs] **A long tube that leads from the mouth to the stomach:** When you swallow food, it moves down your *esophagus* to your stomach. (173)

evaporate
[ee•VAP•uh•rayt] **To change from a liquid to a gas:** The sun's heat causes ocean water to *evaporate*. (230)

evaporation
[ee•vap•uh•RAY•shuhn]
The process by which a liquid changes into a gas: The water level of this lake has dropped because of *evaporation*. (230)

evidence
[EV•uh•duhns]
Information, collected during an investigation, to support a hypothesis: A scientist gathers *evidence* from an experiment. (48)

excretion
[eks•KREE•shuhn] **The removal of wastes from the body:** Sweating is one kind of *excretion*. (182)

excretory system
[EKS•kruh•tawr•ee SIS•tuhm] **The system that removes wastes from the body:** Cellular wastes leave the body through the *excretory system*. (182)

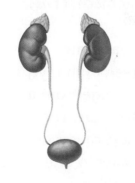

experiment
[ek•SPAIR•uh•muhnt] **A procedure you carry out under controlled conditions to test a hypothesis:** *Experiments* are an important part of the scientific method. (23)

F

feces [FEE•seez] **Solid waste produced by the body during digestion:** *Feces* are stored in the colon. (175)

fermentation
[fer•muhn•TAY•shuhn]
The process that releases energy from sugar in the absence of oxygen: *Fermentation* bubbles are what cause bread dough to rise. (209)

flood basin [FLUHD BAY•suhn] **An area of land that "catches" the runoff from urban areas in a human-made lake:** When people build near a *flood basin*, their houses are at risk of being flooded. (242)

fog [FAWG] **A cloud that forms near the ground:** *Fog* can make it hard for drivers to see the road ahead. (291)

force [FAWRS] **A push or pull that causes an object to move, stop, or change direction:** *Forces* affect the movement of objects. (362)

forecast [FAWR•kast] **The prediction of future weather:** Meteorologists make weather *forecasts*. (300)

formula [FAWRM•yuh•luh] **Symbols that show how many atoms of each element are present:** The *formula* for water is H_2O. (66)

freeze [FREEZ] **To change from a liquid to a solid:** Water *freezes* at 0°C (32°F). (125)

freezing [FREEZ•ing] **Having an air temperature below 0°C (32°F):** Dripping water can form icicles when the temperature outdoors is *freezing*. (125)

front [FRUHNT] **A place where two air masses meet:** Sometimes you can locate a *front* by watching the clouds. (303)

full moon [FUL MOON] **The moon phase in which all of the moon's surface facing Earth is visible:** A second *full moon* in any month is called a blue moon. (365)

fusion [FYOO•zhuhn] **The energy-producing reaction that occurs inside stars:** *Fusion* inside the sun produces solar energy. (336)

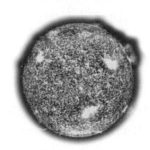

G

gas [GAS] **The state of matter that does not have a definite shape or volume:** These balloons contain helium *gas*. (94)

glacier [GLAY•sher] **A huge sheet of moving ice:** *Glaciers* form in places where new snow falls faster than old snow melts. (226)

graduated cylinder [GRA•joo•ay•tuhd SIL•uhn•der] **A tool used to make quantitative observations of the volume of liquids:** *Graduated cylinders* come in several sizes. (12)

gravity [GRAV•ih•tee] **The force that pulls objects toward Earth:** On a roller coaster, you experience the effects of *gravity*. (362)

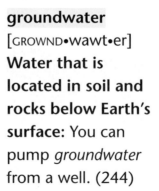

groundwater [GROWND•wawt•er] **Water that is located in soil and rocks below Earth's surface:** You can pump *groundwater* from a well. (244)

H

hail [HAYL] **Raindrops that freeze, are coated with more water, refreeze, and then fall as pieces of ice:** *Hail* sometimes falls in summer thunderstorms. (291)

heart [HART] **An organ that pumps blood throughout the body:** The muscle tissue in your *heart* is very strong. (147)

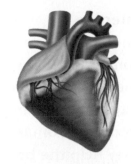

helium [HEE•lee•uhm] **A gas that is the product of fusion inside stars:** *Helium* is lighter than air, so it makes balloons float. (94)

high pressure [HY•PRESH•er] **An area of dense, cold air:** Weather maps often show areas of *high pressure* with the letter "H". (304)

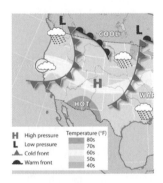

humidity [hyoo•MID•uh•tee] **A measurement of the amount of water vapor in the air:** When the *humidity* is high, your sweat evaporates slowly. (290)

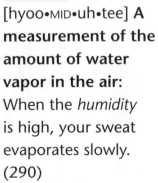

hurricane [HER•ih•kayn] **A large, rotating tropical storm system with wind speeds of at least 119 km/hr (74 mi/hr):** *Hurricanes* form over warm ocean waters. (314)

hydrogen [HY•druh•juhn] **A reactant of fusion inside stars:** Fusion can change *hydrogen* to helium. (336)

hydrologic cycle [hy•druh•LAHJ•ik SY•kuhl] **Another term for the water cycle:** The *hydrologic cycle* and the water cycle are the same thing. (228)

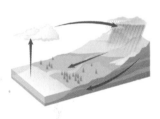

hygrometer [hy•GRAHM•uht•er] **An instrument for measuring humidity:** A *hygrometer* shows the relative humidity. (300)

hypothesis
[hy•PAHTH•uh•sis]
A statement that provides a testable possible answer to a scientific question: These students are testing a *hypothesis* with their experiment. (45)

I

inertia [in•ER•shuh]
The property of matter that keeps an object at rest or moving in a straight line: It takes more force to start something moving due to *inertia*. (362)

inquiry [IN•kwer•ee]
An organized way to gather information and answer questions: You must observe carefully in a scientific *inquiry*. (21)

intestine
[in•TES•tuhn] Two connected tubes, the small and large intestines, leading from the stomach; they help the body absorb water and nutrients and get rid of wastes: Food moves from your stomach to your small *intestine*. (173)

investigation
[in•ves•tuh•GAY•shuhn]
A procedure that is carried out to gather data about an object or event: The student is conducting an *investigation* and recording the results. (20)

J

Jupiter [JOO•pit•er]
The fifth planet from the sun and the largest planet in the solar system: The Great Red Spot on *Jupiter* is a storm that has been going on for more than 300 years. (348)

K

kidney [KID•nee] **The main organ of the excretory system:** You have two *kidneys.* (183)

L

latitude [LAT•uh•tood] **An area's distance from the equator:** Lines of *latitude* are parallel to the equator. (276)

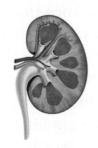

liquid [LIK•wid] **The state of matter that has a definite volume but no definite shape:** Milk is one kind of *liquid.* (96)

local wind [LOH•kuhl WIND] **Wind that results from local changes in temperature:** A land breeze is a *local wind* that blows from the land. (275)

low pressure [LOH PRESH•er] **An area of warm, less dense air:** Stormy weather comes with a *low pressure* area, shown with a letter "L". (304)

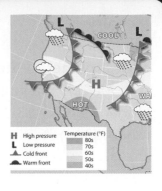

M

malleable [MAL•ee•uh•buhl] **Easy to shape or to form:** Aluminum is a highly *malleable* metal. (79)

Mars [MARZ] **The fourth planet from the sun:** *Mars* has the largest canyon in the solar system. (347)

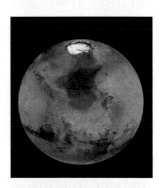

meniscus [muh•NIS•kuhs] **The curved top of a column of liquid:** You can see the *meniscus* when you measure liquid in a graduated cylinder. (12)

Mercury
[MER•kyur•ee] **The closest planet to the sun:** *Mercury* is a little bigger than Earth's moon. (346)

metal [MET•uhl] **A substance that conducts heat and electricity well and is malleable:** Some structures are made of *metal*. (78)

metal alloy [MET•uhl AL•oy] **A solid solution in which a metal or a nonmetal is dissolved in a metal:** Bronze is a *metal alloy* of copper and other materials. (84)

metallic [muh•TAL•ik] **Looking like metal:** *Metallic* objects are often shiny. (79)

metalloid
[MET•uh•loyd] **A substance that has some of the properties of a metal and some of the properties of a nonmetal:** This computer chip is made of silicon, which is a *metalloid*. (85)

meteor [MEET•ee•er] **A piece of rock that travels through space:** *Meteors* are smaller than asteroids. (350)

meteorite
[MEET•ee•er•yt] **A meteor that reaches Earth's surface:** Large *meteorites* can leave craters in Earth's surface. (350)

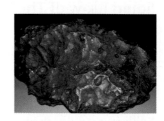

meteorology
[meet•ee•uh•RAHL•uh•jee] **The study of weather:** Students use weather stations to help them learn about *meteorology*. (300)

methane [METH•ayn] **Natural gas containing carbon and hydrogen:** Gas stoves use *methane* to cook food. (66)

microscope [MY•kruh•skohp] **A tool that makes small objects appear larger:** You can use a *microscope* to see things that you can't see with your eyes alone. (8)

mixture [MIKS•cher] **A combination of two or more different substances:** Fruit salad is a *mixture*. (69)

molecule [MAHL•ih•kyool] **A group of two or more atoms that are joined:** This *molecule* has two different kinds of atoms. (66)

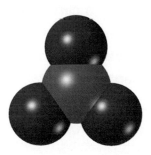

monsoon [mahn•SOON] **A large wind system that reverses direction seasonally:** *Monsoons* often bring rain. (312)

moon [MOON] **Any natural body that revolves around a planet:** Earth's *moon* causes ocean tides on Earth. (364)

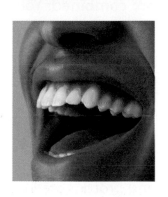

mouth [MOWTH] **The opening through which an animal takes in food, beginning the process of digestion with certain foods:** Your *mouth* is part of your digestive system. (172)

multicellular organism [mul•tih•SEL•yoo•ler AWR•guh•niz•uhm] **A living thing made up of many cells:** A snake is one kind of *multicellular organism*. (146)

N

Neptune [NEP•toon]
**The eighth planet
from the sun:**
Neptune's blue color
is due to methane
gas. (349)

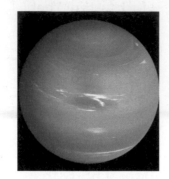

neutralize
[NOO•truh•lyz] **To
make chemically
neutral, as when
an acid and a base
are combined:** You
can use a base to
neutralize stomach
acid. (110)

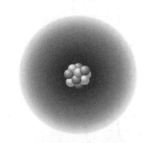

neutron [NOO•trahn]
**One of the particles
in an atom:** *Neutrons*
and protons are in
the nucleus of an
atom. (62)

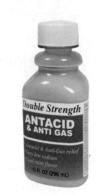

nitrogen
[NY•truh•juhn] **A
nonmetal element:**
Nitrogen is a gas that
makes up most of
Earth's atmosphere.
(94)

noble gas [NOH•buhl
GAS] **An element that
is in the last column
of the periodic
table and doesn't
combine with other
elements:** Neon is a
noble gas. (95)

nonmetal
[nahn•MET•uhl] **A
substance that
does not conduct
electricity and is
not malleable:**
Coal (carbon) is a
nonmetal, because
it does not conduct
electricity and does
not bend easily. (78)

nonvascular plant
[NAHN•vas•kyuh•ler
PLANT] **A plant
without transport
tubes to carry
water and nutrients
throughout the
plant:** *Nonvascular
plants* don't grow
very tall. (194)

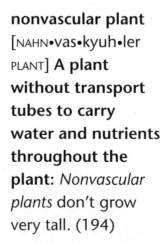

Northern Hemisphere [NAWR•thern HEM•ih•sfir] **The half of Earth that is north of the equator, including North America, Europe, Asia, and parts of Africa:** In the *Northern Hemisphere*, summer is in June, July, August, and September. (276)

nucleus [NOO•klee•uhs] **A dense area in the center of an atom, containing protons and neutrons:** All atoms have a *nucleus*. (62)

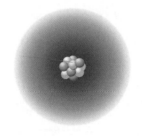

nucleus [NOO•klee•uhs] **In a cell, the organelle that directs all of the cell's activities:** The *nucleus* controls how a cell works. (144)

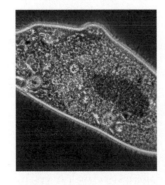

O

orbit [AWR•bit] **The path that one body takes in space as it revolves around another body:** It takes 365.25 days for Earth to complete its *orbit* around the sun. (360)

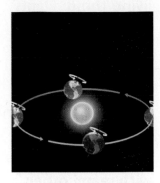

organ [AWR•guhn] **A group of tissues that work together to perform a certain function:** The heart is one of your *organs*. (146)

organ system [AWR•guhn SIS•tuhm] **A group of organs that work together to do a job for the body:** The digestive system is one kind of *organ system*. (147)

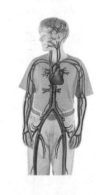

organelle [awr•guh•NEL] **A structure in cells that has a specific function to help keep the cell alive:** A cell has many *organelles*. (143)

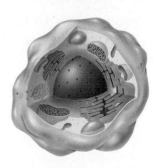

organism
[AWR•guh•niz•uhm] **A living thing:** Plants and animals are *organisms*. (143)

oxygen [AHK•sih•juhn] **A nonmetal element that reacts with many other elements:** Humans need *oxygen* gas to survive. (94)

periodic table
[pir•ee•AHD•ik TAY•buhl] **A table that shows the elements arranged by their atomic numbers:** This *periodic table* shows more than 100 elements. (64)

phase [FAYZ] **One of the shapes the moon seems to have as it orbits Earth:** The moon waxes and wanes during its *phases*. (364)

phloem [FLOH•em] **Vascular tissue that carries food from leaves to the other parts of a plant:** *Phloem* helps transport food throughout a plant. (195)

photosynthesis
[foht•oh•SIN•thuh•sis] **The process by which plants make food from carbon dioxide and water and release oxygen into the air:** Plants need light and water to perform *photosynthesis*. (206)

physical change
[FIZ•ih•kuhl CHAYNJ] **A change in which a substance remains the same substance:** Melting is one kind of *physical change*. (68)

physical property
[FIZ•ih•kuhl PRAHP•er•tee] **A trait—such as color, shape, or hardness—that describes a substance by itself:** Some of the *physical properties* of this animal are its color and shape. (68)

physiology
[fiz•ee•AHL•uh•jee]
The study of how organisms function: Understanding *physiology* can help runners win races. (166)

planet [PLAN•it] **A body that revolves around a star:** Our solar system has nine *planets*. (346)*

planetary
[PLAN•uh•tair•ee]
Having to do with the planets: Information about Mercury is one part of *planetary* science. (68)

Pluto [PLOOT•oh] **The ninth planet from the sun:** *Pluto* is smaller than Earth's moon. (349)*

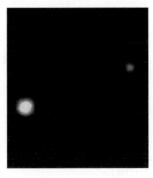

*In 2006, the International Astronomical Union defined a planet as a body that orbits the sun, is spherical, and is large enough to clear its orbit. They reclassified Pluto as a "dwarf planet," because it is not large enough to clear its orbit.

pollution
[puh•LOOSH•uhn] **Any change to a resource that makes the resource unhealthful to use:** Factory smoke is a source of air *pollution*. (254)

precipitation
[pree•sip•uh•TAY•shuhn]
Water that falls from clouds to Earth: *Precipitation* can be solid, like snow, or liquid, like rain. (290)

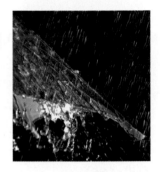

prevailing westerlies
[pree•VAYL•ing WES•ter•leez] **The prevailing winds over the United States that blow from the west:** The *prevailing westerlies* move weather systems from west to east. (277)

prevailing wind
[pree•VAYL•ing WIND] **A global wind that blows constantly from the same direction:** The picture shows Earth's *prevailing winds*. (276)

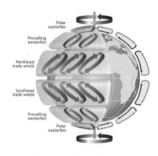

product [PRAHD•uhkt]
A substance that is formed by a chemical reaction: Carbon dioxide is one of the *products* of combining baking soda and vinegar. (120)

propane [PROH•payn]
Gas used in heating some homes and for cooking in outdoor barbecues: This tank holds *propane* for the grill. (66)

properties [PRAHP•er•teez]
The physical and chemical qualities of a substance, such as size, texture, or ability to react with other substances: One of the *properties* of this glass jar is that it is smooth. (68)

proton [PROH•tahn]
One of the particles in an atom: *Protons* have a positive charge. (62)

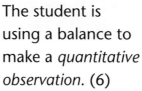

Q

qualitative observation [KWAWL•uh•tayt•iv ahb•zer•VAY•shuhn]
An observation that does not involve measurements or numbers: A description of a smell is a *qualitative observation*. (6)

quantitative observation [KWAHNT•uh•tayt•iv ahb•zer•VAY•shuhn]
An observation that involves numbers or measurements: The student is using a balance to make a *quantitative observation*. (6)

quarter moon [KWAWRT•er MOON] **The moon phase halfway between a new and a full moon:** A *quarter moon* looks like a semicircle. (365)

R

rain [RAYN]
Precipitation that is liquid water: Some forest areas receive a lot of *rain*. (290)

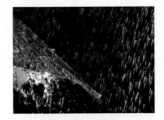

reactant
[ree•AK•tuhnt] **A substance that changes during a chemical reaction:** Vinegar and baking soda are *reactants* when you combine them. (120)

reclamation
[rek•luh•MAY•shuhn] **The recycling of sewage water:** Sewage water can be used again if it goes through *reclamation*. (257)

RECLAIMED WATER USED FOR IRRIGATION DO NOT DRINK

NO BEBAN EL AGUA DE IRRIGACIÓN

recycle [ree•SY•kuhl] **To use something again for a new purpose:** Trees *recycle* oxygen from carbon dioxide. (256)

recycling
[ree•SYK•ling] **Making new products from old ones:** *Recycling* is one way to help the environment. (257)

reservoir
[REZ•er•vwar] **A body of water stored for future use:** *Reservoirs* provide fresh water to many cities. (242)

respiration
[res•puh•RAY•shuhn] **The process in which oxygen is delivered to and waste products are taken away from the body's cells:** Alveoli are involved in *respiration*. (208)

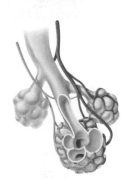

respiratory system
[RES•per•uh•tawr•ee SIS•tuhm] **A group of organs and tissues that exchange oxygen and carbon dioxide between your body and the environment:** The *respiratory system* includes lungs. (160)

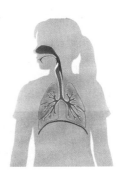

saliva [suh•LY•vuh] A fluid that is produced by the mouth, softens food, and begins the digestion of certain foods: *Saliva* can help start digestion of starches. (173)

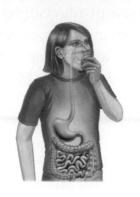

salt [SAWLT] A substance that is made by combining an acid and a base: The table salt you use on your food is just one kind of *salt*. (124)

satellite [SAT•uh•lyt] A body in space that orbits a larger body: Some *satellites* are natural, and some are artificial. (346)

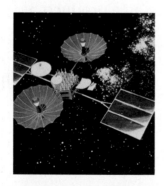

Saturn [SAT•ern] The sixth planet from the sun: *Saturn* has dozens of moons and many rings. (349)

scientific method [sy•uhn•TIF•ik METH•uhd] A series of steps used to plan and carry out an experiment: You can use the *scientific method* to answer your science questions. (44)

sea level [SEE LEV•uhl] The level of the surface of the ocean, used as a standard in measuring heights and depths: Some areas of California are below *sea level*. (272)

seasonal [SEE•zuhn•uhl] Dependent on or determined by the time of year: Some trees show *seasonal* changes in the colors of their leaves. (312)

semimetal [SEM•ee•met•uhl] A substance with some properties of a metal and some properties of a nonmetal: This computer chip is made of silicon, which is a *semimetal*. (85)

sequence
[SEE•kwuhns] **The order in which things happen:** Food moves through the digestive system in a certain *sequence.* (156)

severe weather
[suh•VIR WETH•er] **Extremely bad or dangerous weather, such as hurricanes, tornadoes, or thunderstorms:** It can be dangerous to be outside in *severe weather.* (308)

sleet [SLEET] **Precipitation formed when rain passes through air that is cold enough to freeze water:** *Sleet* makes sidewalks very slippery. (291)

snow [SNOH] **Precipitation that is formed when water vapor turns directly into ice crystals:** Flakes of *snow* are ice crystals. (291)

solar system [SOH•ler SIS•tuhm] **A star and all the planets and other objects that revolve around it:** The largest planet in our *solar system* is Jupiter. (346)

solid [SAHL•id] **The state of matter that has a definite shape and a definite volume:** Sand is one example of a *solid.* (98)

solubility
[sahl•yu•BIL•uh•tee] **The ability to dissolve:** The drink mix has high *solubility.* (68)

Southern Hemisphere
[SUHTH•ern HEM•ih•sfir] **The half of Earth south of the equator, including South America, Australia, and much of Africa:** In the *Southern Hemisphere,* winter starts in June. (276)

sphere [SFIR] **The shape of planets and stars:** A *sphere* is the shape of a ball. (332)

star [STAR] **A huge ball of very hot gases in space:** *Stars* look small from Earth's surface. (332)

stomach [STUHM•uhk] **A baglike organ of the digestive system, with strong muscles that mix food with digestive juices:** The *stomach* uses digestive juices to break down food. (172)

stomata [STOH•muh•tuh] **On the underside of leaves, tiny holes that release waste products:** Some *stomata* can be seen only with a microscope. (185)

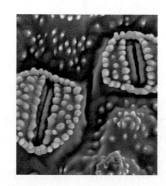

stratosphere [STRAT•uh•sfir] **The layer of the atmosphere that contains ozone and is above the troposphere:** Space shuttles must pass through the *stratosphere* on their way into orbit. (272)

stratus [STRAT•uhs] **A type of cloud that forms low in the atmosphere, possibly leading to light precipitation:** *Stratus* clouds may look as if they are closer to Earth's surface than other kinds of clouds. (290)

structure [STRUHK•cher] **In an organism, a part that can be recognized by its shape and other properties:** This bird's wing is a *structure*. (142)

sublimation
[suhb•luh•MAY•shuhn]
A change from a solid to a gas without becoming a liquid: These ice crystals formed through *sublimation.* (69)

sun [SUHN] **The star at the center of the solar system:** The *sun* provides light and heat energy to our solar system. (332)

 T

teeth [TEETH] **The hard structures in the mouth that grind food into smaller pieces:** People have two sets of *teeth* during their lives. (172)

telescope
[TEL•uh•skohp] **A tool that scientists use to study parts of the universe not visible to the human eye:** Powerful *telescopes* on Earth and in space reveal faraway parts of the universe. (360)

temperature
[TEM•per•uh•cher]
The measure of the quantity of heat in a substance: Thermometers are used to measure *temperature.* (10)

thermal conductivity
[THER•muhl kahn•duhk•TIV•uh•tee] **The ability of a metal to transfer thermal energy easily:** The wires inside the toaster have high *thermal conductivity.* (80)

thunderstorm
[THUHN•der•stawrm]
A storm with rain, lightning, hail, and thunder: *Thunderstorms* happen in every part of the country. (316)

tissue [TISH•OO] **A group of cells that work together to perform a certain function:** The lining of the stomach is one kind of *tissue.* (146)

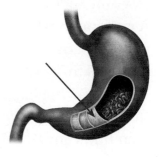

tornado
[tawr•NAY•doh] **A violently spinning column of air that touches the ground:** The inside of a *tornado* has very low air pressure. (317)

trade wind [TRAYD WIND] **A prevailing wind near the equator:** The movement of air near the equator causes *trade winds*. (277)

transpiration
[tran•spuh•RAY•shuhn] **The process by which water moves up and out of plants through tiny holes in their leaves:** Plants recycle water through *transpiration*. (185)

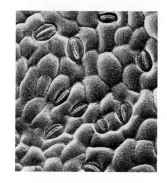

tropical storm
[TRAHP•ih•kuhl STAWRM] **A cyclone in which wind speeds are 63–118 km/hr (39–73 mi/hr):** *Tropical storms* are less severe than hurricanes. (314)

troposphere
[TROH•puh•sfir] **The layer of atmosphere closest to Earth's surface:** Planes travel in the *troposphere*. (272)

U

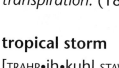

Uranus [YUR•uh•nuhs] **The seventh planet from the sun:** *Uranus* takes 84 Earth years to orbit the sun. (349)

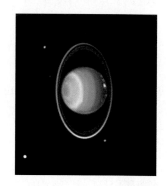

urine [YUR•in] **A liquid waste product produced by the body:** *Urine* is stored in the bladder. (183)

V

vacuole [VAK•yoo•ohl] **A plant organelle that stores material such as nutrients, water, or wastes:** *Vacuoles* are like storerooms for plant cells. (144)

vascular plant
[vas•kyuh•ler plant] **A plant with tubes to carry nutrients and water throughout the plant:** Trees are *vascular plants.* (195)

vascular tissue
[vas•kyuh•ler tish•oo] **Tissue that supports a plant and carries water and food throughout the plant:** You can find *vascular tissue* in tree trunks. (195)

vein [vayn] **A blood vessel that carries blood from different parts of the body back to the heart:** *Veins* (blue) carry blood that has little oxygen. (159)

Venus [vee•nuhs] **The second planet from the sun:** *Venus* is about the same size as Earth. (346)

vesicle [vehs•uh•kuhl] **An animal organelle that stores material such as nutrients, water, or waste until the cell uses or gets rid of it:** *Vesicles* are like storerooms for animal cells. (145)

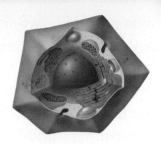

W

waning [wayn•ing] **The process in which the moon goes from full to new:** When the moon is *waning*, the lighted part seen from Earth gets smaller each night. (365)

waste disposal [wayst dis•poh•zuhl] **The removal of waste products from an organism:** Every living thing has some kind of *waste disposal.* (182)

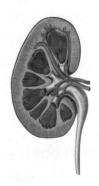

water cycle [WAWT•er SY•kuhl] **The constant movement of water from Earth's surface to Earth's atmosphere and back to Earth's surface:** The *water cycle* includes evaporation and precipitation. (228)

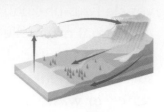

water quality [WAWT•er KWAWL•uh•tee] **The measure of how safe water is for human use:** The *water quality* in the city is tested regularly. (255)

water table [WAWT•er TAY•buhl] **The top of groundwater:** Surface pollution can get down to the *water table* quickly. (244)

water vapor [WAWT•er VAY•per] **The gas form of water:** *Water vapor* is formed when water boils. (228)

watershed [WAWT•er•shed] **An area of land that is drained by a series of creeks and rivers:** Water quality is affected by all the pollution in a *watershed.* (242)

waxing [WAKS•ing] **The process in which the moon goes from new to full:** When the moon is *waxing,* the lighted part seen from Earth gets bigger each night. (365)

weather [WETH•er] **The condition of the atmosphere at a certain place and time:** *Weather* can affect people's activities, especially if it is severe. (270)

weather front [WETH•er FRUHNT] **A place where two air masses meet:** *Weather fronts* often change the weather. (303)

wind [WIND]
The horizontal movement of air: The *wind* is strong enough to bend these young trees. (275)

wing [WING] **One of the limbs that are typically used for flying by animals such as birds, bats, and insects:** A bat uses its *wings* to fly at night. (142)

X

xylem [ZY•luhm]
Vascular tissue that carries water and nutrients from roots to the other parts of a plant: *Xylem* moves water from the roots up to the leaves. (195)

Index

T

Illustration Credits
Introduction Unit
37 Jef Wilson; **45** Mike Wesley; **55** Toby Mikle
Unit One
67 Mike Wesley; **83** Jef Wilson; **98** Jun Park; **100** Peter Bull; **113** Mike Wesley;
120–121 Jun Park; **124** Jun Park; **125** Mike Wesley; **135** Jef Wilson
Unit Two
146 Graphics Articulate; **148–149** Graphics Articulate; **157** Graphics Articulate;
162 Graphics Articulate; **185** Mike Wesley; **211** Mike Wesley
Unit Three
242 Sebastian Quigley; **243** Mike Wesley; **244** Sebastian Quigley; **264** Argosy

Unit Four
301 Mike Wesley; **305** Geoff McCormack; **315** Mike Wesley; **319** Angela Ramos;
325 Argosy
Unit Five
333 Peter Bull; **337** Argosy; **354** Argosy; **375** Argosy
Glossary
R38 Argosy; **R66** Argosy; **R68** Argosy

All other illustration provided by Harcourt School Publishers, BILL SMITH STUDIO